THE SHI'ITE MOVEMENT IN IRAQ

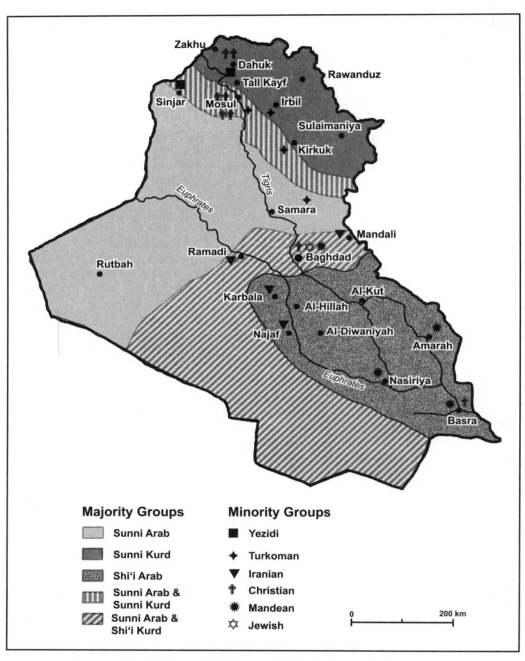

Majority Groups

- Sunni Arab
- Sunni Kurd
- Shi'i Arab
- Sunni Arab & Sunni Kurd
- Sunni Arab & Shi'i Kurd

Minority Groups

- ■ Yezidi
- ✦ Turkoman
- ▼ Iranian
- ✝ Christian
- ✳ Mandean
- ✡ Jewish

0   200 km

Distribution of Religious and Ethnic Groups in Iraq

Faleh A. Jabar

The Shi'ite Movement in Iraq

SAQI

To Fatima

British Library Cataloguing-in-Publication Data
A catalogue record for this book is available from the
British Library

ISBN 0 86356 988 9 (hb)
ISBN 086356 395 3 (pbk)

© Faleh Abdul-Jabar, 2003

This edition first published 2003

Saqi
26 Westbourne Grove
London W2 5RH
www.saqibooks.com

Contents

Contents

Contents

Tables and Maps

Note on Transliteration and Dates

For Arabic words the standard transliteration of the *International Journal of Middle Eastern Studies* has been adopted, but diacritics have been omitted for sake of simplicity. In proper names initial *hamza*s have been omitted. Arabic and Persian words quoted directly from other sources are written as in the original. Some proper names have been given in their current Anglicized form, such as Hussein or Hussain (rather than Husain) or Khomeini (rather than Khumaini).

Arabic words are either printed in italics and followed by their English equivalents, or given after the English word to provide the original concept.

Proper names and family or tribal titles take the Arabic definite article *al-*, hence al-Sadr rather than as-Sadr.

Where necessary, Islamic Hejira (AH) dates of events and publications are followed by their Gregorian equivalents.

Abbreviations

(Journals italicized)

AA *Asian Affairs*
ACI *Association of Iranian Researchers*
AALA *Asia Africa Latin America*
AHR *American Historical Review*
BJMES *British Journal of Middle Eastern Studies*
BRSMES *British Society for Middle East Studies Bulletin*
BSOAS *Bulletin of the School of Oriental and African Studies*
CARDRI Committee Against Repression and for Democratic Rights in Iraq
CC Central Committee
CP *Comparative Politics*
CW Collected Works
DD *Da'wa Doctrine* (four volumes of Da'wa Party internal documents)
DF *Dirasat Filistiniya (Palestinian Studies)*
DD-PS Da'wa Doctrine-Political Section (two volumes)
DP Da'wa Party
DWI *Die Welt des Islams*
ES *Economy and Society*
FJ *al-Fikr al-Jadid*
FO Foreign Office
HT Hizb al-Tahrir (Tahrir Party)
ICP Iraqi Communist Party
IJMES *International Journal of Middle Eastern Studies*
IS *Iranian Studies*
IO International Organization
IOS *Israeli Oriental Studies*
JAS *Journal of Algerian Studies*
LA *Lughat al-'Arab* (Arab Language)
MAI Munazamat al-'Amal al-Islami (Islamic Action Organization)
MB Muslim Brotherhood
MEJ *Middle East Journal*
MES *Middle Eastern Studies*
MERIP *Middle East Report*
MW *The Muslim World*

Abbreviations

NC National Command (of Ba'th Party)
PB Political Bureau (highest body in various political parties)
PP *Past and Present*
PS *Politics and Society*
QF *Qadhaya Fikriya*
RCC Revolutionary Command Council (formerly the highest state body in Iraq)
RC Regional (country) Command (Ba'th Party)
SAB *South Asia Bulletin*
SAIRI Supreme Assembly for the Islamic Revolution in Iraq
SOAS School of Oriental and African Studies
SW Selected Works
TWQ *Third World Quarterly*
WI *The World of Islam*

Foreword

by Sami Zubaida

Iraqi Shi'ism is multifaceted and complex; it is a religious cult, social boundary, political formation and source of ideas and knowledge. It is not socially homogenous, but comprises the clerical classes of the holy cities, urban bourgeoisie, modern intellectuals and tribal peasants and their chiefs. Its politics are far from uniform communal solidarity, but consist of many combinations of interest, ideology and movement, which often transcend communal boundaries. Shi'i intellectuals and activists have been prominent in most of Iraq's modern political movements and cultural currents. The Iraqi Communist Party included many Shi'is in its leadership and cadres, and drew much grassroots support from Shi'ite cities and neighbourhoods. Shi'is were also prominent in various nationalist parties, including the Ba'th, until its 'tribalization' in government.

A unique and rich culture of religion, ritual, poetry and literature, as well as social custom and folklore, was built up historically in the shrine cities of Najaf and Karbala, and from there emanated to Shi'ite communities and locations throughout the country. What may be called the *'Ashura* complex plays a central role in this culture and structures many of its motifs, icons and literary products. These elements have been woven into political ideologies and symbols of dissidence and revolt in recent decades, though historically and for the most part they were contained by a quietist and apolitical culture. These cultural elements are by no means confined to the communal boundaries of the Shi'a, but have been incorporated into the public sphere of an increasingly politicized Iraqi society and in some cases have become symbols of conflict and contest.

There is also, clearly, an intimate connection between Iranian religious personnel and institutions with those of Shi'ite Iraq. Many Iranian clerics have at one point or another taken residence in the shrine cities of Iraq, including Ayatollah Khomeini, and many of the clerical families in Iraq have their origins in Iran. The religious schools of the holy cities are cosmopolitan and comprise students and teachers from many countries, but mostly Iran. Yet Iraqi Shi'ism is distinct from its Iranian neighbour in the pattern of the relation of

13

institutions to the different sectors of the community; the 'Bedouinization' of some of its motifs and rituals in relation to its tribal component; and the Arab culture and identity of its adherents. In the century of development of an Iraqi identity and public culture, Iraqi Shi'ism has been further shaped in its particular form.

Faleh Jabar's book is a unique and impressive contribution to defining in the modern context Iraqi Shi'ism and its society, culture and politics. It draws a fascinating picture of the Shi'ite landscape, its institutions and authorities, personalities, families and factions, the economics of religious life and the financial ebb and flow of its system. The section on Shi'ite cultural spaces is particularly vivid, with narratives of religious knowledge and its transmission, and of ritual and its political construction in relation to events.

The description and analysis of modern Shi'ite political movements and their social and cultural bases is the focus of the book, placed within a wider context, which provides a wealth of information and insight into Iraqi society and politics. The book presents a history of the formation of the Iraqi state and its mutations in relation to the social forces that shaped it. In particular, it contains an important analysis of the social bases and effects of the current Saddamist regime.

Faleh Jabar is uniquely placed to write on modern Iraq. He is a prominent participant in its political and intellectual landscape, first in the country and then, like most surviving Iraqi intellectuals, in exile. His knowledge and research, though impeccably scholarly, are not only archival but born of an intimate connection with events, personalities and cultural currents. Its narratives are informed by a thorough familiarity with the history and politics of the region, lending it a wide comparative perspective, and its analyses are enriched by a grounding in social and political theory. This book is a feast for the student of the country and the region, as well as for the informed and curious reader.

Introduction: The US, War and Iraqi Shi'ism

The ninth day of April 2003 will go down in history as the day of the fall. Barely two days after the anniversary of the Ba'th party (7 April), and twenty-one days after the invasion, the battle Saddam dubbed *Umm al-Hawasim* (The Mother of All Battles) was over, and the whole material edifice of the Ba'th totalitarian regime fell apart. Much to the world's surprise, little resistance was offered. Only the Fedayeen, Arab volunteers, a few Special Republican Guard units and hardcore Ba'th members put up any kind of fight. Arab militants interviewed by Abu Dhabi TV (20–22 April) even bitterly grumbled that they were shot at from behind rather than by US troops.

The vast majority of Iraqis did not want to defend the Ba'th regime. Why? Lack of patriotism? Far from it. Iraqi patriotism has been a vibrant force, but it has been detached from Ba'th rule. And the reason lies in the nature of the patrimonial totalitarian regime Saddam Hussein created in his own image. The 19th-century Russian novelist Fyodor Dostoyevsky once described how, after years of living together, a man and his dog came to look like each other. Never in modern sociological history has a political order resembled its creator as closely as modern Iraq grew to mirror Saddam Hussein.

Modern, secular Iraq was gradually dismantled by the rapacious exercise of power. In its stead a mix of party, tribe, religion, oil and secret police was embedded in the politics of fear, politics of the gift, politics of the patriarchy and politics of manipulating the sacred. The totalitarian patrimonial system completed its life cycle by constantly producing its own anti-thesis. It started by constructing impersonal institutions but ended up personalizing power and promoting a personality cult; it strove to homogenize the nation, but its assimilative techniques deepened ethnic, religious and cultural cleavages, ripping the fabric of the nation apart. A command economy claimed egalitarianism as its ideal, but actually widened the gap between rich and poor, creating crony capitalism and mass poverty. It claimed to embrace the lofty ideals of progress, yet destroyed civil associations and strove to revive outdated traditional value systems, ideology of lineage and fundamentalist discourses.

An enormous gulf developed between official state nationalism (Ba'th Pan-Arab socialism) and popular patriotism. The bulk of the nation was gradually disconnected from the ruling clan-class. Far from being a small group at the helm, the clan-class that ruled Iraq was formed from state, party and tribal elites, and constituted a relatively large core held together with blood ties, intermarriage, ideological bonds, economic interests and, in the words of Charles Tripp, 'communality of guilt'.

The US Perspective

Given the Bush administration's longing for President Saddam Hussein's unconditional surrender, the US military campaign that destroyed Ba'th rule was reminiscent of the 'death foretold' in Gabriel García Márquez's celebrated novel: a rapist is to be eliminated, and everybody knows it; nobody does anything to stop it. There is one difference, though: many voices, like the Russian premier Yevgeny Primakov, advised the patriarch to take the safe passage offered and leave to save his country the ravages of war.

Why the US changed course from its previous strategy of containment to regime removal has been and may continue to be debated. Several major changes prompted this change of direction; religion, or Islam, is part of it.

America's former containment strategy functioned on three main levels: first, sanctions, which impacted hugely on the civilian population, a burden only somewhat alleviated when the oil-for-food programme was agreed in 1996; second, a humiliating and enforced disarmament, supervised by UNSCOM, the UN special committee; and third, reduced sovereignty (with the imposition of 'no-fly' zones in northern and southern Iraq). As Iraq managed to work its way through the loopholes and dislodge inspectors in December 1998, hawkish voices began to be raised in the US.[1]

There are three intertwined factors that may explain why the US shifted from containment to removal. The failure of the previous US strategy is one reason; the tragedy of 11 September 2001 is another. Then the swift success scored in the removal of the Taliban's medieval regime in Afghanistan produced euphoric expectations.[2]

Together, they motivated and provided ammunition for a fourth factor: the rise of the neo-conservative wing of George W. Bush's administration. This ideological trend, sharing and reflecting certain values and global concepts of the rising evangelical right, has a strong unilateral tendency and a conception of the post-Cold War as a realm of a war of civilizations, rather than a globalized and globalizing liberal world. It displaces Adam Smith's[3] vision of a self-regulating market economy with a Samuel Huntington's concept of 'the clash of civilizations'.[4] The former theorizes a world governed by economics rather than politics, where the importance of the nation-states and political and military classes wane and diminish. The latter removes the real world of nation-states and installs an imagined one divided into new cultural blocs, insulated forever and embedded in one marker: religion. From a neo-conservative perspective, this world demands a militarised march of globalization. This is more of a Clausewitzian globalism, with strong US unilateral overtones.[5] As the French fear, this would spell the end of the post-1991 world order. Indeed, it may already have.

The tragedy of 11 September boosted the neo-conservatives' argument. It won worldwide sympathy for the invasion of Afghanistan, but worldwide opposition to the invasion of Iraq.

The attacks were the subject of several interpretations in the West and elsewhere, and will continue to be debated and interpreted for a long time to come. The 11 September offensive was launched by a former US ally: the Wahhabi Hanbalite neo-militancy. Wahhabism was a US ally during the Cold War. It was used as an ideological tool in the face of the radical Gamal Abdel Nasser of Egypt in the 1950s and 1960s; against the Soviet Union in the 1970s; and against Soviet-backed, communist-led Afghanistan in the 1980s. Of course, Usama Bin Laden was the product of anti-communism, rigid Hanabalism, oil wealth and CIA-trained violence. In the aftermath of the 1991 Gulf War, this Frankenstein monster has rebelled against its own creator and ex-global patron, the US. The neo-cons can and may have it inserted into the neatly arranged catalogue of civilizational fracture lines.

Shortly after the collapse of the World Trade Center in New York, the push for regime change in Afghanistan and Iraq was immediately voiced.

The swift success scored by the US in removing the fundamentalist Taliban regime was, and in fact still is, a catalyst for further experiments in surgical removals.

But if the Taliban is part of the fundamentalist realm, how could a secular Iraq fit in? The answer may well be found in two areas. The developing Bush Doctrine conceives the new menace in the potential marriage of pariah states and violent Islamic militancy, the former providing 'weapons of mass destruction and the latter a striking force.[6] Iraq fits in a dual manner, both as showcase and counterweight. It is conceived as a hostile 'pariah' state, a potential threat in the sense stipulated by the Bush Doctrine. If removed, it may serve an example for others, on one hand, and its secular society could well be geared as a counterbalance to militant Islamism across the Middle East on the other. In other words, the new Iraq would constitute an antithesis to the conservative, fundamentalism-infected Arabia.

Iraq has long been such an antithesis: a Hijazi, Shafi'i monarchy ruling over a Hanafi-Shafi'i populace with liberal institutions and anti-tribal modernity, versus Najdi-Hanabalite Arabia with pro-tribal, traditional patriarchy. Republican Iraq was an even stronger antithesis, despite a short-lived marriage of convenience during the Iraq-Iran war.

Disarmament of Iraq is the 'minimalist' approach; its 'democratization' is the maximal. On this score the US administration is split into two flanks, the State Department 'realists' who advocate a 'limited change' geared toward a friendly, stable government in Iraq and the 'idealists, entrenched in the

Pentagon, the office of Vice-President Dick Cheney and the National Security team and backed by congressmen, who envisage full-fledged secular democratization.'[7] Hence the recurrent statements about 'the march of democracy' in the Middle East in the wake of 'liberating Iraq'.

For Iraq to serve such grand designs, two preconditions must be fulfilled: secularism and democracy. Ironically, Iraq's secularism has been in real threat. So has its civil, non-tribal fabric and its Tocquevillean civil associations, the very essence of any viable democracy.[8]

The Shi'ite Perspective in Exile

The Shi'ite Islamic movements have been over-focused on what they see as a rare window of opportunity offered by the Bush administration's campaign to reshape the political order and ultimately Islamize power and/or redress communal grievances. Shi'ite Islamist and perhaps liberal activists from both the older and younger generations seem to agree now that Shi'i politicians in the 1920s made a grave mistake when they fell from favour with the colonial power, Great Britain, which had the keys to mould the political system – much to the Shi'is' distaste. Now, they contend, it is time to undo that error.[9] Seeking US patronage has become almost the norm, with only a few, feeble ideological voices opposing such liaisons with Washington.

From 1992, all Shi'ite Islamic parties, the Da'wa, SAIRI (or SCIRI) and the Munazama took part, one way or another, in the US-sponsored Iraqi National Congress led by the Iraqi Shi'i liberal businessman Ahmad Chalabi. A few years on, they all withdrew, one after the other. The INC was on the verge of disintegration and collapse.

In late 1996, SAIRI initiated regular contacts with the Clinton administration via its bureau in London, headed by Hamid al-Bayati, thereby breaking an old taboo. The Iraq Liberation Act, promulgated by the Congress in December 1998 shortly before Operation Desert Fox, may have further encouraged this change of course on the part of SAIRI from abstention to active engagement with US diplomacy. The election of the reformist Muhammad Khatami in Iran in May 1997 may have also egged on SAIRI along these lines.

Since then, al-Bayati has had several photo opportunities with various US officials, including the ex-Secretary of State Madeline Albright. SAIRI soon became an integral part of the expanded spectrum of Iraqi opposition forces that were regularly consulted and hosted by Washington in the hope of reviving the moribund INC. It was named by the US State Department as being eligible for support as stipulated in the Liberation Act. The Da'wa and Munazama were excluded from this US patronage for having a 'terrorist' record, a reference to their bombing campaign in Kuwait and beyond during the early 1980s.

But SAIRI soon took an active part in the Windsor gathering, where the INC leadership was expanded and rotated. In the run-up to the Opposition Congress held in London in December 2002, SAIRI was one of six major parties to decide the composition of the delegates. Prior to the London Congress, Abdul Aziz al-Hakim, the second man in SAIRI, appeared in Washington to denounce war options and take part in the US-sponsored gathering of the group of six.[10] Through SAIRI's patronage or cooperation, Shi'i delegates from other Islamic groups such as the Da'wa, Munazama, Kawadir al-Da'wa, plus non-political institutions such as the al-Bayt of Sayyid Muhammad Bahr al-'Ulum or the al-Khoi Foundation, were included in the list of delegates invited to the London Congress. This was non-voluntary power sharing, dictated by the simple fact that SAIRI could not, and indeed cannot, claim to be the sole representative of Shi'ite Islamic groups, let alone the Shi'ite community at large.

Officially, the Da'wa Party was a member of an anti-war alliance, inclusive of leftists and nationalists. US-Da'wa contacts were not initiated until 14 October 2002 in London. Three successive meetings between Da'wa representatives and US State Department officials in took place in London. The Da'wa was represented by Abu Ahmad al-Ja'fari (a *nom de guerre* of Ibrahim al-Ushaiqer, a Da'wa spokesman.)[11]

Officially, the Da'wa boycotted the London Congress; individual leading figures like the political bureau member, Sami al-'Askari, defied the boycott and responded positively to SAIRI's invitation. Officially, the Da'wa directed strong criticism towards the London Congress, focusing on SAIRI's claims that it is 'the' representative of the Shi'is.[12]

SAIRI tried to broaden its Shi'ite constituency. Indeed, the Congress was packed with an overwhelmingly Shi'ite representation; all Islamists were, one way or another, invited, endorsed or at least not rejected by SAIRI, which had veto powers. Approximately 56 per cent of the 300 delegates were Shi'is.

But Shi'i delegates did not and will not figure as one bloc, imbued with unity of ideology or social or political perspectives.

Apart from the common goal of removing the Ba'th totalitarian regime, they have little in common. They subscribe to various ideological trends: militant fundamentalist Islam, moderate liberal Islam, Western liberalism, moderate Arabism, Kurdish nationalism and Marxism.

Shi'i liberals of the INC stand for full liberalization of polity and economy, including innovative concepts regarding privatization of the oil sector. The full-fledged, classical *laissez-faire* capitalism in their view has a manifest secular concomitant. At the London Congress, the Iraqi scholar Kanan Makkiya – who hails from a Shi'ite family – called, among other things, for the separation of state and religion. But neither liberalism nor secularism is a welcome to other Shi'i-led organizations. For example, full dismantling of the command economy and removal of oil rentierism are hardly a starter for the Iraqi National Accord (INA), led by the Shi'i leader Iyad 'Allawi.[13]

Similarly, separation of state and religion is a horrible scenario for all strands of Islamists, Shi'i and Sunni alike. Islamic-minded delegates, who were mainly but not exclusively Shi'i Islamic militants, insisted on and got the inclusion of two crucial points in the final statement of the London Congress: one, that Islam is the religion of the state of Iraq; and two, that Islam is 'the' rather than 'a' source of legislation. (The Arabic text read: *al-Islam masdarul tashri'*, i.e. Islam [as per the Shari'a] is 'the' source of legislation; the more liberal English translation replaced the definite with an indefinite article so as to soften the Islamst connotations. Whether or not that is a liberal way of seeing things or a self-deceptive wish will be much debated.)

The Islamic legislative fervour in the final statement of the Congress may have been the result of a reciprocal exchange of favours between the Kurds and SAIRI. In return for full recognition of federalism, a crucial Kurdish demand, the Kurds reciprocated with full endorsement of Islamizing the future constitution. Of course, these agreements could cancel each other out: SAIRI never accepted federalism, and Kurdish nationalists are politically secular and opposed to any assimilation, Islamist or otherwise.

It is well-known that this constitutional article on the *Shari'a* has been and may well continue to be a battlefield for Islamists of every walk. Their *raison d'être* is the re-Islamization of politics and culture. Political Shi'ism gave rise to three distinct schools: the liberal Lebanese, the authoritarian Iranian and the moderate Iraqi. Muhammad Fadlallah and the late Muhammad Mahdi Shams al-Din represent the liberal trend in Shi'ite politics; Khomeini's *wilayat al-faqih* (the governance of the jurisprudent) represents the authoritarian version; Muhammad Baqir al-Sadr's is the 'third-way' theory (See Part IV of this volume on ideology). Iraqi Shi'i Islamists, moderate Islamic dignitaries and charitable institutions are not unified in this regard. Only few advocate Khomeinism, above all SAIRI.

As a result, the terms 'Shi'i' and 'Shi'ism', as we argue in this volume, cannot and should not be deployed as sociological or political categories. Using these terms to signify a monolithic type of compact community imbued with unity of purpose and mono-dimensional political orientation is a naive stereotype created by an ignorant world media. In this oversimplified image, Iraq is neatly cut into three chunks, well-defined in statistical accuracy and unified in the imagination of 'instant experts' who multiply in the wake of every conceivable crisis like mushrooms.[14]

At the London Congress, SAIRI scored many successes. First, it was empowered by the US to decide the composition of the delegates, to mould, in part, the final statement and to emerge as a power-broker in the process of shaping the post-conflict political system.

An important feature of the London Congress was not only the numerical predominance of Shi'i delegates, but also the primacy of SAIRI's men in the

65–man Committee of Co-ordination and Follow-Up that emerged from the gathering. Of the 65 members, 33 were Shi'is; of the 21 Shi'i Islamist members of this committee (moderates, communalists and fundamentalists), 17 were either SAIRI members or protégés and 4 were Islamic moderates with independent status. Only 12 members of the committee were secular liberals and nationalists.(See the list below.)[15]

Beyond the London meeting, SAIRI took two further steps. In the Salahudin conference of February 2003, Aziz al-Hakim of SAIRI was included in a six-man leading committee, the nucleus of a post-conflict authority. The US special envoy Zalamay Khalilzad made it clear to the Salahudin gathering that they should stop short of reaching out for a 'government-in-exile', lest such a measure alienate anti-Saddam institutional and social forces militating for a rehabilitated post-conflict Iraq.[16]

To lend muscle to its politics, SAIRI deployed units of its Badr Army (Faylaq Badr) in Sulaymaniya. The size of the contingent is yet unknown; it may well be symbolic, but it indicates SAIRI' s drive to back its political ambitions with a military presence. Its deployment on Kurdish territory signals a gesture of goodwill and gratitude on the part of Jalal Talibani's Patriotic Union of Kurdistan (PUK) towards SAIRI and their regional patron, Iran. These units are poised to take initiative the moment a power vacuum allows for deployment and activity. SAIRI wishes to affect the course of events and win an early foothold.

But what political strategy underlines SAIRI' s thinking? The Shi'ite Islamic movements of Iraq, a crucial element of the opposition, stand many chances. Conceived as part of a penalized and disfranchised community, they are required to have a positive input for regime change.

Democratic change will be welcomed, but would secularism? For Shi'ite Islamic groups democracy has an oversimplified dual meaning: majority rule and the people as the source of power and legislation; in their minds, the first serves as a conduit for 'automatic' Shi'ite majority government; the latter is a secular antithesis to the 'Islamic' polity some groups call for. A corollary to democracy, the Islamists usually overlook, is pluralism, along with civil and human rights.

Given the secular role envisaged for Iraq, SAIRI' s choices seem limited. A communal-based politics or an Iranian type of fundamentalist-authoritarian rule would trigger Sunni fundamentalist responses, risk a communal cleavage and threaten secularism. In the global anti-terrorism atmosphere such a strategy would spell SAIRI's demise. Sooner rather than later, they will have to further modernize their ideology or risk being sidelined.

Communalism (*ta'ifiya*) in Iraq has thus far been more of a state policy than a culturally embedded social divide. Secularism, often confused with atheism, is the guardian of a peaceful symbiosis between religion and politics, notably in multi-ethnic, multicultural societies.

The Shi'ite Perspective in Iraq

SAIRI and other forces in exile seem to have been oblivious to the unpredictable and uncontrollable Shi'ite social forces that were in the making during the 1990s and unleashed by the fall of totalitarianism. The dream al-Hakim and his aids had of receiving a welcome by millions, like Khomeini's return from France in Janaury1979, may have been wishful thinking.

Barely hours after the fall of Baghdad, the Iraqi Shi'ite Pandora's Box was opened. From that moment to the end of April a series of significant, sometimes macabre, events occurred. Chest-beating crowds on the day of the fall; the assassination of Majid Kho'i in Najaf; demonstrations in Nasiriya and Baghdad; the multimillion-man pilgrimage to Karbala on the Arba'in visitation: these set-pieces were constructed of popular religion, institutionalised religion and old state-religion. The renowned civility and secularism of Iraq's society seemed, for the moment, a bygone myth.

Chest-beating: Non-verbal Symbolism

The chest-beating Iraqis in the shantytown of West Baghdad, dubbed Saddam Town (and renamed al-Sadr Town), constituted a bizarre celebration, if any, on the day Saddam Hussein's statues came crashing down. In addition to the fierce chest-beating, date-palm leaves, green banners and clay tablets were hoisted aloft, all artefacts of Shi'ite ceremonial ritualism. Chest-beating was a coded display of allegiance to the Imam, a display of protest and a physical statement to convey past grievances. In this ritual, pain is a medium of catharsis; it purifies the physical body and releases trapped agonies – it also holds a promise of happiness to come. Green palm leaves were another symbol: a celebration of life, hysterical ecstasy. The actual palm leaves the throng used were yellow and dry. They now assumed a new function. Green banners were the symbol of Imam Ali. His descendants put on green headwear to distinguish themselves as a noble lineage. Clay tablets known as *turba* are made from the soil of Najaf and used in prayers. The forehead of the worshipper would touch this sacred soil in honour of Najaf, the holy burial place of the first Shi'i Imam.

Thus the political language was mute. In this republic of silence one needs to learn how to speak. The crowd on 9 April in Baghdad could not utter even one political slogan. Mute cultural artefacts became a demonstration of identity, representations of identity, declarations of freedom and pronouncements of the unutterable. For once, the crowds went vocal and chanted: *By God we swear never to forget Imam Hussain*. Another, more recurrent line: *No God but Allah*.

Looting and Mayhem

The significance of these manifestations of identity was almost lost in the days that followed. In the ensuing power vacuum, looters ran amok. Banks, Baʿth Party and government offices were set ablaze; the museum, central library, private homes, jewellery shops and UN premises were emptied of their valuables. Hospitals and private hotels were devoured. The animal instincts of the mob were in full swing, and US-UK forces did nothing to stop it. By every norm of international law, an occupying force bears the legal responsibility to protect life and property, above all the invaluable heritage of Mesopotamia. The gangs were a queer mix of Baʿth party officials who destroyed all incriminating evidence and expanded the range of fire to hide their trail. Officials also took part in robbing the country of its valuables, of cash and antiques. Petty thieves did less. More than a quarter of a million of ordinary criminals, who had been released in November 2002 under a general amnesty, roamed the streets to terrorise the populace and strip hospitals of whatever item they could lay hands on. Another set of looters comprised the deprived and the hungry. A looter carrying a fridge and a fan said to an Arab reporter[17] that he had served in two wars, yet he could not provide a fan for his family. It was a redistribution of national wealth previously usurped by the ruling party. In the last category were to be found angry mobs bent on revenge.

Macabre Death in Najaf

The tragic death of the prominent Shiʿi cleric Majid al-Kho'i (age 42) in Najaf on 10 April, is a gruesome reminder of the pernicious legacy Saddam Hussein has left: violence and politicised religiosity. Like his Imam, Kho'i was slain by power-mongers, just few yards from the tomb of his ancestor. His death marks the beginning of a schism in Najaf that may well spill over. Kho'i rushed to Najaf the moment it was clean of Baʿth forces, to save his hometown the horrors of the day after. A group of paramilitaries were entrenched inside the holy shrine, threatening to wreak havoc and cause unnecessary bloodshed. Angry mobs were wild and bent on exacting revenge from pro-government clerical dignitaries, and the power vacuum was worse compared to other cities: US forces here could not approach the holy shrine, let alone invade it. The rage pulsating beneath the city was alarming. Yet Majid Kho'i, an optimist and rationalist, took up the challenge. This hideous episode was reminiscent of Dickens's *A Tale of Two Cities*, as angry mobs went wild, armed with knives, daggers, machetes, sticks and firearms – even rocket-propelled grenades. Mobs are wild entities, united by animal instincts, bereft of rationality and blinded by thirst for blood. Of faith they have none; of commitment they know only blind loyalty to a person, or an empty idea of allegiance per se. Such was the pack that attacked the office of the Custodian of the Shrine of Imam Ali, a few minutes before midday prayer. In the office Kho'i was negotiating with the custodian, Haydar, who hails from the well-known Rufai'i noble family. A delegate of Iraqi exiles had volunteered to escort Kho'i in this perilous journey. The Najafi mob entered the shrine of the shrine and blocked the office, demanding the surrender of the custodian, obviously to have him lynched for past cooperation with Ba'th rule. In response to pleas for sanity by Kho'i, the crowd opened fire – an outrageous act of desecration. Ninety minutes passed, and the besieged raised the holy Qur'an and white handkerchiefs and surrendered. The prisoners were tied and dragged by the frenzied mob to the house of their leader, the young cleric and self-appointed authority Muqtada al-Sadr. An eyewitness and himself a prisoner with Kho'i, the Iraqi journalist Ma'ad Fayyadh, was whisked from danger. A moment later, the crowd preyed on the captives, stabbed them to death, mutilated their bodies and dragged the corpses into the streets. This tale of two factions but one city is a symbolic portent of a new rift in the Shi'ite clerical leadership and, by extension, community. The much-feared and predicted Sunni-Shi'i clash proved as mythical as the monolithic unity of religious class in Najaf.[18]

Muqtada al-Sadr: A New Force

The new rising force behind the rift in Najaf is the al-Sadr family, led now by Muqtada al-Sadr, a bearded, sturdy young man with a melancholy, serious look. With an obvious mass following in Najaf, Nasiriya and al-Sadr City (previously Saddam City), Muqtada may have emerged as a surprise equally to the outer world and to the senior members of the clerical leadership in Najaf and in exile. Muqtada was placed under house arrest after the assassination of his father and two brothers in 1999. His father's followers have since covertly recognized him as the 'heir'. In the nineties, Muqtada's father Sadr II, built networks of novices, mostly sheikhs (i.e. non-*sayyids*), and communities of emulators for whom he provided much-needed social services during the sanctions period. Re-instituting the Friday prayers, a heresy or innovation by the norms of Shi'ite jurisprudence, the father led millions in prayers; his fiery speeches became a source of solace, comfort and motivation. He was also a proponent of homegrown Arab clerical headship, which implied a clerical rivalry with Grand Ayatollah Ali al-Sistani, who succeeded Abu al-Qassim al-Kho'i in the 1990s.

The green *mujtahid* seems engaged in a macabre bid for supremacy. The demonstrations were presumably staged under his direction, in his name and by his own followers, in Najaf, Nasiriya and Baghdad in April; they seemed to suggest he was a new Khomeini striving for political power. The situation he created led observers to think it was to some extent reminiscent of mass politics in Tehran, 1979. However, the two cases are, in many respects, worlds apart. The clerical class in Iran ran to 70–80,000 men, with more than 25,000 in Tehran alone. The mass movement that challenged the Shah had an ideological vision, and could snowball to the point of paralysing the army and culminating in mass, urban civil insurrection.

Muqtada al-Sadr, by contrast is not ideological; he has no clear vision of an Islamic state. His loyal following of clerics runs into a few hundred. His movement had been too weak to challenge the Ba'th regime even at the latter's lowest ebb. The very intellectual legacy of the al-Sadr family upholds a vision that is opposed to Khomeini' s version of the Guardianship of the Jurisprudent. The first al-Sadr, for example, advocated an advisory rather than a leading political role for the *'ulama* (see Part V on ideology). Muqtada al-Sadr is thus far not very political either. His endeavours are geared mainly towards the assertion of his supremacy in clerical headship. In other words, he stands for clerical supreme authority by means of street politics. His 'power' mentality may have been a competitive response largely shaped by the fact that other Najafi families like al-Hakim's have already politicised Shi'ism and shifted their clerical status from the nuances of jurisprudence and ecclesiastical excellence to power politics. Another factor behind his violent drive to religious headship is the politicisation of the name of the al-Sadr family. The Da'wa party upheld Ayatollah Muhammad Baqir al-Sadr, (Muqtada's uncle), as a modern symbol of martyrdom and defiance. Muhammad Sadiq al-Sadr (Muqtada's father), who was assassinated in 1999, became a household name. His followers abroad raised him to a symbol of martyrdom. But theirs was a modern, party-politics symbolism. The young Muqtada simply primordialized this symbolism as a family trust. He evokes Shakespeare's fiery Tybalt. His character, age and style represent one of the most dramatic turns in Iraqi Shi'ism since the 19th-century Usuli-Akhbari clashes in Najaf, in which armed gangs were instrumental.

His attempt is to override the clerical norms of seniority, such as knowledge-based rank, scholarly achievement or age; this his weakest point. His age has been controversial. Rivals say he is only twenty-two; loyalists claim he is thirty-two. His actual age could be anywhere in between. His instrument is street politics; this is his strongest point. But he has already met formidable obstacles.

The clerical class has traditionally consisted of family-based leadership embedded in local city solidarity and supra-national networks of emulators and novices. But the 1979 Iranian Revolution affixed ideological fracture lines; these increased the complexities of the social organization of the clergy. Muqtada al-Sadr is now creating a new cleavage: Iraqi anti-government-domestic versus alien pro-government-exile Shi'ite leadership. Thus far, this position has brought him multiple challenges. His hostile position against the exiles and institutions brought him into direct conflict with ideologically fundamentalist groups such as the Da'wa, SAIRI and Munazama, all based in Iran. Tehran has been grooming Muhammad Baqir al-Hakim and his SAIRI since 1982. Muqtada al-Sadr's attitude, then, threatens SAIRI, the Da'wa and Munazama and targets, by extension, the families of al-Hakim and al-Mudarisi. So far, SAIRI's leader has staged a cautious return to his town, Najaf, in such unwelcoming circumstances. His brother Aziz al-Hakim crossed the border with 400 armed men and could only find his way to Najaf a week or so later.

By the same token, the line of confrontation against the forces returning from exile got Muqtada al-Sadr bitterly entangled with the moderate, rational and influential Kho'i Foundation, and the Kho'i family. This is a formidable, representative institution that enjoys some 80 per cent of the Shi'ite *khums* (religious taxes) worldwide.

Single-handedly, he is waging a war against what he termed 'traditional clerics' as against 'non-Iraqi' clerics, and against pro-Ba'th clerics – in a word, against all but himself. His followers allegedly killed the custodian of Najaf and assassinated Majid Kho'i. His second step was to pressure the old Ayatollah Muhammad Said al-Hakim into paying allegiance to him. His forces also besieged Grand Ayatollah al-Sistani's house in Najaf, but al-Sistani's followers rushed in from nearby towns to remove the mob.

In Najaf as elsewhere, tensions are high between these factions. SAIRI, for example, occupied the offices of the Ba'th Party in Najaf; Muqtada al-Sadr reportedly became entrenched inside the Shrine. Iraqis crossing the borders from Iran are augmenting the strength of the old Islamic Shi'ite fundamentalist parties. Iran has also been sending its agents and protégés. Here and there, they raise the slogan: 'Islamic government'. In response, the pro-Muqtada al-Sadr groups are using the slogan: 'Yes to *Hawza*'. A classical Arabic term, this word has a Najafi connotation, meaning the religious leadership in Najaf (it also means 'centres of religious learning'). Since a collegiate body of clerical dignitaries resides in the holy city, the term *hawza* is politically amorphous or ambiguous.

Polarization is accelerating. The collegiate body of clerical authority in Najaf issued a joint statement denouncing the individuals and groups who claim to represent the *hawza*, i.e. religious authority, by raising banners and slogans in its name. The communiqué also said that 'pro-Ba'th security agents have put on the religious garb and begun to give statements before TV cameras, although they hardly speak proper Arabic'. The statement was signed by four grand ayatollahs: Ali al-Sistani, Muhammad Said al-Hakim, Sheikh Muhammad Ishaq Fayadh and Sheikh Bashir al-Najafi.[19]

In London, Ayatollah Hussain al-Sadr categorically denounced assassination, a clear reference to his nephew in Najaf.[20]

Muqtada al-Sadr's movement is not insignificant, but it is also not all-powerful. It took shape under circumstances of steep rise in popular religiosity, in itself a non-fundamentalist and apolitical phenomenon. This is a periphery that may help augment fundamentalism proper.

The young al-Sadr's movement has three disparate components: the clerical core, formed mostly of young clerics and novices who were loyal to his father; the charity networks his father built to channel services; and spontaneous armed mobs, which emerged after the demise of the Ba'th. Much of the momentum is derived from transitory circumstances: power vacuum, lack of security and services and absence of rival, religious and secular groups. In fact, two factions have already broken away from Muqtada al-Sadr. Further splits may well follow. Young al-Sadr, it seems, is in dire need of recognition from senior high-ranking clerics or from the powers that be.

A TV Preacher Reborn

The rise of popular religiosity has been observed in Iraq nationwide across the communal and religious divide. The massive demonstrations in the largest Shi'ite suburb in Baghdad, the millions of pilgrims marching to Karbala on the Arba'in and the mass demonstrations in Nasiriya and Najaf startled Sunnis, clerics and laymen in the Sunni suburb of Baghdad, 'Adhamiya, Mosul, Falluja and beyond. Mosul and the cities of Anbar Province have traditionally been conservative bastions of explosive mixture: Islamism, tribalism and old-fashioned Arabism. The Muslim Brotherhood originated in Mosul and spread in the Anbar (Dulaim) Province. Two presidents hailed from Anbar; so did some republican prime ministers, dozens of cabinet ministers, hundreds of newly rising millionaires and thousands of high- and medium-ranking military commanders. A sense of loss embitters their lives.

The Brotherhood, dormant for decades under the Ba'th, received fresh air in the aftermath of the defeat in 1991. Sunni preachers were encouraged in state-owned mosques, run by the Ministry of Religious Endowments (*awqaf*). Bearded young men with short robes (the Iraqi *dishdasha*) became regular sights in Baghdad, Mosul, Ramadi, Falluja and beyond. Among the rising stars was a television preacher, Ahmad Kubaisi, who had been promoted in the United Arab Emirates. Shortly after the fall of Baghdad Kubaisi, known for his strong liaisons with the Ba'th government, was flown to Baghdad to start fiery speeches and lead a 10,000–strong demonstration after Friday prayers. Deploying anti-American slogans and motifs, Kubaisi cast himself in a patriotic role. He soon announced the formation of a 'Patriotic Front'. A few days on, an Islamic party – the old Muslim Brotherhood – was announced in Mosul. Less than a week later (30 April) demonstrations started in the conservative and traditional small town of Falluja.

Members of the defeated regime – including military commanders, junior officers from the Republican Guard, and officers of the Security and Intelligence Services – enjoying their newfound freedoms, flocked to these outfits, partly to resist change, partly to influence its course, partly to get recognition from the US and partly to counterbalance Shi'ite militancy.

Kubaisi, for example praised what he called Shi'ite anti-Americanism, and called for a Sunni-Shi'i alliance. Shi'i dignitaries retorted that this was a trap to alienate them from the US and depict them as troublemakers.[21]

While a strong sense of Iraqi nationalism exists, the majority of Iraqis seem to agree that a premature withdrawal of the US-UK forces will be conducive to a power vacuum and civil war. Unless an Iraqi civil administration with solid institutions of power is firmly on the ground, obtaining the withdrawal of the allied forces would be a dangerous cause. The majority, save the defeated regime, shares this pragmatic conclusion. Overstaying, on the other hand, will definitely be counterproductive.

Prospects

Tyranny empties society of its modern self-defences, leaving sacred institutions intact. Religion has worldly roots; it works as antidote to war and death, crime and prostitution; it is an identity marker, a provider of charities, a source of moral support and a substitute for discredited ideologies.

The latter point merits elaboration. In 1967, following defeat in the June 1967 Arab-Israeli war, Nasserism went into decline; popular religion and Islamism were on the rise. Iraq had been an aberration: Arab nationalist-socialism assumed power exactly at that point. Now that the Islamism seems on the decline, can Iraq prove to be yet an aberration?

The focus on Islam and Islamism in this introduction may convey a larger-than-life, hence misleading picture. These forces are prominent by default. Modern forces and rational clerics supportive of secular politics have not said their piece yet. Unlike armed mobs from shantytowns that used to agitate on the left in the 60s, modern secular forces now are not wanting – but they are seemingly inactive, at least for the moment. Perhaps that is why Iraq seems a land overwhelmed by tribal chiefs and turbaned clerics. The situation as a whole seems undecided. What will remain of mob-street politics if decommissioning is effected, or if services are reintroduced to render religious charities and clerical supervision superfluous, or if, in addition, secular, civil associations are rehabilitated?

Much will depend on what the *de facto* US civil rule will do or be willing to do. Will it go for the minimalist approach or opt for democratisation and secularisation? Iraq's true challenge now is to find the answer for which Majid al-Kho'i willingly risked his life.

Faleh A. Jabar
London, 2 May 2003

PART ONE

State, Nation and Islamism

ONE

Overview

Shi'ite militant Islam and Shi'ism in general have been the focus of sustained attention since the phenomenal success of the Iranian Revolution in 1979. Yet, beyond the Iranian case, research on the role of Shi'i Islam in politics across the Middle East has attracted little academic writing (Cole and Keddie, 1986). Even less attention has been given to Shi'ism and Shi'ite militancy in Iraq, which preceded the Iranian Revolution, and still less to their nature, origins, the social movements they have developed, social actors involved, ideological responses they gave rise to and the specific sources of power and legitimacy their *'ulama* (doctors of religion) wielded. These aspects remained relatively obscure or under-studied.

One of the main sources of ambiguity is the lack of differentiation between the various national settings in which Shi'ism developed and the divergent historical trajectories they took, common theological traits notwithstanding. This research is an attempt to fill the gap in our understanding of the social origins, actors and ideology of Shi'ite Islamism in Iraq which forms both part of the general and gradual rise of social movements of militant Islam (Islamism, fundamentalism) on one hand, and, on the other, constitutes a renewed response on the part of Iraqi Shi'ite activism. This is what makes it a *sui generis*, unique case which defies oversimplified reductionist concepts.

The rise of modern Shi'ite Islamic militancy in Iraq can be dated to the late 1950s (after the demise of the monarchy in July 1958), although its roots go back much further. By the mid-1960s, under the authoritarian/military regime of the 'Arif brothers (1963–68), Islamic activism thrived beyond the expectations of its own originators. By the mid-1970s, mass Islamic protests and the executions in 1974 of many Shi'i Islamic leaders by the Ba'th regime revealed the extent to which Shi'ite Islamism was in action and capable of defying a formidable regime long before the rise of Khomeini. In 1977, mass anti-Ba'th protests and demonstrations in Najaf, Karbala and Khan al-Nus, during the Marad al-Ras (Arba'in) pilgrimage to the shrine cities, shook political life, causing splits in the ruling elite. Since then, the upsurge of Shi'ite Islamism has been a major feature of Iraq's political and social development. Before, during and after the Iranian Revolution, this trend influenced national politics and was one among many catalysts contributing to the outbreak of the Iraq-Iran war (1980–88). It contained the organizations or groups that played a major role in the destabilizing, violent campaign during the first Gulf war, and an even greater part in the February 1991 anti-Ba'th uprisings which gained control of thirteen out of seventeen governorships. These groups and organizations still hold strong positions in the opposition inside Iraq or in exile, wielding cultural influence, economic power and mass political potency. They are supported by vast social networks, military organizations and autonomous, informal institutions with relatively large clerical revenues. They also count as influential actors in regional politics.

The Literature

Compared to the vast literature on religion in relation to state and society in Iran, which is covered by various disciplines (history, sociology, politics, anthropology), research on religion in Iraq in recent decades – and Shi'i Islam in particular – has not received sufficient, if any, attention. The few exceptions include Wardi's *Lamahat,* Fernea's *Shaykh and Effendi,* Salim's *al-Chibayish,* Nafisi's *The Political Role of the Shi'a of Iraq,* Ruhaimi's *History of the Islamic Movement in Iraq* and Nakash's *The Shi'a of Iraq.* These scholarly works, however, focus on the pre-1958 period. In half of them, the main research is only partially focused on Shi'i Islam. This paucity of scholarly work stems partly from the insurmountable difficulty of conducting field research in Iraq under the Ba'th totalitarian regime.

Standard political or social histories which cover the post-1958 period are confined to a few paragraphs or a section, providing a general profile on the Shi'a in what may be termed the 'problem of the Shi'a'. The 'problem' figures in the briefest of manners, the sole exception being the Slugletts' corpus of work, which dedicates several separate papers to the topic. Generally, most sources used in the standard histories are either secondary or, when primary, are insufficient and meagre. These sources include official, mostly biased Iraqi documents, some concise British Foreign Office reports or scanty statements by Islamist informants who were still clandestine activists. Thus most authors have been more inclined to present a general overview or an analysis of single, often isolated episodes. There has, moreover, been a degree of 'recycling' of information in these works.

In the mid-1980s and early 1990s, Shi'ite Islamism in Iraq and beyond assumed greater importance, and the flow of relevant information increased. Consequently a number of papers, essays, books and dissertations on the topic appeared, the more important ones from Batatu, Mallat, Baram, Bengio, Wiley, Jens Uwe-Rahe and Ibrahim Ferhad.

Depending on their topic, these studies include either:

(i)   an overview on the Shiʿa of Iraq to assess the 'communal factor';
(ii)   a study of certain Shiʿite Islamist movements;
(iii)   an analysis of the doctrinal innovation in law (by al-Sadr)
(iv)   an examination of single political episodes (the 1974 executions, the 1977 confrontation).

While insight into these and other aspects of Shiʿite Islamism is provided, understandably little consideration is given to the social and doctrinal origins of various movements; their organizations; command structures; the nature of actors as segmentary-lineage status groups or modern classes; analyses of ideology; and the structure of Shiʿite cultural spaces, with their supportive resources or inhibiting barriers.

Meticulous as these papers and studies are, they still fall short in the quantity and depth found in studies of the Iranian case. What we have in the Iraqi case is no more than a dozen papers (Batatu, three; Cummings, one; Bengio, two; Haim, one; Baram, two; Mallat, one; Slugletts, three; Kedourie, two; Stapleton, one); three books (Wiley, Mallat and Ferhad) and two dissertations (Uwe-Rahe and Clark).

Theoretical Approaches

Three distinct approaches underpin the literature on Shiʿism and Shiʿite Islamist activism in Iraq: communal, cultural-essentialist and conjunctural.

The basic concepts of the communal pattern revolve on the community versus society (*gemeinschaft/gesellschaft*) dichotomy, which looks at the Sunni minority-dominated state *vis-à-vis* the Shiʿite majority-oppressed community. Within this framework Islamist militancy among the Shiʿis is seen as an expression of grievances arising from this tense dichotomy. Many authors subscribe to or share some aspects of this approach (Baram, Bengio, Luizard, Ferhad and, to a lesser extent, Nakash). In most cases, Shiʿism, Shiʿis and Shiʿite Islamism figure almost as one and the same thing, as if they were a sociological category: a homogenous, monolithic sociocultural entity. This approach lends a fixed essence to communal spaces and structures and the identity (or identities) they produce, sometimes imbued even with a mono-dimensional social or political activism as if religious culture in and of itself creates a unifying space of a social and political nature under any circumstances. It therefore overlooks social and cultural diversity within the Shiʿis, whether during the agrarian or modern epochs or the transformative phase from the one to the other.

The reality that religious culture, to use Victor Turner's term, is a multivocal space, and that forms of religiosity (Weber, *The Sociology of Religion*) differ widely from one social group to another is to some extent blurred or ignored in the communal approach. *Gemeinschaften*, as is clear from Batatu's voluminous work, have constantly been caught in the process of transformation to modern forms of social organization and culture, so that old forms existed at different levels of transformed symbiosis with new, modern forms. Their reality is far more complex and richer in terms of social organization and culture than the communal approach allows: the tribe, the clan, extended families, urban guilds, status groups, city neighborhoods and city solidarities all split religious spaces and cut across such totalizing categories as Sunnis, Shi'is or even Kurds.

As distinct from the communal, the *culturalist* approach was more often than not recurrently applied after the 1979 Islamic Revolution in Iran in an attempt to explain Islamic militancy in general or Shi'i Islam in particular. Cultural essentialism attributes the rise of Islamism to the resilience of Islam as such (Lewis, Gellner, Huntington and others). This notion derives from Orientalist traditions as well as from Weber's Orient-Occident cultural polarity. Incompatibility with modernity, or the absence of 'sufficient' separation of the secular from the sacred, is thought by this school to plague Islam and cause a cyclical motion, i.e. the revival of fundamentalism; a traditional upheaval; a harking back to the past; and a rebellion against modernization and modernity. A variation of this approach is the notion that Shi'ism as such is a radically anti-modern-state doctrine. Here, the concept of the Hidden Imam, which denies legitimacy to worldly powers, is claimed to have been the source of a cultural rejection of modernity of which the ruling elites in the Middle East were a part. Shi'ism is held to be radical by dint of the logical structure of the theo-jurisitic doctrine itself; its social and political activism and action is deduced from this source with no due consideration to sociopolitical, economic and other factors. Both the communal and cultural approaches therefore share a common reductionist methodology.

A subtler framework can be found in the conjunctural approach, which has provided us with a range of comparative studies of Shi'ite social movements (Batatu, Zubaida, Cole and Keddie, among others). According to Cole and Keddie, Shi'ite Islamist militancy in the Middle East (Iraq, Lebanon, Saudi Arabia, Afghanistan and Iran) might be classified according to two different patterns. The first is the *social pattern* where Islamist protest is caused and stimulated by many catalysts and factors among which are the 'factors of economic and social change that are common to many Muslim countries, and sometimes Third World countries'. (1986, p. 3) The second pattern is *local*, where Shi'ite activism is spurred by protest against group discrimination under authoritarian regimes in specific nation-states.

Among the outstanding research into the dynamics of ramified social change relative to Shi'ite Islamist militancy are the works by Batatu and the Slugletts. Batatu (1977) carries sociological analyses far beyond the oversimplified Shi'i-Sunni antagonism. In the words of the Slugletts (1991):

The notion of the heterogeneity of Iraqi society is another theme that needs further definition and refinement. The facts are that the population of Iraq, now about 18 million, is divided on both ethnic and sectarian lines. Of course, *neither the communities nor the sect constitute homogeneous or monolithic single entities*. A *simplistic image* of Iraqi society has emerged, largely under the influence of Middle Eastern 'experts' of the US defence establishment, of 'Arab Sunnis' supporting the 'Sunni' regime of Saddam Hussein and the allegedly 'somewhat less Arab' Shi'is (a sort of Iranian fifth column) bitterly opposed to it ... (*The Historiography of Modern Iraq*, 1991, pp. 1412–3. Italics added.)

Wider literature on the rise of Islamism across the Middle East, including Shi'ite Islamism, has provided ample evidence that religion has various institutionalized forms and social actors, different cultural forms and various modalities operating within distinct and changing contexts (Kepel, Sivan, Akhavi, Abrahamian, Mortimer, Enayat and Mottahedeh, to name some examples). In addition, research on the case of Iraq has shown that Shi'ism in that country, in comparison to other nationally embedded 'Shi'isms', is *sui generis* in cultural and sociological terms (Batatu; Nakash, 1994).

Shi'ite Islamism, it has been argued, is either part of the general rise of Islamism across the Middle East (Islamism proper) or simply a 'local response' in the narrow sense of the word. Our argument is that Shi'ite Islamism is a combination of the two and that it is a much more complex phenomenon. We can begin to establish this proposition by identifying the social origins, structures and cultural spaces of Shi'i Islam in the micro and macro sociopolitical settings under which they evolved, and the system(s) of ideology they produced in this context.

This thesis is premised on a theoretical framework made up of three interconnected themes:

(i) Political Islam or Islamism, including Shi'ite Islamism, is a conjunctural phenomenon, not a simple cultural or traditional response to or rejection of modernity and modernization. Shi'ite Islamist activism in the broadest sense of the term has been part of successive Islamic responses, first to the liberal-constitutional reformation of the late 19th and early 20th centuries; second, to the cultural-exclusivist response of the second half of the 20th century (which may be termed fundamentalist); lastly, the authoritarian-populist response of the late 20th century (which may be designated Islamist). The Iraqi version of Islamic responses has, to varying degrees, been influenced by these three successive 'waves', all of which reveal a great deal of discontinuity in terms of bearers, movements and platforms, although they have some degree of doctrinal continuity in their reference to Islam, tradition or some Islamic paradigm (early pristine Islam, or Fischer's Karbala paradigm).

(ii)   The pre- and post-national social structures in Iraq are conceived in the theoretical framework of Batatu's *Old Social Classes* as fluid and in constant change, shifting from segmentary, lineage or local traditional solidarities to modern ones as result of the transformation of Iraqi society. In these structures, local solidarities of the guild, the clan, the neighbourhood, the city and the tribe rather than 'religious' configurations were the elementary, basic forms of social cohesion and allegiance – and these were eroding.

(A critical remark here should be added. In Batatu's meticulous work, status groups like *sayyids*, tribal sheikhs or social structures, develop in a lineal-type motion. Social change during the last decades of the twentieth century, however, has provided evidence of the resurgence, for example, of *'ulama*, *sayyids* and tribal sheikhs. The rise of Iranian *'ulama* to power in 1979 boosted the social status of *'ulama-sayyids* in Iraq, thereby inhibiting the previous process of their decline. This change was partial and limited to political movements. The dislocations caused by two Gulf wars and international sanctions imposed since 1990 weakened the state and created a social void which was filled by local community structures: familial, clannish, tribal and communitarian. Thus the seemingly lineal trajectory of social development turned cyclical. Tribal organization was revived, and so were status groups like *sayyids* (nobles), sheikhs and the like. While reducing the validity of the lineal aspect in Batatu's analysis, this line of development does not in the least touch the basic assumption that local community structures rather than pan-religious ones form the reference point for analysis.)

In this approach, Shi'is do not form a monolithic, homogenous, cultural/social entity bestowed with a uniform identity and imbued with a unity of interests and purpose, but are rather diverse, even sundry groups adapting and reacting to their changing reality and subscribing to various ideological constructions – of which Shi'ite Islamism or Shi'ite communalism was only one among many cultural and political discourses.

(iii)   Within political or cultural units such as the nation-state or a particular religion or doctrine, forms of religiosity differ radically from one social group to another (Weber). The major distinction here is made between the literate, textual/canonical doctrine of the clerical class or the *'ulama* on one hand – a Weberian ethical religion *par excellence* – and on the other hand, the Durkheimian, expressive, community-centred ceremonial rituals in the city quarters and small provincial towns – the habitat of the lower, petty classes. Islamism as a modern construct bridges, transcends or even substitutes for the two in a novel unity or replacement. This differentiation is meant to conceptualize the culture of the clerics as distinct from the culture of community rituals (*'Ashura*, lamentation assemblies, processions and passion plays) (Fischer, 1980). This differentiation may apply to Sunni Islam as well, to mark off Sufi orders – with their autonomous social organization and passionate rituals – from the state-sponsored, scriptural religion of the *'ulama*, with its legalities and ethical terms (Eickelman, 1976).

The empirical research presented in this thesis studies the three major agents or bearers (the Hegelian *traeger*) of Islamism:

(i)   the clerical class;
(ii)   the mercantile class in Najaf;
(iii)   the modern middle-class intellectuals.

The segmentary lineage or local divisions and networks, and the sources of social power, interests and culture of these social categories, are examined in historical sequence. By examining their relative microcosms (the family, social group, city) and the way they are conditioned by and react to the macro setting – the Iraqi nation-state and the wider Islamic environment across the Middle East – the nature of the Islamist responses will be brought into a clearer relief as they originate, evolve and mutate. The discourse through which these agents or actors conceive of their own transformation and reality is brought into contrast with these changes on one hand, while on the other hand the logical structure of the discourse is examined separately as an ideology.

The study is empirical, relying on a considerable volume of primary sources: documents and literature (some of which is emerging for the first time), extensive interviews and field observation.

Major Primary Sources

Shi'ite Islamist movements and groups remained cloaked in tight, underground secrecy for almost two decades from 1958–59 to 1980 and even beyond. In the aftermath of the 1979 Iranian Revolution, they started to release regular publications: weeklies or monthlies, party circulars, statements, press interviews, research reviews and platforms. Compared to the almost total obscurity that had prevailed in previous years, these materials provide some useful sources of information. Yet, they remained insufficient and hence partly unreliable.

After the Iraq-Iran war (1980–88), a massive migration brought a considerable number of the members, cadres and leaders of these movements to Western Europe and the US. The rigid atmosphere of secrecy among them – caused by the fear of secret police infiltration and concern over security – decreased, while a greater confidence and better appreciation of the importance of public relations and media developed. The true change in this respect came after the first Gulf war in 1991, when most groups came more boldly into the open. Their activists authored a host of works on their history, action and clandestine organization. Public meetings, open lectures and other similar activities unveiled detailed, though, academically speaking, inconsistent accounts of their history, strategies, structures and schisms. Nevertheless, quarrels among different splinter groups helped to reduce areas of obscurity. In this atmosphere access to classified Shi'ite Islamist party documents became less difficult.

On the other hand, the official archive of the Iraqi security services contains a wealth of information. Opposition groups confiscated a considerable part of this archive, some 40–50 tons of documents, during the 1991 uprisings. A great portion of this confiscated archive is being processed in Washington (Makkiya). Another portion is at the disposal of opposition groups, and there is easy access to it. Although this second portion is still disorganized, it is of paramount importance to the study of various aspects of social and political life in Iraq, including Shi'ite activism. The full publication of all the available documents will doubtless greatly widen our horizon.

High-ranking Ba'th officials who have defected to the West or elsewhere, and who include important military, security, diplomatic and party figures, are another source of information, although still of a fragmented kind.

Finally, Foreign Office reports and correspondence on Iraq are useful for the early phases of the movement after 1958, particularly under the 'Arif regime, although it focuses on the general relationship between the 'state' and 'the Shi'a'. Most of these documents have been collected and published in Arabic translation and with commentary by SAIRI's speaker in Europe, Hamid al-Bayati.

We may classify our primary sources as follows:

(i)   *Islamist Party Organs* These include various regular political weeklies, monthlies and quarterlies published from 1980 in Tehran, Damascus, London and other locations: *al-Jihad, al-Da'wa al-Islamiya, al-'Amal al-Islami, al-Badil al-Islami, Tariq al-Thawra, Liwa' al-Sadr* and others. These provide good information on party history, interviews with leaders, biographical details on leaders and activists, coverage of some episodes (violent operations such as bombings or assassination attempts) and political positions and statements. Quarterlies such as *al-Jihad* or *Majalat Dirasat wa Buhuth* are a good source of ideological and intellectual production on political theory, economic doctrines, theological issues and ideological debates against nationalism and Marxism.

(ii)   Islamist Party Indoctrination/Educational Literature: Besides their party press, various organizations have produced countless booklets designed to educate their membership in party discipline, dogma or history. They give a wealth of information on organizational issues, party history and problems of strategy. Of special importance in this respect are the volumes of Da'wa documents titled *Thaqafat al-Da'wa* (*Da'wa Doctrine*). These are printed in six volumes, two of them subtitled 'The Political Section'. These six volumes, still reserved only for advanced cadres of the party, provide the richest source on the Da'wa during the years 1958–79. Thanks to a leading figure in the Da'wa, I have had access to them. The text of these volumes is not well-organized and the table of contents needs to be reorganized to establish order in terms of sequence and topic.

(iii) Islamist Literature: Works produced by writers and activists on the political development and activities of various groups, and biographical studies of leading figures such as al-Sadr, Sahib al-Dakhil and others – though possibly tainted by inaccuracies, discrepancies, inconsistencies, partisan bias and posthumous eulogizing – contain a wealth of internal material and some first-hand information, in addition to biographical details of activists which helps to establish sociological profiles.

(iv)   Theoretical Works of the Spiritual or Actual Leaders: These works, such as al-Sadr's, al-Mudarisi's or Shirazi's various economic, political and philosophical treatises are of tremendous importance to study the ideology of Shi'ite Islamism in its long and contradictory development. Only al-Sadr's works have been studied so far (see Mallat, 1993 and the German edition of *Iqtisaduna*, translated and introduced by Andreas Rieck, 1984).

(v)   Interviews and Conversations: Around forty leaders, advanced cadres, ex-ministers, practising politicians and functionaries have been interviewed or questioned. The term 'interview' denotes a lengthy session of no less than three hours. This is meant to establish a personal profile (biographical details), family history and political history. The interviews were also sessions geared towards studying political motivation and gaining information on the internal structure of the party, forms of agitation, operation, mobility, schisms and the like. They were additionally designed to scrutinize details and check various accounts of different episodes, and gain insight into states of mind during various periods of action. 'Conversations', by contrast, were more informal and the use of this term denotes a shorter meeting with a fixed set of questions to clarify certain points from the interviewee who, by dint of his or her official position, direct experience or family membership could provide information on various points and issues. The number of interviewees fixed in the table of interviews is confined only to leading figures. Rank-and-file individuals from various organizations have not been included, although their experiences were made use of in the text.

While interviews and conversation provide first-hand information, this material – as is well known in field – has many shortcomings. It may contain inaccurate recollections due to faulty memory or, perhaps, bias. Self-interested presentation of events, posthumous eulogies of certain charismatic leaders or 'martyrs' and a change of alliances or sides and other factors taint such information, and scrutiny becomes all the more necessary. When no concrete evidence helps to determine the issue, a set of hypothetical combinations has been presented. Due to family values or official position, some interviewees withheld permission to be directly quoted – as is the case with some Kho'i and Sayyid Hamid Husuna's and Sayyid Jamal al-Din's kin or associates.

(vi)   Ba'th party documents, booklets and directives.

(vii) Iraqi government publications archive: statistics, military and security directives and miscellaneous correspondence.

TWO

Islamism, Fundamentalism, Communalism and the Nation-State

The Complexity of the Iraqi Case

The analysis of Shiʿite Islamist activism in Iraq presents an intricate case in the light of two facts. One is the resilience and spread of Shiʿite and Sunni Islamism and fundamentalism across the Middle East from the early 1970s. The other is the concomitant rise of sectarian militancy in multi-communal societies.

Religious militancy in Egypt, Iran, Sudan and Algeria is an example of Islamism and fundamentalism proper. The cases of Shiʿite activism in Lebanon, Saudi Arabia (the eastern province) and Afghanistan are examples of communal militancy. The coincidence of these two overlapping phenomena has, at times, obscured the fact that they are two distinct cases, at least in their origins and strategies.[1] The complexity and richness of the Iraqi example derives from the fact that it is a unique combination of the two cases.

Broadly speaking, Islamism constitutes a populist movement and ideology of the middle and lower middle classes and strata who seek to defy post-colonial, authoritarian nationalist regimes in their mutation from corporate *étatisme* to the liberalized, deregulated economy that has caused sociocultural tensions under new or enhanced conditions of alliance with the West.[2] This was triggered by a combination of domestic sociopolitical change and external national defeat. These movements opt for radical, extra-institutional politics and/or communitarian activity to achieve their conception of the re-Islamization of society and polity through the application of the *Shariʿa* (Islamic law). Communal militancy, by contrast, seems to be a responsive, segmentary movement(s) caused by political, economic or cultural group-discrimination, and opts to remedy these and other grievances in multi-communal societies.[3]

The first case is mainly the result of sociopolitical, economic and cultural dynamism common to so many Middle Eastern, and in some cases Third World, countries; the second is the result of certain unbalanced nation-building and state-formation processes and policies. In both cases, there are

41

unrepresentative, unresponsive, exclusivist regimes, mostly single-party systems. The processes and policies resulting in communal militancy differ widely from country to country. The case of Lebanon differs radically from that of Saudi Arabia or Iraq. Having different political systems and different forms of legitimacy, political or economic participation, national integration and social configuration, each case has become *sui generis*. True, the sets of processes in the first (Islamist) and second (communal) cases overlap and interact, particularly when we consider the nature of the symbiotic relationship between socio-economic change and state formation and nation building. Yet these two sets can and must be separated, at least conceptually.

The understanding of the Iraqi case of Shiʿite Islamic militancy requires the analysis of the nature of Islamism and fundamentalism on one hand and of the nature of state formation and nation building in Iraq, on the other, in order to delineate the boundaries and various forms of Shiʿite Islamic activism of Iraq. In this chapter, we shall analyse the changing phases of Islamism and fundamentalism as well as the specific development of the Iraqi nation-state and society relative to Shiʿism.

The Changing Phases of Islamic Response

Defining the Boundaries of Islamism

During the 1970s, the terms 'Islamism' and 'fundamentalism' began to circulate as synonyms for the new waves of a surging political Islam. More than a decade later, a thorough scrutiny of the conceptual basis underlying the usage of these two terms led to a questioning of the validity of the term 'fundamentalism',[4] the differentiation between the two,[5] and the application of the term 'Islamism' as a substitute, to describe contemporary political Islam as a modern and novel construction.[6]

As a discourse or movement, Islamic activism dates back to the late 19th century, when Muslim thinkers attempted to restructure and reform the traditional tenets of their religion in order to meet the needs of modernizing society and polity, to better challenge the superior West on an equal footing and to achieve progress. This went down in history as the reformation movement and was mistakenly depicted as the only major reformation and defiance to the West in the world of Islam. This is an extremely narrow conception for the following reasons:

(i)   It excludes all forms of Islam which had an encounter with the West but produced no innovation of religion.

(ii)   It excludes those who effected innovation in religion without being stimulated by such an encounter.

(iii)   It excludes those who experienced neither such an encounter nor such an innovation, but were still socially and politically effective in institutional, cultural or political terms.

There are abundant examples on each count. They include the Usuli versus the Akhbari controversy, or the Babi movement versus the orthodox school, disputes which dotted 19th-century Shi'i Islam and involved a renewal of the creed. The self-generated interpretation of Islam, as with the Wahhabi Hanbalite school of Ottoman Arabia in the early 19th century – the prototype of fundamentalism proper – is an example of reformation and political crusade. Sufi traditionalism, on the other hand, involved a military and cultural encounter with the West without any reform of dogma. The Sufi Qadiriya fought the French, and the Mahdiya Sufi movement in the Sudan defied British-Egyptian domination in the late 19th century; other Sufi movements were politically decisive, as they created a central agrarian polity *à la* Sanusiya in Ottoman Libya.[7]

As we can see, from the late 19th to the late 20th centuries Islamic activism has included movements from a spectrum ranging from radical and liberal reformation to cultural, essentialist conservatism, all of which have presented a specific interpretation of Islam and mounted challenges to the West.

Students of and actors in these movements may well be struck by the seeming similarity of theological and other themes common to most of these trends. Their pivot is the theme of the centrality of religion. Either the traditional religion is conceived to be eternal and true, transcending any need for innovation, or a paradigm of pure, pristine Islam is constructed and deployed together with the call to retrieve it. This involves a move to purify Islam, and to redefine it so as to exclude accretions and untrue, existing interpretations. This purified, all-embracing version of Islam is then reintegrated into polity and society, whether in the moral, social or political life of the individual, the community or the life of the nation (in whatever term this word is interpreted).[8] This concept, so recurrent among reformers, would divide the high-cultural space of Islam into a true, pure Islam which stands in antagonistic contradistinction to 'untrue', 'corrupt' versions of Islam and/or alien ideologies; it would also set this newly constructed version of purified Islam in contradistinction to the traditional orthodox Islam, Sufi Islam and low, popular religious culture.

In the course of a century or so, the theme of a pure, all-embracing Islam has been held by various social actors produced different discourses and a variety of strategies under changing historical contexts: we may find it in al-Afghani's liberal-constitutional activism, 'Abdo's pedagogical reformation,

Wahhabi warrior centralizing conservatism, Hassan El-Banna's cultural essentialism or Khomeini's populist authoritarianism.

The multitude of these trends and movements may be classified, for the sake of clarity, into three successive waves which have flowed through a century or so and have different natures despite the existence of some elements of continuity: the first is the 19th-century Islamic reformation as distinct from the fundamentalism proper of Wahhabi Hanbalism and anti-Western Sufi movements of the 19th and early 20th centuries; the second is the movement initiated by the Muslim Brotherhood in 1928 in Egypt, which we can consider as a new version of fundamentalism which marked the colonial era; the third is the most recent wave best exemplified by the Iranian Revolution, which we will term 'Islamism'.[9] The diversity and mutation of these waves will be discussed below.

An Attempt at Classification

The question as to whether or not Islam has a fixed essence has been, and will continue to be, a much debated subject.[10] Our argument is that this question in itself has generally been devoid of the historical context necessary for the examination of a creed which extends over vast areas and continents and is embraced by a multitude of social agents in the context of many and varied rural or urban, verbal and literate cultures – each in different degrees of transformation.[11] This becomes clear when we look in more detail at the three waves of Islamic activism.

The 19th-Century Landscape

The 19th century was an era of massive change for Islam, caused by the dynamics of the West's advance into its domains or sustained by dynamics operating from within the Muslim world itself. Both these sources of change brought about a diverse range of theological, social, political and military movements within both Sunni and Shi'i Islam.

In the 19th century Sunni Islam developed various trends:

(i)   the rational reformation and Islamic nationalism of al-Afghani and 'Abdo (in Egypt and the Ottoman domains) and Khair al-Din Pasha (in Ottoman Tunisia), or the theological and pedagogical reformation (the case of Sayyid Ahmad Khan of India);

(ii)   the theological revival of mediaeval Hanbalism in the form of Wahhabism in Ottoman Arabia;

(iii) the Sufi or Sufi-tribal orders of Qadiriya (Algeria), Mahdiya (the Sudan) or even Sanusiya (Libya).

Of these three different trends, only (i) and (ii) involved a new interpretation of Islam to meet different challenges. The third involved challenge without reform. Case (i) represents Islamic reformation; Case (ii) is the prototype of fundamentalism; Case (iii) represents traditionalism proper. We will now compare the theological aspects, social actors, strategies and medium of action in these cases. Some of these trends, as we shall see, continued well into the early decades of the 20th century. Some perished (Sufi warriors), others triumphed (Wahhabism) and others mutated.

The Islamic Reformation: Theology, Pedagogy and Politics of Modernization
In the face of the advancing and advanced West, Muslim state functionaries and thinkers sought ways and means to stem the tide of decline which was felt in the military and economic fields. As early as the 18th century, the Ottomans lost a series of military encounters (notably against Russia), while their revenues from the provinces plunged because the pattern of world trade had changed as a result of European commercial expansion.[12] Reform sprang from state functionaries, and had a military aura coming mainly in the guise of reorganized standing armies and new military-industrial projects.[13]

A second generation carried reform further to the very heart of political structures. On the heels of centralization, constitutionalism and nationalism followed as aspects of reform. At this point, the internal battle between advocates and adversaries of reform shifted from the arena of the state and its structures to cultural innovation. The urgency of this reform was brought home by the great loss the Muslim empires had sustained and were sustaining: the demise of the Muslim Moghuls in India; the occupation of Egypt by Britain; the secession of Greece and Bulgaria from the Ottoman Empire; and the increasing fragility of Qajar Iran in the face of British and Russian encroachment − not to mention the fate of Algeria, Tunisia and Morocco, which fell prey to French colonial control.

It is in this context that Islamic reform was initiated to introduce modernity and its accompanying principles of constitutionalism, science and rationality. Undoubtedly the figure of Jamal al-Din al-Afghani stands in bold relief, but thinkers like Khair al-Din Pasha, al-Afghani's disciple Muhammad 'Abdo or Sayyid Ahmad Khan made no less an impact on the 19th-century reform movement. With the exception of Ahmad Khan who studied economics in England,[14] these thinkers were educated in traditional Islamic learning.[15] Yet, all shared the conviction that religion, Islam, is the decisive driving force of civilization, and that the reformation of religion was a major starting point whether for pedagogical ends (Khan and 'Abdo) or political ends (Pasha and al-Afghani).[16]

But what kind of reform, and in what direction? The main thrust of religious and political reform sought out by this mainly, but not exclusively, intellectual movement was the introduction of modern concepts and theories into the realm of Islamic thought. This was perceived to be the only effective way to stand against Europe on an equal footing. The Reformation involved reason versus tradition, secular sciences versus religious 'knowledge', constitutionalism versus 'sacralized' dynasties, rational theology versus fatalist dogma and Sufi traditionalism.[17] It was a cultural revolution often visualized by some of its authors as a parallel to Lutheran Protestantism.[18] As a response to decline it was an onslaught against traditional and Sufi Islam. These thinkers sought to 'prove' to their fellow countrymen, and above all to the political and traditional-minded religious elites, that Islam and science were not in disharmony; that *'aql* (reason) is central in the teaching of Islam; that the Qur'anic principle of *shura* (consultation) is akin to the constitutional arrangements of polities; and that the *ahl al-hal wal 'aqd* concept (people who bind and loose, i.e. the traditional leading elite) is the equivalent of the modern parliament. Al-Afghani went even further to de-sacralize the supreme seat of power by proclaiming that the selection and deposing of rulers are worldly matters, a daring breakthrough in a world of 'sacred' dynasties.[19]

These arguments aimed to create secular spaces for human cultural and political agency. The reformers could deploy the rich heritage of classical theology, notably that of the mediaeval Mu'tazilite school, against fatalism, conservatism and Sufism, and depict these as accretions which tainted pristine Islam.[20] The cutting edge of the concept of *tawhid* (unity of God) for example, was directed by the reformers against traditionalism.[21] The terms *'ilm* (science) and *'aql* (reason) were the most recurrent terms in their discourse. Pro-British Ahmad Khan notwithstanding, the reformation had the aura of Islamic nationalism.[22] Al-Afghani combined his anti-imperialist, pan-Islamic designs with an innovative concept of human cohesion. He specified two forms of collective bond in society: that of religion and that of ethnicity (*jins*, in his own word). He even challenged the long-accepted idea of the community of believers by stressing that certain communities could change their religion without renouncing their ethnicity.[23]

The agents of reform were men of the pen or religious dignitaries who belonged to the small literati class of the agrarian Muslim world of the 19th century. They were an urban, educated elite who, in this battle of ideas, could deploy the most advanced tools of communication of their time: the printed word and the telegraph line. The Islamic reformation represented a modernization of Islam in the battle for survival. Paradoxically, it was called the Salafi movement, a designation deriving from *salaf al-salih*, the pious ancestors who stand as the symbol of idealized, pristine Islam free of accretions.

The reformation movement was contradictory, and had a secular and traditional mix. Where it continued into the 20th century, it split into different trends. The secular nationalist movements in Egypt and elsewhere inherited constitutionalism, secular politics and rational theology.[24] This tendency culminated in the rise of the national movement in Egypt, and the constitutional revolutions of Qajar Iran in 1906 and Ottoman Turkey in 1909.

In the post-World War I period, the nationalist independence movements of the Muslim world inherited these secular aspects of the Islamic reformation. Meanwhile, under the impact of 'Abdo, pedagogical religious reformation continued elsewhere – for example, in Algeria at the hands of Abdul Hamid bin Badis in the 1930s.[25] Al-Afghani's Islamic activism also bequeathed the traditional aspects of its discourse to a new form of cultural essentialism represented by the Muslim Brotherhood launched by Hassan El-Banna in 1928.

Archetypes of Fundamentalism: Pristine Islam, Desert Warriors and the Centralized Pre-National Polity

Before, during and after the advance of the reformation as a modernizing trend, a theological call developed in Najd, Arabia, advocating a return to the pristine Islam of the *salaf,* a call for *tawhid* and an onslaught against the accretions (*buda'*) made by other, non-Hanbalite schools of law, the ritualistic Sufi orders and the animistic patterns of elementary forms of religion which tainted Islam.

The major themes of this theology strike an amazing resemblance with the themes of al-Afghani's and 'Abdo's theology of reformation. 'Abdo's *Risalat al-Tawhid (Treatise on the Unity of God)* reminds us, at least in topic, of *Kitab al-Tawhid* by Muhammad bin Abdul Wahhab,[26] the Najdi theologian who initiated what has come to be known as the Wahhabi or Salafi movement. The centrality of religion and retrieval of an idealized, pristine Islam were common to both the Islamic reformation and Wahhabism, yet the two movements were worlds apart. The Najdi theologian based himself solely on the reading of the tenets and writings of the mediaeval Hanbali theologian from Aleppo, Ibn Taimiya (1263–1328). Opposed to all intellectual trends from a rigid, orthodox position, Ibn Taimiya rejected mystical philosophy and Sufism in general, denounced Shi'ism and attacked the Tatars for their application of the Mongol political code known as *yasiq* (also, in another version, *yasa*).[27] His rigid code of worship and conduct was asserted in the true, unwavering Hanbalite spirit. Bin Abdul Wahhab reproduced these tenets in a more stern and rigorous manner. Theologically, his school attacked all non-Hanbalite forms of informal or organized religion in Arabia including Sufi orders, the animistic practices of isolated nomads, the Hanafism of the Ottomans, the more open religious practices in the mercantile, Shafi'i Hijaz and the Shi'ism of the eastern parts of Arabia.[28] These were all declared to be alien to the 'pure' essence of Islam and its fundamental teachings, hence un-Islamic. This theology matured and developed into a military/theological campaign. The unity of God became a symbol of the political unity of Arabia.[29]

The movement was based on the alliance of the Najdi clerics (the house of bin Abdul Wahhab), the class of noble warriors (tribal chieftains from the house of Ibn Saud) and an extended army of tribal warriors reinforced by dislocated Bedouins.[30] The movement was socially and politically directed against segmented and fragmented tribal Arabia. In the realm of theology, it elevated the Hanbali-Hanafi split in Sunni Islam or the Sunni-Shi'i division to an absolute and bloody level. That is why the movement was much abhorred and detested in the 19th century, and the charge of Wahhabism constituted a serious accusation of blasphemy.

The movement would have replicated the Khaldunian pattern of puritan, tribal polity and expanded and disintegrated in three generations were it not for the fact that the Saudis were opposing a post-Khaldunian Ottoman empire which crushed them twice, and were approaching the era of nation-states upheld by Britain, the dominant colonial power in the region. This kept the Wahhabi-Saudi movement within the confines of Arabia when it scored its final triumph in the 1920s. Nevertheless, its central role as custodian of the holy shrines in Mecca and Medina, and later its oil wealth, enhanced the power and clout of this polity.

The theology of Wahhabism represents a prototype of fundamentalism. It played a crucial role in resisting both rational reforming theology and modern ideologies of nationalism and socialism across the Middle East and beyond. In some respects it presented a model for fundamentalists in Egypt and beyond of the application of the *Shari'a*, the purity of religion, the return to Islam and the unity of religion and politics. It was in this spirit that Rashid Ridha wove links with Saudi Arabia in the 1920s and 1930s, a line continued by the Muslim Brotherhood of Hassan El-Banna.[31]

Sufi Traditionalism: Flexible Social Organization

Sufism has been a major social organization and ritual in Islam since the 11th century. Its flexibility has enabled it to accommodate and integrate with a variety of social settings, whether they be the guilds and neighbourhoods in mediaeval Islamic cities; the rural, sedentary agricultural communities; or even the nomadic tribal environment.[32] Some Sufi orders initiated puritan military movements. When discussing the example of Islamic reformism and fundamentalism, we saw that both these trends stood against Sufi orders whether in theological, social or political terms. Sufi fatalist theology was attacked as irrational and an obstacle to modernization (the view of al-Afghani, 'Abdo and bin Badis), its ceremonial ritualism was denounced as *shirk* (blasphemy) – the view of Wahhabism – while its social organization was seen as segmentary and hostile to the centralized polity (as in the case of Arabia).

Yet some Sufi orders had important input in the 19th-century military challenge to the West and also contributed towards the agrarian centralization of the polity. The Mahdiya Sufi movement of the Sudan and the Qadiriya of Algeria provide an ample number of examples of the military challenge, while the Sanusiya Sufi movement of Libya achieved – through pan-segmentary Sufi organization – the centralization that Wahhabism in Arabia could only effect through the destruction of autonomous tribes and Sufi organizations.[33] The West defeated these Sufi movements as a military power and managed to cultivate the collaboration of other Sufi orders, while social and economic change contributed to their gradual disintegration and reformed Islam weakened them in theological terms. They were reduced to mere local *zawaya* (Sufi lodgers) of popular, mostly rural or provincial, religion.[34] In their gradual disintegration in the 20th century, Sufi orders constituted one of the sources of the cultural essentialism of modern fundamentalism, as the case of the Muslim Brotherhood in Egypt shows, but elsewhere they led a peaceful symbiosis with reformed Islam.[35]

Contemporary Fundamentalism: Cultural Nationalism

From the 19th century three currents and movements of Islamic reformation, fundamentalism and Sufi traditionalism reached out to the 20th century. If, according to Hobsbawm,[36] the long 19th century ended in 1917 and the short 20th century started thereafter, then for the world of Islam the latter was one of doom and gloom. It was the century of the dismemberment of the Ottoman empire and the complete colonization and abolition of the caliphate, the symbol of almost fourteen centuries of a real or imagined glorious and powerful Islamic civilization.[37] It was an era of vast socioeconomic change which saw the detachment of territories from their natural habitats and their re-linkage with the world capitalist market, accelerating the displacement of subsistence economy through rapid commercialization and crisis (the 1929 crash) and the disintegration of artisan industries and their guilds, and the forcible settlement of nomadic tribes as sedentary agriculturists, and the development of landlordism. The old social groups and classes began to disintegrate.[38] A new, massive Western culture and Western-educated elites emerged to dot the landscape with liberalism, nationalism and socialism, and the drive for the liberation of women grew stronger.[39]

A new life was created that bewildered and intrigued those who sat on the borderlines of the clash between the old and new modes of social organization watching their lifestyles, value systems and intellectual environments rapidly change. When they reacted against all this, contemporary fundamentalism was in the making. It is not surprising that the response came first from a modern teacher from a Sufi family and an inhabitant of the port city of Isma'iliya: Hassan El-Banna.[40] Port cities were most prone to the change brought by Western colonization, and Sufi orders and leaders were the most affected by the decline of the old forms of social and cultural organization. This new, mature version of fundamentalism constitutes the direct antithesis of Islamic reformation.

Whereas the major thrust of the reformation movement had been to restructure Islam so that it could meet the demands of modernity, the preservation of Islam from Western influences constituted the substance of the new form of fundamentalism. This was a cultural-essentialist trend, a break with rather than a continuation of the 19th-century reformation. The trend, as we shall see, was composed of many groups, and it constructed a cultural/political exclusivist response to changes brought about by World War I. It was an inwardly insulated cultural protest, aggravated by the inter-war global crisis and the spread of Western culture imposed by direct colonization, or even the loss of power and land caused by ethnic division and strife (the Hindus in Pakistan or Zionism in Palestine).[41]

As noted earlier, this new current inherited from the Islamic reformation its traditional aspect which was above all the centrality of religion, inasmuch as liberal nationalists acceded to the modern elements of the same system. The Egyptian form of contemporary fundamentalism was enhanced by the Saudi or Salafi prototype. Egyptian fundamentalism developed and spread across Muslim countries from 1928 through to 1958. The first arrival was the Muslim Brotherhood of Egypt,[42] followed two decades later by similar branches in other Arab countries; Nabhani's Hizb al-Tahrir al-Islami also emerged in the late 1940s, calling for the restoration of the caliphate.[43] Another group in this trend was the Jama'ati Islami of al-Maududi in India.[44] The last organization in this broad fundamentalist trend was the Da'wa Party of Iraq, founded after 1958.

This fundamentalist trend was invariably initiated by old status groups who projected their sense of alienation, decline or national doom as 'the loss of Islam'. Among the initiators we find Sufi leaders, clerics, religious judges, traditional preachers, notable leaders of popular rituals, artisans and even dislocated segments like rural and urban refugees. Social decline, dislocation and cultural nationalism were the major sources of this trend. Their ideology was one of cultural-exclusivism, drawing upon much of the previously mentioned original or elementary fundamentalism (the Salafiya paradigm of pristine Islam). Their strategy was either political (to assume power), pedagogical (to indoctrinate society), a combination of both or a shifting from one to the other. Their medium, paradoxically, was modern party politics or conspiratorial groups which shifted activism from the politics of the notables to mass politics.[45]

These movements had one foot in the colonial era and another in post-colonial nationalist regimes. They fought the latter, opposing the rising tide of radical nationalism and agrarian reform, nationalization and corporate economy; but they lost the battle. When nationalist regimes went into crisis, these movements were crippled and/or changed in character.

Islamism: Populist Authoritarianism and Third World Economic Nationalism

In 1968, after the 1967 defeat in the Arab-Israeli war, the Egyptian media reported the 'appearance' of the Virgin Mary in Cairo.[46] In the aftermath of this episode, leaders of the socialist nationalist regimes in Egypt and the Sudan turned to Islamist symbols and themes. The ideological shift was a portent of a change of direction from state corporatism (Arab socialism) to a liberalized and deregulated economy, an alliance with the West and peace with Israel.

Saudi wealth and influence seemed to replace the revolutionary discourse of Nasserism, starting what the renowned Egyptian journalist Mohammed Hassanayn Haikal called 'the shift from the era of revolution to the era of [oil] wealth'(*min marhalat al-thawra ila marhalat al-tharwa*).[47] This ushered in a new era: the political crisis of post-colonial socialist nationalism in its pan-Arabist garb (Nasserism, the Ba'th) or in a more regional version (Algeria's FLN or Tunisia's Bourgiba).

An ideological prelude was in the making; its centrepieces were the *jahiliya* (godlessness) concept developed by Sayyid Qutb in Egypt, al-Maududi's *al-hakimiya al-ilahiya* (the governance of the deity) in Pakistan and the *wilayat al-faqih* (governance of the jurisprudent) of Khomeini.[48] These were the preparatory steps in the period of transition from the second to the third wave.

Islamism developed a populist ideology of protest against the failures of the authoritarian modern nation-state and its nationalist elites. This tendency grew sharper with the shift from a corporate-command to a market economy, or with events that were perceived as national disasters such as the defeat of June 1967 and the secession of Bangladesh. Along with social protest, these trends developed and enhanced cultural and economic nationalism.[49] The major actors were the modern-educated urban lower classes and the marginalized classes of recent rural origin, or provincial towns.[50]

While attacking the state-controlled religious institutions or apolitical clergy, some movements forged an alliance between militant intellectuals and clerics.[51] While 19th-century Islamic reform worked towards a modernization of Islam, the ideology of Islamism aimed at the Islamization of modernity[52] at a point in time when the West's grand narratives (Marxism, socialism) seemed to collapse in a globalizing world. Islamism absorbed into its discourse an eclectic amalgam of modern nationalist and leftist concepts of the nation-state, economic dependency and world imperialism, carving a third way which defies capitalist and communist projects.[53] In both the Shi'ite and Sunni version of Islamism, a design was sought to unite religion (reduced to an ethical system) with society and polity through a political strategy of power.

During this period wave after wave of Islamist and fundamentalist groups were either revived, as is the case of the Muslim Brotherhood and Hizb Tahrir, or evolved. Under these conditions a new ideological atmosphere of Islamist colour spread across the Middle East. In Egypt, Takfir wal Hijra, al-Jihad or the Jama'at Islamiya emerged alongside the revived Muslim Brotherhood or Hizb Tahrir.[54] In the Sudan, the Muslim Brotherhood of Hassan Turabi (frequently changing names) gained momentum.[55] A similar trend developed in Algeria and Tunisia.[56] Jordan, the West Bank and Gaza soon followed.[57] When the Iranian Revolution triumphed in February 1979, the political culture in the Middle East had already been transformed.

In terms of methods, some groups opted for extra-institutional violence; others, for communitarian ethics (charity, Islamic dress and conduct). Some opted for mass politics while others organized for conspiratorial *coups d'état*.

Finally other groups adapted to institutional politics under controlled liberal experiments.[58] Shiʿite Islamic activism was an integral part of this change.

State, Society and Community

State Formation and Segmentary Society

The formation and development of the Iraqi nation-state constitutes the historical context within which various forms of Shiʿite Islamic militancy emerged. Like many Third World countries, the Iraqi nation-state was a product of the colonial era created in the aftermath of World War I. Carved out of the domains of the 'sick man', i.e. the Ottoman empire, the Iraqi state was formed from an amalgam of three provinces: Baghdad, Basra and Mosul. The random area defined and protected by the British contained a heterogeneous mix of ethnic and religious groups of the most diverse nature. It was manufactured by the colonial power in terms of its system of government (capital, flag, monarchy, bureaucracy); legitimation and representation (constitution and parliament); forms of control and defence mechanisms (military and police); legal structures (basic law and penal codes with a system of courts and special judicial arrangement for tribes); definition of the national community in legal and territorial terms (demarcating the borders and fixed laws of citizenship); creation of a central economic system (national currency, regulation of commerce and taxation);[59] standardization of national culture (educational system);[60] and, lastly, through the insertion of the new entity into the international system of nation-states (treaties with other sovereign states, mandates and membership in the League of Nations). In a word, Britain constructed a modern nation-state.

In the Hegelian tradition,[61] the modern state takes on the following roles, as:

(i) an agency emanating from, but geared to regulate, the inherent contradictions among various conflicting groups and individual interests within 'civil society';

(ii) a system of institutions (the Crown, the executive and the legislature) administered by the 'universal class' (read: the political and bureaucratic classes);

(iii) an organization of a certain national group (a representative of a 'nation');

(iv) an actor in the world: sovereignty, international law and world history.

The reality of the Iraqi nation-state, however, contrasted with the Hegelian concept. It was based on a predominantly agrarian-Bedouin society with feeble, semi-autonomous cities lacking 'civil society' or national cultural homogeneity, i.e. the developed institutions of markets, corporations and a legal system, or standardized national cultural spaces. It had to develop in order to coincide with the concept of modern nation-states. The inclusion of Iraq into the world markets and the international system of nation-states was coercive and, initially, fragile. The circumstances under which the Iraqi state took shape and mutated lent this modern universal agency of governance and sovereignty specific characteristics, some of which are shared by many states across the Middle East:

(i)   It is a young phenomenon, belonging to the 1920s, i.e. it is the product of colonial rule and lacks historical depth and long-rooted institutions.

(ii)   It is a territorial state, a unit where it is not a nation searching for statehood, but rather a state searching for nationhood.

(iii)   It is relatively detached from the power relations of its own 'society' either by dint of external military support (formerly, the British army and administration) or external material sources, or both (oil rentierism or foreign allocations.)

(iv)   In addition to political power, it wields economic power, first as an *owner of land* and/or *regulator and promoter*, then as an *owner-producer*, commanding the bulk of national wealth and gradually removing the distinction of the economic from the political field.

(v)   The institutional structure of the state is characterized by the supremacy of the executive power, which overwhelms and dominates the judicial and legislative powers and gradually absorbs these functions in their entirety.

(vi)   It is monopolized by a thin political class drawn from 'old social classes' or, in a later stage, from equally small groups of middle-class origin (radical officers, revolutionary party functionaries, and clannish groups). It lacks universally inclusive representative regimes and is unresponsive to demands of power sharing.

(vii)   The nature of nation-building gives precedence to, although it does not entirely rely on, coercion and lends the means of violence and their organizers, the military class, a paramount importance.

(viii) Control of the state itself as an agency of governance is as problematic as its control of society. Conspiratorial conflict among different ruling elites is a chronic feature, intensified by the lack of institutional accountability, transfer, replacement or renewal of power holders.

(ix)   Consent is invariably generated through a combined system of clientele networks, benefit-distribution and manipulation of ideological legitimacy.

(x)   Allegiance to the state is contested by different sociocultural and ideo-political loyalties which are focused either on sub-national, segmentary lines of the city, tribe, clan or community, or on supra-national, ideological or cultural imagined community (pan-Arabism or pan-Islamism).[62]

The history of the Iraqi state provides three major phases, each imbued with a distinctive system:

(i)   the traditional-constitutional, liberal monarchy (1921–58);
(ii)   the modern authoritarian-military (praetorian) regimes led by middle-class nationalist radicals (1958–68);
(iii)   the totalitarian-patrimonial social-nationalist regime of the Ba'th (1968–present).

We shall touch upon each of these phases of state formation and nation-building briefly.

Traditional-Constitutional, Liberal Monarchy, 1921–58

Ending four centuries of Ottoman rule (1534–1918), the monarchy emerged in 1921 as a result of the decisions taken by the British Colonial Office in Cairo to install a national government in line with the 'spirit of the age' (the Wilsonian programme)[63] and to affect a cheaper, more solid system of control of colonized territories.[64] The new government was based on a constitutional parliamentary system with an Arab Muslim monarch of noble descent, King Faisal bin Hussein at the helm. This arrangement reflected the nature of the forces at play: the British with their Westminster-type constitutional monarchy and the Arab ruler who meets the demands of the nascent, ethnic Arab nationalism embraced by the rising modern military class, the ex-Ottoman, so-called Sharifian officers.

This nationalism was heralded by Kawakibi, who demanded a return of the caliphate from the Ottoman usurpers to the Arabs, a sign of the historical shift from the sacred empires to modern nation-states.[65] These constitutional-national conceptions were familiar among the Shi'ite clerical class in Najaf who supported national independence and constitutionalism in colonial Iraq.[66] The choice of a *sharif*, a noble member of the household of the Prophet Muhammad, also reflected the traditional nature of a tribal-religious society which places emphasis on the lineage and the sacred community of Muslims.

Mindful of the heterogeneous nature of the Iraqi pre-national space, the colonial power tied the new administration to two restrictions of sovereignty: the imposition of a dual legal system, one for the state (urban), the other for tribes – the so-called Tribal Disputes Regulation Act – and the protection of the non-Muslim minorities, Christians and Jews.[67]

The new state was too fragile to stand on its own. Militarily it was weak even against its own tribes, let alone its neighbours. King Faisal complained that the government had only 15,000 rifles (infantry) versus 100,000 armed tribesmen.[68] On national cohesion, he had an even more bitter complaint:

Iraq is among the countries which lack the most vital element of social life: cultural, nationalist and religious unity. It is so segmented and divided that her politicians should exhibit a great deal of wisdom and discretion and at the same time they should be powerful in substance and essence.[69]

Warning against partiality or particularism, King Faisal described the social divisions in his kingdom as follows:

In Iraq there are highly contradicting thoughts and tendencies which may be classified as follows:

(i)   young modernists, including the government elite;
(ii)   conservatives;
(iii)   Sunnis;
(iv)   Shi'is;
(v)   Kurds;
(vi)   non-Muslim minorities;
(vii)   tribes;
(viii) sheikhs (tribal chieftains);
(viii) the ignorant masses who are prone to embrace any foul idea without any thought or consideration.[70]

The pre-national diversity of the population of Iraq presents an extremely complicated picture. A glimpse may be taken from the 1947 census. In ethnic terms the population divided into Arabs, 3,244,000 (71.1 percent); Kurds, 870,000 (19 percent); Persians, 52,000 (1.2 percent); and Turkomans, 92,000 (2 percent). In religious terms, Muslims constituted 93.3 percent; Christians (Assyrians, Chaldeans and others), 3.1 percent; Jews 2.6 percent; Yazidis and Shabak, 0.8 percent; and Sabaeans, 0.2 percent. Arabs and Kurds were split by the Shi'i-Sunni divide, whereas Muslims as a whole were split by ethnic or communal divides: Shi'i Arabs counted 2,344,000 (51.4 percent); Persians, 52,000 (1.2 percent); Shi'i Kurds, 30,000 (0.6 percent); Sunni Arabs, 900,000 (19.7 percent); Sunni Kurds, 840,000 (18 percent); and Sunni Turkomans, 50,000 (1.1 percent).[71]

Despite the fact that awareness of ethnicity and religious and communal affiliation was present, the focus of allegiance was invariably linked to local social organization, the tribe, the clan, kinship groups, village (*salaf*), city solidarity or quarter (*mahalla*), the latter often organized along ethnic, tribal, religious or sect/guild lines. Within these social configurations old classes or estates existed: aristocrats; *ashraf* (*sayyids*, or nobles from the Bani Hashim – the clan of the Prophet); *chalabis* (merchants); sheikhs; *aghas* (tribal chieftains); artisans (organized in guilds); and peasants and the like. These groups are also classifiable into larger aggregates: the political class of rulers, the military class, the mercantile class, the clerical class and the rural chieftain class all developed, each in its own right, some common economic interests in the 1940s and 1950s. With the redistribution of land estates, these various categories converted into landed and business classes.[72]

Yet, in 1933, King Faisal lamented:

> In Iraq, and I say this with a heart torn by agony, there is yet *no Iraqi people*, but unimaginable human masses devoid of any patriotic idea, imbued with religious traditions and superstitions, connected by no unifying tie, prone to mischief, bent on anarchy, always ready to rise against any government whatever. Of these masses we want, in this respect, to create a people whom we would refine, train and educate ...[73] (Italics added.)

Integration processes were characterized by inclusive and coercive policies. Through national institutions and systems such as schools, the army, the parliament (low and high chambers) and the administration, various segments were incorporated by the central government into a larger society. The development of modern communication systems, roads, steamboats and railways, helped erode the antediluvian isolation of urban and rural communities. Cities, hitherto self-contained entities, emerged from their isolation to operate and interact in a newly created national space. Within them, the lines separating the *mahalla* began to dissolve and new neighbourhoods based on modern professions and modern social standing began to crystallize.[74]

On the other hand, tribes first settled down and large confederations dissolved. Rivalries over water and land accelerated the disintegration of these mini-states. With the transformation of tribal sheikhs into a big landed class, the patriarchal unity of the tribe collapsed.[75]

Economic leverage was also crucial. As the owner of land and natural resources, the government distributed land titles to sheikhly landlords, *aghas* and the high command of the military and bureaucrats, so as to create a solid social base for the new state. The market-oriented economy caused the disintegration of isolated subsistence economies and helped link the previously disconnected areas into national and international markets.

Coercive measures were also deployed by the new central state. The army launched massive and decisive campaigns against rebellious Kurds, Assyrians, Yazidis and Shi'ite tribes of the south.[76] The violent phase of integration marked the 1920s and 1930s, but soon waned thereafter. In the 1940s and 1950s less coercive, more peaceful political and economic leverage promoted integration.

Reconnecting old segments to the central state and consolidating traditional classes, the constitutional monarchy solved the major and preliminary tasks of transformation from the segmentary agrarian to a centralized modern epoch. Marr and Batatu, who have studied government and economic elites, suggest that under the monarchy, integration processes were dynamic and positive, in general.[77] State elites were drawn from the old and very small upper classes of Sharifian officers, *chalabi*s, *sayyid*s and *sheikh*s, who were all drawn from different regions: north, middle and south. The selection processes involved not only a consideration of regional equilibrium but also ethnic and communal balance in terms of Kurds, Arabs, Shi'is, Sunnis and Christians, rural-urban and centre-periphery groups. In different phases of the lifespan of the monarchy, the representation or inclusion of different groups and segments varied, but integration mechanisms were geared towards pan-national inclusion.[78] With the exception of Assyrians (1930s) and Jews (1948–49), this orientation continued for all segments, groups and regions. Arab Shi'is and Kurds figured prominently in lists of cabinets, parliaments, mercantile elites and large landowners.[79] No sooner was this achieved than a new set of antagonisms emerged from the very transformation the centralized state carried out.

In social terms, the processes of integration were conducive to the creation of new classes: namely the landed aristocracy and upper mercantile, business and modern middle classes. At the bottom of the ladder, the decaying artisans and tribesmen were transformed into serf-like sharecropping peasants in the countryside and waged workers and marginal strata in the city. The middle, working and peasant classes were alienated from the political process and economic benefits. Unresponsive to the very social change it had initiated and promoted, the monarchy was met with fierce urban-rural resistance by ideological politics engineered, steered and controlled by the rising and expanding modern middle classes. These groups constituted some 28 percent of the urban population in 1957.[80] This was indeed a minority, given that the urban population was 36 percent and 48 percent of the nation in 1947 and 1957, respectively.[81] Yet, these modern classes were at the cutting edge of the opposition movement and relied heavily on the most active urban forces: students, workers, migrants, impoverished peasants and marginalized craftsmen.

The most crucial role, however, was played by an elite group of the new generation of career officers whom Batatu has called 'soldier/politicians'.

The Revolutionary Period: Military-Authoritarian Regimes, 1958–68
The downfall of the monarchy in July 1958 was, in a sense, a middle- and lower-middle-class rebellion backed by an angry class of serf-like peasants and small landed peasantry against the small pro-British ruling class, which monopolized power and wealth (land and oil revenues).[82]
The 1958 revolution turned state structures, social configurations and the relation between them upside down. A series of middle-class, military-dominated, populist and authoritarian regimes assumed power. The new regimes destroyed the landed and old ruling classes in economic and political terms and reshaped the political system. With the abolition of legislative institutions and the installation of the system of military courts, the relative

(classical) separation of powers was destroyed. Executive power ruled supreme. Legitimacy was shifted from the mandate of the ballot and the noble descent of the crown to modern populist-nationalist ideologies (Iraqi nationalism, pan-Arab nationalism, Marxism). With no institutional-constitutional procedure to regulate power holding and accountability, the centralized means of violence and those who controlled them assumed a crucial role, becoming the arbiters of power.[83]

The new military regime, under General Qassim in particular, improved representation and met the social and economic interests of middle classes; but, as Batatu observed, it also disturbed the processes of national integration.[84] This point is brought home when we remember that the officer corps was, historically, Sunni Arab-dominated. In this light we can understand why, during the military-revolutionary era and particularly after November 1963, the mechanisms of national integration weakened and failed to represent the ethnic, religious and regional diversity of Iraqi society.

The composition of state elites in this period, as Marr has suggested, revealed three major tendencies: an increase in the role of the career officers, a decline in Shi'ite and Kurdish representation and, lastly, a shift from upper- to lower-middle-class provincial elites.[85] While the monarchy could create multi-ethnic, multi-religious landed and upper business classes across the nation, the authoritarian regimes could not.

As an agency of governance, the state itself was now, thanks to increasing oil revenues, relatively more detached from the power relations of social wealth.[86] The means to control the state itself, i.e. instruments of coercion, became decisive, and those who controlled them – the military – became arbiters of power. As control of the state passed into the hands of those who wielded the means of violence (the 'revolutionary officers') and became devoid of the institutional devices that could channel the different, contending claims of the various social groups and classes, the only possible means of power struggle among the ruling elites and oppositional social movements were conspiratorial, extra-constitutional and clandestine.

The nature of the middle classes engaged in this process aggravated these tendencies. For one thing, most of these classes were economically and socially dependent in their mobility on the state itself, hence their glorification of the state as an end in itself and their tendency to use and abuse it. Their social reality was fraught with all sorts of schisms. These classes were, by definition, neither homogenous nor cohesive. Economically, sections were propertied, others salaried. Some were traditional and artisan-like, others modern-educated. In terms of income, they may be divided into high, medium or low groups. In ethnic and religious terms they were also diversified. Another source of cleavage centred around regional divisions in the guise of provincial towns versus large urban centres. These rifts entailed disparities of interests which reflected themselves in conflict-ridden, ideo-political spaces and currents: Iraqi nationalism, pan-Arab nationalism, Marxism, Kurdish nationalism, Sunni fundamentalism and Shi'ite Islamism.[87]

The divisions among the middle strata can also be seen among the class of soldier-politicians who were the major vehicles of power struggle and power seeking in this period. Paradoxically, elite power struggle among the military assumed both a modern, ideological garb and a traditional, clannish spirit. The former aspect stemmed from the wider political culture introduced and sustained by ideological politics; the latter emanated from the locally embedded social organization of the clan, the family and city solidarity, which was still in force in provincial townships and among the military themselves, who descended from these regions: the Mosulite group, the Jumailat group, the Takriti group and the like.

The more ideological and political bonds of military discipline proved precarious or insufficient to lend stability to the state, as was the case throughout the military period, especially during the bloody, short-lived first Ba'th takeover in February–November 1963, the more clannish solidarities and kinship networks were deployed to generate cohesion and loyalty among the ruling elites. The latter aspect grew to an unprecedented degree under the 'Arif brothers (November 1963–July 1968) with a Mosulite-Jumailat alliance emerging among the top ruling military. Yet, the middle-class military remained unstable. The number of actual and would-be *coups d'état* in this period is one indication among many. There were four successful military takeovers and at least half a dozen failed attempts in ten years.[88]

The Totalitarian-Patrimonial Ba'th Regime, 1968–Present

The incessant schisms and rifts among the ruling elites in their search for power produced the need for stable, secure and durable sources of political cohesion. The rise of the totalitarian, patrimonial political system promoted by the Ba'th from 1968 was a response to these conditions. This system differs radically from both the traditional-liberal monarchy or the modern-authoritarian military regimes. The new model seems to have come into being as a result of the marriage between populism in its Ba'th version, state rentierism and civilian-military kinship groups.

There are two analytically separable aspects in the structure of the Ba'thist totalitarian state: the single-party system and the single-family (or clan) system. In its first aspect, the state resembles the totalitarian German model under the Nazis with its single party rule, command economy, national socialist ideology, idealized unity of the nation, and state leader as the focus of power, law and allegiance.[89]

A combination of ideological homogenization, severe repression, control over the economy and a centralized state-monopolized cultural system are major attributes of the totalitarian type. Yet in contradistinction to the European model, the clan system reveals traits in common with the patrimonial type. However, this is not the only difference. In contrast to the

European model, Iraq lacked a mature and solid base of private property and mature social classes with vested interests independent of the state. The fusion of modern forms of mass, populist politics with primordial solidarities as a medium for organization, cohesion, mobilization, control and regulation is a unique mix which lends the Iraqi state a novel character.

In institutional terms, the new model carried the centralization of all powers to a higher potency: the executive, legislative and judiciary powers were all subsumed under the tight control of a self-defined, self-absorbed body, the Revolutionary Command Council (RCC).[90] According to the 1968 provisional constitution (amended in 1970 but still in place), the Ba'th party is proclaimed as the 'leading party' of both 'state and society', idioms borrowed from the Soviet ideological discourse, and the RCC is theoretically its tool. However, actual power relations were the opposite.[91] Since 1970, all members of the Regional Leadership (RL), the highest leading body of the party, were incorporated in the RCC, thus reducing the duality of the RCC and RL and fusing them into one.[92] With the RCC as the decisive centre of power, the cabinet below it has had limited authority, functioning mainly as an executive arm of the RCC. As the cabinet contained some RCC and RL members, it was, in effect, totally under the latter's control.[93] In 1980, in the wake of intense power struggles and the Iranian Revolution, a National Assembly was introduced under a controlled ballot.[94] The Assembly aimed to operate as a model 'rejecting both liberal democracy [the Western model] or dictatorship of the proletariat [the Soviet model]'.[95] The General Secretary of the party was, constitutionally and actually, the Chairman of the RCC, President of the Republic, Commander-in-Chief of the armed forces and, at times, the Prime Minister and grand patriarch of the kinship groups.

In its functions, this model looked like a Leviathan, but premised on hegemony rather than covenant. The totalitarian-patrimonial state monopolized not only political life but also controlled the bulk of spheres of production and the distribution of social wealth[96] (despite partial privatization and deregulation in 1987),[97] dominated production and distribution of culture (education, print and electronic media, culture industry) and absorbed into itself most forms of social association (trade unions, societies, professional unions, social clubs, business trusts, chambers of commerce and so on). It built itself into an omnipotent, omnipresent Leviathan which surpassed the wildest dreams of its original creator Hobbes and his possessive individual who, in the Iraqi model, figured as an atomized, dispossessed monad.

Under the Ba'th, a formidable controlling machine was created.[98] State bureaucracy and the military and security forces grew massively. The fastest growing agency was the military, which had 62,000 men in 1970 (2.9 percent of national work force and 6.6 per 1000 of the population); by 1980 these figures had risen to 430,000 men (13.4 percent and 31.8 per 1000 respectively).[99] Only after the first Gulf war were these apparently ever-growing trends reversed. In 1990–91, the size of the armed forces went down from approximately one million to 385,000 men (7.8 percent of the work force, 20 per 1,000 in 1992).[100] At different points during the 1980s and 1990s, the proportion of the armed forces to the population ranged between 7.3 per 1,000, in 1975, to 60.6 per 1,000 in 1988 (at the peak of the Iraq-Iran war).[101] In the aftermath of the first Gulf war, this ratio dropped to a stable 20 per 1,000, which is still among the highest in the world.[102]

Whereas the expansion of the military and security forces signalled the emergence of a formidable control system, the expansion of the bureaucracy indicated the increasing roles and functions of the state as it built up into the greatest single owner-producer and employer. As the state monopolized the bulk of social wealth, state employment became one of the cardinal means for distributing economic benefits among various classes and groups.

The ruling elite, which controlled the administration, the military, the security forces and the sensitive party organs, formed a small unique class-clan in its own right.[103] To expand the narrow social bases of the ruling Ba'th, distributive mechanisms and clientele networks were extended to middle and upper classes.[104] As the state installed a command economy, feeble propertied and moneyed classes could thrive only if and when they were integrated into the clientele web of state patronage. While taking *étatiste* tendencies to the extreme, and giving the enfeebled private sector only a restricted space for expansion, the Ba'thist state managed this process through various economic, regulatory and associational mechanisms. It could use its bulky contracts, import-export licences, tax exemption and supervisory powers over social and economic associations as a lever to restructure the mercantile, industrial, contractual and private banking classes and subsume them entirely under its firm control. This manipulative strategy was also geared toward generating absolute political loyalty and ensuring the smooth running of private economic activity. The upper classes grew in terms of wealth and numbers, but they were restructured in ethnic, religious and regional terms.[105]

One indication of the growth of this class of capital is that while the number of millionaires in 1958 was around 23, in 1982 there were more than 800, taking into account that the rate of the Iraqi dinar (ID) against the US dollar was $3.30 and $3.10 in 1958 and 1980 respectively.[106] By the end of the Iraq-Iran war, at least 3,000 families commanded private social wealth.[107] On the other hand, the composition of this upper class changed. Preliminary research in the field, though partial and inconclusive, has shown that random samples taken from upper-class groups contain numerous elements which have ascended the social ladder by dint of tribal affinity, party affiliation or both, and that the old upper classes reveal a great degree of restructuring in ethnic and religious terms carried out in order to weaken previously powerful groups. The selective inclusion of Kurds from pro-government tribes of Surjis, Hirkis and Zibaris, or of certain Shi'ite families in the business classes matched the calculated attempt to provide kinship groups and pro-Ba'th Sunni families with the means to enter these upper classes. A client business class was thus created with powerful pockets occupied by loyal families with clan and/or party liaisons.[108]

The widest and greatest social space the totalitarian state tried to harness and win over was that of the modern middle classes. By dint of state-secured employment, the salaried middle classes increased rapidly. In 1958, the major categories of the modern middle classes accounted for 28 percent of the urban population; by 1968 (on the eve of the Ba'th takeover) this figure had increased to 34 percent and by 1990 it had reached 54.4 percent.[109] These classes formed the social space from which the Ba'th recruited their growing party apparatus, which reached some 1,800,000 members and supporters, the bulk of whom were absorbed into the administration. The extent of this process can be clearly seen in the following: in the period between 1950–80, the population more than trebled (from 5,100,00 to 17 million), while the administration grew tenfold, from 58,000 to 277,000 in 1968 to 828,000 in 1980. The latter percentage constitutes 16.8 percent of the labour force.[110]

This whole process involved widespread economic and social benefits; yet it was neither even nor all-inclusive, or even consistent across the regional, ethnic or religious spectrum of the nation. Inclusive policies towards various ethnic or cultural groups were changing according to circumstances. Party and state organizations in charge of implementing these policies varied in their method and tempo in different regions, and were affected by changing political circumstances and inherent particularist preferences. Such factors limited the efficiency of these gigantic, inclusive, integrative policies in terms of generating allegiance and consent. But there was a structural deficiency that limited the range of such distributive tendencies, namely an over-reliance on oil revenues. With no real growth in primary and processing productive units, the over-growth of services in terms of volume and manpower was not benign.[111] The moment any pressures or constraints on oil revenues emerged, the distributive capability of the state was weakened. This, in turn, curtailed its political manoeuvrability, thus causing social disparities and tensions. This predicament was startlingly evident during the Iraq-Iran war and after.

The negative effects of these changes were aggravated by constant internal migration. This process changed the social landscape as it turned Iraq from an agrarian society in the first half of the 20th century to a modern, urban mass society during the second half. In 1947, for example, urban centres contained only 36 percent of the population, estimated at around 5 million. In 1987, the ratio was turned upside down: urban population constituted 72 percent of the nation,[112] a ratio matching the European average.[113] Almost half of city dwellers in 1987 were newcomers who had migrated in the previous fifteen years or so.[114] Cities were not only inflated to such an extent that they could not cope with the expanding need for social services, but were also subject to social and cultural changes. In the capital, Baghdad, which contained more than one third of the entire population, there occurred an apparent ruralization of the city with far-reaching social, cultural and political effects. The regional, religious and ethnic composition of the population of Baghdad also changed.[115]

A combination of soaring military expenditure, increased pressures on social services and inflationary tendencies in the 1970s and 1980s reduced most migrants to urban poor.[116] Even at the peak of the mid-1970s oil boom, the size of urban marginalized strata, i.e. the un- or semi-employed, was estimated at between 350–400,000. In 1987, the official figure was put at 342,000 nationwide, and 254,540 in the urban setting.[117] This was at a time when the bulk of the nation was mobilized for the war effort, and when around 1,500,000 Egyptian guest workers were filling in labour shortages.[118] With the end of the Iraq-Iran war in 1988, the demobilization of conscripts inflated the ranks of these marginalized underclasses.

In the aftermath of the first Gulf war, the situation worsened. With sanctions and the massive havoc wreaked upon the country's industries, infrastructures and capabilities, it is now the salaried middle classes, the backbone of the totalitarian regime, who have been wiped out. Among the prewar deprived were many Shi'is, Kurds and other groups. Among the pre- and postwar privileged were many Sunnis from the north and west of Baghdad with selectively included, lucky groups from among the Shi'is or Kurds. Outwardly, the social disequilibrium assumed a sectarian garb. According to Batatu, this was a result of the authoritarian nature of the regime.[119]

Shi'ite Social Structure

So far, we have outlined sociopolitical change in general terms. Now we should review the specific changes among the Shi'a. As already indicated, the term 'Shi'a', contrary to widespread usage, is not a sociological category but a loose cultural designation, which may differentiate a certain group from another in religious terms but never specifies social, cultural (not to mention political) differentiated aspects within this 'group' itself. Such distinctions can be made between the Bedouin and rural inhabitants; the illiterate, landless peasants and wealthy *sheikh* landowners; the clerics and city artisans and merchants or, indeed, the very social stratification within the clerical class where one may discern a lower class of shrine servants, medium-ranking or poor or rich *'ulama*. Each social group among the Shi'a is characterized by a definite form of social organization, specific lifestyle, distinct value system and independent economic activity and interests. In the words of Batatu:

When the modern Iraqi state was formed in 1921, Iraq's Shi'a did not constitute a closely knit body of people. Though sharing similar traits, they were split up, like other inhabitants of Iraq, into numerous distinct, self-involved communities. In most instances, they did not identify themselves primarily as Shi'a. Their first and foremost loyalty was to the tribe and the clan. This was especially true in the villages and the *salafs* (clusters of rural dwellings). But even at Najaf, which was the principal centre of Shi'ite learning, the feeling of the tribe, or the *mahalla* (city quarter), was in a political sense stronger than the tie of Shi'ite sentiment.[120]

There are three major phases of evolutionary development which transformed the social structure of the Shi'a and other groups as well.

In the first phase, the major change was in the direction of imposing, or regaining the supremacy of, central authority seated in the city over the powerful tribal world of nomadic and semi-settled tribal warriors. It was also a move to reassert the central authority of the state over the autonomous mini city-states. These processes were initiated by the Ottomans during the late 19th century reforms known as the Tanzimat. Under the Mamluks of Iraq, larger tribal confederations were encouraged, while under the post-Mamluk Ottoman *walis* (governors) a settlement strategy was vigorously pursued.[121] This transformation had many far-reaching results, such as the disintegration of the tribal confederations into factions fighting over land and water resources. Another change was the transformation of tribal chieftains, hitherto selected along primitive 'democratic' lines, into state-appointed *mallaks* (landowners) and the clan members into landless peasants, destroying thereby the most cherished primordial unity.[122]

The disintegration of tribal confederations and tribal unity led to a crisis of identity and alienation which was eased out by cultural reformulation: a shift from Bedouin non-religiosity to a form of Shi'ism reconstructed to suit tribal values and conceptions.[123] Shi'i Imams were presented as gallant knights and brave warriors who, by dint of their noble lineage, were saints, friends of God, protectors of life and crops and guarantors of commercial and property contracts.[124] These services were much needed in the growing cash economy of sedentary agriculture. Emissaries from the clerical class in shrine cities and the roaming, free-travelling *sayyids*, helped this transformation of Ottoman Iraqi tribes to Shi'ism in the 19th century. That is why Iraqi Shi'ism is often depicted as 'Bedouin' and 'Arab' in contradistinction to the 'Sufist' and 'Persianized' Shi'ism of Qajar Iran.[125] In general, however, the tribes were more closely linked to their resident local *sayyids* rather than to the *mujtahids* (religious authorities) in Najaf.

In the shrine cities, the Shi'ite social structure under the Ottomans was more complicated. Shrine cities were mini-states in their own right.[126] The greatest division was between the clerics and the lay groups. The clerical class of *mujtahids*, who resided in the shrine cities, most notably in Najaf and Karbala and to a lesser extent in Kazimain and Samara, were not in the least unified. They were divided along ethnic lines: Persians, Azeris (Turks) and Arabs. The Persian and Azeri *mujtahids* had their networks interwoven with their fellow Persians and Azeris.[127] The Arab clerics, however, lacked institutional infrastructures (networks of mosques, places of worship or financial networks) to mobilize and effectively influence urban classes and tribal life in Iraq. The clerics were further divided by primordial solidarities: the family and the city. Rivalries among Kazimain, Najaf and Karbala clerical families were apparently tense and could be seen in street fights among the local followers of different *mujtahids*, such as those involving gangs from Najaf against others from Kazimain.[128] The *mujtahids* were unable to govern their own shrine cities, as they lacked organized power.

Najaf, for example, was governed by armed guilds known as *Shmurt* and *Zugurt*, who controlled the four quarters of the city and provided security and defence against external hazards. The armed guilds forged exchange-liaisons with the clerical class on one hand and the city artisans, merchants and even pilgrims on the other.[129] These involved security service-for-money relations. The *Shmurt* and *Zugurt* were organized along tribal lines of the *mahalla* and had tribal values of collective solidarity.[130]

The extent of divergence among the tribal *sheikh*s, *mujtahids*, merchants and armed guilds may be illustrated by the following. While some clerics issued *fatwas* for *jihad* (holy war) against the British in defence of the – nevertheless Sunni – Muslim Ottoman rule, and even took part in this *jihad* campaign in 1914–17, laypeople in both Najaf and Karbala rebelled against the Ottomans in 1915 and 1916 respectively.[131] Both these cities asserted their autonomy and were ruled by notable lay families who showed no tendency towards establishing religious rule. On the other hand, in 1920 some Arab tribes responded favourably to the call of the *mujtahids* in Najaf for anti-British armed insurrection, while others cooperated with the colonial administration or took a neutral stance.[132] Those who rebelled did so for reasons other than the *fatwas* of the *mujtahids* – namely in protest against certain British administrative policies.[133]

In the second phase there were deeper changes. From 1921, nomadic tribes ultimately lost their significance as a sedentary form of agriculture was firmly and universally established. In 1867, nomadic tribes formed 35 percent of the population of Ottoman Iraq; in 1890 the proportion dropped to 25 percent; in 1905 it plunged to 17 percent and by 1930, they were less than 1 percent.[134] In contrast, the rural population increased from 41 percent in 1867, to 50 percent in 1890 and 59 percent in 1905. By 1930, the rural population figure had reached 72 percent.[135] Tribal chieftains were transformed into landlords with vested interests in land tenure which was protected and guaranteed by the Crown and the British. As the vast Arab tribal domains were mainly Shi'ite, rural Shi'ism was integrated, controlled and manipulated by the new emerging political class in Baghdad.

The clerical class, who were vigorously involved in the political agitation for independence in 1920–21 and staunchly opposed the British Mandate or the ratification of the Iraq-British Treaty, were soon ejected from the political process by the deportation of non-Arab *mujtahids*.[136] The clerical class was thus weakened and rendered apolitical by firm secular measures.

Under the monarchy, the major Shi'ite social classes – landlords, merchants and clerics – developed little in the way of common interests. Three political trends evolved: cooperation, opposition or apoliticism. Opposition during this phase was again divided along two lines, one symbolized by the anti-British, pan-national, patriotic movement of Ja'far Abu al-Timman , al-Hizb al-Watani (The National Party),[137] the other by al-Hizb al-Nahdha (The Renaissance Party) of Amin al-Charchafchi, who stressed communal Shi'ite grievances.[138] These two parties denote how the politically active Shi'ite mercantile classes of the period actually developed along two opposing lines: on one hand advocates of Iraqi nationalism, on the other, local communalism. Even the communal-embedded group recognized the Iraqi nation-state and got involved in the institutional and constitutional politics it provided. The divergent economic, social and political interests among the Shi'ite classes were unfavourable to the growth of a Shi'ite identity. So were the pan-national integrative processes pursued by the Crown. These processes were restricted in the last years of the monarchy, excluding the vast rural Shi'ite and Sunni areas; but the July 1958 revolution ended this exclusion.[139]

In the third phase, after the deportation and migration of the Jews in 1948–49,[140] the predominantly Shi'ite mercantile class gained strength and power and emerged as a strong social class. Shi'i tribal landlords established firm positions and gained more wealth and power. A strong Shi'ite political class also matured. On the other hand, a new Shi'ite middle class was also emerging and expanding. The migration of the Shi'i *fallahin* (peasants) to the cities, notably to Baghdad, changed the sociological profile of the Shi'is from a predominantly rural to a predominantly urban population. However, it was the Shi'i migrants who augmented the ranks of marginalized, disenfranchised urban poor. The Shi'ite modern middle classes and urban poor were thus alienated from their affluent and upper-class co-religionists by social, political and ideological divides.[141]

Thus, while the bulk of the Shi'is were rural poor *fallahin* in the first half of this century, in the second half they were transformed into poor and middle-class city dwellers. Just as the transformed Bedouin found a cultural antidote to their alienation in Shi'ism, the landless, migrant Shi'i *fallahin* found their salvation and emancipation in communism. As soon as the Shi'i *fallahin* migrated to the city they lost their natural social habitat, the *salaf* or *dira* (tribal domain). In the city they faced a harsh reality: a loss of subsistence economy, of the social solidarity of the *dira*, a lack of social and personal security and a sense of alienation from the city environment.

Like the city's impoverished artisans and declining *sayyids*, the *fallahin* found in the clandestine social movements a conduit for self-expression and protection. The Shi'ite (and other) sections of the modern middle classes were at the cutting edge of opposition to the monarchy. They provided the bulk of the leadership for modern mass political movements. After the heavy blows dealt by the successive agrarian reforms to the landlord class, who also lost their political leverage in the now-abolished national assembly, the Shiʿite mercantile class received a similar succession of devastating blows, first under the ʿArif brothers and later under the second Baʿth rule. Crippled as a social and political power, the mercantile and landlord classes became too weak to act. The Shiʿite political class of the monarchy was also disenfranchised in the Republican era. This increased the social and the political weight of other social groups and their mass political and radical movements. Yet the destruction of these movements, and the disruption of national integration processes unleashed by the successive military takeovers, created a vacuum that was soon filled by Shiʿite Islamic groups. Common grievances were narrowing the gap between different Shiʿite social groups and creating converging tendencies. A reconstruction of Shiʿite identity along communal and Islamic lines was accelerated by the sectarian policies under the regime of the ʿArif brothers and the authoritarian, secular policies under the Baʿth.

Areas of Conflict: the Shiʿis and the Modern State

At different times in the history of the modern Iraqi nation-state, various and often changing Shiʿite groups took an oppositional stand against the state. Five major issues played a pivotal role in Shiʿite agitation:

(i)   The first is political, premised on under-representation. This issue was acute during the first two decades of the monarchy and waned in its last decade, but resurfaced under ʿArif and the Baʿth. The issue had been a cause for rapprochement between some mercantile, sheikhly landlords and clerics in the 1930s, when the population census showed the Shiʿis to be in the majority. Yet their proportionate weight in the government was much lower, if not insignificant.[142] This recognition involved a new sense of 'nation-ness' defined in terms of an electoral, numerical majority and minority. The issue of under-representation has been a constant theme in contemporary Shiʿite literature which invariably refers to Shiʿis as an 'oppressed majority'. Under-representation is seen by Shiʿi activists as a premeditated, discriminatory policy which bars their community from decision-making bodies and other sensitive organs like the military, security forces and bureaucracy. Even today Shiʿi secular liberals explain the absence of a democratic, representative system in terms of the fears of 'Sunni' ruling elites losing power to the Shiʿis.[143]

(ii)   The second issue centres on economic grievances. Different propertied and landed Shiʿite groups opposed land reforms in 1959 and the nationalization and regulation of trade in 1964 and 1970 on communal grounds, as a drive to weaken the Shiʿis, while in the nationalist or Marxist jargon, these policies figure in the form of *étatiste* or non-capitalist progressive measures, i.e. in social-national terms. The clerical classes were the oldest agitators in this respect, lamenting their lack of sufficient *waqf* resources (religious endowments) and attributing this situation to Sunni political bias.[144] Under the Ba'th, for example, commercial, industrial and estate-owning Shi'ite groups were depicted by the regime as a menace to the nation.[145] These groups had their property confiscated and were deported in the 1980s. Some Shi'ite religious endowments had been expropriated during the 'Arif reign,[146] while others were appropriated by the Ba'th regime – as was the case with the funds of the Kufa University Project. Yet, under President Saddam Hussein, attempts to 'mend fences' were made and budgetary allocations were expended on the holy shrines in Najaf, Karbala and Kazimain.

(iii)   The third issue is that of cultural encroachment. With the inception of the modern state in Iraq, Arab nationalism replaced Islam as a political focus of allegiance and unity. Various forms of Arab nationalism existed and developed, from Sati' al-Husri's cultural version based on language and history,[147] to the ethnic forms of Ba'thism which secularized and Arabized Islam as in the case of Michel Aflaq. These secular trends, which emerged in the Arab Mashriq, were constructed in order to achieve at least three aims: to remove religious unity by stressing the ethnic distinction of Arabs from Turks and later from Persians; to overcome the Christian-Muslim divide among Arabic-speaking people in the Mashriq; and to reconstruct history in order to establish the Arabs' right to a nation.[148] Reconstructing history in support of the claim to nationhood is a recurrent element in modern nationalism. Glorification of past Arab empires or the attribution of their decline to the inclusion of alien elements in Islam such as Turks and Persians were recurrent themes.[149]

These discourses involved inherent contradictions within both Sunni and Shi'i Islam. First, they reduced Islam to a predicate to ethnicity, thus destroying the centrality of religion, a theme abhorred by conservative Muslims, Shi'is and Sunnis alike. Second, by giving priority to ethnic over religious affiliation, the previous supremacy of Muslims over other religions – notably Christians and Jews, who were *thimiz* (protegés) in the eyes of jurisprudence – was destroyed. Lastly, the glorification of past empires implied the legitimation of Sunni dynasties and contradicted the essence of Shi'i Islam revolving around the legitimacy of the household of Imam Ali.

The Nusuli affair in the late 1920s serves to exemplify this problematic.[150] Nusuli, a Syrian secondary-school teacher of nationalist leanings, glorified the Umayyad dynasty which was, in the eyes of the Shi'is, the usurper of the caliphate from the rightful Imams. His book on the topic embittered Shi'i intellectuals in Iraq and caused a political crisis.[151] Latent in the thought and practice of al-Husri and his pan-Arabist followers in Iraq during the 1930s was the idea that the ethnic purity of the Arabs was not only crucial but was endangered by the Persians. Shi'ism was therefore suspect.[152] In the 1950s and 1960s, Abdul Aziz al-Duri, a Sunni historian and dean of Baghdad University under 'Arif, raised this theme time and time again.[153] The continuing bitterness created among Shi'is is reflected in the fact that decades later, in the 1990s, Hassan al-Alawi, Abdul Karim al-Uzri and a host of other secular writers launched a vigorous counter attack to prove that Shi'ism is originally Arab in character and that Persian Shi'ism is a latecomer.[154]

(iv)   The fourth issue is citizenship rights. Rights to citizenship in the modern Iraqi nation-state have been an issue from the first years of its inception right up to the present day. It faced two major developments, one relevant to Persian Shi'is, the other to Arabic-speaking Jews. The latter erupted on the eve of, and after the emergence of, Israel in 1948 as a nation-state for the nation-less Jews.[155]

For the Persian Shi'is, the issue of nationality has ramified historical roots. At the heart of it lies the legacy of centuries of Ottoman rivalry with Safavid and later Qajar Iran (1501–1917). Wars have not only plagued the relations between the two 'sacred' empires, but their rivalry over the domination of Iraq overshadowed the destiny of the communities which inhabited this space. Both empires, the Sunni Ottoman and the Shi'ite Safavid and Qajar dynasties in Persia, extended their protection over their co-religionists and their cherished shrine cities, the 'Atabat (Shi'ite shrines) in Iraq.[156]

Communal regional relations were part of pre-national rights. The shift from the notion of subjects to the notion of citizenship has been problematic worldwide. It involved long processes of turning erstwhile porous and flexible territorial boundaries into fixed ones, of removing pan-territorial protection rights for co-religionists, and of recognizing the right of the territorial state to sovereignty over all inhabitants of this nascent national space. The Peace of Westphalia in Europe marked this shift; in the domains of the Ottoman Empire, particularly in Iraq, the modern notion of citizenship was installed by the British and first deployed against Persian *mujtahids* in 1924 to silence their opposition to the British and the monarchy. Persian *mujtahids*, given the choice of naturalizing or leaving[157] Iran under the Reza Shah regime, never recognized the newly born Kingdom of Iraq partly because of issues relevant to rights of Iranian residents of Iraq.[158] Persians in Ottoman Iraq were protected by Iran in accordance with official agreements signed with Istanbul. Arab Shi'ite groups or individuals were encouraged by the Iranian consul to seek Iranian citizenship, known as *taba'iya*.

When the monarchy was installed, the population of Iraq was officially registered as either Ottoman or Persian. Many Arab families had sought Persian 'naturalization' to avoid military service in the Ottoman standing army, notably during general mobilization in World War I; they were officially registered as 'Persian' subjects. Some Shi'is managed to avoid such fate.

An anecdote relating to the well-known industrial family of Fattah Basha may serve to illustrate this aspect. Fattah Basha is originally from a Shi'ite family in Kirkuk. The father sought a career for his son in the Ottoman army. He was advised to change his *mathhab* (religious school of law) from Shi'ism to Sunnism in order to accomplish this. The son rose to prominence and became one of the wealthy few in monarchal Iraq.[159]

Apart from the legalities of citizenship, Shi'ism was equated with Persianism. This conception was part of a local prejudice reinforced by the fact that the shrine cities of the Shi'a had Persian cultural traits, strong trade relations with Persia, and a strong presence of Persian *mujtahids*.

In their mutual struggle, both governments in Iraq and Iran tried to exploit this issue for their own ends. In an attempt to pressure Iran, for example, the Ba'th government deported Iranian nationals *en masse* in the early 1970s. On the eve of the Iraq-Iran war and after it, the Iraqi government deported vast numbers of Shi'is, the bulk of whom were Arabs of past 'Persian subject' status. The number of deportees expelled differed dramatically from one source to another. Figures ranged between 60,000 at the minimum and 160,000 at the maximum.[160] The issue of citizenship rights has been and may continue to be a source of grievance among the Shi'is at large whose very identity as Iraqis has been assaulted.

(v)   Secularization is another problem. Driven by modernization, the state assumed a multitude of functions that had previously been the monopoly of the autonomous clerical class such as administering the law, education, or the collection of taxes. These processes contributed to the eclipse of religion. Impelled by *étatiste* urges, successive regimes in Iraq tried hard to control religious cultural spaces and maintain a controlled separation of state from religion. As the Sunni religious establishment was already incorporated into the administration, the secularization drive was directed against the autonomous, Shi'ite establishment with its vast, pan-national financial networks of emulators, institutions of learning, shrines and worship centres. Intentionally or otherwise, secular policy damaged the welfare of shrine cities as it affected the flow of pilgrims, seminarians and corpses for burial in holy soil. It also detached the clerical class from the realm of politics and weakened their position and standing.

Secularization affected the realm of penal code, commercial law and family statutes. If the absorption of the judicial functions of the *'ulama* by state agencies was easily enforced, the reformation of family statutes along secular lines was met with Shi'ite and Sunni resistance. The re-Islamization of these statutes and acts has been a major issue on the Islamist agenda, both Sunni and Shi'ite.[161]

PART TWO

Genesis and Mutation

Introduction

The Shi'ite Islamic movement originated at the holy shrine of Najaf during the aftermath of the July 1958 revolution. It was a direct response to the changes this revolution symbolized and completed. These changes involved the decline of old social classes, including the clerical class. Such a decline involved a multitude of social, economic, cultural and political facets and was obviously a complex historical process.

As outlined in Part One, the revolution destroyed the political hold of the old social classes and passed power to the modern middle classes. It initiated radical socioeconomic reforms such as the abolition of the Tribal Dispute Act, the appropriation of large landed sheikhly or aristocratic classes and the enactment of a new family law. Modern associations such as workers' unions and women's and students' leagues were enfranchised. The new but short-lived freedoms opened up opportunities for the rise and expansion of modern ideologies – Marxism in particular.

At least three major issues affected the clerical class and their lay collaborators and attracted their fierce opposition: the demise of sheikhly landlordism, the family law and the mass spread of Marxism. In the eyes of the clerics, Marxism was a threat to Islam as a creed and sacred source of law-giving, a social force that would threaten its hold over the urban and rural Shi'i laypeople. The degree of participation in a communist-led political life was unprecedented and absorbed the energies and attention of vast masses, especially amongst the middle, lower and manual urban and rural classes. For example, the pilgrimage to Karbala and Najaf on the Marad al-Ras in 1959 registered the lowest numbers ever. The scene at the shrine cities that year, visited by a few scattered hundreds compared to the huge crowds of tens of thousands in previous years, was horrendous and appalling to the clerics' who came face-to-face with the alienation of the huge peasantry and poor urban crowds from the holy shrines due to their involvement in communist-led street politics and trade-unionism.

The communist youth, student or other associations posed another kind of threat when they controlled the Shi'ite popular rituals and harnessed them to their own ends. The influence of the Communist Party after 1958, notably during the first two years of the revolution, was unprecedented.[2] In retrospect, this influence peaked in 1959 after the crushing of Colonel Shawaf's short-lived military insurrection in Mosul in 1959. General Qassim leaned more and more on the communists. Their power in the people's militia was unchallenged, and they were in full control of the workers' trade unions, peasants' associations, student and youth organizations and women's federation – in addition to, and above all, holding strong positions among the rank-and-file and non-commissioned officers in the army.[3] To many *ulama* this signified the Apocalypse.[4]

The demise of sheikhly landlordism was another source of alarm. This social class, part of which was Shi'ite, lost power and status in the wake of the abolition of the parliament and the upper house (Majlis al-A'yan), the stronghold of the semi-feudal class of tribal *sheikhs*. Agrarian reform destroyed their power and wealth.[5] As the tribal code was rescinded, tribal sheikhs lost their state-endorsed legal authority in the countryside. To some extent, this class had been a source of handsome *khums* (religious taxes) to the clerical class in Najaf and beyond.[6] Its demise thus not only deprived the higher stratum of clerics of revenues and social and political support, but also caused concern over private property in general among the propertied classes.

The family law reform, which envisaged equal inheritance rights for women, the imposition of monogamy and the regulation of other aspects of family life was another shock to the clerical class and conservatives in general. For the clergy, it symbolized the sweeping influence of secularization and the decline of the *Shari'a*.

The *ulama* of Najaf and the traditional-thinking social groups in their service were taken aback by changes which were the culmination of a half-century or so of continued decline: the dwindling status of the *ulama* in Najaf, the decline of the *madrasa* (theological seminary),[7] the diminishing returns of the *khums* and the decline of the welfare of the holy cities. The clerical Shi'ite class and their Najaf mercantile allies answered the challenge and developed two different responses.

The first was initiated and sponsored by the senior generation of the conservative *ulama*. It was pedagogical and philanthropic in character and centred on expanding and renewing the *madrasa* and extending social services. Publications were also instrumental in attacking 'atheism' (meaning the Communist Party) and propagating conservative Islam. As a result of these strategies, the Society of the 'Ulama in Najaf was born. The second response was initiated by a Najafi group of reforming junior, apprentice *ulama* and Shi'i lay activists from mercantile families. This was ideological and political in character; namely, it opted for the creation of a universal Islamic ideology to supersede Marxism and the formation of a modern organization to spread it. This is the origin of the Da'wa Islamic party – a novel phenomenon and one that, although responsive in nature, was extremely fragile because it was compelled to surmount formidable obstacles of apolitical conservatism of every conceivable kind.

Some developments in the Middle East, however, helped this line of mutation. In Iran, for example, Grand Ayatollah Burujerdi, the supreme Shi'i authority of the time, cast off his apolitical attitude and launched a crusade against the Shah's attempts at agrarian reform in 1959 – thus ending decades of quietism and non-interference in the world of the Shi'i *'ulama*.[8] Sunni Islamic activism was another factor. The Iraqi branches of the Muslim Brotherhood and Hizb al-Tahrir al-Islami (Islamic Liberation Party) of Nabhani were all politically active in a daring anti-communist crusade. Radical junior *'ulama* in Najaf found these actions inspiring, effective and, in terms of the *Shari'a*, a lawful means of activism.[9]

In this part of the study, we shall examine the genesis and development of these two responses, their divergence, limitations and mutation.

THREE

The Da'wa Founding Group: Defining the Self (1960–64)

The formative period of the Da'wa group extended from 1958–59 to at least 1964. During this phase the founding group of junior *'ulama* and Najafi merchants focused their energies on defining self, perspectives and discourse, and on propagating their new ideas. Two major themes were constructed: an Islamic utopia and the creation of a new political instrument – a party. This endeavour met with stiff resistance on the part of clerical conservatives.[1] The various aspects of the Da'wa group's self-definition will be examined below.

The Legitimizing Process

The question that stood before the Da'wa nuclei was to create an ideology matching Marxism and to legitimize a new form of organization with a clear strategy and tactics.

From the discussion that took place over these issues, the intellectual framework, known in Da'wa jargon as *al-Usus* (the Foundations or Fundamentals), emerged. The *al-Usus* were written by al-Sadr, probably in 1960, and were approved by the founding group. The text of the manifesto may be divided into three major sets of argument:

(i)   The establishment of a modern organization to disseminate the party's ideology and carry out its mission;

(ii)   The schematic periodization or categorization of the stages of activity, or the programme of action leading to the ultimate goal;

(iii) The foundations of the concept of an Islamic polity as the ultimate goal of the Da'wa.

The founding group sought to create a Leninist organization based on cells, chain of command, discipline and obedience. This type of organization had been introduced into the region through the communist (Third) International from the 1920s, and through Fascist and Nazi channels.[2] In the late 1920s and 1930s, this mode of organization was adopted by different currents: the communists in Syria, Egypt and Iraq and the Muslim Brotherhood in Egypt. Radical nationalists, Ba'thists and pan-Arabists, together with the Hizb al-Tahrir al-Islami of Nabhani, adopted the cell party in the late 1940s.

As the Leninist model proved its superiority over the politics of notables, which was centred on elite figures and saloon gatherings with no root organization, it overwhelmed the imagination of some young Islamic-minded Najafi lay groups. These young men observed with admiration and awe the appeal of the Marxist utopia and the efficiency of the clandestine communist organization in Najaf which even competed with them in organizing the 'Ashura rituals. They were eager to command such powerful instruments of recruitment and mobilization. Young clerics also shared this fascination.

The Party

The first theme in the manifesto relates to the movement. The Da'wa is described as a *haraka taghyiriya*, a movement for radical and revolutionary change,[3] the vanguard of the nation, conscious of the needs, limits and interests of Islam and aware of the conditions of the *umma* (global Islamic community) and its concerns.[4] The term also describes the Da'wa as the bearer of a mission that serves the cause of God, a sacred cause that transcends vulgar existence and mundane trivialities. The term 'party' or even 'movement' is implicit. Eschewing it was a conscious choice to avoid using a well-known secular category. Other terms were used freely: the Da'wa (a call) is depicted as *inqilabi* (revolutionary) rather than *islahi* (reformist). The first concept is derived from the word *inqilab*, i.e. radical as opposed to evolutionist. Al-Sadr used the term *inqilabiya*, the Ba'th Arabic equivalent for revolutionary, in contrast to the communist-circulated word, *thawriya*. In the late 1960s the term was dropped by the Da'wa as its Ba'th genealogy became embarrassingly apparent. *Islahiya*, evolutionist reformism, was rejected, since it only modified '"super structures" (*buniyat fawqiya*) rather than [changing] the basic and deep-rooted structures'.[5] Concepts such as culture; education; construction; action; change; movement; radical revolution; conscious vanguards; radical consciousness; and fighting spirit all derived from radical secular ideologies and coloured the new discourse.[6] The movement was therefore entrusted with a mission, namely to 'establish an Islamic government and install a ruling apparatus until favourable conditions arise to enable the nation give its opinion in a referendum'.[7]

The tasks of the missionaries in the first stage (see further below) were:

(i)   *tashkhis al-fikr*, constructing the ideology;
(ii)   *tarbiyat al-du'at*, educating the new members or missionaries;
(iii)   preparing and training an organized and disciplined vanguard (*talia wa'iya*);
(iv)   bringing consciousness to the masses;

(v)   developing the concepts and theories for the future polity and society of Islam.[8]

This form of organization is justified on practical and doctrinal grounds. The practical argument runs as follows: organization is highly appreciated in contradistinction to spontaneity, planning to improvisation and cohesion to sporadic and scattered efforts.[9] The doctrinal justification has ramified aspects. It argues that the *Shari'a* does not specify any particular form for preaching Islam and advocating change, therefore it is legally permissible *(shar'i)* to adopt *any useful method* to propagate the tenets of Islam. Second, it argues that *'amr bil ma'ruf wal nahi 'an al-munkar,* 'to command the good and forbid the evil' is an imperative whose fulfilment demands *organizing* the *umma.*[10] Third, it argues for obedience and discipline in the name of Islam.

This notion of party obedience involves an irresolvable contradiction with Shi'ite theology. In Shi'ism, authority is rooted in the doctrine of emulation. Unless they are *mujtahids,* all Shi'is have to act in accordance with the injunctions of the *'ulama.* With the Da'wa's demands, however, obedience would be owed to two centres of authority: the new party leadership which issues directives and the old *marja' taqlid* (religious authority) who issues *fatwas.* If this duality is established, the doctrine of emulation is practically annulled. This is clear when the Da'wa confirms that its members are God's missionaries[11] and that guidance should be sought not from human mortals but from God and his apostles.[12] There is no mention of the *Imam* or *mujtahids.*

The justification for the 'dual authority' runs as follows:

(i)   it is a social contract *('aqd ijtima'i)* that the member obeys the person in charge *(al-mas'ul)*;

(ii)   the collective opinion of a college *(al-majmu')* which includes experts *(ahl al-khibra)* is better than the opinion of one individual;

(iii)   in the leadership of the Da'wa there is a *faqih* (jurisprudent).

These three factors oblige obedience and submission *(ta'a).*[13] From a purely theological point, the existence of a *faqih,* presumably a *mujtahid,* would have been sufficient to demand obedience. In fact, this third point is couched in a very vague Arabic form, which reveals an uneasy attempt at avoiding a sensitive issue.[14]

The novelty of the Da'wa argument lies in the fact that the traditional chain of command, which runs from God to the Prophet to the Imams and down to the *mujtahids,* is broken. The assertion that the missionaries do not take their decision to join the party from a human mortal, but from God, only reinforces the tendency to break the traditional chain of authority as the choice is left to the individual's own discretion. This is similar to Protestant ethics, which demolished the mediating role of the church as guardian of the true faith and opened up the way for a direct relation between the deity and individuals.[15]

The Stages of Struggle

The second theme in the *al-Usus* is the stages of struggle. This was the most important topic in the founding members' lengthy discussions.[16] It was also a recurrent issue on at least ten occasions from 1961–79.[17]

The stages of political struggle are conceptual designs aimed at lending collective activity a sustained, organized nature in space and time. They define the nature of human society, the moving factors responsible for its change and transformation and the role of the human actor in both cognizing the process and steering it in a desired direction. The nature of this concept is pedagogical. The stages of struggle are:

(i)   *al-marhala al-fikriya*, in which Islamic ideas and concepts are to be constructed, disseminated and consolidated by means of a group of dedicated missionaries. This phase was later renamed *al-marhala al-taghyiriya* (the phase of change).

(ii) *al-marhala al-siyasiya*, the political stage, during which the Da'wa Party, having built its bases and won enough mass strength and following, would shift to the political level to wage struggle for power.

(iii) *al-marhala al-thawriya*, the revolutionary stage, is focused on removing the ruling, presumably un-Islamic, elite.

(iv) *al-marhala al-hukmiya*, the phase of a ruling Islamic regime when the ideal Islamic polity and society are constructed.

The four-stage model echoes themes from the Muslim Brotherhood of Egypt and the Hizb al-Tahrir al-Islami of Nabhani (Jordan-Palestine). Both groups had active branches in Iraq, and their publications were familiar in Najaf. In fact, the first sources of indoctrination for the Da'wa missionaries were drawn from the works of Egyptian thinkers like Hassan El-Banna, Sayyid Qutb, Muhammad al-Ghazali and others.[18]

Tables 3.1 and 3.2 show how the Da'wa envisaged the periods of struggle in general and how, in this respect, they were keen on self-differentiation from other Islamic groups. The periodization envisaged by the Muslim Brotherhood is in three stages: first, propaganda, communication and information; second, formation, selection and training of militants in a disciplined organization; third, the phase of implementation.[19] In the late 1960s, Muslim Brotherhood splinter groups reduced the stages to two, one of weakness and concealment and the other of strength and *jihad*, holy combat.[20]

Accordingly, the period under study here is part of the first phase, the '*fikriya*' or '*taghyiriya*' stage. This phase remained effective from 1960 until the beginning of the Iranian Revolution in 1979. Until then, the Da'wa group conceived of itself as an educational, intellectual movement rather than a political organization. The shift to the political stage, as will be seen, was, in the words of Da'wa documents and the recollections of leaders, forced upon them by the Ba'th. They were, to use their own wording, 'dragged into the political stage'.[21]

Table 3.1: Stages of Classical and Modern Islamic Action as Envisaged by the Da'wa

Organization or Period	Stage One	Stage Two	Stage Three	Stage Four
1. Early Islam	Building the nuclei	Propaganda and action	Building the state	nil
2. Muslim Brotherhood, Egypt	Preaching (*ta'rif*)	Building the organization (*takwin*)	Struggle (*tanfith*)	nil
3. Tahrir Party	Study and preaching (*dirasa wa ta'lim*)	Political (*siyasiya*)	Taking power	nil
4. Da'wa Party	Ideological (*fikriya* or *taghyiriya*)	Political (*siyasiya*)	Assuming power (*thawriya*)	Building polity (*hukmiya*)

Table 3.2: Characteristics of Each Stage of the Da'wa's Struggle

Stage	Name	Method	Objects
One	*fikriya***	Intellectual/ clandestine	Forming and spreading ideology
Two	*siyasiya*	Political action Open/clandestine	Weakening the regime
Three	*thawriya*	Unspecified	Unseating the ruler
Four	*hukmiya*	Unspecified	Constructing the ideal society

* Earlier designation was: *inqilabiya* or *fikriya*, but later was renamed as *taghyiriya*.

The Utopian Islamic Polity

In the *al-Usus*, al-Sadr sets the foundation of a universal Islamic polity as the strategic end of the Da'wa. Unlike secular states, this pan-Islamic polity is held tightly together by a creed, which makes it a *dawla fikriya*,[22] a doctrinal state, 'highly superior' to any other model.[23] Muslims have equal rights in this polity.[24]

The territorial space of this *dawla* spreads across the lands in which Muslims live, but it also has territorial claims beyond. One such claim is juristic, that is to retrieve *kharaj* (taxed) land that had been conquered by early Muslims. The other is doctrinal. The *dawla Islamiya* has the right to claim the earth in its entirety on behalf of the deity.[25] The *Shari'a*, in this polity, will regulate all social, economic, political, material and spiritual aspects of life and the *'ulama* will hold a monopoly on judicial power.[26]

The political system of this *dawla*, as al-Sadr presents it, is based on *shura*, with no Shi'ite traits of the infallible Imam or *wilayat al-faqih*. He says two forms of government theoretically exist: The theocratic (or deistic, *ilahi*) and the *shura* (consultative):

> The deistic governance means the rule of the infallible individual (*al-fard al-ma'sum*, i.e. the Imam).[27] The second form of governance is the *shura* rule or the rule of the *umma*.[28]

Al-Sadr concludes:

> In a word, the *shura* in the age of occultation (of the Twelfth Imam) is a *permissible form of government*.[29] (Italics added.)

This abstract roaming into the far future in search of a universal Islamic world power, detaches the group from day-to-day reality. As the desire and need to deal with real politics was strongly felt by the group, al-Sadr added three classifications for the existing Muslim nation-states:

(i)   the state that truly applies the *Shari'a*;
(ii)   the state that only partially applies *Shari'a*;
(iii) the state that never applies *Shari'a*.

The first case commands obedience from Muslim subjects; the second needs to be guided and advised; in the third, it is imperative to remove and replace the ruling elite or at least attempt to deter disobedience (*ma'siya*) when removal proves unattainable.[30] Into which category the Iraqi state fell is not stated; but judging from the kind of activity undertaken by the Da'wa in Iraq, it is of the second type, that of partial rather than total deviation.

The somewhat abstract, dry nature of this vision has its strong and weak points. The vague, remote, utopian goal of a pan-Islamic polity to be established when all Muslims or the majority embrace the 'true' Islam, as envisaged by the Da'wa, gave the movement both a *raison d'être* and a hope; it also relieved it of any risky, premature involvement in volatile politics. The educationalist character of action was, at least at that point, almost philanthropic, rather than militant. In terms of thought, it detached the group from traditional conservatism; in terms of spaces of action, however, the budding movement remained within traditional confines (the mosque, the *madrasa*, the *husayniya*, the 'Ashura assembly) which it tried to transcend.

Contrary to the local spirit of the lay members whose supreme goal was to create an active sub-national Shi'ite movement, the clerics – as is clear in the strategy they moulded – looked for supra-national ideals. This reflects the international nature of Shi'ite theology, of the Shi'ite *madrasa*[31] and of Shi'ite *mujtahid*-lay networks. It also matches the ideological culture prevailing across the Arab world at the time, such as Marxist internationalism and pan-Arab nationalism, both movements which aimed to transcend the nation-state and legitimize larger supra-national polities. This could be the reason why the Da'wa group expanded to include the Lebanese, Persian and perhaps Bahraini clerical seminarians and junior apprentice *'ulama* residing in Najaf.

The *al-Usus* advocated a universalist approach to Islam. There is hardly any explicit reference to Shi'ism; even the infallible Imam is introduced as 'the infallible individual'. The Islamic nation envisaged in the programme is neither Sunni nor Shi'ite. The same applies to the *'ulama* and *fuqaha* who are entrusted with judicial powers in this prospective polity. This universalism attempted to override mediaeval and contemporary Shi'ite schools in matters of political legitimacy. This daring thrust was, perhaps, utopian on the part of its authors, who were over-encouraged by the short-lived Shi'i-Sunni cooperation under al-Hakim.[32]

Challenges to the Da'wa

Two major challenges faced the Da'wa: one from secularists, the other from clerical traditionalists. We lack documented evidence from these opposing actors. However, the Da'wa's written self-defence gives us some idea of their nature:

> We found [in 1959–60] that the prevailing conviction among Shi'ite circles is that the *'ulama* and *fuqaha*, religious doctors and jurisprudents, *denounce any involvement in politics* ... In fact the ideal image of the most pious and pure of the *'ulama* is the one most remote from the world of laypeople.[33] (Italics added.)

The first, secular, challenge came from General Qassim's supporters and communists who attacked the Da'wa as reactionaries.[34] Ba'thists and pan-Arab nationalists considered Islamist militancy a natural ally at the time. But as soon as the communist threat waned, their attitude changed.[35] In all these cases, Islamist militancy was conceived to be a regression.[36]

The second challenge came from the senior Najafi *'ulama* and the Karbala group,[37] led by Hassan Shirazi,[38] who directed their onslaught with different themes and motifs along a traditionalist/Usuli line.[39] Traditional quietists[40] contended that Shi'is have their religious authority, the *hawza* as it is called in Najafi jargon, and they do not need *effendis* (administrators).[41] Senior *'ulama* feared the growth of a political party would create a rival to the centre of authority and compete with them over diminishing resources and mass loyalty. The fierce competition among them was too strong to admit a newcomer.[42] A doctrinal challenge was also raised against the Da'wa, namely that the application of Islam or the call for establishing an Islamic state is impossible and contradicts the *Shari'a*, which commands quietism until the return of the Hidden Imam.[43] Other anti-Da'wa clerical views explained that party politics were not *haram* (impermissible) but politically dangerous.[44]

The Karbala-based Shirazi group had a different doctrinal argument: the *wilaya 'amma*. This argument says that militancy should be endorsed by a *fatwa* (religious edict), i.e. it should be a *Shari'a* imperative[45] and that party activity must be led by a supreme *mujtahid* who enjoys the *wilaya 'amma* (general command). Driven by family and city rivalries (see Chapter Twelve), the Karbala group did not oppose party politics in general but did oppose the Da'wa politics in particular.[46] On this argument, the Da'wa commented:

> One of those who quarrelled with the Da'wa [Hassan Shirazi] published a book defending his concept that *marja'ism* should lead the party ... When the Da'wa was severely hit [by the Ba'th regime in 1974] this concept resurfaced.[47]

The above debate, so neatly expounded by the different contenders, was associated with a smear campaign directed principally at prominent figures of the Da'wa. Muhammad Baqir al-Sadr was, again, the main target. Not only were accusations of Sunni heresies made, but harsher and more devastating criticisms were unleashed against him. His treatise on *fiqh* was said to have been of a superficial quality, a devastating critique indeed for a junior jurisprudent who had set for himself the grand mission of producing a universal Islamic theory to replace not only Marxism but any Western ideology. Should the *hawza* consider his works 'superficial' or 'shallow', then his prospects for dissemination beyond Najaf were gloomy indeed.

Al-Hakim's position on the matter was unfavourable and decisive (see Chapter Four). There are vague *fatwas* attributed to al-Hakim on party politics. In the first he forbade such line of action. In the second, he sanctioned it, provided that the identity of leaders is disclosed to the members; he demanded transparency rather than clandestineness.[48]

The Da'wa's Reaction to the Attacks

The Da'wa launched a counter-attack, producing interesting arguments. It contended that *marja'ism* (the collective body of senior *'ulama*) could not achieve success unless it relied on a political organization different from itself. This was for the following reasons:

(i)   The activities of *marja'ism* were functionally sporadic, focusing on recruiting *wukala'* (agents), collecting revenues, distributing them and competing with other *'ulama*, hence the activities were feeble because they were individualistic, disorganized and sometimes chaotic or unfocused.

(ii)   *Marja'ism* could not publicly practise politics, as it would be exposed to persecution, and the creation of an Islamic party is meant to give them an instrument in this field.

(iii)   *Marja'ism* collapses with the death of the supreme *marja'*. The re-affiliation of the deceased's followers with other competing senior authorities ensues, leading to a great waste of assets.[49]

(iv)   The Da'wa denied creating a duality of Islamic authority. The reassurances given by the Da'wa, unintentionally perhaps, were counterproductive. In a lengthy article,[50] the Da'wa explains that 'there is no double centre ... no duality,' as both the Da'wa and *marja'ism* call for Islam. The Da'wa, it is asserted, supports *marja'ism* and defends the *'ulama* and their students whether or not the latter are emulators.

(v)   The Da'wa tried to attack apolitical *'ulama*. According to its view, *marja'i'sm* is of three types: traditional, reformist and a handful who support change, implying a criticism of the first two types.

(vi)   The Da'wa pledged to strengthen the clerical class: 'The number of *mujtahids* is *less* than the demand of the *umma*, hence the Da'wa wants to bring talented religious students up the ladder to assume the rank of *ijtihad*.'[51]

(vii)   Al-Sadr and the group of initiators also tried to ignite Shi'ite competitiveness through highlighting the Sunni's successful creation of their own political instruments, the achievements their organization had accomplished and the modern literature they had produced and widely circulated.

(viii) Lastly, the Da'wa promised to install a *faqih* sitting permanently on the leadership board of its intended political organization, or even above it, to supervise the righteousness of the latter's actions, thereby symbolizing the supremacy of the *mujtahid* over the lay.

These and other arguments, however, did not in the least please opposing clerics or soften their firm challenge.

Early Schisms

A number of pressures began to erode the confidence of the Da'wa group and even caused some final breaks with it. After the first cells were formed and expanded, political, social and doctrinal pressures mounted and drove some members to withdraw. Consequently, the group was reduced to 'a handful of homogeneous militants of conscious believers, *hawza* apprentices and few individual *'ulama'*.[52]

Out of fear and caution, the number of attendants at al-Sadr's elementary lectures at the *hawza* declined. Ayatollah al-Hakim[53] spread the word that *marja'ism*, the centre of absolute *ijtihad* (interpretation of the *Shari'a*), was for all, whereas the party is only for a few. The brevity and clarity of the message was decisive. Al-Hakim's aide at the Dar al-Ifta' (The Bureau of Issuing Religious Opinion) reprimanded and reproached both Mahdi and Muhammed Baqir al-Hakim, the two sons of the Grand Ayatollah, for delaying the emergence of the Hidden Imam by their childish indulgence in clandestine movements.[54]

Along with others, al-Sadr realized at this point that the time had come to keep a distance from the political organization in whose creation he had been so deeply and passionately immersed from its very inception. The group was advised of his position.[55] The Da'wa chronicle starkly describes these moments as 'severe shocks and upheavals caused by the withdrawal of members under political and social pressures …'[56] The intrigues of a certain rival from another party forced some Mujahidin of great weight [al-Sadr and others] to suspend their membership or leave the party.'[57] Al-Sadr was said to have expressed readiness and willingness to support the party in ideological terms, since there was no *amr shar'i*, a ruling by a *marja'*, for him to quit. He never returned to the party. In the course of time he not only distanced himself but also, in 1974, his students from the Da'wa.

In the early 1980s, this latter point developed into an intricate political battle among rival Shi'ite groups. Almost two decades after the episode, the debate was centred on the actual relation between the Da'wa and al-Sadr. The

Tehran-based, pro-al-Hakim weekly, *Liwaʿ al-Sadr*,[58] for example, stressed the following points:

(i)   Al-Sadr established the Daʿwa Islamiya in 1958 but did not give it any specific name.
(ii)   He left the movement in the 1960s because he had not adopted the concept of the absolute *wilaya*, command or guardianship of the *faqih*.
(iii)   Tensions built between him and the rest of the leadership.
(iv)   In his later days, he rejected being linked to one specific Islamic party.

The article was based on the biased recollections of Mahdi al-Hakim and his brother Aziz al-Hakim, both active in a group separate from the Daʿwa during the period in question. The Tehran-based *al-ʿAmal al-Islami* took up the same issue in an attempt to dissociate al-Sadr from the Daʿwa when it said:

> Al-Sadr invested his intellectual and practical energies to patronize Islamic militancy and Islamic movements, dealt with all Islamic organizations of whatever colour, showing sympathy and benevolence … He had channels with all contingents of Islamic movements.[59]

These two assertions were challenged by the Daʿwa's prominent *faqih*, Kazim al-Haʾiri. Al-Haʾiri claimed he asked al-Sadr several questions on these matters:[60]

(i)   Have his students distanced themselves voluntarily?
(ii)   Did he wish them to distance themselves?
(iii)   If so, was this a temporary measure?
(iv)   Or was it a matter of principle?

Al-Haʾiri confirmed that 'the answer in his [al-Sadr's] own honourable handwriting was: "I meant the first, second and the third but not the fourth."'[61]

That was al-Sadr's major retreat. He felt the weight of the criticism and sensed the perils of being isolated at such an early stage of his thorny career. Decades later, some of his disciples would reverse the motive, saying al-Sadr withdrew from the party to protect it, that he was determined to fight his way up the clerical ladder until he reached the status of grand *mujtahid*, so that with a word from him 'millions would join the party'.[62] Whether or not such a vision ever crossed al-Sadr's mind is impossible to judge, but the predicament reveals the dilemma of clerical modernization in Shiʿite *milieux*: without the support or acquiescence of a grand patron, modernization by junior agents is unthinkable.

The reliance on the proxy support of the Grand Ayatollah Muhsin al-Hakim or his silence proved to be double edged. In 1959–60 al-Hakim's political stand was of paramount importance in sustaining, indirectly of course, the drive to the new, innovative generation that sought to renew Shiʿite thought, a generation symbolized by al-Sadr himself. A year later, al-Hakim became an obstacle and al-Sadr was too fragile to resist these pressures. Another possible source of his withdrawal might have been the proxy liaisons some of the Da'wa leaders established with the Shah.

It is not clear why, apart from al-Sadr and the two sons of al-Hakim (who all withdrew upon the command of the Grand Ayatollah), other clerics remained within the newly born Da'wa. It is equally unclear why lay persons like the merchant Sahib al-Dakhil, the engineer Salih al-Adib or even clerics like Murtadha al-'Askari, 'Arif al-Basri and other leaders should pay no due attention to al-Hakim's *amr shar'i*. Either these actors claimed to emulate other *mujtahids* or simply claimed to have a potency which needed no *fatwas*. Or, perhaps, such an *amr shar'i* was never issued by al-Hakim, who was only critical of al-Sadr and his two sons. Whatever the case, al-Sadr was now relieved from party politics and had more space to concentrate on his literary work. In a sense, he and the Da'wa Party were freed from each other's shackles.

The Voice of the Party

Early on, the group launched an organ, *al-Da'wa al-Islamiya* (The Islamic Call). This clandestine, handwritten leaflet-like publication carried in ten successive issues the exposition of the *al-Usus*. *Al-Usus* was, probably in 1961 or 1963, renamed *Sawt al-Da'wa* ('The Voice of the Da'wa').[63]

The fact that both organs were handwritten leaflet-like affairs testifies to the poor material and financial resources possessed by the group. The first issue available in a typed format is No. 22, dated Thil Qi'da 1397 (15 October 1977). It was presumably typed abroad in exile. Only after the 1979 Iranian Revolution did the first printed edition emerge.

In its chronicles, the Da'wa Party speaks of how the central organ of the party carried on its front page the Qur'anic verse:[64]

And we wished to be
Gracious to those who were
Being oppressed in the land
To make them *leaders*
And make them *heirs*
(Sura 28:5; italics added.)

The format of the first typed issue (No. 22) tells a different story, however. It is very simple, less than A4 size. The logo on the cover page, *Sawt al-Da'wa*, is engraved in clumsy, bold handwritten calligraphy, flanked by two Qur'anic verses. On the right:

Who is better in speech
Than one who *calls* (men)

To God, works righteousness,
And says 'I am of those
Who bow in Islam?'
(Sura 41:33; italics added.)

On the left:

God has promised, to those
Among you who believe
And work righteous deeds, that He
Will, of surety, grant them
In the land, *inheritance*
(*Of power*), as He granted it
To those before them.
(Sura 24:55; italics added.)

These two *suras*, i.e. Qur'anic verses, reveal the state of mind of the initiators. The first verse describes missionaries as fighters for Islam and the real embodiment of the truth of God, which lends them a sublime status and sacred character.[65] The second gives hope of victory, as Muslims are promised security and the final assumption of power.

Twenty-one pieces, commentaries and articles written and published during the period 1960–63 make up 112 pages in three years, roughly 37 pages annually: 54 in 1960; 20 in 1961 and 38 in 1963. Twelve of these pieces are purely abstract ideological formulations; six relate to organizational themes; one is programmatic and only one is political. Clearly, the focus was on ideology and organization.

The sole political piece emerged in the spring of 1963, and interestingly enough it was a feature on the struggle between the Iranian *'ulama* and the Shah. There is also a report on the communiqué released by the rector of Azhar, Cairo, Mahmud Shaltut, in solidarity with Iran's *'ulama*.[66] The first commentary stressed that the battle going on in Iran revealed the following:

(i)   that the US was behind the Shah in his endeavours to carry out their scheme;

(ii)   the Shah's reforms could not deceive the nation even though the latter were of shallow thinking. Both *'ulama* and *wataniyin* (nationalist) leaders were opposed to the reforms;

(iii)   it was the *'ulama* who enjoyed real popularity. If only they decided to go into action, the nationalist leaders could do nothing but follow the example of the *'ulama*;

(iv)   although popular support was massive, the *absence of organization* on the part of the *'ulama* renders that support impotent.[67] (Italics added.)

Right up to 1964, *Sawt al-Da'wa* was still engaged in defending the party's non-political stand. In an article titled 'Why do we refrain from discussing important political events in our regions?' it is asserted that:

> Many missionaries [*du'at*, i.e. members] had raised the above question in the aftermath of so many political upheavals in the Mashriq and Iran. The Da'wa was reproached for not satisfying this vital need for any militant fighting at a time when political discussions are heard even among ordinary [apolitical] laypeople ... Many missionaries were emotionally carried away by some current ideas ... They have forgotten that we are different from other politicians and political groups who passionately endeavour to change rulers at random. We do NOT wish to sit on the ruler's chair, nor are we professional politicians ...[68]

It added:

> The [Islamic] nation's attention, at present, needs to be redirected towards Islam so that they would embrace it, and this process needs huge efforts ... And the missionaries are the agents to achieve this task. If they get involved in explaining political events, who would then work for the Islamic thought?[69]

These publications also testify to the irregular nature of the activities of the group and the obscurity of the line of action they wished to pursue. Not a single word was ever jotted down in this period (1960–63) on organizational form, no directions as to whom should be won over to the party and how, why, where. The activities of the group, it seems, were focused on the *hawza*, the religious academy and its population, apprentice and junior turbaned.

The analysis of the data displayed in Tables 3.3 and 3.4 on the publication of *Sawt al-Da'wa* extends beyond the preliminary period of 1960–63 and may thus carry us to the 'Arif brothers' era and the two Ba'th regimes. The latter two periods will be dealt with in due course. But it should be pointed out immediately that of the four general periods of action, the first (1958–63) was the weakest. This was mostly due to clerical pressures from within Najaf.

Table 3.3: Sawt al-Da'wa: *Dates and Periods of Publication, 1960–80*

Issue	Date AH	Date AD	Source*	Period
1	N/A	N/A	N/A	Qassim era
2	1381	15 Jun. 1961–14 Jun. 1962	V.4, p. 215	same

Issue	Date AH	Date AD	Source*	Period
3	Rabi' Thani 1383	Aug. 1963	V.4, p. 52	First Ba'th regime, Feb. – Nov. 1963
4	Sha'ban 1383	18 Dec. 1963	V.4, pp. 58,75	'Arif brothers, 1963–68
5	Thil Hija 1383	15 Apr. 1964	V.4, p. 282	same
6	Rabi' Thani 1384	11 Jul. 1964	V.4, pp. 63,68	same
7	Jamadi Awal 1384	8 Sep. 1964	V.4, p. 309	same
8	Jamadi Awal 1385	28 Aug. 1965	V.4, p. 309	same
9	Sha'ban 1385	25 Nov. 1965	V.4, p. 304	same
10	N/A	N/A	N/A	same
11	Jamadi Awal 1386	17 Aug. 1966	V.4, p.315	same
12	N/A	N/A	N/A	same
13	Thil Qi'da 1386	11 Feb. 1967	V.4, p. 400	same
14	Thil Qi'da 13867	31 Jan. 1968	V.4, p. 123	same
15	Rabi' Thani 1388	29 Jun. 1968	V.4, p. 328	same
16	N/A	N/A	N/A	The second Ba'th rule before the Iranian Revolution, 1968–79
17	N/A	N/A	N/A	same
18	N/A	N/A	N/A	same
19	N/A	N/A	N/A	same
20	N/A	N/A	N/A	same
21	N/A	N/A	N/A	same
22	Thil Qi'da 1397	15 Oct. 1977	V.4, p. 3	same
23	Sufar 1398	11 Jan. 1978	V.4, p. 165	same
24	N/A	N/A	N/A	same

Issue	Date AH	Date AD	Source*	Period
25	Shawal 1398	3 Sep. 1978	V.4, p. 320	same
26	Muharram 1399	2 Dec. 1978	V.4, p. 127	During and after the Iranian Revolution
27	N/A	N/A	N/A	same
28	N/A	N/A	N/A	same
29	Muharram 1400	21 Nov. 1979	V.4, p. 285	same
30	N/A	N/A	N/A	same
31	N/A	N/A	N/A	same
32	Shawal 1400	13 Aug. 1980	V.4, p. 217	same

*This table has been constructed on the basis of the *Da'wa Doctrine*, vol. 4.

Table 3.4: Sawt al-Da'wa: *Frequency of Publication 1960–80*

Period	Number of Issues	Duration	Frequency	Remarks
Qassim era	2	3 years	18 months	Slow activity due to weakness & ambiguity
First Ba'th regime	2	10 months	6 months	
'Arif brothers	11	4 years	4.3 months	Severe interruptions in 1965 and 1968, but activity is intensified compared to previous periods
Ba'th regime				
A. 1968–79	9	10 years	13+ months	Published in Iraq; reduced activity due to state terror

Period	Number of Issues	Duration	Frequency	Remarks
B. After 1979	10	2 years	2.4 months	Regularity established when publication resumed abroad
Subtotal	19	12 years	7.47 months	
Total	32	20 years	7.5 months	

FOUR

Social Origins and Actors

Beginnings

The genesis and later development of the Da'wa Party was the combined work of two social groups: a young generation of reforming *mujtahids* who emerged in the late 1950s, and various disadvantaged Shi'ite lay groups, notably mercantile families descending mainly, but not exclusively, from Najaf. The role played by these two groups in the movement is unique and merits examination.

There are several contradictory accounts on the date, place and actors who were involved in the foundation of the Da'wa. Such inconsistencies are common to the accounts of both scholars and party records. According to the six-volume records of the party, known as *Thaqafat al-Da'wa (Da'wa Doctrine*, hereafter DD):

> [T]he call [literally *Da'wa*, although it is not a proper name but rather a noun] started its march or first steps as from 17 Rabi' al-Awal 1377 [October 1957], and focused on studying [Iraqi] society, specifying its ills and features ...[1]

This quotation never states in clear words that a political organization was established, the word 'party' is clearly avoided, and the text vaguely refers to an idea, a 'call'. This contradicts two other statements in the DD, Volume 3. One asserts that the Da'wa Party was established in 1958 and the other refers to 1959, 'during the period of the struggle between the two leaders of the 1958 July Revolution', namely General Qassim and Colonel 'Arif, who split ranks.[2] Hence we have three different dates of foundation according to the DD itself: 1957, 1958 and 1959.

Different years are also given by individual leaders. Murtadha al-'Askari, for example, could not determine whether the Da'wa was founded before or after the 1958 Revolution. Talib Rifa'i, another founding (if not *the* founding) member, says the party was started a few months after the July 1958 revolution.[3] However, his partner in leadership, Salih al-Adib, confirms that the first cell of the party was formed in 1957.[4] Different dates have been given by various scholars: late 1960s or late 1950s (Batatu),[5] 1957–8 or late 1950s (Baram),[6] 1968 (Slugletts),[7] 1969 or late 1960s (Marr),[8] 1957 (Wiley, Joyce) or 1958 (Farhad).[9]

Accounts of the place where the party was founded are similarly conflicting. Some sources assert that the Da'wa was founded in Najaf at Muhammad Baqir al-Sadr's residence, at Muhsin al-Hakim's place,[10] at the house of an unnamed 'prominent *mujtahid*'[11] or in Karbala.[12]

Different sources in the leading circles of the party, or in Da'wa literature, give different accounts of the composition of the group of actors who initiated the Da'wa.[13] Another ambiguity is who exactly established the party: Baqir al-Sadr, Mahdi al-Hakim, Talib Rifa'i, Sahib al-Dakhil or others? Different claims exist. Talib Rifa'i and Mahdi al-Hakim credit the achievement to themselves while other leaders have given credit to al-Sadr.[14] The lists of original initiators are as varied as they are interesting to the study of the origins of the Da'wa. They have at least five combinations (see Table 4.1).

Table 4.1: Possible Variations or Combinations of the Da'wa Founding Nuclei

Version 1[15]	Version 2[16]	Version 3[17]	Version 4[18]	Version 5[19]
1. Mahdi al-Hakim	1. Mahdi al-Hakim	1. Mahdi al-Hakim	1. Mahdi al-Hakim	1. Mahdi al-Hakim
2. Talib Rifa'i	2. Talib Rifa'i	2. Talib Rifa'i	2. Talib Rifa'i	2. Talib Rifa'i
3. Baqir al-Sadr	3. Baqir al-Sadr[a]	3. Baqir al-Sadr	3. Baqir al-Sadr	3. Baqir al-Sadr
4. Anonymous[b]	4. Sahib al-Dakhil	4. Sahib al-Dakhil	4. Sahib al-Dakhil	4. Sahib al-Dakhil
	5. Murtadha al-'Askari[c]	5. Murtadha al-'Askari	5. Murtadha al-'Askari	5. Muh. Bahr al-'Ulum
		6. 'Arif al-Basri		6. Muh. Baqir al-Hakim[d]
		7. Hadi Fadhli		7. Muh. Hadi Subaiti
		8. Mahdi Simawi		
		9. Muh. Sadiq Qamusi[e]	6. Muh. Sadiq Qamusi	8. Muh. Sadiq Qamusi

This table has been constructed on the basis of information provided by sources quoted in endnotes 15, 16, 17, 18, and 19.

a. Rifa'i claims he had recruited al-Sadr. Al-Dakhil also claims to have recruited al-Sadr.
b. Identity is withheld for security reasons.

c. Al-'Askari, a cleric of Persian origin, was recruited by al-Sadr.
d. Muhammad Baqir al-Hakim was still an adolescent, some fourteen years old. At present he is the chairman of SAIRI.
e. The committee was expanded to include the following: Muhammad Sadiq Qamusi, Salih al-Adib and Muhammad Hadi Subaiti.

The puzzles raised by these contradictory statements become somewhat redundant when we consider that the notion of forming a modern, Shi'ite ideological party was in the air as early as 1952.[20] Since most of the actors were not only from the same town but also school colleagues and even neighbourhood companions, they must have shared their experiences and conceptions in such a way that these ideas assumed a collective nature. Political organizations do not emerge ready-made, and their foundation may well take some time before they can crystallize. Since recollections on this formative period began to surface some twenty years on, it is possible that the statements by different actors may refer, in retrospect, to different phases in this process. Personal competition, factional splits, familial rivalries and ideological differences, which plagued those individuals who carried the work for few decades, have developed into conflicting interests. This gives rise to under- or overestimation of self or family roles.

Table 4.2: Known Da'wa Party Initiators and Leading Members, 1958–59

Name	Occupation	City	Born	Source
Category A: Initiators				
Muhammad Baqir al-Sadr	cleric	Kazimiya*	1930 or 1931	a, b, c
Mahdi al-Hakim	cleric	Najaf	1940?	a, b, c
Muhammad Baqir al-Hakim	cleric	Najaf	1944	a, b
Muhammad Bahr al-'Ulum	cleric	Najaf	1930	
Talib Rifa'i	cleric	Najaf	1930?	a, b, c
Muhammad Sadiq Qamusi**	merchant	Najaf	1930?	a, b, c
Sahib al-Dakhil***	merchant	Najaf	1932, d. 1972	a, b, c
Murtada al-'Askari	cleric	Najaf	1915 or 1919	?, b, c

Name	Occupation	City	Born	Source
Muhammad Salih al-Adib	engineer	Karbala	1930?, d.1996	?, b, ?
Muh. Hadi Subaiti****	civil engineer	Najaf	1930?	?, b, ?
Category B: Karbala figures*****				
Hassan Shirazi	cleric	Karbala/Iran	1934, d.1980	d
Mahdi Shirazi	cleric	Karbala/Iran	1930?	d
Muhammad Shirazi	cleric	Karbala/Iran	1932?	d
Hadi Shirazi	cleric	Karbala/Iran	1930?	d
Category C				
Five anonymous persons from among the Najafi initiators; one is presumably still in Iraq, and his identity could not be disclosed by interviewees.				

This table has been compiled on the basis of information provided by the following sources: a: Muhammad Bahr al-'Ulum; b: Sami al-'Askari; c: Muhammad A. Jabar; d: Muhammad Taqi and Ahmad al-Katib.

*	Originally from Kazimain but based in Najaf.
**	Source b claims it is Abdul Razaq Qamusi.
***	Al-Dakhil worked as a trader in Najaf and an accountant for other merchants in Shurja, Baghdad. Al-Dakhil is said to have attended some religious courses in Najaf. His writings in the Da'wa publication reveal a literary talent with a lucid, emotive style.
****	Subaiti is Lebanese on the side of his mother.
*****	The Karbala group withdrew from preliminary meetings in protest. They then embarked on a project of their own.

Another reason for these conflicting accounts is that the Da'wa Party never kept records of membership or minutes of meetings; indeed, it never issued a statement or political communiqué carrying its signature in the first two decades. This kind of systematic action was only started in mid-1979. For example, the Da'wa Party first published its programme, *Bayan al-Tafahum* (Declaration of Mutual Understanding) and started printing its clandestine mouthpiece, *Sawt al-Da'wa* in 1980, one year after the Iranian Revolution and almost twenty-three years after its officially recognized day of establishment in October 1957, or twenty-one years after the second equally officially recognized date of its formation, 1959.

Conflicting Meanings

Each version of the spaces, places and actors has a different symbolic and contextual meaning which is of paramount importance for current claims to leadership. The first version asserts that the party was established on 17 Rabi' al-Awal 1377 (12 October 1957),[21] when a meeting was held at the residence of the Grand Ayatollah Muhsin al-Hakim, who was second in the Shi'ite hierarchy only to the grand *marja'* Ayatollah Burujerdi in Qum, Iran. The 17 Rabi' al-Awal (1957) is celebrated by the Da'wa Party as their anniversary, or Party Day. Since it coincides with the Prophet Muhammad's birthday, the date assumes a symbolic meaning. It lends the party a universal rather than particular Islamic aura. It also serves to indicate that the party came into being out of sublime ideals to further the cause of Islam even under the monarchy, rather than as a reaction or response to the rise of communism in Iraq in 1959. Instead, the party leaders are more inclined to lend their movement a positive, offensive character, one associated with renewal and reform.

By the same token, the claims that the founding group held its meeting at the house of al-Hakim or of al-Sadr in Najaf, or, rather, in Karbala, convey different meanings conducive to different claims to legitimacy. However, the notion that Ayatollah Muhsin al-Hakim endorsed such a project is refuted by the positions he took in 1960 against the Da'wa. Even if it is claimed that such meetings were convened without his previous knowledge or approval, the choice of his home and the inclusion of one or two of his younger sons (Mahdi and Muhammad Baqir) could imply that the endeavour was patronized by the 'house of al-Hakim' and suggests that the party was a unanimously approved, pan-Shi'ite organ. Such claims reveal the extent to which such a political gathering was in need of the social patronage of a grand or senior *mujtahid*. Other claims have similar patronage-seeking ends, whether they relate to persons (al-Sadr) or cities (Karbala).

Views on who pioneered the idea of the Da'wa or who was the source of organizing the initiative differ greatly. The initiative, it is contended, came from Muhammad Baqir al-Sadr;[22] another view gives credit to Mahdi al-Hakim; a third to Talib al-Rifa'i;[23] a fourth to Sahib al-Dakhil.[24] These diverging contentions may be due, in part, to human inconsistencies and error; but their significance has also a great deal to do with present conflicts among various contenders who wish to claim radical credit for themselves or deny their rivals such credit.

Our assumption is that intentions to start a Shi'ite party had actually been in the air before 1958 Revolution, but had never gone beyond contemplative thinking. When that line was crossed, the sociopolitical context had changed radically. So, too, had the leading actors. Indeed, one of the contenders who claimed credit for establishing the party, Mahdi al-Hakim, asserted that there had been a Da'wa in 1957, but it was yet unnamed.[25] This conclusion is verified by various facts. There are no records or recollections which suggest that the group, before 1958, had any concrete activity, such as producing a publication, holding regular meetings or even drafting or thinking of drafting a platform and document of whatever nature. Meetings may have taken place, but these could have been more akin to social liaisons than to any kind of political endeavour. The accounts relevant to the year 1957 have little logical or historical coherence. For example, in his two-volume study on party politics under the monarchy, the Shi'i historian Hassan Shubbar provides details on a number of Shi'ite Islamist groupings organized in Najaf, such as Harakat al-Shabab al-Muslim (The Movement of Young Muslims) in 1950 or the Ja'fari Party (named after the sixth Imam, Ja'far al-Sadiq) in 1952. Yet he makes no mention of the Da'wa of which he is a member.[26]

In contrast, 1959 was a year of visible, tangible Islamic agitation, whether in the form of the Da'wa Party, the Jama'at al-'Ulama or the Hizb al-Islami (Sunni Islamic Party) which was supported by Ayatollah Muhsin al-Hakim. Many Da'wa Party propaganda articles are signed and dated in 1959, a framework which signifies a strong turnabout in the Shi'ite world of *marja'ism*, and the life of the clerical class in Najaf itself.[27] We have already outlined the way in which the demise of the monarchy threw the clerical class into a headlong encounter with secular change in social, economic and legal areas. Aggravated by their sense of decline,[28] their responses were encouraged by the Iranian[29] and Sunni Arab examples of activism.[30] These factors emboldened the *'ulama* and enhanced the drive of the lay groups in Najaf, who were highly dependent on the *mujtahids* or at least very close to them. This framework was crucial in the shift from quietism to activism and the growing militancy of traditional groups in Najaf, Karbala and Kazimiya.

Leadership

The notion of creating a Shi'ite political organization as active, modern and appealing as the communist movement originated in the minds of the lay elements of the group. Two candidates are possible, Talib Rifa'i and Sahib al-Dakhil. By vocation and learning, turbaned *'ulama* are more inclined to doctrinal and pedagogical reforms; lay Najafis are more bent on social action.

In 1957, however, circumstances were unfavourable for launching the Islamic Shi'ite party. When conditions changed, the project was taken over (hijacked) by the junior clerics. It is important to note here that, historically, Shi'ite political parties were initiated by lay figures who sought support from *mujtahids*, not the other way round. It is most probable, therefore, that Talib Rifa'i and Sahib al-Dakhil had been the original masterminds, with al-Dakhil playing the most active role, even if Rifa'i was the nominal leader.

Al-Dakhil's record seems to suggest he was a natural-born organizer and mobilizer. It was al-Dakhil who, back in 1952, initiated the Jaʿfari (Shiʿite) party in Najaf with Hassan Shubbar and Sadiq Qamusi.[31] He was also a member of the Munatada al-Nashr (Publication Club), an innovative literary group influenced by the great Shiʿi reformer Muhammad Rida al-Muzafar in the early 1950s[32] and was also the co-founder of the Lijanat al-Thakafa wa al-ʿAmal (The Committee for Culture and Action), another Najafi literary-political movement of the same period. Both these cultural formations were part of the Najaf intellectual awakening to modern life in the second half of the 20th century. In both groups, Sahib al-Dakhil was a young activist influenced, along with other young Najafis, by the innovative endeavours of Sheikh al-Muzafar, a well-known advocate of *madrasa* renewal in Najaf.[33] The group was also under the influence of the great religious figure Muhammad Hussain Kashif al-Ghita, who took a clear-cut anti-Western (and partly anti-Marxist) position and posed Islam as an alternative.[34] Sahib al-Dakhil actually was the leader of the Daʿwa organization in the 1960s[35] and continued to play an active role in the movement and formation of the Daʿwa Party until his execution in the early 1970s.

In many ways al-Dakhil symbolizes the role and activism of the traditional Najafi merchants who descended from a tribal or rural origin. He came from the Bakr bin Waʾil clan, a branch of the Shiʿite sections of the Shammar tribe. This clan settled down in Najaf, and some of its members extended trading links with the countryside, mainly in cereals. The Shurja cereal trade centre in Baghdad was delicately linked to the countryside. Al-Dakhil himself was a cereal merchant in Shurja in Najaf at one point, and had previously been a worker at a spice store owned by the al-Turaihi family, a well-known family of noble lineage to whom he was related by marriage.[36]

Sahib al-Dakhil was also an active *khums* collector for Najaf. His strong links with the high echelons of the clerical class in the shrine city put him in a strategic position to sense both the grievances of the Najafi merchants, whose business was strongly linked to the welfare of Najaf as a holy centre, and the reactions of the *mujtahids*. Another feature to consider is that Sahib al-Dakhil, like many other notable mercantile/tribal families, was a leading organizer of the ʿAshura rituals, a ceremony which provides prestige and enhances business for this class of petty merchants.

Secular encroachment, economic reforms and the decline of cultural traditionalism were felt by the Najafi/Karbalai section of the Shiʿite mercantile class. The collective interests of the latter did not merge until 1964. However, as the budding lay group allied itself to the enthusiastic junior clerics in mid-1958, the centre of leadership shifted to the latter. The need to break traditional barriers, together with the need for theological potency and intellectualism, family status and patronage connections, were all forces that enhanced this transfer of leadership. These circumstances would boost Muhammad Baqir al-

Sadr's standing within in the group.[37] In this context, al-Sadr's leading role seems inevitable.

Born around 1930,[38] al-Sadr must have been twenty-eight in 1958, an age of maturity, intellectual choice and even leadership. The other participants were either of his age (Bahr al-'Ulum, Sahib al-Dakhil) or far younger than himself, as was the case with both Mahdi al-Hakim and Muhammad Baqir al-Hakim, who were in their adolescence, or were less prominent than himself in theological terms. Rifa'i was 'turbaned' too, but more inclined to family business.[39] Compared to lay members, then, al-Sadr had a higher status.

Yet, in 1958 al-Sadr was still a *murahiq* (a junior or apprentice *mujtahid*), and by the rigid standards of the Shi'ite clerical hierarchy, he was in the early stages of the long, arduous process of ascent to the grand status of *ijtihad/mujtahid*. In the realm of the clerical class in Najaf, family, age and learning play an important role in defining one's status. al-Sadr's rank would therefore have given him precedence over his colleagues within the founding group. Outside it, however, his standing was inferior to other high-ranking religious figures in Najaf, Karbala and Kazimiya. Thus, without the patronage of other, higher *mujtahids*, his own career was in jeopardy – not to mention his aspirations towards innovation and reformation.

His family status, however, was solid. He descended from a very old, well-known noble, clerical family originating from Jabal Amil in Lebanon. As the name itself denotes, the family occupied the position of al-Sadr, i.e. a leading ministerial post in the Safavid administration. It was also counted among the prominent *sayyid* families in Kazimiya.[40] His elder brother Isma'il was already a prayer leader and religious figure there. His maternal uncle, Sheikh Murtadha al-Yasin, enjoyed high esteem and played a prominent role in Shi'ite religious activism during the 1950s. Indeed, the status of both the al-Sadr and the al-Yasin families was so high that together they enhanced the position of the young al-Sadr in Najaf.

His relationship with the Grand Ayatollah Muhsin al-Hakim was a third source of his comparative strength. It should be remembered here that al-Sadr, as his biography confirms,[41] wrote a commentary on his patron's major work, *Riyadh al-Salihin* (The Gardens of the Pious). Usually junior *mujtahids* attain a higher rank by commenting on the works of an already established authority, as was the case with Khomeini, who produced a commentary on a treatise by Burujerdi.[42] By dint of such notes, the commentator would win good offices and patronage from the higher *marja'*, including financial support. He would also seek to strengthen the position of his master by winning him more and more imitators or followers. However, while this patronage might help raise the commentator's status, it could also inhibit any moves towards innovation or reform in doctrinal terms. Al-Sadr, along with the other Da'wa initiators, was caught in the informal networks of the decentralized, multiple and loose Shi'ite hierarchy from which they would not have been able to free themselves unless they ascended the theological ladder of the sacred class to achieve an untouchable grand status.

In the combined clerical-lay group of the Da'wa, al-Sadr was authorized to prepare the constitution and the programme of the party and make some contacts with candidates and supporters. Although the group was still unnamed at this stage, the intention, presumably, was to create a political movement. Directly or through junior members of the group, al-Sadr liaised with his maternal uncle Murtadha al-Yasin and Murtadha al-'Askari. The latter was a prominent, elder cleric of high social standing who was to join the leadership of the party.[43] Al-'Askari and Murtadha al-Ansari were both elders and by definition patrons of the group. Contacts had also been made with some Karbala clerical figures.[44]

The group of initiators moved cautiously and in total secrecy. No document was ever produced, and no direct publication ever started, even though the need for drafting a charter and party rules was recognized and presumably decided upon. The main decision, it seems, was to formulate and produce a modern Islamic theory. The second task was to approach the Shi'is at large in order to re-indoctrinate them in a peaceful, ethical, educational manner.

Intellectual work was the preserve of the clergy. Judging by later developments, the lay section must have been allocated a different set of tasks and expectations, namely organizing supporters into some form of discipline. Entrusted to define the philosophy, al-Sadr set about writing a set of ideological premises known in Da'wa Party jargon as *al-Usus*. Al-Sadr also embarked on preparations to author his *Falsafatuna* and *Iqtisaduna*, 'Our Philosophy', and 'Our Economics', which appeared successively in 1959 and 1961. In this phase of hectic agitation, the group swelled its ranks to twenty members and around one hundred sympathizers.[45]

The Nature of the Initiators

The list of participants involved in the formation of the Da'wa [see Tables 4.1 and 4.2], though far from complete or free of partial error, demonstrates that the group included fifteen members who represented a variety of social categories. We have split the members into three groups: Group A includes the initiators, Group B the Karbala participants and Group C the anonymous members. Judging by regional affiliation, family descent, occupation, age group, class and national origin, we may observe the following:

The initiators of the Da'wa Party were exclusively Najafi (nine out of ten). Only al-Sadr is from Kazimiya. His liaison with Kazimiya is of a relatively minor importance as it is the Khalisi family which dominated clerical circles and activity there, while the al-Sadr family was relegated to a secondary position. The residence of Muhammad Baqir al-Sadr in Najaf was a further indication of this reality.

Karbala (Group B) was, it is suggested, present at the preliminary contacts and discussions but not represented at the organizational level. The inclusion of the Karbala group in the discussions to form an Islamic political party indicated both the desire on the part of the Najafi initiators to expand their constituency and the demand by the Karbala group to be recognized. The nature of the liaisons between the two groups remains unclear. But these contacts ultimately failed to achieve unity of purpose. Inter-city and by extension inter-family rivalries overshadowed the exchanges between the two groups. To this very day, Da'wa leading figures deny the Karbala group any role in promoting Islamic militancy while the Karbala figures, who formed their own organization, inflated their own part in these preliminary steps.

However, the Karbala group did play a prominent role in the years to come, and their late-1960s activism can also be traced back to this moment. Other Shi'ite or predominantly Shi'ite cities like Hilla, Basra and others were absent at this point. Karbala was itself unrepresented in the end.

The most influential religious, noble families were present: the al-Hakims, the Bahr al-'Ulums, the al-Sadrs, the Shirazis and the al-'Askaris (five out of ten); but other prominent families of the time were not included, such as the Khalisis, the al-Jawahiris, the al-Ghitas and others. The participating families had, at the time, colossal social status, religious weight and even relative wealth.

In terms of profession, six out of ten in the list are clerics and students of religion (in Najafi jargon, 'turbaned'). In terms of nationality, all known participants were Iraqis by birth, the only exception being Murtadha al-'Askari who is believed to be of Iranian origin (one out of ten). This proportion could possibly be altered if the origin of members of Category C, which is unknown, could be taken into account.[46] In any event, were Category B, the Karbala group, to be included, the proportion of Iranians would rise sharply.

The New Generation

The average age of the participants in 1958 would gather the majority of known initiators (nine out of ten) under two age groups: seven are between 25–35 (70 percent), two are between 14–20 (20 percent), and only one is over 40 years old (10 percent). This profile reveals a generation gap within the clerical class. Apart from Murtadha al-'Askari, all the participants were young men, junior or apprentice *'ulama* and students of a new generation. This same conclusion is drawn when we look at the Karbala group (B).

This generation was predominantly born during the 1930s, and had been brought up under the turbulent impact of the second British occupation of Iraq in 1941; the 1948 Palestine war; the Iraqi Wathba upheaval of 1948; the 1954

Najaf revolt; and the reform movements of Kashif al-Ghita, Muzafar and others. Its experiences are not the same as those of Muhsin al-Hakim's generation, who fought in defence of the Ottomans in 1917,[47] took part in the anti-British 1920 tribal-urban revolt or had to get involved in the futile battle against the newly born monarchy in 1921 – and afterwards had to withdraw from the political arena under the combined pressures of the Sunni elite of the newly born nation-state and the British Mandate authority.[48]

The new generation of mostly noble, junior clerics and seminarians gradually matured on the eve of, during and after the era of World War II, when life was rapidly being secularized and new non-Islamic ideologies – communism, Arab nationalism, national socialism and liberalism – began to make their great advance. This was the post-Burujerdi generation, which was less insulated by rituals and mere preaching and more inclined towards taking an active role in the world of political and intellectual action. More members from this Najafi generation were soon attracted to the call, although they faced staunch traditional resistance. Nevertheless, in less than two decades the leading figures of Shi'i Islam in Iraq, Lebanon and beyond would emerge from this milieu.

Social Differentiation

The lay members in the group were either medium or small merchants, or belonged to mercantile families. As noted earlier, one of them was Sahib al-Dakhil, a cereal merchant linked mostly to rural areas. The other was Qamusi, a linen merchant. The other two lay participants were from the modern professions – agricultural and civil engineering – but by social origins they were from notable, mercantile families. Their presence signifies a social transformation in traditional mercantile groups whose sons were then included as new, modern-educated middle class professionals. Social origins apart, their attraction to the Shi'i-Islamist discourse may well signify the extent to which the family and city environment determined social action. Their presence was a portent of the forthcoming rise of this category which would, as from the late 1970s, assume a leading role in terms of numerical, intellectual and organizational weight.

The proportions given so far must be read in relative terms. This is because the evidence used for our calculations is based upon ten members, whereas the presumably 'complete' list contains fifteen. According to many Islamist activists, most of those who are missing from the list were men of religion, i.e. junior students or jurisprudents and one or two possible merchants.

The developments that invigorated the *'ulama* and their lay Najafi mercantile emulators involved different social, cultural and doctrinal interests. The *'ulama*, as a traditional status group, were losing their previously held pivotal position. As a consequence of secularization, not only was religion being relegated to a secondary, ethical system but the pedagogical, juristic and social roles of this clerical group were also diminishing. The revenues they derived from their command over the production and distribution of religious knowledge and services were plunging (see Part Three). Their main interest was to preserve Islamic law, the *Shari'a*, defend their autonomous institutions and retain their monopolistic authority over the Shi'ite lay community. Their means to achieve this end were the *madrasa*, the pulpit, the book and the customary social networks of emulators. Their response was geared towards pedagogy and charitable work. The decline of the clerical class was part of a general social transformation which, in the words of Batatu, destroyed 'older social forms attaching value to noble lineage, or knowledge of religion or possession of sanctity, or fighting prowess'.[49]

In other words, the *'ulama* customarily perceived their own decline as the decline of religion, and their self-preservation as the defence of religion. However, while junior clerics were caught in the same web of decline and shared the same doctrinal/pedagogical concerns as the senior clerical class, their sense of loss was geared more towards creating effective, innovative instruments that could take reform well ahead of the conservative confines set by their elders. These junior clerics sought innovation on every front, but in doing so they were inhibited by the rigid fetters of traditionalism.

Despite the divergence, however, there was a high level of collaboration and mutual support between senior and junior clerics. Both generations were working together in the *madrasa*, the pulpit and the ritual and both cooperated in the Society of 'Ulama and the clerical publications. The younger group was financially, socially and vocationally dependent on the patronage of their grand *mujtahids*. Thus they were tied to the clerical class in general, but were also alienated from the formidable centres of conservatism this class harboured.

On the other hand, there was a political convergence between the junior *'ulama* and the lay merchants in the sense that both categories had lost faith in traditional modes of mobilization and were inclined to modern ways and means. However, these two groups did diverge in other respects.

The other status group, the petty merchants in the shrine cities – particularly in Najaf – harboured a similar sense of peril. They suffered a double loss of status because of the dual nature of their calling. This group had one foot in a worldly occupation, i.e. trade and commerce, and another in a sacred calling, the organization of Mawakib Husayniya. Najafi merchants were dependent on religious tourism and trade with the countryside. In each trade circle they had mutual vested interests with the clerical class and the sheikhly landlords respectively. As their prosperity depended heavily on the welfare of the countryside in general, any disruptions in the trade cycle caused by ruptures in rural production, as was the case after agrarian reform in 1959, or any state regulatory impediments of free trade, would damage the well-being of this predominately Shi'ite class.[50] Some may have narrowly benefited from such changes, and others may have adapted to the new conditions. Part of this group, however, did suffer.

Some of the merchants figuring in Table 4.2 were also leaders of 'Ashura rituals which preserved their cultural identity, sustained their leading social roles and authority and enhanced their economic interests. In ceremonies, they functioned as leaders of the community. As we shall see in Chapter Nine, the religious tasks they assumed brought them social prestige and enhanced their secular calling, and might also have been a source of additional income. Najafis, Karbalais and Kazimites have a special term to denote such figures: *wujuh husayniya* (notables of the Hussein rituals). Nowadays, more political terms are used: *qiyadat husayniya* or *qiyadat mawakib*, meaning 'leaders of processions'.

Their high status in the community is hereditary in most cases. This status, for certain mercantile families, is enhanced by noble lineage (*sayyid*). Some members of this group are actually *sayyids* or allied to *sayyid* families through intermarriage, a further bond uniting them with the clerical class which is predominantly, but not exclusively, of *sayyid* descent. This group occupies a social space where the clerical class and lay believers meet and merge. They act as intermediaries and as a medium of exchange, so to speak, both in the marketplace and in the quarter-based ritual. This group is also devoutly religious. Their religiosity is distinct from the scriptural niceties of the clerics and dense with rituals as a form of popular action. Inasmuch as the clerical class dominates the scriptural realm of religion, the *wujuh husayniya* merchants control popular rituals.

With secularization this group came to suffer, as people's allegiances, economic importance, political loyalty or spiritual certainties were being steadily located in areas outside the circle of the clerical class and their allies, the lay organizers of the rituals. This group was so emotionally and socially attached to popular rituals that any encroachment or limitations set on these rites would trigger fierce reactions. As noted earlier, some members of this group started the so-called Ja'fari Party in 1952 in Najaf because they felt Shi'ism as a creed, ritual, symbol and reality was threatened. This reaction came in the aftermath of an assault against Persian pilgrims on their pilgrimage to the shrine city. In the words of Hassan Shubbar:

> The government, people thought, had a hand in the physical assault [on the Iranian pilgrims on pilgrimage] which was perpetrated by some thugs [*shaqawat*] of Najaf ... The victims went around crying for help, urging the Najafis to denounce such acts and put an end to them ... *The markets went on strike and the* 'ulama *stopped giving lectures or leading prayers in protest.*
>
> In that atmosphere, the martyr Sahib al-Dakhil came to me arguing that Najaf has a *holy status* and should therefore be *governed by the* 'ulama themselves in a *local administration* [*hukuma mahaliya*] to supervise the implementation of the penal Islamic code and keep order.

We searched for a third person to form a delegation. We visited Sayyid Muhsin al-Hakim, Sheikh Muhammad Hussain Kashif al-Ghita, Sheikh Abdul Karim al-Jazayiri and Sheikh Muhammad Jawad al-Jazayiri and others. The *'ulama* expressed sympathy with our views, but nothing practical came out of it.

Sahib al-Dakhil, Sadiq al-Qamusi and I started party political activity in 1952 *after this incident. Fearing the general atmosphere in Najaf which rejects such actions*, we moved in *secrecy*. We mobilized friends and acquaintances to … adhere to *Islamic rituals*, night prayers and *purposeful Majlis Husayniya* (Hussein Assemblies) … As we failed to organize a Majlis Hussein exclusively in the name of the party, the project collapsed.[51] (Italics added.)

What this group lacked was independence. Its union with the clerical class exceeded the notion of an 'ideal attachment'. As the group lacked the legitimacy or literary ability to mould an independent ideology or launch their own movement on behalf of the Shi'is without sufficient endorsement, the ties to the sacred classes were only tightened. Leaders they were, indeed, of local communities but, to some extent, on behalf of supreme religious authority and in its service. Their inherent weaknesses lay in their localism and lack of social alliances, appealing ideology and legitimizing authority.

Their world was limited by these obstacles. The clerical class was, for them, the universal but reluctant class which commanded both legality and financial power. Of course, the clerical class needed them as *wukala'*, mobilizers and preservers of mass following. But the relationship was unbalanced. The lay mercantile group was not only motivated by the decline of religion and the decay of older social forms in which status groups enjoyed esteem and prosperity, but was also extremely and explicitly aware of this decline and the meaning of social change. In 1963 they lamented the eclipse of the *'ulama*, tribal sheikhs and the notables (meaning themselves) as the *Da'wa Doctrine* states in plain words:

Our society is *disintegrating* and losing direction because people in *villages* and *towns* have *lost authentic leadership*, unlike the previous society which had figures assuming leadership, and this *leadership* was original and was *obeyed by the community* because it was formed by the *'ulama* in the first place and the *notables* and *sheikhs*. And no matter how many weak points these kinds of leaders had they nevertheless, possessed some framework which tied them together. In a word, previously members of society would resort to the nearest *sheikh*, notable (*wajih*) or doctor of religion (*alim*) to seek solutions for their problems; today, however, disintegration (*tamazuq*) is the order of the day, the *older form* has been *destroyed* and the *new leadership forms have not yet filled the void*. Certain [political] parties seem to replace this old form but they had not yet achieved that.[52] (Italics added.)

Unlike the pedagogical endeavours of the *'ulama*, the lay petty merchants of the holy cities were inclined to politics, action and debate more than texts and theological argument. Witnessing the modern classes advancing their cause by means of organization and mobilization, they advocated the creation of a political movement. Some members of their families who had received a secular education came to appreciate the modern forms of agitation they had experienced during their student years. It was from this social group that the lay founders of the Da'wa emerged.

FIVE

The Formation of the Jama'at al-'Ulama in Najaf, 1960

As the Da'wa Party was in the making, a parallel process was taking place among the clergy driven by the same circumstances and for the same purpose. The general alarm felt by the *mujtahids*, senior and junior, prompted a drive to form an organized body to combat communism and reassert Shi'ite values and Islamic tenets. This body was the Society of *'Ulama* in Najaf (Jama'at al-'Ulama fil Najaf).

Senior *'Ulama*

The initiative for the society came from different sources. Senior *'ulama*, even the most conservative and apolitical, were stunned and dismayed by the declaration of a new, secular family law (No. 188) in December 1959.[1] In the aftermath of the well-known Burujerdi *fatwa* against the Shah's attempted agrarian reform in Iran,[2] in February 1960 the grand *marja'* Muhsin al-Hakim discarded his caution and issued a *fatwa* against communism.[3] The contacts to form the Jama'at al-'Ulama began in mid- or late 1959, but the body was proclaimed in 1960 on the anniversary of Imam Ali's birthday in Najaf.[4]

The composition of this group has some features in common with that of the known initiators of the Da'wa Party in 1959. Its real sponsor was undoubtedly Grand Ayatollah Muhsin al-Hakim. Without his consent, any such gathering of the *'ulama* would have been unthinkable.[5] Unlike the Da'wa Party, the work of this group was based on pure, simple, traditional theological, educational and charitable ideas. Its activity was also run exclusively by the clerical class, which acted as the sole and legitimate agency under the strict supervision of the grand centre of religious authority.

Again, the overwhelming predominance of Najaf is evident in the group. However, the family representation and Najafi familial base is wider than that of the Da'wa. In addition to al-Hakim, Bahr al-'Ulum, al-Sadr and other families, there are also the al-Jawahiri, the Radhi, Rumaithi and others. The presence of Kho'i is a case in point. Although Kho'i's opposition to clerical politics is well known, and although he maintained this position almost to his last day, the dismay clerics felt at the time over the radical changes in social policy during the post-1958 era agitated even the most apolitical elements in this class.

Table 5.1: The Composition of the Jama'at al-'Ulama in Najaf, 1960

Name	City	Age	Rank[a]	Source[b]
Category A: *Senior 'ulama group attending meetings*				
Murtadha al-Yasin	Kazimiya	61–70	A	a, b, c
Muhammad Taqi Bahr al-'Ulum	Najaf	61–70	H	a, c
Mosa Bahr al-'Ulum	Najaf	61–70	H	a, c
Muhammad Jawad Sheikh Radhi	Najaf	61–70	H	a, c
Isma'il al-Sadr[c]	Kazimiya	51–60	H	a, c
Muhammad Abu al-Qassim Kho'i	Najaf	61–70	H	?, b, ?
Muhammad Baqir al-Shakhsi	Najaf	61–70	H	a, ?, ?
'Abbas al-Rumaithi	Najaf	61–70	H	?, ?, c
Muhammad Hassan al-Jawahiri	Najaf	N/A	H	?, ?, c
Hussain al-Hamadani	Najaf	51–60	A	?, ?, c, d
Khidhir al-Dujaili	Najaf (residence only)	51–60	A	?, ?, c, d
Category B: *Unspecified ranking*				
Muhammad Juwwa		N/A		?, ?, c
Muhammad Jamal al-Hashimi		N/A		?, ?, c
Category C: *Junior supportive, novice 'ulama and apprentice students*				
Muhammad Baqir al-Sadr	Najaf/ Kazimiya	21–30	J	a, b, c
Mahdi al-Hakim	Najaf	21–30	J	a, ?, ?
Muhammad Hussein Fadlallah	Lebanon	21–30	J	a, ?, ?
Muhammad Mahdi Shams al-Din	Lebanon	21–30	J	a, ?, c
Baqir al-Qarashi	Najaf	21–30	J	a, ?, ?
Hadi al-Qarashi	Najaf	21–30	J	a, ?, ?
Muhammad Bahr al-'Ulum	Najaf	21–30	J	a, ?, ?
Ali al-Wa'ili	Najaf	N/A	J	?, ?, c

Name	City	Age	Rank[a]	Source[b]
Salih al-Kharasan	Najaf	21–30	J	a, ?, ?
Abdul Hadi al-Fadhili	Najaf	N/A	J	?, ?, c
Muhammad Amin Zayn al-Din	N/A	N/A	J	?, ?, c

a. A: *ayatollah*; H: *hujjat al-Islam*; J: Junior or *murahiq* ; the rest are novices.
b. a: Muhammad Bahr al-'Ulum (interview); b: Ahmad al-Katib (interview); c: W. Joyce,[6] quoted from Ibn al-Najaf;[7] d: Kazim al-Ha'iri.[8]
c. Isma'il is Muhammad Baqir al-Sadr's elder brother.

The exclusive city solidarities between the two groups – the Da'wa and the senior *'ulama* – are not entirely identical. True, in the *'ulama* group there is no Karbala connection, and the influential Khalisi family of Kazimiya is also absent; but there are figures from Dujail, Baghdad and other urban locations. Unlike the known participants of the Da'wa, the ten major figures of the Jama'at al-'Ulama were over sixty years of age, with a medium or high-ranking clerical status. This was to cause generational tension in terms of innovation.

At the helm of the society was Murtadha al-Yasin, the maternal uncle of Muhammad Baqir al-Sadr. In certain accounts, al-Sadr is categorized as belonging to Category A of the senior *'ulama*, i.e. as a member of the Jama'a.[9] Other accounts include him in Category C, that of the junior and apprentice *'ulama* who were not full members of the Jama'a but instead acted as mere assistants.[10] In both cases, his participation in the activity of the group is certain. Both Murtadha al-Yasin, his maternal uncle, and Isma'il al-Sadr, his elder brother, would give him a strong position.

The numerical weight of the Jama'at al-'Ulama and their assistants is also impressive compared to the initiators of the Da'wa. In line with the norms of status derived from family descent, learning, age and wealth, senior *'ulama* occupied the leading, directive positions.

The appointment of Murtadha al-Yasin as the head of the Jama'a may be attributed to a host of factors. First, he was an *ayatollah*; he had connections with both Najaf and Kazimiya, which would enable him to link the two centres and build bases for al-Hakim in Kazimiya – traditionally controlled by the Khalisi family. In accordance with clerical hierarchical traditions, the junior *'ulama* were not given any prominence in the leadership.[11] The members of this group fell within the age brackets of 20–30. Al-Sadr was among the eldest and most advanced in terms of religious study. He had already finished his *dars al-kharij*, the final stage in the religious school curriculum. Backed by family status, kinship networks and al-Hakim patronage, al-Sadr was in a strong position to assume a leading role among the junior *'ulama*. However, this strength itself was also a major source of his weakness.

Members of the junior group, Category C, were entrusted with executive tasks. They were to run the mouthpiece of the Jama'a, a publication that came to be known as *al-Adhwa' al-Islamiya* (Islamic Lights). Al-Sadr assumed what became the position of a *de facto* editing manager. On what was effectively the editorial board sat Muhammad Hussein Fadlallah, the well-known Lebanese *mujtahid* and spiritual father of the Lebanese Hizballah, Muhammad Amin Zain al-Din; Abdul Hadi al-Fadhili; and possibly others.

The junior *'ulama* were not only a wide but also nationally varied group. For the first time, two figures from Lebanon were included. Judging by titles, some Iranian elements must also have existed among them. In fact, the steering committee of the society contained two figures representing Arabs and Persians respectively.[12] The junior *'ulama*, who were more radical in terms of reform and political ambitions, controlled the propaganda and educational work. But senior *'ulama* controlled financial resources, mass charisma and, of course, religious legitimacy. The contradiction between the two categories would surface in different areas at different points.

Welfare and Education

The Jama'at al-'Ulama was announced in 1960 on the anniversary of Imam Ali's birthday, a symbolic, emotive occasion. Significantly, the Da'wa strove to link its Party Day to a wider Islamic occasion, the birthday of the Prophet Muhammad, a more universal symbol transcending the Shi'i-Sunni divide.

The Jama'a set out to pursue a peaceful programme of educational and welfare work. Along the lines of Egypt's Muslim Brotherhood, the Jama'a established medical care centres and a social assistance fund (The Society of the Charity Islamic Fund) to help the needy, the poor, the blind, invalids and orphans. The main thrust was in the realm of education, which was particularly geared towards reviving and modernizing the *madrasa* (see Part Three). Apart from using these strongholds for Islamic ideological education, they also served to create areas that were uncontrolled by the state itself, thus amounting to a kind of Shi'ite civil society.

The number of schools established was impressive. No less than ten elementary, secondary and higher schools were founded in Baghdad, Basra, Hilla and Nu'maniya – all in addition to the College of Theology (Kuliyat Usul al-Din) in Baghdad, which was supervised by Mahdi al-Hakim and Murtadha al-'Askari.[13] The educational network was thus cast far beyond the seat of Najaf. The vast funds needed for such schemes were provided by al-Hakim and private donors.

Under the unifying motto of combating atheism, Najaf witnessed a plethora of weeklies, books and booklets authored by various *'ulama*, most of them junior. The subject matter of these publications, as is evident from the titles, reveals a strong tendency to approach contemporary problems such as: *Labour and Workers' Rights in Islam*; *The Political Order in Islam*; *The Problem of Poverty in Islam; Wealth in Islam; Government and Administration in Islam; Financial System and the Distribution of Wealth in Islam; Communism: a Subversive Principle; Communism is the Enemy of the People; The Family Organization in Islam; Birth Control in Islam; An Experience with an Atheistic Friend.*[14]

The titles listed here were authored by a number of clerical writers who later became leaders of various Shi'ite establishments. Amongst them are names like al-Sadr, Mahdi Shams al-Din (now vice chairman of the Higher Shi'ite Assembly in Lebanon), Muhammad Hussein Fadlallah and others.[15] The books reveal the extent to which the activist sections of the sacred class believed in the need for building a social and political theory in defence of Islam.

Adhwa' and the Ideological Battle

Al-Najaf, al-Tadhamun al-Islami (Islamic Solidarity), *Risalat al-Islam* (The Message of Islam) and *al-Fayha'* weekly were among the reviews issued in Najaf, Nasirya and Hilla that aimed to disseminate ideas and educate followers in the new views formulated by the *mujtahids* under urgent circumstances of ideological threat.

Adhwa', the mouthpiece of the Jama'at al-'Ulama, was officially owned by Sheikh Kazim al-Hilfi, a Najafi *alim* who was of no particular prominence.[16] Al-Hilfi's name never appeared on the list of the Society of the 'Ulama, nor among the activists, elder or junior. It appears that he was willing to put his name on a publication as a matter of social patronage. This was a shrewd tactic which lent the publication a neutral garb. *Adhwa'* carried a unique tone, and in it al-Sadr ran a regular column under the heading *Risalatuna* (Our Message).[17]

The very fact that the Najaf *'ulama* resorted to publishing a periodical that relied upon the polemic of ideas was significant in the hitherto sedate environment of Najaf.[18] Indeed, up to a few years before this point, the idea of any clerics reading modern magazines or literature would have been scandalous. Muhammad Shams al-Din described how he once had to hide magazines and read modern books in total secrecy.[19] Bahr al-'Ulum recalls how the verse he wrote during that time was disclosed to close friends only decades later for fear of accusations of indulgence in modern heathenism.[20] Although *Adhwa'* did not run for more than two or three years[21] it played an important role in establishing new intellectual traditions and providing a sense of meaning and identity to the junior *'ulama* and their close lay collaborators. In a sense, *Adhwa'* filled an actual ideological void in the movement of the Najafi *'ulama* in general. In the words of Muhammad Hussein Fadlallah, the publication of this periodical '… opened the eyes and hearts of the people (*al-nas*) to conceive the new challenges':[22]

It [*Adhwa'*] could inject the *new Islamic thought* in the consciousness of the *new generation* of the religious students there [in Najaf] and could, through this injection, *open the bitter struggle* inside the *hawza* [religious school and establishment] between the conservative and innovative [*'ulama*] ... As a consequence, the *hawza* was set off on the trajectory of *political struggle between Islam and the authorities* [sulta].[23] (Italics added.)

Al-Sadr's contribution to *Adhwa'* has been collected in single book titled, like his column, *Risalatuna* (Our Message), which was first published in Najaf in 1968 by Abdul Hussein Baqqal.[24] The second edition appeared in Beirut in 1981, with an introduction by Muhammad Hussein Fadlallah and presumably edited by Muhammad A. Jabar.[25] Both editions contained sixteen articles which touched upon various topics and were cast in the Islamic, Najafi style renowned for its clarity, emotive charge, agitative spirit, oversimplified ethical totalities and universal concepts, suffused with a sense of grief, lamentation and hope. The third edition, published in Tehran, wrongly claims that the whole set of the sixteen articles are by the 'Martyr al-Sadr'. According to the Beirut edition, which was classified by the Da'wa activist Muhammad A. Jabar after publication, al-Sadr contributed only to the first five issues of *Adhwa'* and had to resign under circumstances we shall touch upon shortly. If al-Sadr had four, possibly five, contributions in five issues only, why then do we have sixteen leader commentaries attributed to him? Jabar asserts the articles are by Shams al-Din and al-Sadr. Only three articles are identified as being actually authored by al-Sadr; one is ambiguous, possibly written by him.

Fadlallah's editorials and other contributions to *Adhwa'* were published in Beirut in 1980 under the title *Afaq Islamiya wa Mawadhi Ukhra* (Islamic Perspectives and Other Topics).[26] All pieces published in the al-Sadr and Fadlallah collections reveal the mood and mode of thinking prevalent among the novice *'ulama* of Najaf at the time. Al-Sadr's four pieces revolve around a major issue, that of the revival of the Islamic *umma* (nation or community), the need for a mission (*risala*, also a messianic message) to cope with the challenges of two civilizations, the capitalist and the Marxist. Their fears and hopes are couched in a philosophical jargon of Islamic exclusiveness, echoing the ideas set in al-Sadr's volume *Falsafatuna* (Our Philosophy). No political issues are raised, no concrete political events ever mentioned. The language is purely abstract. Al-Sadr's basic, civilizational themes will be discussed in Part Five. At this point, however, we may touch upon the themes of *Adhwa'* in the briefest manner.

In Article No. 1 (see Table 5.2) titled 'The Basic Condition for the Rise of the Umma', al-Sadr emphasizes the need for a system he calls 'principle' (*mabda'*). He says:

The basic condition for the rise of the nation [*umma*] – any nation – is to have the righteous principle [*al-mabda' al-salih*] which would define for her targets and ends and determines for her supreme ideals [*muthul ulya*] ... By the right principle we mean the existence of such a principle [first], the comprehension of the nation of it [second], and her belief in it [third].[27]

[T]his principle exists and is represented by Islam as a religion ... which would remain forever ... to guide the nation and raise her from the debacle to her central position among other nations of the world.[28]

Table 5.2: Authors and Dates of Publication of Adhwa' *Editorials*

Editorial	Author	Date AH	Date AD
1	al-Sadr	15 Thu al-Hijja 1379	11 June 1960
2	al-Sadr	1 Muharram 1380	26 June 1960
3	al-Sadr	1 Sufar 1380	26 July 1960
4	Shams al-Din	15 Sufar 1380	9 August 1960
5	possibly al-Sadr	N/A	N/A
6	Shams al-Din	1 Rabi' Awal 1380	24 August 1960
7	Shams al-Din	15 Rabi' Awal 1380	7 September 1960
8	Shams al-Din	15 Rabi' Thani 1380	7 October 1960
9	Shams al-Din	20 Jamadi Awal 1380	23 October 1960
10	Shams al-Din	1 Jamadi Thani 1380	22 November 1960
11	Shams al-Din	1 Rajab 1380	21 December 1960
12	Shams al-Din	1 Sha'ban 1380	20 January 1961
13	Shams al-Din	Ramadhan 1380	19 February 1961
14	Shams al-Din	1 Shawal 1380	17 March 1961
15	Shams al-Din	15 Shawal 1380	1 April 1961
16	Shams al-Din	15 Thi al-Qa'da	1 May 1961

The problem then is 'that the *umma* has the principle and generally believes in it, but does not have the third element, i.e. the comprehension of her own principle'.[29] 'This contradiction seems bizarre at first sight ...'[30] The divergence is attributed to:

> ... sinister intrigues (*mu'amarat dani'a*), implicit or explicit, by the sons of the crusaders and colonialists, the historical enemies of Islam. These grand intrigues resulted in the armed colonial invasion, and the invaders who had

destroyed the international entity of Islam have no other aim but to divorce the nation from her principle [religion].[31]

The periodical *Adhwa'* declared that it would take upon itself the task of ending this divorce and work towards a reunion. The second article,[32] titled *Risalatuna wa al-Du'at* (Our Message and the Missionaries), says that the Islamic message has three facets: 'One is the *doctrinal* character of the message (*'aqa'idiya*) which lends it a sacred and certain feature.'[33] The second is *'hope'*, and the third is '... *subjective motive [al-dafi' al-thati]'*.[34] These elements would mobilize the Islamist missionaries (*du'at*).

In the third article[35] al-Sadr defines the messianic message in abstract, philosophical terms. The message is based on:

> First, a spiritual view of life and the universe in general, which does not mean the negation of the material aspects of the universe ... Islam recognizes spiritual and material facts but links them to one prime mover, God ...[36] Second, the rational method of thinking (*al-tariqa al-'aqliya fil tafkir*) as against the empirical method which excludes reason ...[37] The third is the practical measure preached by Islam in its general view to life and universe ... This practical measure covers all human individual, social, political, economic or ethical fields.[38]

Al-Sadr's new 'grand narrative' is presented as a civilizational confrontation and exclusive cultural marker. The fourth article by al-Sadr in this collection specifies Islam as the basis upon which a whole civilization should be built.[39] According to al-Sadr, Western civilization is 'anchored in an ideological basis which is "democracy", that is, major liberties in the realm of thought, religion, politics and economy'.[40] The other civilization, 'the Marxist one which competes with the capitalist civilization, has the material view of universe, life, society and history as its ideological basis'.[41] Muslims are warned against both the uncritical acceptance or the gross rejection of Western thought.[42] This pragmatic position is soon almost reversed when al-Sadr urges: 'Second, conscious Muslims should make Islam the ideological basis and the general framework for all civilizational thought and concepts about the universe, life, human beings and society.'[43]

Shams al-Din's articles, on the other hand, touch upon wider themes and issues: social unity and cohesion; Muslim disunity and the need to reunite; colonialism; Crusaders; the usurpation of Palestine by Jews; Islam and progress; Islam's spirituality versus European materialism; Islam and reform; Islam and history; Islam versus colonialism. These themes lament the decline of Islam as a religion and civilization, the loss of the unity of the Islamic nation (*umma*) and the triumph of the Crusaders. This is the first Najafi Islamic text to feature the Palestinian-Jewish question (the only previous example available is the *Muhawarat* of Kashif al-Ghita).

As in al-Sadr's essays, Shams al-Din presents Islam as the only alternative to Western civilization. It is a cultural marker, philosophical worldview, social cohesive force and source of renewal and progress. The ideas briefly outlined here echo in general terms the call by Muhammad Hussain Kashif al-Ghita.[44] The main themes of this *mujtahid* are:

(i)   A strong onslaught on Western European colonialism and the colonization of the Arab and Islamic worlds. The West is held responsible for the deterioration of Islam.

(ii)   The threat of communism is a byproduct of the poverty, backwardness and weakness of Arab and Muslim countries caused mainly by the West.

(iii)   The loss of Palestine to the intrigues of the West.

(iv)   Islam contains sublime ideals for the reformation and progress of Muslim societies.

(v)   The *'ulama* are obliged to interfere in politics in terms of advice, guidance and preaching.

The wording of this call is cast in an Arabist spirit which speaks in terms of anti-Westernism, reformation and activism.[45] It is interesting to note how far al-Sadr reflects and stresses the first, second and last aspects; whereas Shams al-Din and the Lebanese *'ulama* (the Lebanese school in general) stressed other themes and aspects linked to Palestine and Arabism in general, even at that early stage.

As we can begin to see, the *Adhwa'* periodical carried through a momentum that had already been in existence since the early 1950s. However, in this instance, 'the momentum' was not carried through by the writings of first-rank *mujtahids* such as Kashif al-Ghita who enjoyed world repute, but by the writings of fragile, novice *mujtahids* who were seeking survival. It was also part of a collective project rather than a single call.

Born in 1876, Kashif al-Ghita had a long and successful career. When, in 1953, American and British ambassadors urged him to combat communism, al-Ghita was 77 years old and already had vastly numerous contacts all over the Islamic world. During his long career he attended conferences in Pakistan, Iran, Lebanon and Egypt and was present at every major Islamic gathering during the first half of the 20th century. He had played a prominent role in resisting the British invasion of Iraq and was moulded in that acute era of anti-imperial confrontation.[46]

Kashif al-Ghita's call was essentially political. That of the other reformer, Hussein Muzafar,[47] was mainly pedagogical. The two aspects were united in the activities of the novice section of the Jama'at al-'Ulama fil Najaf, who reflected their views in *Adhwa'*. Eventually, the Jama'a was expanded to encompass the *'ulama* of Baghdad, such as Murtadha al-'Askari, who lectured at the Husayniya al-Mubaraka in Karrada Sharkiya, Baghdad.[48]

Schisms and al-Sadr's Retreat

An organizational/doctrinal and political rift soon erupted in the group and caused the resignation of al-Sadr from *Adhwa'* in the summer of 1960. The column in *Adhwa'* which al-Sadr had edited under the title of *Risalatuna* drew a barrage of criticism from different quarters of the senior *'ulama* inside and outside the society. Al-Sadr was accused of presenting his own personal 'philosophical' views as if they were representative of all the *'ulama*. Critics noticed that some leader comments by al-Sadr repeated verbatim paragraphs from *Falsafatuna*. Al-Sadr also failed to refer the initial drafts of *Adhwa'* to the steering committee, thus violating their right to supervise the paper.[49] Some *'ulama* even wondered whether *Adhwa'* was the mouthpiece of the society of senior *'ulama* or the paper of a junior, even apprentice figure like al-Sadr who was, after all, not even fit for membership yet. Critics attacked al-Sadr in person and demanded more control of the publication.

The critique fell partly along the lines of traditional Najafi inner rivalries. It also, however, had a doctrinal motive, namely the conservative *ulama*'s rejection of the innovative ideals espoused by the editorials. There was also a strong political motivation in connection with the Iran-Egypt conflict. Da'wa circles believe there was another political campaign against al-Sadr on part of Hussein al-Safi, a Ba'thist and Najafi lawyer who had strong links with Muhsin al-Hakim, and was also, in addition, a backer of Islamist action against communism and an opponent to the formation of the Da'wa Party.

Al-Sadr himself was unclear about the exact motives or identity of the different sides behind the attack. The letters he wrote to Muhammad Baqir al-Hakim shed light on some aspects of the episode:[50]

After you [had left for Lebanon], gossip, rumours, sound and fury erupted all against your companion [al-Sadr himself] to smash him ... The campaign started in the circles of the steering group which supervises *Adhwa'*, in fact among some of them and their followers ... Then it grew stronger, [with agitation coming from] another group with figures like Husseinal-Safi[51] – I do not know if there is a causal relation or connection between the two campaigns ...[52]

On 6 Rabi' Awal 1380 (31 August 1960) al-Sadr wrote:

[T]he campaign against *Adhwa'* by the Jama'at al-'Ulama relapsed after they were advised that it is they who supervise the paper ... The *Adhwa'* editorial group ... now submit their articles to the three[53] [*mujtahids* in the steering committee].[54]

Al-Sadr resorted to his maternal uncle, who appeased those offended by his neglect. Murtadha al-Yasin also advised them that al-Sadr would stop his contribution to the paper.[55] Al-Sadr resigned to avoid what seemed like unnecessary tension. The Lebanese junior cleric Muhammad Hussein Fadlallah took charge of the publication under the supervision of the society, and *Adhwa'* resumed its work without much ado. Obviously the campaign was not against *Adhwa'* as such but against al-Sadr himself, and by extension against his innovative work and political stand.

Baqir al-Hakim contends that the campaign was also planned by the Ba'th party. His deduction is based on the role played by the ex-turbaned lawyer Hussein al-Safi, mentioned by al-Sadr in his letters. Al-Hakim's view is that:

The façade in this attack [against al-Sadr] were some of the *'ulama* circles, but the hand of the Ba'th party was behind it, since the Sayyid master [al-Sadr] in some of his letters confirms that the lawyer Husseinal-Safi, who had a turban on his head before and descends from a clerical family, who has strong connections with some influential *'ulama* and is the one in charge of the Ba'th organization in holy Najaf, was behind the campaign.[56]

It is worth noting that, during this period, there had been no ideological clashes between the clerical class and the Ba'th party. Indeed, both groups shared a common cause in their bitter fight against General Qassim and the communists.

The political attacks against al-Sadr had a great deal to do with a major schism within Shi'ite *mujtahid* circles in Najaf and beyond. This rift was caused primarily by the confrontation of two opposing ideologies: Nasser's Arab nationalism and the Shah's pro-Western, pro-Israeli position.

To understand the full implication of the event in the Najafi framework it is necessary to go back to February 1959 when Mahmud Shaltut, the rector of al-Azhar University/mosque – a Sunni religious establishment – issued a *fatwa* recognizing Twelver Shi'ism as a legitimate Islamic school along with the other four Sunni schools of law.[57] Shi'ite jurisprudence was included in the hitherto purely Sunni curriculum of al-Azhar. The *fatwa* based itself on 'historical and pragmatic' arguments.[58] Muslim unity, a tolerance of different schools in Islam and a denunciation of prejudice was voiced in the *fatwa*. Shaltut also published 'Amili's *Wasa'il al-Shi'a*, an authoritative Shi'ite source of traditions, and the Tabarsi's *Majma' al-Bayan*, a Shi'ite exegesis of the holy Qur'an.[59] These steps fostered Shi'i-Sunni clerical understanding and rapprochement. Shaltut's *fatwa* had been preceded by a series of similar Shi'ite initiatives. In 1947, the Iranian

Shi'i Muhammad Taqi Qummi established *Dar al-Taqrib* in Cairo for greater Shi'i-Sunni understanding. In 1953, the leading Iraqi Shi'i *mujtahid*, Muhammad Hussain Kashif al-Ghita, exchanged letters with the Egyptian provisional president Muhammad Nagib. Kashif al-Ghita had paid many visits to Cairo earlier in order to foster such developments.[60] Shaltut had 'a series of friendly communications' with two Shi'i leaders in Iraq, Muhammad al-Khalisi and Muhammad Hussain Kashif al-Ghita.[61]

In the light of this background, we can now begin to consider the confrontation, in July 1960, between Nasser of Egypt and the Shah of Iran. In response to Iran's *de facto* recognition of Israel, Egypt, in retaliation, broke all diplomatic relations with Iran. Shaltut called on all Muslims to wage *jihad* against the Shah for his pro-Israeli position, and his appeal was despatched to various Islamic centres.[62] Al-Sadr, it is confirmed, asked a question of the Grand Ayatollah Muhsin al-Hakim about his attitude towards the Iranians.[63] He received a reply that expressed displeasure at the Shah's pro-Israeli position.

Al-Hakim's stance was somehow leaked by al-Sadr, and it is perhaps this leakage – unintended or otherwise – that caused the uproar against al-Sadr. Al-Sadr's complaints (in letters sent to Baqir al-Hakim) are dated in Sufar and 6 Rabi' Awal 1380, and these are dates that coincide with 26 July and 31 August 1960, a period directly after the Nasser-Shah episode. The presence of the Lebanese Fadlallah and Shams al-Din, who both had Arabist leanings and voiced clear resentment against the loss of Palestine in line with Kashif al-Ghita's attitude, was perhaps another factor which influenced al-Sadr's enquiry and the leakage of al-Hakim's position.

Fadlallah says explicitly:

> We were influenced by the Egyptian revolution, although it was a nationalistic revolution, we lived through the experience of the Palestinian problem in a responsible manner from the very beginning.[64]

The Lebanese *mujtahid* also recalls that at the age of twelve he wrote verse in defence of Palestine in 1947–48.[65]

It seems that religious circles in Najaf split into antagonistic opinions. Some supported the Shah as the representative of a Shi'ite state against which, arguably, no attacks should be levelled and that Egypt was, after all, a Sunni state. Others supported and hailed Nasser against the Shah. A third line pleaded for impartiality.[66]

It is clear that Grand Ayatollah Muhsin al-Hakim was unwilling to compromise his relations with the Shah of Iran. His reply to al-Sadr may have been confidential. True, al-Hakim was pressured by telegrams and requests to disapprove of the Shah's pro-Israel move and he responded. In his cautious, diplomatic manner, he sent a letter to Ayatollah Bihbihani in Tehran advising him of the commotion and protests among Muslims as a result of the Iranian recognition of Israel, and expressing his hope that Iranian officials would be counselled of their Islamic duties.[67] The letter neither expresses direct protest nor mentions the Shah in person. The telegram was published, but it is not clear whether or not its publication in *Adhwa'* and the Sunni journal *al-Hiyad* was actually authorized by al-Hakim. The press leakage must have gone beyond the fine diplomatic thread in Najaf and angered pro-Shah figures, and must have contributed to the wide, intricate campaign against al-Sadr. *Adhwa'* resumed publication without al-Sadr. The overconfidence he gained from his family, patron or advance in academic life proved self-destructive.

Al-Sadr's retreat from *Adhwa'* widened his range of activity in the intellectual production of new Islamic treatises. He could now dedicate his efforts to *Iqtisaduna* (Our Economy), a large volume of 700 pages.

In a sense, this retreat was a setback which would be followed by another related to his involvement in Da'wa Party politics, but it was also hard evidence that the Jama'at al-'Ulama was not only far from being under the influence of al-Sadr but also had no connection with the Da'wa Party, let alone being under the latter's influence or patronage.[68]

According to the tables of the initiators of both the Da'wa and the Jama'a (see Table 5.1), the only link between the Da'wa project and the organized body of the Jama'at al-'Ulama was al-Sadr and Muhammad Bahr al-'Ulum. Since the latter withdrew from any commitment to the Da'wa in 1960 after the death of his father in the spring of that year,[69] there remained only one person: al-Sadr. Again, as a junior cleric, he could not subsume the Jama'at al-'Ulama under the influence of a party which had not yet taken shape.

Jama'at al-'Ulama and the Islamic Party: Sociopolitical Issues

The two flanks of the Shi'ite world, Iraq and Iran, reciprocally interacted during the years after the July 1958 Revolution, as did developments in both countries.

The agrarian reform proclaimed by General Qassim in September 1958, barely two months after the July revolution, provoked a reaction in Iran. The successful communist-led peasant revolutions in China, Southeast Asia and Cuba were alarmingly fresh, and the Egyptian and Iraqi agrarian reforms were in force. The US pressed Iran and Ethiopia for similar reforms to avoid destabilization in the Middle East, and similar concerns were sensed by part of the Iranian ruling elite as well.[70] Against the December 1959 land reform bill, Grand Ayatollah Burujerdi issued a *fatwa* declaring it to be inconsistent with both the *Shari'a* and the Iranian constitution.[71] The bill was passed on 17 May 1960, but remained inoperative. In March 1961 Burujerdi died. Both his opposition and death marked a turning point in the clerical involvement in politics and in their hierarchical arrangements.

Burujerdi's position 'marked a break in cooperation between the clergy and the [Iranian] state in public policy'.[72] It is after rather than before Burujerdi's death that anti-Shah agitation was started by Khomeini and other leading *mujtahids* in Iran.[73] Not only the Iranian but also the Iraqi *mujtahids* felt delivered from the apolitical constraints which had resulted from years of timid non-interference imposed by the state and accepted by grand religious authorities.

Not without the Shah's encouragement, *marja'ism* shifted back to Iraq.[74] Upon Burujerdi's death, the Shah despatched his letter of condolence to al-Hakim, signalling a recognition of al-Hakim as the new grand authority. This move was intended to remove the clerical pressure on him and relieve Iran of a leading centre of religious opposition. A double effect was produced by this change of hands at the top of the hierarchy: it freed the new generation (Khomeini, Milani, Taleqani and Shari'atmadari in Iran) to develop their own trends under the circumstances of a leadership vacuum, and it boosted the Iraqi flank of the Shi'ite establishment at a time when it was bent on resisting social and cultural change.

It is interesting to note the proxy nature of al-Hakim's responses. He never publicly or directly condemned the agrarian reform or explicitly criticized the family code, promulgated in September 1958 and December 1959 respectively. These issues were attacked by other, less prominent *mujtahids*. It is also said that he instructed four of his sons – including his eldest, Muhammad Yusif al-Hakim – to send telegrams to the prime minister, General Qassim, to assert that land reform violated Islamic law which protects private property.[75] His anti-communist *fatwa* came also at this point. It was issued in February 1960, a few days after Burujerdi's *fatwa* on the Iranian land reform bill.[76]

Al-Hakim's decision to refrain from directly opposing both bills might be attributed to his cautious nature and his desire to steer away from such sensitive issues which affected the lives and welfare of almost a quarter of a million peasant families, the bulk of whom were Shi'is. When peasants were told of al-Hakim's alleged ruling that prayer on land confiscated under the agrarian reform bill was unacceptable, they demanded a written text as a proof that this was true. In other cases, peasants simply denied that al-Hakim would oppose the transfer of land to them, for they were Shi'i and poor. Other shrewd peasants denied such a *fatwa* was issued at all, saying that al-Hakim was too wise to take such a position.[77] The liaison with the Shah was perhaps another factor behind al-Hakim's cautious, proxy attitude.

The fact that landlords opted for political help from the Ba'th party, as Batatu confirms,[78] may indicate how ineffective al-Hakim's position on this issue was. It is only in the face of the Communist Party that al-Hakim was explicit. His *fatwa* runs as follows:

Any connection with the Communist Party is unlawful. Such a connection is in the nature of disbelief and infidelity, or it is supportive of disbelief and infidelity.[79]

Two other figures joined in the *fatwa* campaign. On 3 April 1960, Murtadha al-Yasin, the head of the Jama'at al-'Ulama and al-Sadr's maternal uncle, issued a *fatwa* published by the Hilla-based *Fayha'* weekly (from) on 23 April, in which it was stated that: 'adherence to the Communist Party or lending it support is one of the greatest sins which religion denounces'.[80] Mahdi Shirazi, based in Najaf, ruled in the same month that prayers and fasting by Muslims who had embraced communism were 'unacceptable because of lack of faith'. Later in June, Shirazi further affirmed that it was not permissible for Muslims to buy meat from a butcher who believed in communist principles, and that a youth of this persuasion was not entitled to inherit from his father.[81]

The support for the formation and activity of the Islamic Party in Iraq was al-Hakim's second step. The party was originally the making of the Muslim Brotherhood.[82] The movement was headed by a religious dignitary in Mosul, 'Abd Allah al-Nu'man. Among its figures were Muhammad Mahmud Sawaf, a doctor of religion, and Abd al-Rahman Sayyid Mahmud, who assumed leadership of the movement in 1958. The Muslim Brotherhood spread its organization from Mosul to Baghdad. It withdrew its original support to Qassim and opted for a confrontational line, believing Qassim was sympathetic to the communists.[83] Shi'i-Sunni contacts must have occurred in late 1959 and early 1960 to launch a joint, anti-communist struggle.

The opportunity to bring into the realm of open, legalized party politics an Islamic party, perhaps for the first time in modern Iraqi history, came when General Qassim promulgated the Societies Law (*Qanun al-Jam'iyat*) legalizing political parties. The Law was declared on 2 January 1960, and on 2 February two applications were submitted to the Ministry of the Interior to licence two Islamic groups, the Islamic Party (Hizb al-Islami) and the Islamic Liberation (Tahrir) party. The latter was an offshoot of the mother party established in Jordan by Nabahani.[84] Ibrahim Abd Allah Shihab and Nu'man Abd Razaq Samara'i were among the leading signatories to the application. The former was the actual leader of the party, the latter assumed leadership a month later when Shihab withdrew. Muhsin al-Hakim was mentioned among the group of sponsors supporting the party.[85] According to the Societies Law at least ten individuals should apply and a number of sponsors was also needed.

The party's programme submitted to the Ministry of the Interior, named *Dustur* (constitution), envisaged a state based on Islamic law and a government deriving its legitimacy from defending the *Shari'a*. Atheism, especially communism, was to be eradicated. Arab unity was inconceivable unless embedded in the *Shari'a*. A *shura* (consultative) assembly should be elected; in its turn it would elect the head of the state who, again in his turn, would select a cabinet and a legislative body from the members of the *shura*.

Official objections were raised against the programme, and the initiators were ready to compromise on amendments. The official point of view was that only the state had the right to have a constitution, and a party should not label its documents as such. Fears that the party had links with the banned Egyptian Muslim Brotherhood were implied. The application was turned down by the Minister of the Interior at the end of March on the grounds of Item 4 of the Societies Law, which prohibits any foreign connections of whatever nature.[86] The founding members took their case before the Court of Cassation[87] and on 26 April the court decided in their favour. Yet the party could not start a daily, *al-Jihad*, since the information ministry declined to grant them permission; the party leaders had to resort to other 'friendly' papers, such as the Arabist-leaning *al-Hiyad* daily, which volunteered to publish the party's programme, or the Shi'ite weekly *al-Fayha* issued in Hilla, which printed some of its statements and memoranda.[88] The former, *al-Hiyad*, was suspended following its venture to extend help to the newly born Shi'i-supported Sunni party.

The emergence of such a party signifies many aspects relevant to Shi'ite religio-political activism. For lay Sunnis, it has always been easier to enter the political field. Organized religion in Sunni Islam is incorporated into state bureaucracy. No 'emulation' principle exists to subsume the lay population under the authority of the clergy. The Sunni religious establishment could easily be attacked as part of the 'corrupt' regime if and when it attempted to de-legitimize the oppositional Sunni-Islamist movement. For Shi'is in Iraq, above all for the person of Grand Ayatollah Muhsin al-Hakim, it was a novel break with past tradition. At a closer look, it seems that al-Hakim was ready to fight with the hands of others. He encouraged the formation of the Jama'at al-'Ulama without being directly involved in it, either as a member or as a sponsor. He urged his sons to denounce agrarian reform, but never ventured to utter a word in public against it. Lastly, he sponsored a Sunni Islamic party but never let Shi'i clerics indulge in party politics. He always kept himself at a distance – necessary both to lend the position of grand *marja'* an aura of higher authority, standing above all contending parties, and to shield this position should such politics backfire.

The very fact that the Sunni-led but also Shi'i-sponsored Islamic party was the only active Islamic political organization reinforces the hypothesis that the Da'wa Party in 1960 was still in its embryonic phase, just one step ahead of the pre-1958 conceptual views. The assumption that the Islamic party was formed by both the Muslim Brotherhood and the Da'wa lacks documentary evidence.[89] The Da'wa Party, so keen on stressing pan-Islamism, provided no party document to such past cooperation with the Muslim Brotherhood of Iraq in 1960. The oldest document the Da'wa Party could claim to have issued as an ideological or political statement dates back to late 1960 or early 1961.[90] This is not to deny that the Da'wa Party had no existence or that it was not in an early formative process.

The Islamic party had a full-fledged offensive agenda during its short life span. The anti-communist agitation this party undertook began with two emotive memoranda – the first submitted on 31 May 1960 and the second conveyed on 24 July 1960 – both arguing for a ban against the Communist Party and the Islamization of laws under the supervision of a committee of *'ulama* and religious experts. The Jama'at al-'Ulama in Najaf endorsed the memorandum of 30 May 1960 without voicing any direct criticism.[91]

The campaign culminated in a harsh memorandum submitted on 15 October 1960 to the prime minister, General Qassim.[92] The Hilla-based Shi'ite weekly *al-Fayha'* published its full text, which carried a point-blank accusation of General Qassim. It said the Iraqi people were divided in an unprecedented manner; the communists were solidly placed by dint of proxy support extended by the government; contrary to the spirit of Islam criticism was prohibited; the economy was in a shambles; the people were hungry; public funds were squandered on statues; land appropriation was criminal and fruitless; social justice as envisaged by Islam was wanting; atheistic, communist teachings such as the equality of the sexes were espoused; communism should be abolished; finally, all the religious leaders who had been arrested in the previous two years should be released. Lastly, responsibility was laid on General Qassim 'because you are the prime minister, and ministers carry out your orders'.[93]

The licence of the Islamic party was suspended but not abolished, its offices in Baghdad and Mosul were shut down and fifteen of its leaders were arrested. The pro-Arab nationalist papers now and then published more moderate statements by the Islamic party. Despite its apparent weakness, the party scored an astounding success at the third congress of the teachers' union in February 1961, barely a year after its legalization. The Islamic party won 465 of approximately 1,200 votes, i.e. 40 percent of the total.[94] The short history of the Islamic party, with the staunch support it was given by the *mujtahids*, was solid evidence of the new spirit prevailing in Najaf and displayed by various *mujtahids* in different degrees and forms.

The importance of this turn lay in several major points:

(i)   it opened the door for clerical general activism;
(ii)   it reasserted the hitherto waning authority of the *'ulama*;
(iii)   whether intentionally or not it fostered the renewal of Islamic thought conceived by the junior *'ulama*;
(iv)   it indirectly encouraged Shi'ite party politics, and
(v)   it helped, along with other factors (regional and international), to re-establish Najaf as the seat of grand *marja'ism* under Muhsin al-Hakim.

These changes were implemented gradually from late 1959 up to late 1961. The momentum waned later, and came to a standstill with the demise of the Qassim regime in 1963. The eclipse of the Islamic party and the Jama'at al-'Ulama was, paradoxically, the portent of the strengthening of an alternative response, that by the Da'wa Party, which would be delivered now from the heavy clerical shackles that had tied its hands during the Qassim era.

SIX

The Daʿwa Party, 1963–68: From Universalism to Particularism

In the aftermath of the first short-lived Baʿthist rule from February–November 1963, a new phase began in the life of the Daʿwa gathering.

The demise of the Qassim and Baʿth regimes brought about both short- and long-term changes. As shown in Part One, these were years of chaos, turmoil and successive bloody *coups d'état*. They changed the political system, the social/ethnic and religious structure of the ruling elites, disturbed national integrative processes, altered the role of the state and led gradually to the destruction of radical movements on the left and right, creating thereby an ideological/political vacuum.

These mutations enhanced the militancy of various sections of Shiʿi Islamists on one hand, and changed the nature of the movement from a fundamentalist entity with a universal Islamic aura to a traditional/particularist response fighting against group discrimination. They also opened up the stage for the Daʿwa movement, which was fresh, intact and consciously bent on filling the ensuing void – although it lacked the strategic vision and political instincts. In this section, we shall outline the crucial aspects of these changes and their impact on the Daʿwa.

The February 1963 Coups

In February 1963, a coalition of Baʿthists and pan-Arabists of various strands toppled the General Qassim regime and massacred communists and leftists. Internal contradictions among the rival factions of the ruling elite erupted barely a few months after the seizure of power, in November of the same year, and a second military regime was installed which was to survive for the next five years. It was now the turn of the Baʿth party to face physical elimination.[1]

With the elimination of the communists and the Baʿthists consecutively, a political void among the Arabs opened up. For the Kurds, the Kurdistan Democratic Party, led by the legendary Mullah Mustafa Barzani, was still strong despite a continuation of armed clashes in the period under consideration.

Both the communist and the Ba'thist parties were instrumental in Shi'ite social and political activity. They constituted a political space for middle, lower-middle and underclasses, which were manifestly strong in Shi'ite areas. The Communist Party, in fact, had thrived on the migrant Shi'i peasants to Baghdad from southern provinces, and the Shi'i poor in urban centres. Studying the ethnic, religious and sectarian composition of the Communist Party leadership before and after the 1958 July revolution, Batatu concluded that the Shi'is' political mobility through and attraction to communism was mainly social; their percentage in the leadership almost matched their proportional weight in Iraq society.[2]

In a sense, the communist movement was a major political space for different social classes of urban poor, of labouring, lower and middle classes, Shi'i, Sunni, Arabs and Kurds in general; yet the presence in it of Shi'i poor peasants and lower-middle classes was significant indeed.

Inasmuch as the anti-Qassim 1963 military takeover was conceived in class terms by indoctrinated communists, namely as a pro-imperialist, petty-bourgeois right-wing *coup d'état*, ordinary affiliates thought of it in communal idiom, as an anti-Shi'i conspiracy. The general secretary of the Communist Party, Salam 'Adil, was a *sayyid* from Najaf; many Central Committee members and most leading cadres were Shi'is; General Qassim himself was Shi'i on the side of his mother; the resistance to the coup came from overwhelmingly Shi'ite suburbs in Baghdad, like Kazimain, Khalaf al-Sadda and others.[3] Such a communal representation given to the perplexing developments was, so to speak, characteristic of disenfranchised cultural groups deprived of modern instruments of self-expression. Yet Shi'ite weight was not insignificant in the Ba'th party or government. In a cabinet of twenty, there were twelve Ba'thists, five pan-Arabists, two Kurds and one independent. But of the twelve Ba'th elements, six were Shi'is.[4]

The Shi'i ministers were: Hamid Khulkhal, Sa'dun Hummadi, Naji Talib, Hazim Jawad, Talib Shibib and Salih Kubba. This is not to mention other leading Ba'thists who wielded influence and power, like Hani Fukaiki himself.

The existence of so many Shi'i leaders at the top served, through family connections, as patronage channels. Grand Ayatollah Muhsin al-Hakim used these conduits, inasmuch as the Shi'i Ba'thists reprinted his 1959 anti-communist *fatwa* to further their cause. In the early months of the 1963 Ba'thist coup, al-Hakim arrived at Kazimain on his way to Samara, where the holy shrine of Hassan al-'Askari (the eleventh Imam) and the occultation site of the Hidden Imam al-Mahdi are located. Such a pilgrimage was a regular occurrence and usually merited official regard.

The [Ba'th ruling] party and the government should have despatched a representative to greet and welcome such a prominent Shi'i celebrity as Grand Ayatollah Sayyid Muhsin al-Hakim, but [President] Abdul Salam 'Arif objected at the beginning on the pretext that al-Hakim's visit was a communal challenge to the government ... As a result of pressures [on the part of the Shiʿite members of the cabinet], ʿArif retracted on the condition that [the Sunni military] Tahir Yihiya would greet al-Hakim.[5]

Sensing a positive change towards him, al-Hakim took another step. In his calculated manner, he sent Sheikh Ali Saghir and his son Mahdi to call on Fukaiki's father to ask the latter

... to convey his wish that his two envoys, Saghir and Mahdi, would like to meet with four Shiʿi leaders, Hamid Khulkhal, Muhsin Sheikh Radhi, and myself [Hani Fukaiki]. The gathering took place at my father's place in Adhamiya. The envoys expressed al-Hakim's wish to see the four of us.[6]

In the above session, the al-Hakim envoys put forward

... a few humble requests similar to the kind the small, non-Arab minorities would ask for: matters relating to the curriculum, administrative affairs, the inclusion of Twelver Shiʿism in the College of Jurisprudence, extending aid to [Shiʿite] educational centres, to [Shiʿite] *awqaf* and holy shrines. No political demand was ever made except two points: bringing to an end the massacre against the communists and the abolition of the family law [promulgated under Qassim].[7]

Al-Hakim's move demonstrated an inclination to use family/communal networks for peaceful, extra-institutional pleading to achieve the desired ends. It was also insensitive to popular apathy towards the first Baʿth regime evident among the vast Shiʿi poor.

Ironically, it was the Sunni military men ʿArif and al-Bakr who pressed for the abolition of the family law. The cancellation of the law was taken by Sunni military out of conservative social positions against the expressed will of the highest ruling body, the National Revolutionary Command.[8] Traditional Sunni *ʿulama* had the same goal as their Shiʿi equals and both supported the measure.

The Baʿth party received a heavy blow at the hands of their military comrades and allies in November 1963. The collapse of the first Baʿth reign was the result and cause of a civilian/military split which ran roughly on ideological/political lines parallel to the communal fracture line. Almost all military Baʿthists were Sunni; the majority of the civilian party apparatchik was Shiʿi. With this turn of events another political space was lost to modern, middle-class Shiʿis.

Under 'Arif

The destruction of both the Ba'th and the communist currents led to a sharp political void in the realm of social movements. For vast numbers of Shi'is who had been hitherto attracted to and mobilized by these spaces it was a sudden, even inexplicable, vacuum. The generation approaching social and political awareness at that period conceived the situation neither in class terms, as in Marxism, nor in a nationalistic/ideological idiom, in the manner of the Ba'thist concept, but had to spontaneously construct or receive a third form of representation – a discourse embedded in communal identity. This has much to do with the rise of Shi'ite identity as such. Batatu contends that there have been ramified sociopolitical and economic processes which began under the monarchy but continued during the post-1958 revolution, in which national integration processes, inclusive of Shi'is, were damaged or weakened.[9]

Changes in the social movements were coupled with mutations at the top of the political hierarchy. The military, which had gained the upper hand in national politics, further enhanced its position. It is generally agreed that while the military regimes of 1958–68 improved the representation of the modern middle classes, they disrupted the delicate, relative equilibrium among different ethnic and religious groups. The military was, and to a great extent still is, a predominantly Sunni apparatus.[10] Among the two major and reserve committees of Free Officers who led the July 1958 anti-monarchy revolution, only three officers were Shi'is.[11] The continued ideological and political power struggle among different military groups and factions reduced the Shi'ite military at the top to a mere one: Talib Shibib, who by dint of his pan-Arab ideology and big-landlord social descent was alienated from the poor masses of Shi'is.

The narrow sectarian outlook of president Abdul Salam 'Arif and his close military associates, notably premier Tahir Yihya, a Takriti from the Shiaysha clan, and premier 'Arif Abdul Razzak from the Dulaim tribes, exacerbated under their reign a sense of sectarian oppression amidst sections of the Shi'a. Some anecdotes from 1964 serve to illustrate this atmosphere. In one incident related by Fukaiki, President of the Republic Abdul Salam 'Arif alleged that the Egyptian president Gamal Abdel Nasser refused Shi'i officers; on this basis 'Arif advised the cabinet to nominate only Sunni officers for military scholarships in Egypt. Another anecdote related that upon a visit to the Shurja cereals trade centre in Baghdad, a predominantly Shi'ite line of business, premier Tahir Yihya was irritated by the critical remarks voiced by the *rawzakhan* Ali al-Wa'ili, which reflected the grievances of Shi'i merchants over detrimental regulations imposed on the business class and the flight of capital. Yihya threatened to take harsher measures against this powerful class of Shurja.[12] The security apparatus, on the other hand, were lenient on Sunni dissidents but harsh against Shi'i militants from the Ba'th party, the main target of official wrath.[13]

Lack of access to informal, regional and kinship networks with the ruling elites rendered the extra-institutional, clandestine political activism on the part of disprivileged Shi'is inevitable. Political under-representation was soon coupled with an onslaught on the economic strongholds of private capital in 1964. The so-called 'socialist' decrees were enacted in July 1964. The scheme was the brainchild of Nasserite technocrats, prominent among them Khair al-Din Hasib, governor of the Central Bank and a devout pan-Arabist.[14] Ideological and political motives were mainly behind the move.[15] 'Arif was not for socialism, a term he tried to soften by adding the adjective 'prudent' (*rashida*) to it. His Islamist and pan-Arabist inclinations were stronger and most professed. Yet it was Nasser who insisted that union should not proceed before a degree of uniformity in social, economic and political structures was achieved. 'Arif's endorsement of the nationalization decree was partly anchored in his passionate drive to pan-Arab unity, and partly in a strong *étatiste* concept. For Hasib and his group, it was an *étatiste* ideological belief with economic overtones that nationalization would enhance the role of the state as the bearer of progress and development.

Plans were drawn up in the utmost secrecy to strike at the private sector so as to create homogeneity with the United Arab Republic (UAR), i.e. the Egypt of Nasser, to pave the way for the desired unity without fear of grave social resistance by propertied classes against any public appropriations. Such a reaction had occurred in Syria in early 1960 and caused the breakup of the UAR in 1962.[16]

On 14 July 1964, twenty-seven large industrial, four commercial, nine insurance and five banking companies were nationalized. These accounted for 42 percent of the already feeble private sector of Iraq.[17] The measures changed the power relations of social wealth. The state was already self-sufficient in terms of finances. Oil revenues covered almost 70 percent of the government budget. Services provided by the state were the source of other returns. Only a tiny, negligible part of state revenues was derived from various taxes.[18]

The 1964 nationalization decree destroyed the private sector. There is a similarity here with the effects of the agrarian reform of 1959. Both these laws weakened the power base of a hitherto strong social class, then sheikhly landlordism, now private capital. But whereas land reform redistributed the confiscated social wealth among members of other social classes – the poor or landless *fallahin* – with the state acting as an arbiter or supervisory agency, the nationalization act shifted a significant part of social wealth to the hands of the state itself in its capacity as an owner-producer. The social power of big wealth was thus subsumed under the direct control of the state.

In terms of ethnic/sect correlations, the nationalized capital was now controlled by state-economic agencies which fell under civilian, mostly Arab/Sunni technocrats. The newly created public sector was placed under the management and administration of the Economic Organization headed by Khair al-Din Hasib, which comprised three sub-departments: the Public Insurance Establishment, the Public Establishment of Commerce and the

Public Industrial Establishment; their directors were, respectively, Talib Jamil, Khalid Shawi and Hassan Ahmad Salman, all staunch pan-Arab Sunnis.[19]

The class of private capital is, of course, heterogeneous in ethnic, religious and sectarian terms. The mercantile class was predominantly Shi'ite. So, relatively speaking, was the industrial class. The financial upper elite might also have had Shi'is in greater proportion than the Shi'ite population. Multi-functional capitalists were not rare.

The nationalization act, which was officially proclaimed as being part of a 'socialist transformation' and viewed by the communists as a progressive 'non-capitalist development',[20] disadvantaged Shi'i merchants, and capitalists conceived of it in both social and sectarian terms: an assault by abhorred socialism against sacred, efficient private property[21] and/or a Sunni onslaught against Shi'ite strongholds, that is a deliberate act to reduce the power of Shi'ite merchant and other upper classes, a further step towards an almost gross exclusion of Shi'is from political and economic life and total Sunni hegemony.[22]

To add to this, a general Sunni fervour blatantly surfaced in various forms: measures were taken to impose restrictions on the entry of Shi'i foreign students to Najaf. Processions in Muharram, the 'Ashura and other rituals, received fresh restrictive controls. 'Ulama, notably of non-Iraqi origin, were harassed.[23] Disadvantaged Shi'is received these measures with alarm. The livelihood of the holy shrine cities was affected by a diminishing number of pilgrims and theological students.

Harsh state measures stemmed partly from ideological bias and preconceived misgivings towards the national loyalty of Shi'is – partly from the uneasy relations between a pro-Western Iran and the pro-Nasser, Arabist Iraqi elite, and partly from the *étatiste* official creed and its authoritarian nature.

A series of other implicit and explicit actions by the government and its protegés attacked the Shi'is. Mention should be made first of the leniency with which Sunni Ba'thists and other dissidents were treated compared to the harsh double-dealing the defiant, oppositional Shi'is received. Batatu and other social observers attributed this abuse or double standard to the ethnic/sectarian structure of the security service apparatus, namely the overwhelming presence of personnel from the Sunni province of Dulaim (renamed al-Anbar).[24]

Other implicit dubious ideological attacks questioning the very national loyalty of the Shi'is themselves were in the air. Abdul Salam 'Arif spoke of *Shu'ubiya*, a contemptible label to designate the Shi'is of Iraq. Abdul Aziz al-Duri, the dean of Baghdad University under 'Arif, published a book titled *al-Juthur al-tarikhiya lil shu'ubiya* (The Historical Roots of Shu'ubiya).[25] Jalal al-Sayyid, a Ba'thist Syrian pedagogue politician and ex-minister, attacked the Shi'is of Iraq directly in his book *Tarikh hizb al-Ba'th* (The History of the Ba'th Party) where he explicitly contends that 'the Shi'ite community (*al-ta'ifa al-shi'iya*) is unfaithful in its affiliation to Iraq; it has a dual loyalty, divided between the Shi'ite Iran and Arabic Iraq'.[26]

Such ethno-nationalist views, embedded as they were in the idea of the ethnic purity of Arabs, were held aloft by many pan-Arab nationalists influenced by the Nazi German school in the 1930s in Iraq. Pedagogues like Abdul Razzak al-Hassan, Muhammad Bahjat al-Athari, Sami Skawkat and others accused Shi'is of being *Shu'ubis*, that is, anti-Arab.[27] Alawi contends that Taha Yasin al-Hashimi, a prominent Sunni politician and premier under the monarchy, disseminated the view that '[Iraqi] Shi'is were against [pan-Arab] unity, for they feared that should they be integrated with another Arab country in a unity project their relative proportion would decrease'.[28]

These views remained, a carryover from the days of the monarchy, and were shared by many Sunni politicians and even Arab historians and sociologists like Batatu, Khadduri, Kedourie and others. In fact many Syrian pedagogues in the 1930s like Nusuli or the Arab ideologue Sati al-Husri showed similar sentiments.[29] Both ethnic and cultural nationalism tended to incorporate a reconstructed or imagined Arab history into their discourse, producing a paradigm of the eternal Arab nation.[30] This design transcended the Christian-Muslim divide in greater Syria. In the Iraqi context, however, it ignited a communal/segmentary feud over the meaning of history. Other pan-Arabists in Iraq simply put their sectarian bias in a nationalist mould to achieve political ends or were, *à la* Abdul Salam 'Arif, capable of simultaneously embracing pan-Arabist themes and a clannish/communal spirit. Such trends were invigorated under 'Arif into a fierce campaign.[31]

Al-Shibibi's Memorandum

The 'Arif regime aggravated the sense of injury among vast numbers of Shi'is, even the secular and modern-minded. The negative atmosphere enlivened a communal view of political and social events. Da'wa leaders held such views. For them, 'Arif was an anti-Shi'i ruler who attempted to destroy:

(i)   religious authority (Najaf and the *'ulama*);
(ii)   their economic leadership (the mercantile class);
(iii)   their political representation (i.e. the Da'wa).[32]

Perhaps the memorandum submitted by the aging literary and political figure, Muhammad Ridha al-Shibibi to the then-premier Abdul Rahman al-Bazzaz in 1965 was palpably expressive of this mood. His grievances were manifold. Below are significant and relevant excerpts from the memorandum which appeared at a moment when there was a civilian prelude in government and a promise, offered but not delivered, to liberalize both polity and economy. The text might have been co-authored or collectively discussed by many Shi'ite circles with the encouragement of higher religious authority.[33] The memorandum was enthusiastically reprinted and distributed by many Shi'i and spontaneous activists in many grand mosques in Baghdad, a fact testifying to what extent it was expressive of a general mood.[34] The text opens as follows: 'Among what encourages [us] to submit this memo at this moment is that the government is headed by a jurist [by profession, i.e. al-Bazzaz himself], and this is a good step.'[35]

Describing the differences, infighting, discrimination, doubts and grievance felt generally by his peers, al-Shibibi goes on to enumerate the problems as he saw them:

1. ... We stress the necessity to quickly draft electoral laws, put them before the people to endorse them until *elections* are *held* at the period specified by the provisional constitution, provided the elections will proceed under an *unbiased, neutral administration* which should guarantee *freedom of press and freedom of expression and opinion.*

2. ... The issue of *Arab unity and federal union* ... The geographical, historical unity and common destiny can at any time create a unity of action [among Arabs] to face challenges and threats. In our opinion, Arab unity is an issue on which there should be a referendum. Arab solidarity is the means to protect [unity].

3. ... *Sectarianism* [*ta'ifiya*; by Iraqi standards the word denotes the Shi'i/Sunni divide, more specifically the Shi'ite grievances of Sunni prejudice] *has been held by the current laws to be a criminal offence ... but what matters is not abstract formulae or written legislation but actual implementation and observance of the spirit of these laws. Never has sectarian bias been such an open practice* [*mushkila safira*] *by the government as it is today. It has never been a source of concern for the people who have always denounced, fought and demanded the abolition of such discrimination as an abominated practice. The devoted people* [to this country] *have always advised* [the government] *to adopt a different approach which would bring off the absolute equality upheld by divine and positive laws.*

    More often than not, the Iraqi people have rebelled against the policy of *blatant discrimination*. Since their first revolution in 1920 they endeavoured to build a *national democratic polity*, the fruits of which would be enjoyed by *all* sons of the people *irrespective of race, religion or sect*. The people hailed the July 1958 revolution and ... anticipated it would uproot the *divisive confessional prejudice* [*na'ra ta'ifiya*] by uprooting the bases and pillars of colonialism. But recent developments [the 'Arif takeover] proved, unfortunately, that the *divisive spirit* has been revived and is stronger and wilder than ever before.

    It is no longer a secret that the *majority of the people* [Shi'is] are extremely indignant, they feel their *dignity is humiliated* and their *rights are violated*, the more so when some of their *representatives* in the government are *wrongly chosen*. If this majority overlooked some of their rights to hold government posts, or overlooked *unemployment among their young graduates* who obtained higher degrees, or if it is possible that this *majority* ignored the deliberate [state] negligence *to develop their cultural, economic or social life*; or ... the disregard [shown by the government] to their honourable contribution to *jihad* [against British colonialism in 1920] and sacrifice, they can not accept to have their *Arab affiliation*, their noble descent, their dignity, their *loyalty to their fatherland and to the state* which they have built on the skeletons of their devoted martyrs, *flagrantly slandered by certain public figures and hired newspapers.* [The reference is to books on *Shu'ubiya* mentioned above, as well as official remarks by 'Arif and his associates] ...

4. ... Since *Arabs and Kurds* are partners in this homeland ... our Kurdish brothers should be entitled to enjoy their *legitimate rights* in the framework of *administrative decentralism* in a unified Iraq ...

5. ... Trade unions in Iraq have been subjected to different forms of political pressures which distanced them from their duty to defend their members ... The labouring classes have been suffering from dismissal or incarceration; their families have been deprived of their breadwinners. The government has to reconsider the regulations of the Labour Act ... and allow the establishment of trade unions which genuinely defend the interests of their membership.

6. We do not intend to debate *whether or not socialism is valid for Iraq*, but [we shall] confine ourselves to turn to the reality of things and what has actually occurred to give a judgement based on reality rather than fantasy. As a result of the socialist decisions enacted on July 14 1964, *Iraq's financial and economic situation has been deteriorating: increased unemployment, dwindling production, waste of public funds, flight of national capitals and chronic budgetary deficit* ...

    The government should *reverse this improvised policy* [of nationalization] ... the *fields of public and private sectors should be accurately defined* so that citizens would freely do their business in an atmosphere of security and full confidence.

    The agricultural sector is a major source of general wealth, and the agrarian reform has led to errors which caused backwardness, hence the very foundations of the act should be reconsidered ... the appropriated [*landlords*], *including those with lazma* [usufruct] *rights, should be compensated.* For we do not recognize confiscation of property in principle.

    Taxes need to be *reviewed* ... Other hastily legislated bills which contravene our *Shari'a*, Islamic law, should be reversed ...

7. Law No. 80, 1963, and the [establishment of the] National Oil Company are two national achievements that should be preserved ...

8. The *Ittihad al-Ishtiraki* [the official Socialist Union] ... was unsuccessful in spite of the material and moral support it had from the government. This is because it was plagued by conflicting [narrow] interests; in addition it rested on the *monopoly of political activity* and the concept of the *single-party system*, which we do not accept as a guiding principle for the governance of this country.[36]

No other Shi'ite political group could, at this stage, put forward such a daring and lucid programme in which liberal political demands, liberal social interests (of the big landlords and private capital), the Kurdish question and the national oil question are combined with Shi'ite grievances of political under-representation, social and cultural negligence and official sectarian bias. The whole wording of the memorandum is a typical mixture of liberalism, universal Islamic fervour and Shi'ite protest. Al-Shibibi was a transitional figure who had one foot in the monarchal era renowned for its relative legality and institutional political action, compared to the military era with its authoritarian overtones. But al-Shibibi had also another foot in the post-monarchy, revolutionary era with whose prerequisites he tried hard to cope and reconcile himself. His text contains many points in common with previous Shi'ite endeavours in the 1930s, Mithaq al-Najaf for one,[37] but the present document has a wider political horizon. It shows a pan-Iraqi and Arab spirit, liberal and Islamic sensibilities, all intertwined in a programme for political parliamentary pluralism.

The significance of the above text stems from two factors. First, it was expressive of a general mood of different Shi'ite social classes, and second, it was mindful of various social classes and groups – the landlords, private capital and the clerical, middle and lower classes – whose demands are clearly defined: reversal of nationalization, land appropriations, trade unions, more scope for educated middle-class Shi'is and the like. Al-Shibibi was a Najafi literary celebrity who had a prominent role in the movement for the independence of Iraq in the 1920s, and the various political agitations by leaders of Najaf or by the Shi'is in general in the 1930s, and who also had been appointed Minister of Education in the 1940s.[38] Hence his memorandum symbolizes the ethos, the spirit, the *mood* prevalent at the time among wide sections of the Shi'is. This is not to imply that the programmatic points he raised were a pan-Shi'i project, or that these demands enjoyed unanimous agreement among the Shi'is as a monolithic, social-political congregation.

The Growth of the Da'wa

The al-Shibibi memorandum depicts the atmosphere in which the Da'wa was now agitating. But it may also reveal the extent to which the Da'wa was far away from a concrete political vision. It was still, according to its theory of stages, in the first, pedagogic phase which confines the party to propagating Islam (see Chapter Three). The Da'wa group had by now changed hands. At the helm, al-Sadr withdrew into the shadows of the *hawza*, whereas Sahib al-Dakhil stepped in. Al-Sadr was a universalist Islamic man of letters, al-Dakhil a particularist communal man of action. His social liaisons differed from those of the clerical class. While clerics were confined to traditional networks of emulators, al-Dakhil ranged far beyond them to other modern, social groups like students and professionals. But whereas the clerical class had pan-national spaces in their perspectives, al-Dakhil was limited to sub-national spaces. His new mercantile calling in Baghdad drew him nearer to modern bonds. Being a man of action with keen practical instincts, he looked beyond the limited horizon of abstract jurisprudence. But being also socially and intellectually secondary to what he conceived as the grand, black-turbaned, senior *mujtahids* of his time, he was attached to the latter and highly dependent on them. These changes would affect the development of the Da'wa group.

During this period al-Dakhil moved swiftly to fill the void created by the weakened, secular movement and to expand on Shi'ite grievances which impacted on the party. This reality changed the nature of the Da'wa from a universalist Islamic group in defence of Islam to a segmentary organization fighting in defence of group interests. Al-Dakhil concentrated on the creation of wide, solid networks of membership. This endeavour was, nevertheless, caged within the *husayniyas*, the small mosques where only Shi'i believers would gather to say prayers, observe Shi'ite ceremonies and socialize in their neighbourhoods. As is obvious, the *husayniya* is named after Imam Hussain, around whose death the 'Ashura ritual is focused. These mosque-like centres were traditional social locations of Shi'ite interaction. Each *husayniya* constitutes a point of gravity for the Shi'a on the basis of the *mahalla*, the city quarter. They are run by *sayyids* usually despatched from Najaf. Through this figure a link is established between the religious authority and the various Shi'ite communities.

Under al-Dakhil, the Da'wa Party moved to sustain the intellectual momentum which it had internally initiated in previous years. Adhering to the intellectual nature of its activity, the Da'wa approached Ayatollah Muhsin al-Hakim with an innovative project: to establish a series of religious public libraries in the *husayniyas* across the country. These would be named the al-Hakim Libraries, their mission being to provide Shi'ite communities with the intellectual food produced by Najaf. It is presumed that the idea was conveyed to al-Hakim the father by his two sons, Mahdi and Muhammad Baqir, and he seemed to have given his consent.[39]

The al-Hakim libraries did appear in many *husayniyas* beyond Najaf, particularly in Hilla, Basra and Baghdad. Some libraries were based in *husayniyas*, others, perhaps for lack of space or other reasons, were located in ordinary premises, a small house rented in a Shi'ite neighbourhood. Naturally, they needed logistical support in cash and kind. Being outwardly free from any direct political aura or partisan appearances, they won the sympathy and appreciation of many circles, including, of course, al-Hakim himself. The libraries turned into an attractive meeting point for many Shi'i youth, frustrated and disenfranchised as they were in the mid-1960s.

Husayniyas were thus no longer restricted to traditional, practising Shi'i Muslims who came to say their prayers, ask for a *fatwa* from the *sayyid* or try to obtain social services like marriage or divorce contracts, interpreting dreams or *istikhara* – a sort of divination – as well as gather socially with co-religionists to mourn the dead or for other reasons. The *husayniya* now became an intellectual centre supplying a reading public with literary services. To give one example, the Jami' Khulani in the centre of Baghdad provided its reading public with a wide range of works: books by Balzac and Stendahl stood side-by-side with those of Pushkin, Lermontov, Gogol, and Dostoyevsky in their Arabic translations. Books on physics, chemistry, history, poetry and the like were as available as the works of Sayyid Qutb, Hassan El-Banna and the various Shi'ite Qur'anic exegeses.[40]

Hence the libraries broke off the narrow limits in which the *husayniyas* were formerly caged. As leading Da'wa Party activists in Baghdad admit in retrospect, they brought a rich catch of new, young, energetic supporters and sympathizers. This success brought leading Da'wa figures the blessings of the grand *marja'* in their capacity as supportive, lay-emulators on one hand, and gave them on the other hand the opportunity to build informal networks to circulate ideas, forge personal bonds, distribute party literature and mobilize the young who responded. Through these libraries, it seems, some university students were recruited, and a new inroad into the universities was opened. Many factors fostered this orientation. The universities were drained of leftist and radical nationalist elements, the main trends in this milieu. With the Nasserite followers inherently weak and lacking traditions of action among the students because of their overemphasis on winning over the military, all strands of Islamist tendency became active.

Salih al-Adib, a student at the College of Agriculture in Baghdad at the time and an active leading member of the Da'wa, helped to carry its activity over into student circles inasmuch as Sahib al-Dakhil secured similar avenues to mobilize merchants in the Shurja. Sensing the early successes in this new, and hitherto difficult field, al-Dakhil took charge of the universities and applied his full energies there.

Another, perhaps more important factor, was that the Da'wa group was intact. Not a single detainee from this group, let alone political prisoner, was ever reported by the party or security records during this period. The intellectual innovation started earlier by al-Sadr (*Iqtisaduna, Falsafatuna*) provided a new brand of intellectualism to fill the ideological void stemming from the failures of both the Ba'th and the communists.

The Da'wa seized the opportunity for semi-open action. Contrary to its programme, it was tempted to test its popular strength in the students' union elections at the university level, in the academic year 1964–65, within the Qa'ima Mustaqila, 'the Independent List'.[41]

This modern student organizational activity was not released from traditional vision: the *mawakib husayniya*, processions of Imam Hussain. The Da'wa incorporated the newly mobilized student masses into these *mawakib husayniya* and lent them a new form. Each faculty would now arrange its own *mawakib*. Detached from the traditional community and re-inserted into a modern educational institution, the university, the *mawakib* relied on student-Shi'i solidarity and proved to be a surprising success. The new *mawakib* were, however, given a modern, refined character. They were, in fact, organized in the form of political street demonstrations with banners and slogans. Marching in the streets, these *mawakib* – wherever they could emerge – attracted public attention and, in certain cases, enthusiasm. The verse these educated *mawakib* used was written in classical Arabic to lend the traditional commemoration a refined, sophisticated character. Thus the *mawakib* from Baghdad University, and later from other universities as well, were now on the scene side-by-side with the *mawakib* of traditional neighbourhoods and guilds. Speeches, sermons, poems and slogans were imbued with oppositional spirit. The defiance was not directly political, but it was assertive of Shi'ite ethos and identity which permeated these gatherings and lent them a specific meaning, in a political context of an authoritarian rule insensitive to the ethno-religious-communal diversity of Iraqi society. In a sense, Shi'ite identity was more powerfully reconstructed among sections of the modern-educated middle and lower middle classes, which had hitherto been alienated from such traditional leanings.

In 1964, however, the Da'wa sponsored a massive popular reception organized in honour of the golden decoration for the tomb of 'Abbas (Imam Hussain's half brother, who is buried in Karbala). The golden, engraved tomb structure was donated by wealthy contributors, *khums* payers in Iran, to the holy shrine of 'Abbas in Karbala. Delegations waited for the gift on the Iraq-Iran border. Crowds were gathered, either spontaneously or otherwise, to escort the procession. In Baghdad, the reception turned into a massive, peaceful demonstration. Rows of devout Shi'is marched in front of the golden tomb and behind it. A few banners were hoisted aloft. The poems were recited harmoniously, and there were visible overseers and stewards who were acting in a concerted, disciplined manner. Observers could hardly avoid the conclusion that there was a well-knit body of organizers behind the procession.[42]

These episodes betrayed the existence of a shadowy body pulling the invisible strings from behind the scenes. As the Da'wa Party had circulated no leaflets on its own behalf, rumours had it that there was a ghostly, religious group known as the Fatimid Party, *Hizb Fatimi*, with suspicious connections with the Jordanian monarch King Hussein, behind these moves. Such rumours had also surfaced back in 1963.[43] In fact, no Fatimid party ever existed.[44] Talk of it may have been the result of inaccurate reports by informers, or of political intrigues by the government. Da'wa Party leaders solemnly confirm that the circulation of the Fatimid name by their rivals was meant to smear the Shi'a, since the term was degrading and communal. The fabricated linkage with the Jordanian monarch was further evidence of an attempt to discredit their party.[45] But why did the party not issue a clarification? A counter-argument runs as follows: fearing untimely disclosure, the Da'wa Party adhered to the concealment (*taqiya*) principle. Some of their militants even took part in sustaining those rumours on the Fatimid Party to lead the security organs astray.[46]

Whatever the case, the Da'wa *mawakib* and other activities alerted the military regime of the 'Arif brothers to a newcomer to the political stage. The General Directorate of Security was instructed to keep a vigilant eye on the Shi'ite Islamist area, and a new, fifth branch was organized.[47]

The Da'wa sustained several major changes. First, its thrust was no longer inclined to the intellectual, universal form of Islam, but rather to a local Shi'ite ethos and identity. Secondly, the social composition of the movement altered. The flow of modern educated groups, notably from recent migrant peasant families, inflated the ranks. Third, the political inactivity of Grand Ayatollah Muhsin al-Hakim, coupled with the success of the 'Arif regime in recruiting Mujtahid Ali Kashif al-Ghita, proved to many Shi'is that the clerical class was impotent.[48] This conclusion increased, in the eyes of young Shi'i activists, the need for a modern political tool.

Finally, the Da'wa thrived and expanded with members and sympathizers, who by now were estimated at a few thousand.[49] It might be possible to conclude at this point that the weaker the communist and Ba'thist clandestine movements which overwhelmed the political scene earlier, the stronger the appeal of the alternative provided by the Da'wa and perhaps other Islamist groups. The more secular ideologies are discredited and weakened, the stronger the appeal of a sacred ideology becomes. The less the secular ideologies and movements are sensitive to ethnic and communal diversity and grievances, the more the need arises for cultural-political representation of the affected groups. The more national integration is deformed, the stronger the drive for an identity constructed along religious lines becomes. Finally, the more the religious class is in decline, the greater the need for a separate protective identity to endure decay and remain side-by-side with other ideologies on equal footing.

Table 6.1: Known Leaders and Leading Figures in the Da'wa Party, 1960–65

	Name	Education	Occupation	Social origin	Age group	City	Ethnic origin	Remarks
1	Muh. Baqir al-Sadr	*madrasa*	cleric	poor *sayyid*	20–29	Najaf/Kazimiya	Arab	left party in 1961 or 1962
2	Mahdi al-Hakim	*madrasa*	cleric	*sayyid*	20–29	Najaf	Arab	left party in 1961 or 1962
3	Muh. al-Hakim	*madrasa*	cleric	*sayyid*	10–19	Najaf	Arab	left party in 1961 or 1962
4	Murtadha al-'Askari	*madrasa*	cleric	sheikh	40–49	Najaf*	Persian	left party
5	Talib Rifa'i	*madrasa*	cleric	*sayyid*	20–29	Najaf	Arab	based in the USA
6	Sahib Dakhil	*madrasa*	merchant	Shammar tribe	20–29	Najaf	Arab	
7	Salih al-Adib	university	agricultural engineer	middle class	20–29	Karbala	Arab	died in Tehran, 1996
8	Muh. Hadi Subaiti	university degree	civil engineer	middle class	20–29	Najaf	Arab	Lebanese on side of mother
9	'Arif al-Basri	*madrasa*	cleric	petty middle	20–29	Baghdad/Karrada	Arab	left Hizb al-Tahrir and joined the Da'wa Party
10	Hassan Shubbar	university	lawyer	middle class	20–29	Najaf/Kazimiya	Arab	

* Compared to Table 4.2, three clerical figures withdrew; they are: Bahr al-'Ulum, al-Khalisi and al-Qamusi. There are two newcomers: one cleric and one lawyer.

PART THREE

Shi'ite Cultural Spaces: *Marja'ism* and Popular Rituals

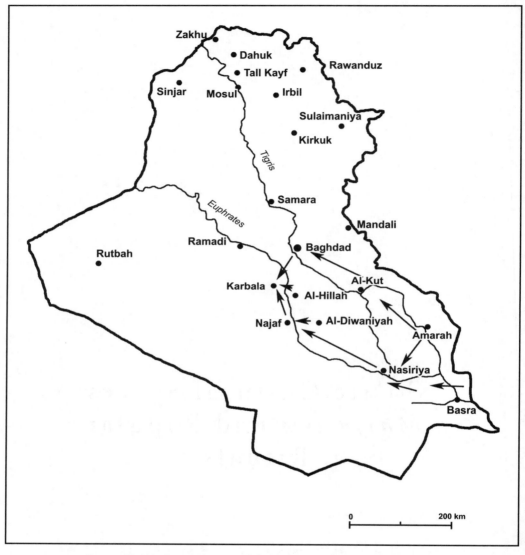

Route of Arba'in Pilgrimage; All Pilgrims Converge on Karbala

Introduction

As a religion, Shi'ism,[1] like Islam in general,[2] has different institutionalized and popular forms.[3] It comprises a mode of ethical/juristic religion of the clerical class, which resembles the typology Weber has given to ethical prophecy and ethical deity. This Weberian-like ethical/juristic[4] religion contrasts with community-based ceremonial ritualism, which may well be typified as a Durkheimian elementary form of religion – which constitutes a self-reflection of the community and its inner cohesion.[5] The two forms overlap in certain areas, yet they live partly in peaceful symbiosis and partly in cultural clash. Both function as social cement, an instrument of collective control, a source of legitimacy and social exchange, and as potential ready-made structures for mass politics.

It is from these two spaces that the actors who initiated this modern movement come; it is from them that they try to make their movement function as a bridge linking the two cultures. It is upon these spaces that they try to build, it is from them that they draw their symbols, signs, ethos, legitimacy and formations and this is the periphery on which they rely for recruitment and mobilization. But in these spaces they also meet formidable obstacles. Here, then, lies much of the momentum or inertia the modern movements of the Shi'is of Iraq have had or will have in the future.

An analysis of the nature of these two cultures is vital to an understanding of the functioning, limitation and development of Shi'ite Islamist movements in Iraq. In this section we will first investigate the high religious culture of the clerical class with its Weberian ethical legalities and specific sources of authority over the lay community. We will then move on to examine the structure, functions and the nature of social actors involved in the low culture of Durkheimian popular religiosity.

SEVEN

Sacred Money

The power of Shi'i *ulama* stems from three major, interlinked sources:

(i)   knowledge of the sacred text;
(ii)   monopoly of its interpretation and transmission through the *madrasa*;
(iii) control over religious taxes.

But these would count for little if the sacred were not itself dominant as a system of beliefs, a dominance that is to be explained by the macro social context of the pre-modern or the agrarian age. The rise of modern nation-states sets in motion socioeconomic and cultural processes under which the power and clout of the *ulama* constantly decline.

The interpretation of the sacred relates to this world, the other world and to the relation between them.[1] Under certain historical conditions religious knowledge is held superior to other forms of mundane knowledge, and those who control it – the clerical class – assume power over the laypeople.[2]

Through this knowledge the *ulama* gain a high rank in the segmentary agrarian universe. Their functions enable them to exchange services with the lay population at large in return for payments. The *khums* (religious tax) and *zakat* (alms), together with other payments, accrue to the *ulama* in their capacity as agents in charge of administering the execution of the sacred law (the *Shari'a*) and as individuals labouring in this field – scholars, jurists, judges, trustees, arbiters and *muhtasibs* (market overseers). The revenues received enable them to gradually solidify their position and generate an autonomous power base and infrastructures. This autonomy is one of the features that distinguishes Shi'ism.[3]

The accumulation of wealth and systematization of the production and transmission of learning were the preconditions for the development and maturity of the highly autonomous clerical class that came to be known in the 19th and 20th centuries. Below we analyse the doctrinal and social origins of sacred money and their relative decline.

The Collector of *Zakat*

Both Shi'i and Sunni jurists stress the importance of *zakat* as an essential part of the imperative of *'ibadat* (religious obligation). Quoting from the Imams, Khomeini describes *zakat* as 'one of the imperative pillars of faith, he who denies it is a *kafir* ... He who retains a carat of it [unpaid] is excommunicated from [the community of] believers and Muslims'.[4] Or, in the words of Muhammad Hussain Kashif al-Ghita:

> For the Shi'a, *zakat* is the second pillar of faith after prayer. Some traditions (transmitted from the guiding Imams) have it that the prayer of he who pays no *zakat* is void.[5] In the words of [the Abbasid jurisprudent] al-Mawardi, *zakat* (or *sadaqat*) functions as both *purification* for the donor and *support* for the recipient.[6] (Italics added.)

In the Qur'an *zakat* is mentioned as *sadaqat*, i.e. charity or alms. Both words are considered to convey one and the same meaning. *Zakat* is both a religious ritual (on the part of the donor) and social income support to the recipient.[7] The *zakat* donor should be a sane adult Muslim who possesses productive wealth gained from cattle breeding (pastoralism), cereals (agriculture) and/or gold and silver money (trade). With the commercialization of the economy, *zakat* came to be calculated in money equivalent, 2.5 percent of disposable annual income.

Eight categories of persons (according to the Tawba Sura of the Qur'an, 9:60 and 9:103), classifiable into three distinct groups, have the right to receive *zakat*:

(i)   as social charity for five categories of recipient – the poor; the needy; those in bondage (*fil riqab* – slaves or, according to other interpretations, captives); those in debt (*al-gharimun*); the wayfarer (*ibn al-sabil*);

(ii)   as administrative pay for one recipient: those who collect and distribute *zakat* on behalf of the community (*al-'amilun 'alaiha*);

(iii)   as military costs in the cause of God for two categories of recipient: *fi sabil Allah*, i.e. *jihad*) and *al-mu'alafa qulobahum* (literally, 'reconciled with Muslims') military or political allies.[8]

The *zakat* tax was paid annually and had three main parameters: quantity, time of payment and intention. The *fuqaha* (jurisprudents) differed little as to the nature of payment, its timing or intention. But they greatly diverged as to the method and agency of collection and distribution.

The Sunni school endorsed the payment of *zakat* either directly by the donor or through the rulers, as did Shafi'i in the eighth and ninth centuries.[9] Later Sunni jurists legitimized 'the practice of *de facto* [ruling] powers [*amir*]' in collecting *zakat* on behalf of recipients.[10] Emerging in the second half of the tenth century, the perfected Imami *fiqh* (Shi'ite jurisprudence) dropped (*saqit*) the three last shares set aside for administrative and military purposes – the *'amilun, jihad* and *mu'alafa qulobahum* – from the *zakat* imperative during the age of the occultation of the Hidden Imam.

The Shi'i-Sunni difference was related to the legitimacy of government. If there was no Imam or *sa'i* (messenger of the Imam), the donor should distribute *zakat* himself and never hand it over to the unjust ruler.[11] Or better, he should 'deliver *zakat* ... to the *'ulama'* because they were more knowledgeable 'about matters of distributing *zakat*'.[12] Gradually, the Shi'i *fuqaha* reintroduced the previous *saqit* categories of *zakat*, the ones related to *jihad* and administration, which meant that they should take over these military and administrative functions. They even included their group, the *fuqaha*, in the five categories of the needy recipients of the *zakat*.[13]

Defining and Redefining the *Khums*

Khums, like *zakat*, has been a religious imperative for early Muslims. Unlike *zakat, khums* is derived from a proportion of the spoils of war (*ghana'im* or *anfal*) and from all taxes paid by non-Muslims in return for truce, i.e. without fight, *fai'*. The rule regulating the distribution of this war booty accorded the noble warriors four out of five shares and retained one fifth (*khums*) for the Prophet Muhammad. Pre-Islamic conventions had it that the warrior chieftains would acquire for themselves a quarter (25 percent) of the booty. Islam dropped the percentage to 20.[14] The *khums* is mentioned in the Anfal Sura (8:42) as the part taken from the spoils of war.[15] The *sura* categorizes the source of booty, the allocations and the beneficiaries who enjoy the *khums*. They are: God, the Prophet, near relatives, the needy, orphans and wayfarers.

Relying on this verse, Shi'i *fuqaha* established a six-share division of the *khums*, the first three shares belonging to the Imams, since they represent God, the Prophet and his kin. The other three shares belong to the poor, orphans and wayfarers from the Bani Hashim (Muhammad's clan),[16] as *sayyids* or *ashraf*. That is why modern Shi'i *mujtahids* call their share as clerics *sahm al-Imam*, which is half of the *khums*. They may also take the other half if they are *sayyids*, descending from the Bani Hashim.

Sunni classical jurists confined the *khums* to *anfal* (spoils of war), as did Abu Hanifa, Shafi'i, al-Mawardi and Ibn Taimiya, to name but a few.[17] Shi'i jurists, by contrast, combined the *anfal* and the *fai'* (tribute without war, i.e. truce, or the mere threat of war). They also expanded the sources from which *khums* is to be claimed to seven categories of goods:

(i)   spoils of war;
(ii)   minerals;
(iii)   treasure found with no owner;
(iv)   what is gained from the sea by diving;
(v)   annual disposable income derived from trade, agriculture and craft;
(vi)   non-Muslim (*thimi*) land if bought from a Muslim;
(vii)   any *halal* (pure, lawful) goods mixed with *haram* (impure, unlawful) goods.[18]

Now with *khums*, the goods and wealth involved were the property of the Imam and the Bani Hashim. None but the Imam himself has the right to receive and dispose of that part of the *khums* that accrues to him by dint of his lineage. This was problematic in the era of the great occultation. *Khums* payers were given many options, the main and most crucial of which are (according to the eleventh-century jurisprudent al-Tusi's position):

(i)   the *khums* might be buried;
(ii)   the *khums* might be preserved by the payer as long as he is alive, but he should, before death, appoint a trustworthy Shi'i as *wasi* (guardian). A chain of guardianship would then go on until the advent of the Imam;
(iii)   the *khums* might be divided into two equal parts: the tithe should be paid to the Bani Hashim, with the Imam's tithe to be either buried or handed over to a guardian, as in points (i) and (ii).[19]

It was the practice to bury the share of the Imam in mosques or in the shrine. Certain *fuqaha* were *sayyids* and had their share in the *khums*. As judges they had actual judicial control over the Imam's tithe but as a *wadi'a* (deposit) or *wasiya* (will). Until the time of Muhaqqiq al-Hilli (d. 1277), there was ambiguity as to how the share of the Bani Hashim should be distributed. As for the Imam's portion, Muhaqqiq al-Hilli affirmed the right of the *'ulama* to control it in their judicial capacity as trustees.[20] He coined the concept of 'deputation' (*niyaba*), i.e. the role of the *fuqaha* as deputies to the Imam on the basis of their functioning as the rightful judicial power.[21] Both Shahid al-Awwal (d. 1347) and Shahid Thani (d. 1558 during the Safavid era), perfected the concept of deputation of the *fuqaha*. The power of the *'ulama* was justified and enhanced on the basis of their function as judges, lawyers and even actual leaders of the various Shi'ite communities. The enhancement of this role took almost six centuries to mature.

The Shi'i *fuqaha* thus grew richer and more powerful compared to their Sunni counterparts.[22]

Rising and Diminishing Returns

The 19th century was, perhaps, the golden age for the clerical class. Royal donations and endowments, the collection of *khums*, *zakat* and votive offerings, pilgrim traffic, corpse traffic and the concomitant trade with the shrine cities in Ottoman Iraq turned the latter into centres of wealth as well as of law and theology.[23]

When the Wahhabi (Sunni-Hanbali) warriors raided and pillaged Karbala in 1801, they carried away with them as spoils of war vast quantities of oriental precious coins in addition to 4,000 doubloons, 350,000 silver pieces, 400,000 Dutch ducats and 250,000 *thalers*. In the 1850s (half a century later), the Grand *Marja'* Murtadha al-Ansari received 200,000 tomans annually. By contrast, the total annual revenues of the Qajar treasury barely amounted to 3 million tomans. The ratio between the two was 1:15. By the early 20th century, the revenues of Najaf from charities, *khums* and offerings were estimated at around 1 million pounds sterling.[24]

Revenues were at this point derived from *khums* and *zakat*, votive offerings and endowments. *Khums* was totally under the control of the *'ulama*, who organized a body of *wukala'* to collect and transfer these taxes. The stronger the clerical-lay relations and the wider the social and political roles of the *'ulama*, the greater these revenues became. The late 19th-century growth of urbanism and the prosperity of commerce augmented the capacity of the artisan and mercantile classes to pay religious taxes. These revenues would, in the course of time, symbolize the drive of urban classes and their clerical patrons to oppose the powers that be and assume a political character, as was the case in the Tobacco Revolt and the constitutional revolution in Iran.

Votive offerings were paid in exchange for religious services. The more these services were sought after, the greater the revenues. This type of payment dwindled with the eclipse of the role of the *'ulama* as judges or providers of such services as adjudication, contract trusteeship and the like as these functions passed into the hands of the central bureaucracy.

Endowments (*awqaf*) were controlled by the state. Under the Safavids or Qajars, shrine and land endowments were regulated and administered by the *sadr* (a bureaucratic, state-appointed functionary) and the noble estate class, which shared not a single iota of their resources with the *'ulama*.[25] In fact, endowments were used by different dynasties as a leverage to pressure the clerical class. The tighter regulations imposed on endowments under Reza Shah (in the 1930s)[26] or under the Iraqi monarchy ended this line of financing.[27]

As an independent source of finance, *khums* and *zakat* were maintained as far as the modern state's controls and regulations are concerned. The regulations imposed by both the authoritarian modernizer Reza Shah and the newly installed monarchy in Iraq could affect *awqaf*, corpse traffic and pilgrimages but not *khums* and *zakat*.

The *'ulama* of Najaf and Karbala were highly dependent on the Iranian urban mercantile classes. But these were now distanced by the national divide. Inside Iraq, the clerics had not woven similar liaisons with the merchant class. The shift of the *marja's'* centre from Najaf to Qum in late 1940s further weakened the financial position of the *'ulama* of Najaf and Karbala.[28]

The lack of state patronage, *awqaf*, and social alliances with the indigenous Iraqi mercantile class further reduced the flow of sacred money. Another factor was the rural nature of the Shi'ite wealthy classes, the landed tribal chieftains. Iraqi Shi'i peasants and sheikhs paid their *khums* to their *sayyid* (noble) families rather than to Najaf. A piece of land called *tawali'* (front land) was usually allocated to the *sayyids*. *Fallahin* would till the land, deduct their material input (seeds, fertilizers or pump fuel) but not labour input, and hand over the net product to the living saint, the *sayyid*.[29] Visiting or residing *sayyids* also received fees for other social services such as registration of marriage or divorce contracts, distribution of inheritance or auditing and writing correspondence for illiterate sheikhs.[30]

Sociopolitical change, which brought the demise of landlordism and the rise of modern, secular-minded middle classes, thus further weakened the financial/social base of the Shi'i *'ulama* in Iraq. The advent of political Islam and the oil boom of the 1970s provided the stimulus and the means to augment *khums* payments. The Shi'is of the Gulf, lacking spiritual leaders of their own and facing what they conceived as communal oppression,[31] directed their *khums* to leading Najaf *maraji'* (high-level *'ulama*).[32] The flow of money was facilitated by the international web of banks and financial houses in the Gulf and the easy access to the Western world in terms of banking or tourism. Iraqi Shi'i *mujtahids* also established cultural and other institutions in Western countries to avoid regulatory impediments in the Middle East. The flow of *khums* was estimated in late 1980s and early 1990s at $3 million per month, or $36 million per year. Compared to the oil revenues of the region, the *khums* is a negligible amount indeed.

Earlier, Iran was considered a net contributor to the *khums* money; now it has become a net receiver. Burdened by state taxes, fewer Iranians are inclined to pay the *khums*, but most of those who pay, pay it to their own *'ulama*. This involves rivalry between the Islamic state and the autonomous *'ulama* class on one hand, and creates a secular/religious duality in the system of taxation on the other.

The $36 million sum is not directly accessible to the *marja'*. Each has a host of *wukala'* who usually have a mandate to carry out several charitable and social welfare payments and projects. Independent clerical dignitaries also launch campaigns for their own share of this principal.

EIGHT

The Transmission of Knowledge: The Traditional *Madrasa* and its Decline

The *madrasa*, or theological college, is a central institution in Shi'i Islam. In it, a complex cultural space is created, through which scriptural discourse(s) and specific social networks are built and sustained. Within its framework intellectual renewal, political agitation or schematic reform of the creed, the definition of Shi'ite dogmas or the defence of Shi'ism as such may take place. And in this frame, the informal hierarchies and social networks may serve as underground structures of political activity.

Our argument is that at times of crisis the *madrasa* and other ritual-related institutions (such as the *husayniya*-mosque) with the extended networks they have, operate as a substitute for the modern social organizations which have been destroyed by years of state terror. Where and when the *madrasa* and other religious institutions such as *husayniya* or mosques remain intact, they provide an alternative organizational tool. The Iranian experience is a case in point. Fischer argues that the revolution of 1978–79 used the networks of preachers and the administrative structure already in place in alliance with people outside the *'ulama* hierarchy.[1]

When the *madrasa* as a part of the institutional foundation of organized religion is much too weakened, an alternative is created – that is, a clandestine modern party. This is the case in Iraq.

Clash of Institutions

The *madrasa*, which emerged in the late 9th and early 10th centuries, stands between two contrasting institutions. Its forerunner is the classical mosque (*masjid*); its successor is the secular school. There is a functional continuity common to all three: they have been centres of producing and transmitting learning. Yet, they are worlds apart.

For centuries, learning and the transmission of knowledge were autonomously conducted in mosques proper. The mosque was a unifying space of Muslim worship irrespective of sect or school of law; yet, as a space of learning, it was the arena of divisions and antagonism between different sects or schools of law, theology or even grammar. Before the rise of the *madrasa* in the late 9th and 10th centuries there were some 500 competing schools of law.[2] Originally, *masjid*s were founded by individuals who retained the power to determine the informal curriculum (theology, Islamic law and other Islamic sciences) and the school of law (whatever sect). By dint of the *waqf* (religious endowment) legalities, the mosque

> ... became free of its founder's control. Its *waqf* was said to be a *waqf tahrir*, a '*waqf* of emancipation'. The relationship between it and its founder was thus likened to that existing between an emancipated slave and the emancipating master who relinquishes his rights over him.[3]

Mosques are the property of God. By contrast, 'the *madrasa* came under the control of its founder, and that of his descendants in perpetuity, if so he desired'.[4]

The *madrasa* brought structural – legal, textual and social – change to the institution of learning. For the first time learning was brought legally under the strict control of *madrasa*'s patron-founder; structurally the *madrasa* combined the lodging (*khan*) and library (centre of records and books) with an ancillary mosque (or, alternatively, a *khan* and library were added to an existing mosque); the curriculum of the *madrasa* was confined to only one school of law and, finally, it employed the *'ulama* as a social group in a specific ideological-political cause. The Seljuk dynasty, for example, provided for the schools, salaries for the *'ulama*, stipends for students and premises for the institution financed by *waqf*. The Madrasa Nizamiyah, named after the Seljuk vizier Nizam al-Mulk, developed into a network of state-sponsored centres of education.

The development of the institution of learning under the Fatimids in Egypt or under al-Tusi in Najaf, had a similar ideological cause but a different institutional pattern: the strict promotion of the *masjid* into an exclusive centre of learning. In Madrasat al-Azhar,

> ... the Commander preached and gave out proclamations during Friday prayers. Several times a week there would be court sessions ... as well as gatherings for ... tax agreements. Archives were stored in the inner parts of the building [of al-Azhar].[5]

The Nizamiya and al-Azhar were integrated into the state. The legal knowledge they produced was to function as an instrument of social cement, social control and political legitimacy. Within the traditional division of labour, the graduates assumed the functions of judges, jurists, prayer leaders, *waqf* administrators (*mutawalis*) or market supervisors (*muhtasibs*).

Under the Seljuks, the *madrasa* propagated the Shafi'i school of law; al-Azhar under the Fatimids taught the Sevener Shi'ite school. Under the Ottomans, the Nizamiya recognized three schools of law, the Hanafi (of the

Ottomans), the Shafi'i and the Hanbali. The Ottoman al-Azhar had four Sunni schools of law. In North Africa, the Zaituna mosque-*madrasa* adopted the Maliki (local) and Hanafi (Ottoman-endorsed) schools.

Shi'ite *Madrasa*: The Drive to Autonomy

From its inception in 1056 down to the rise of the first Twelver Shi'ite empire in 1501, the Safavid, Shi'ite *madrasa* developed autonomously. Changing political circumstances, i.e. the rise and fall of dynasties, forced the Shi'i *'ulama* to migrate and move about over the centuries from Najaf to Hilla, Aleppo, Jabal Amil and the like.[6] But this lack of state patronage kept the *madrasa* weak and vulnerable.

With the rise of the Safavid dynasty, the autonomy of the *madrasa* was curtailed. It was now the turn of the Shi'ite *madrasa* to have the same organic merger with state power, because the Safavids (1501–1722)

> ... inherited and preserved many of the religious institutions of the Sunni Iran ... Consequently, in the 16th and most or part of the 17th centuries, the structural relationship between the religious and political institutions in Shi'ite Iran did not differ appreciably from the 'caesaropapist [King-Pope]' pattern to be found in the Sunni world. The mosques and educational system under clerical control were integrated through the centralized administration of the religious endowments (*awqaf*) by the highest clerical functionary of the state, the *sadr,* on behalf of the king. Furthermore, the *qadis*, appointed by the ruler, manned the judiciary branch of the Safavid state. Caesaropapism in Safavid Iran had two sources: the legitimacy of the *dawlat* as God-ordained turn in power in common with Sunni Islam, and the charisma of the Safavid lineage as the putative descendants of the Imam and the Viceregents ... of the Hidden Imam.[7]

After the fall of Safavids in 1722, there was a massive exodus of clerics to the holy shrines in Iraq. Isfahan and Qum lost their prominence as centres of learning while Najaf and Karbala regained their positions. By the time the Shi'i Qajar assumed power in 1797, the Shi'i *'ulama* had already developed their independent power base in the holy shrines, the *madrasa* included.[8]

Change and Transformation: The Phase of Decline

The advent of the modern secular school in the 19th century (particularly after the mid-19th century) set the stage for the eclipse of the traditional *madrasa*.

Being part of modernity, secular schools appeared first to meet the need for standing armies in Egypt under Muhammad Ali, Ottoman Turkey and Qajar Iran. The effects of these reforms spread to other areas – Ottoman Iraq, Syria and Lebanon.[9] In 1876 the Ottomans enacted a law to organize and supervise modern schools. Western missionaries and the colonial powers continued the development of modern schooling, as was the case in Egypt and Iraq under British colonial occupation (1888 and 1918 respectively).

Secular schools were directly linked to a newly developing social division of labour created by the bureaucracy, the military and relevant services. The new system, which had been military-oriented, developed into civil education.[10] Under the Ottoman decree of education in 1869, elementary compulsory learning from the age of seven was declared. Private schools, native and foreign, were also brought under state regulation. The system was developed further with Rushdiya intermediary and Sultaniya secondary schools. Students were recruited to enter the military academy (open to Sunnis only), school of medicine, civil administration, faculty of law and letters.[11] A similar trend began in Qajar Iran.[12]

In this new era, the *madrasa* system lost its previous centrality as an educator of functionaries, jurists, judges, *muhtasibs* and *mutawalis*, in addition to other experts.[13] The creation of modern secular schools brought a novel and powerful mode of knowledge to the social space, the secular versus the sacred. The duality was intense on the social level. The *effendis*, the symbol of the new secular-learned class of civil servants, became sources of information and knowledge and gained the respect and even the trust of people at large. The new system also created a powerful bureaucratic and military elite. Students, officers and modern-educated functionaries came to play important roles. This gradually eroded the social value of religious knowledge and enhanced secular education as an achievement-oriented system. There were also other sources of tensions.

The secular school system is identified with nationhood, stressing various aspects of nationalism (language, history, culture), whereas the *madrasa* is either sub- or supra-national in character. In Najaf, for example, the *madrasa* was confined to Shi'is as a community in a certain national setting, or as a community across nations. Although there were different lodgings for Turks, Iranians, Shi'is from the Indian subcontinent or Lebanon, the class of tutors was international.[14] This supra-national nature of the *madrasa* would be brought under strict state control.

Another source of clash between the two systems is cultural. Even the most liberal-minded clerical figures could not view secular learning without scepticism. The great 19th-century Islamic reformer Muhammad 'Abdo emphasized the necessity of learning modern sciences but expressed fear of Western cultural influence over the minds of pupils in terms of religious belief and ethical norms.[15] The dislocations and disruptions caused by World War I diminished both pilgrimages and reduced the flow of sacred money and clerical students to Ottoman Iraq. The heavy-handed Ottoman policy against Najaf and Karbala in those years further weakened the status of the shrine cities, and the *madrasa* suffered. By the mid-20th century, the *madrasa* had reached its lowest point. One indication is the diminishing numbers of the student population in shrine cities. At the beginning of this century, seminarians were estimated between 10,000–15,000.[16] Less than a decade later, i.e. in 1918, their number had dropped to 6,000.[17] By 1957, the decline was deeper and clearer. The number and ethnic origin of students in Najaf in 1957 was as follows:

Table 8.1.a: Students in Najaf Religious Schools[18]

Country of origin	Number	Percent
Iran	896	45.85
Indian subcontinent	665	34.03
Syria and Lebanon	47	2.40
Bahrain, Ahsa & Qatif	20	1.02
Iraq	326	16.68
Total	1954	100

The situation in Qum reveals a linear, rather than cyclical pattern, as shown in the following table:

Table 8.1.b: Students in Qum Religious Schools[19]

Year	Number of religious students
1930s	6,500
1961	5,000
1972	1931*

* includes *mujtahids*, teachers, servants and students.

Decline generated two responses: one for the development and expansion of modern schools for the Shi'is, led by Najafi modernizers; the other for the reformation of the *madrasa* from within in terms of curriculum, formalization of admission procedures, certificates and graduation. Both attempts met stiff resistance from conservative *'ulama* but received some support from a few reforming *mujtahids*.

The first attempt was initiated by the Najafi Ali al-Bazirgan in 1906 and continued by the well-known poet and notable Muhammad Sa'id al-Habbubi, the Baghdad merchant-politician Ja'far Abu al-Timman and other Shi'i lay figures in 1908. The group applied for the establishment of the Ja'fari-Ottoman Progress School. The application was granted, and the school opened on 12 December 1908. The Shi'ite pro-modern school movement soon gained momentum.[20] To ease counter-pressures from the conservatives, al-Timman convinced a number of Shi'i *mujtahids* to endorse the drive for modern schooling with *fatwas*. Indeed, in 1909, the text of the *fatwa* was published in the *al-Raqib* journal. Part of it read:

> The sons of Ja'faris may attend schools (*makatib*) to study various sciences, knowledge, arts and languages the ignorance of which should be removed out of necessity, provided that the Islamic creed and principles are preserved.[21]

The other reform trend was best represented by Sheikh Muhammad Ridha al-Muzafar. In the mid-1930s, al-Muzafar led a crusade to renew religious learning which, in his view, was the essential instrument in reforming religion itself. He organized the Muntada al-Nashr (Publication Club). The name concealed the real agenda of the group behind a literary title in order to avoid unnecessary clashes with the conservative *'ulama*. The club was, in fact, a higher institution for religious learning with a new curriculum. The modernization of theological colleges culminated in the establishment of Kuliyat al-Fiqh (The College of Jurisprudence) in 1958, under the auspices of al-Muzafar. Its curriculum included modern philosophy, sociology, psychology, history, English language, comparative literature and the like.[22]

The *Madrasa*: Social Group and Social Organization

One of the *madrasa*'s functions is to produce new, qualified members of the clerical class in order to maintain its numbers. A long period of common living, joint study and common intellectual influences, covering some five to twenty years, turns novices into a relatively cohesive social group who share values, lifestyle, political leanings and social prestige or frustration. Intermarriage, common ethnic, regional or kinship descent at times further foster these bonds. This social group retains most of their links after graduation and constitutes a local or national, or at times even supra-national, Shi'ite civil society.[23] Students go through three stages of study known as *muqadamat* (preliminary), *sutuh* (secondary) and *dars al-kharij*, the graduation phase. A student may spend some twenty years or so to reach the final phase.

The *madrasa* was the major realm in the pre-industrial society for achievement-oriented upward mobility. Through it, many rural and poor students with no family clerical status managed to reach the highest echelons of Shi'ite *marja'ism*. Stories of rural families despatching their sons to Najaf or Qum to ascend the social ladder are not rare.[24]

But this rise is only a possibility. Many provincial and poor students drop out in the first or second phase of learning to constitute a lower clerical stratum relegated to secondary places and spaces, such as prayer leaders in villages, guardians of a small community mosque or *husayniya*, or simply rural preachers. On the clerical scale, dropouts form an underclass. Other students may manage to reach a medium rank, but only a few reach the upper echelons. Not every student can definitely become a *mujtahid*, let alone a leading one; but there is no *mujtahid* who can go up the ladder without having been a diligent student. This differentiation stratifies the group socially into poor, medium or rich strata.

Students are provided with lodging and paid stipends by their tutors, the *mujtahids*. They are attracted by the more renowned and most generous. The reliance of students on the *mujtahids* for their livelihood, academic progress and their certificate (*ijaza*) builds into patronage networks. These networks are not in themselves political. But when a *mujtahid* turns political, they function like a ready-made organization that, at certain times, may surpass a clandestine Leninist-type party in efficiency. Khomeini started his agitation among his students. His treatise *Wilayat al-Faqih* was a series of lectures to seminarians in Najaf. And it was at the Faydhiya *madrasa* in Qum that the anti-Shah agitation originated in 1978.

In this respect, the *madrasa* functions as a social web that may, in certain instances, replace the state-controlled or state-destroyed civil society organizations and associations at times of crisis, as was the case in Iran in 1979. When this role is relatively weak, the *madrasa*'s radical novices would seek a modern substitute: a clandestine modern political organization.

NINE

The Rise and Centralization of *Marja'ism*

The other centre of Shi'ite power is *marja'iya*, the autonomous religious authority. It has a history of its own.

The notion that *marja'ism* as an institution has been there since the time of Kulaini (d.940) or even earlier, and is as widespread among the clerical class and their lay emulators as *marja'iya* is challenged.[1]

Ayatollah Muhammad Baqir al-Sadr, for example, postulates that '*marja'ism*' dates from the time of early Shi'ism (Ashab al-'A'imma al-Ma'sumin) down to the present. In his words, there were four successive stages in the history of *marja'ism*:

(i)   the subjective *marja'ism* (*marja'iya thatiya*) starting with the deputies of the Imams (the last died in 939) down to 'Allama Hilli (d. 1325);

(ii)   the administrative *marja'ism* (*idariyya*) started by al-Shahid al-Awal, Abu Abdullah Muhammad ibn Jamal Din 'Amili (d. 1374);

(iii)   the central *marja'ism* established by Sheikh Ja'far ibn Sheikh Khidr Janagi Najafi Kashif al-Ghita (d. 1813);

(iv)   the popular *marja'ism* which emerged against the Western colonization of the Muslim world.[2]

Whether or not al-Sadr's conceptualization is historically sound, it clearly underlines a path of development in which religious authority assumed different forms and functions. Yet he projects the present reality of *marja'ism* on the past, claiming that all these forms of authority were centralized and instituted. Some Shi'i jurists and most students of Shi'i Islam challenge this conceptual projection. Muhammad Hussein Fadlallah of Lebanon, for example, maintains that:

> In past history, there had been no supreme, central *marja'ism* because long distances did not allow scattered communities [of Shi'is] to refer themselves to religious authorities [residing] in remote locations [presumably in Najaf] although there was a degree of contact ... That is why communities consulted the religious authority in their vicinity.[3]

The idea that *marja'ism* was there from the time of Kulaini or even earlier is clearly a myth. No less mythical is the idea that the institution of *marja' mutlaq* (the most senior *ayatollah*) emerged almost ready-made.[4] Students of Shi'i Islam agree that the institution of *marja'ism* appeared in the early or mid-19th century. Some refer to Kashif al-Ghita, others to the author of *Jawahir al-Kalam* (d.1849); but most single out his disciple, Murtadha al-Ansari (d.1865), as the first *marja' mutlaq.*[5]

The inception of this novel, religious institution denoted the growing autonomous power, wealth and social networks of the *'ulama* embedded in a widely recognized juristic-theological legitimacy. This recognition was also supported by state patronage and popular allegiance.

In this chapter we will study the formative process of this institution mainly in juristic-theological and sociopolitical terms. The chapter also focuses on the inner segmentary structures and external forces, which kept this institution in constant attraction and repulsion towards poles of centralization/ decentralization or order/disorder to this very moment. The major aspects of this process took some two centuries or so.

To clarify the presentation, five major aspects will be examined:

(i) The juristic-theological concepts of knowledge and power which paved the way for the inception of *marja' taqlid mutlaq.*
(ii) The relevance of the 17th–18th century Usuli-Akhbari juristic, social and theological/cultural conflict.
(iii) The drive to centralization in the mid-19th century.
(iv) The disorder of the informal order of *marja'ism.*
(v) Modern attempts at the formal institutionalization and modernization of *marja'ism.*

Knowledge and Power: Major Concepts

Legitimization of the authority of *'ulama* or *mujtahids* revolves, in juristic-theological terms, on the nature of knowledge.[6] Hence concepts of knowledge preceded those of power.

Concepts of Knowledge

Knowledge is one of the cornerstones of Shi'ism. The infallibility of the Imams as heirs of worldly and spiritual leadership is the basis of the legitimacy of the God-chosen Imam, the source of learning, jurisdiction and saintly mediation with the divine. The notion of the infallibility of the Imams, it seems, has two origins. One is the nature of God as all-knowing and all-good. From this Mu'tazalite premise, a theo-political theory was derived, namely that if the ruler is not infallible he would lead the community of believers astray, and this contradicts divine grace, for God can not command humans to do evil.[7]

The *'ulama* inherited their high status, community leadership and other roles, first in their capacity as transmitters and codifiers of tradition, *akhbar*, from the infallible Imams. Early Shi'i *fuqaha* in the age of occultation focused on codification and collection: al-Kulaini (d. 941), al-Sadduq (d. 991) and al-Tusi (d. 1067).[8]

Knowledge is dual, the sacred and infallible versus the mundane and fallible. The former is absolute and in harmony with heavenly justice and grace; the latter is probable and liable to go astray. The boundaries between these two realms of knowledge were debated, challenged, reinterpreted and modified throughout centuries of turmoil and change. Three major changes are discernable:

Reason and Ijtihad

An epistemological domain was created for the *'ulama* to share the Imams power to interpret texts and traditions by means of reason, *'aql*, and *ijtihad*.

The concept of *'aql* (reason) as a fundamental step towards *ijtihad* was first developed in a very limited form by Sheikh al-Mufid (d. 1022).[9] Like the Akhbaris, al-Mufid specified the fundamental sources of Islamic law as three: the Qur'an, the *sunna* (customs) and the *hadith* (sayings) of the Imams; but the methods leading to what is contained in these sources are: *lisan* (language), *akhbar* (traditions) and *'aql* (reason).[10] Hence the concept of *'aql* was not seen by the Akhbaris as a *source* of the *Shari'a* but as a *method* of investigation.

Muhaqqiq al-Hilli (d. 1277) took the concept of *'aql* another step forward, but he fell short of accepting *ijtihad*. It was left to 'Allama al-Hilli (d. 1325), who represented the second wave (or phase) of Shi'ite jurisprudence, that of mediaeval Shi'ism in the Mongol era, to establish the concept of *ijtihad* with reason as a *source* not merely a method.[11]

The concept of *ijtihad* constituted 'a crucial step in the enhancement of the juristic authority of the *'ulama*'.[12] From the epistemological point of departure, this led to the division of knowledge into two realms, that of absolute knowledge (the sacred text, infallibility of the Imams) and presumptive or probable knowledge (*zann*) based on the human (i.e. limited and fallible) exertions of powers of reason by the *'ulama*. It was centuries on that *ijtihad* was extended to stand on equal footing with absolute knowledge.[13]

Emulation

The superiority of clerical over lay knowledge was established through the concept of emulation, *taqlid*. It seems the notion of emulation appeared independently of *ijtihad* in the 11th century. In a cautious and qualified manner, al-Murtadha (a disciple of al-Mufid) expressed the desirability of *taqlid*, emulation, in the sense that laymen should seek the legal advice of the jurist.[14]

Three centuries on, 'Allama al-Hilli would again reiterate the argument of emulation, *taqlid*, premising it on practical needs. A differentiation of knowledge is inferred by him from the division of labour: the lack of legal expertise by the laymen due to their lack of time for acquiring this knowledge since they have to earn their living.[15]

The incumbency of *ijtihad/taqlid* was not conceptually defined and refined until well into the 16th century. According to John Cooper, it was the Muqaddas al-Ardabili (d.1585), in his *Zubdat al-Bayan*, who refuted

> ... the arguments against *taqlid* and [he] formally conjoin[ed] the ideas of *ijtihad* and *taqlid*. This conjunction greatly enhanced clerical authority in Shi'ism. If *ijtihad* legitimized the juristic authority of the *'ulama*, *taqlid* made compliance with their injunctions and opinions an ethical obligation for the laity.

Thus,

> ... a new trend has set in. The layman is no longer the voluntary seeker of legal advice (*mustafti*) of mediaeval Shi'ite literature, and is gradually assigned the *fixed legal status of 'follower'* (muqallid) as *subject to clerical authority*. (Italics added.)[16]

Stratified Knowledge: The Most Knowledgeable ('Alamiya)
The *'ulama*'s knowledge itself was differentiated through the concept of *'alamiya*, the most knowledgeable, creating thereby a hierarchy of junior, medium and supreme *mujtahids*, although this did not curtail the autonomy of each *mujtahid* in whatever grade he was. The concept of *'alamiya* was born in the 19th century:

> [T]he jurists of the Qajar period, after having established the principle of *taqlid* in its broad sense, started to accept the *marja' taqlid* as being of the *same superior level of knowledge* ('ilm) *as the Imam*. (Italics added.)[17]

The term *'alam* (most-knowledgeable)

> ... first appeared in *Ma'alim al-Usul* by 'Amili. But he seems essentially to have been concerned with the quality of being more precise in reporting tradition'.[18] In the mid-19th century, al-Ansari 'claimed *ijma'* [unanimity] *on* the *necessity of emulating the most learned mujtahid.*' (Italics added.)[19]

Only late in the 19th century was the principle of *'alamiya* clearly defined by Ayatollah Tabataba'i Yazdi who claimed,

... It is *obligatory* to follow the most learned *mujtahid* of the time. The most learned *mujtahid* ... is he who is most informed about the rules and sources of jurisprudence and is most capable of deducing religious ordinances.[20] (Italics added.)

Knowledge, by its very nature, is cumulative and capable of quantitative comparison and qualitative differentiation. The new Usuli concept of *'alamiya* enhanced the confidence in human mind. The elite of *'ulama* turned into *mujtahids* is, accordingly, stratified into grand, medium and low clerics. In this context, the system of knowledge-related concepts reflects and reinforces the hierarchical grading within the *'ulama* class. *Mujtahids* were ranked into *mujtahid mutlaq, mujtahid juzi'* and apprentice *'ulama* whose *ijtihad* is still short of both, i.e. cautious *ijtihad*. The validity of specialized and cautious *ijtihad* were depressed and restricted.[21]

Concepts of Power

As concepts of knowledge were endorsed, they took on a life of their own, penetrating the religious culture of both clerics and laypeople, binding them in mutual covenant. Through this social bond knowledge becomes power, and those who control it generate a system of power that coexists, in an uneasy tension, with the worldly centres of political power.

The notion that *'ulama* or *fuqaha* have some sort of authority is as old as the time of al-Tusi. According to Bahr al-'Ulum, a debate on their authority was triggered among Shi'i *fuqaha* when discussing the meaning of *uli al-amr*. In Sura 4:59, we read:

> O ye who believe!
> Obey God, and obey the apostle,
> And those charged
> With authority among you [*uli al-amr minkum*].[22]

Three sources of authority command obedience: God, the apostle, and the *uli al-amr*. The last term is interpreted as those charged with authority, responsibility, decision or the settlement of affairs.[23] The nature of *uli al-amr* is as ambiguous as any term could ever be. The above interpretation never states what sort of decision, responsibility or settlement is meant, or what areas these terms cover.

Classical Shi'i scholars interpret *uli al-amr* as designating the Imams, since to obey them means to obey the canons of God, and this obedience should by definition be based on correct, non-deviant, comprehension of the divine law; hence those obeyed should be infallible, and the latter are the Imams. Otherwise, it would have been contradictory of God to ask believers to follow a wrong path.[24]

By contrast, the Sunni reformer Muhammad 'Abdo (d. 1903) interpreting *uli al-amr* as being, 'princes, rulers, *'ulama,* commanders of the soldiery and all chieftains and leaders to whom people [*al-nas*] resort for their needs and public interests.'[25] In fact, this is the general understanding.

As early as the days of al-Tusi, the Shi'i *'ulama* argued that the *uli al-amr* are the *'ulama* themselves. Against this concept al-Tusi retorted:

> Those who argue that the term denotes the *'ulama* have gone astray, because His saying *'uli al-amr'* means to obey those who have control [*al-amr*], and the *'ulama* are not of this category.[26]

This internal Shi'ite debate conducted some nine centuries ago was perhaps among the earliest manifestations of the *'ulama's* drive to assert concepts of power supporting their authority as functionaries in charge of executing the Imam's functions. The functions attributed to the Imam are:

(i)   Leading the Holy War (*jihad*)
(ii)   Division of the booty (*qismat al-fay*)
(iii)   Leading the Friday Prayer (*salat al-jum'a*)
(iv)   Putting judicial decisions into effect (*tanfith al-ahkam*)
(v)   Imposing legal penalties (*iqamat al-hudud*)
(vi)   Receiving the religious taxes of *zakat* and *khums*[27]

Gradually these duties were performed by the *'ulama* on a *de facto* basis in their capacity as community leaders. Two major concepts were contrived to justify the expanding role of the *'ulama* on behalf of the Hidden Imam: one is *na'ib al-imam,* vice-regent of the Imam; the other *wilayat al-faqih,* the governance of the jurisconsult. The vice-regency of the Imam is an older term, attributed to Muhaqqiq al-Hilli. Both al-Karki (d. 1533) and Shahid Thani (d. 1558), took up the concept. In the first cases the concept was related to certain functions such as collection of *zakat, khums,* arbitration and the like. In the case of al-Karki it was expanded to cover the legitimation of the Friday prayers and *kharaj* farming (land rent and taxes) under the Safavid Shah 'Abbas.[28] The other term, *wilayat al-faqih,* was coined by Mullah Ahmad Naraqi (d. 1828) who developed this 'obscure notion' into a doctrine. He argued forcefully for the right of the *mujtahid* to act as a successor to the Imam and vested him with all the power of the Imam.[29]

Wilayat al-faqih was not a new concept different from *niyabat imam* but an elaboration of the powers the latter denotes.[30] These powers were either limited (*khas*) or general (*'amm*). It is only with Khomeini in the 20th century that the concept reached its full development to include political leadership with a shift from the old, segmentary community to the modern nation-state.

The Social, Cultural and Juristic-Theological Divide: Usuli versus Akhbari

The development of Shi'ite concepts outlined in the previous sections was the product of the Usuli-Akhbari conflict, inasmuch as they were the product of a constant adaptation and accommodation by the Shi'i *'ulama* to changing realities. In the words of Juan Cole, 'schools of thought should be seen as ideologies supporting the position or aspirations of differing groups of *'ulama*'.[31] In other words, the *'ulama*, as a social group, acted in and reacted to changing social, political and economic conditions. They also lived according to a given set of doctrines which at times hindered their coping with the new realities. Reinterpretation, modification and new readings of old tenets and principles were all the more imperative.

The Usuli Challenged

The Usuli school had dominated the scene in Persia from the beginning of the Safavid era in the 16th century. The recruitment of al-Karki by Shah Isma'il and his appointment as the 'seal of *mujtahids*' by Shah Tahmasb was unprecedented in the Shi'ite history of ruler-*mujtahid* recognition. This novelty received two challenges, one explicit, the other implicit. They came first from Ibrahim Qutaifi, a Shi'i *mujtahid* who was opposed to the appointment of al-Karki. Rivalry was at the root of this defiance.[32] Al-Karki was keen on having the favour of the royal Safavid court for himself. Qutaifi's attacks against al-Karki's authorization of the Friday prayers were a means to discredit the latter. His dashing criticism would have been unthinkable without the fact that several Shi'ite communities, notably of Syria, Bahrain and Iraq, were in existence beyond the reach of the Safavid power. This geographical extension helped maintain theological pluralism. The significance of Qutaifi's position, opposing clerical alliance with worldly powers, might well be interpreted as being an expression of discontent on the part of the disadvantaged section of Shi'i *'ulama* in the Arab lands, those who gained no patronage in the Safavid era or simply rejected the Safavids.[33]

The other challenge to al-Karki's and other Arabic-speaking Shi'i' *ulamas'* incorporation into the Persian political, social and cultural life came from a different quarter, what Arjomand termed the Persian 'clerical estate'.[34]

The differences between the Arab *'ulama* and the indigenous noble 'clerical estate' underlay fierce competition between two social groups over posts in the administration, religious services, *awqaf* revenues and religious-tax collection. They were split by differences of language (Arabic versus Persian), culture (theology-jurisprudence versus theosophy) and status (learning versus noble lineage). As Arjomand put it:

In fact, the clerical notables bitterly resented both the intrusion of the Shi'ite religious professionals under the protection and patronage of the ruler, and their pre-e[m]ption of the term *'ulama*-the learned.[35]

The Arab *mujtahid* class from Iraq, Bahrain and Syria 'displaced, to some extent, the indigenous "clerical estate" of landed notables who had held official religious office'.[36]

It seems that these two reactions against the alliance of the Usuli school – represented by al-Karki and his group – with the Safavid dynasty formed the basis of the revival of Akhbari school as a protest movement in the 17th century. This revival took a century or so during which the Persian 'clerical estate' shifted from Sunnism and theosophism to Twelver Shi'ism, gaining enough confidence to '[counter] the Shi'ite doctors' bid for hierocratic domination with a radically different interpretation of Shi'ism and a counter-ideology of their own'. So,

> ... once the intellectual representatives of the clerical estate set forth to create their distinct variant of Shi'ism, they rediscovered the rich heritage of the pietistic traditionalism of Qum and reconciled it with the gnostic philosophy. In reviving Akhbari traditionalism, they discarded the legalistic exoteric rationalism of the *mujtahids* in favour of a gnostic rationalism that advocated inner-worldly salvation through the hermeneutic comprehension of the sacred texts.[37]

This onslaught, it seems, was assisted by political factors, namely the desire of the Safavid dynasty in the late 17th century to weaken the growing influence of the Usuli school, whereas the Ottomans, as has been suggested by Qazwini, wished to sustain the schism within the Shi'ite school.[38]

The Theological-Methodological Onslaught: Astarabadi and the Rise of Neo-Akhbarism

The reinvigoration of the Akhbari school in the 17th century is associated with the name of Mirza Muhammad Amin Astarabadi, a descendant of the Persian clerical estate.[39] The Akhbari current was present in Shi'ite schools from its early days.[40] The oldest reference to Akhbarism and Usulism came in *Nihayat al-Usul fi 'Ilm al-Usul* by 'Allama al-Hilli where it was asserted that Abu Ja'far al-Tusi was an Usuli who was challenged by Murtadha and his associates on certain issues.[41] Differences, however, were mostly methodological relative to sources and method of law deduction.[42]

With Astarabadi, Akhbarism 'crystallized in separate movements elevating the theological-methodological differences to the level of ex-communication'.[43] The animosity between the two reached such a point that Akhbaris would not touch any Usuli textbook without using a handkerchief to avoid impurity.[44]

The clash implied an acute power struggle with a deep cultural/social rift extending beyond juristic issues.

Astrabadi started his onslaught on the Safavid-allied Usulism from the Hijaz, Arabia. Residing in Mecca, he could act freely, supported by notable Shi'i figures in Jabal 'Amil such as Hurr 'Amili and in Persia, such as the Sheikh al-Islam in Mashhad; and the movement soon flourished in Bahrain, Ottoman Iraq and pockets in Persia.[45] In his *Fawa'id al-Madaniyya*, Astarabadi rejected the concept of *ijtihad*, *'aql* and the probable (*zann*) knowledge, stressing the importance of *akhbar* (traditions) transmitted through the infallible Imams and restricting the sources of doctrine and law to two, the Qur'an and traditions, with no place to *'aql* and *ijma'*. To him, these were Sunni traditions and Sunni deviations. *mujtahids*, in the Akhbari view, are, like their lay followers, *muqalids* of the Imams. No human has the right to be emulated.[46] The list of differences between the two schools was expanded to 29 points; some sources enlarged the list to 43, or even 86.[47]

The Akhbari doctrine aimed at shaking the very basis of Usuli clerical authority based on knowledge. The clerical-lay duality and the right of the *mujtahids* as vice-regents of the Imam were abolished. The Akhbaris, in Arjomand's view, served the interests of the Persian clerical estate against the Arab-Usuli jurists by challenging the 'hierocratic dominion' of the latter. Placing emphasis on the charisma of lineage, the Akhbaris stressed their importance as *sayyids* and reduced the status of *'ulama* based on knowledge. They also attracted the mass of ordinary believers through 'devotional piety' reconciling, thereby, Sufi-influenced popular traditions with dry, canonical jurisprudence.[48]

Prior as well as parallel to this line of development, the Akhbari trend was strengthened in Ottoman Iraq, Bahrain and Hijaz right from the time of Qutaifi who, in his challenge to al-Karki's alliance with the Safavid shahs Isma'il and Tahmasb, based his criticism and opposition on Akhbari lines, i.e. rejection of the Friday prayer performance, tax collection, *kharaj* farming, deputyship to the Imam by the *faqih* and other duties performed by the Shi'i *fuqaha* under the unjust ruler.[49] Qutaifi's position symbolized an Iraqi (even beyond) Akhbari-based opposition to al-Karki.[50] The two trends met and reciprocally enhanced each other's influence.

The temporary triumph of Akhbarism was brought about by other factors.

Loss and Transformation

The Shi'ite world in the 17th century was now split into three circles: a pro-Safavid Usuli domain in Persia, an independent Arab Usuli school in Jabal 'Amil and an Akhbari realm in Ottoman Iraq, Bahrain and Hijaz. The sudden downfall of the first circle under the Sunni Afghan conquering tribes (1722) demolished the solid, state-patronized base of the Usuli school in Persia. The endowments supporting the clerical class were confiscated; the patronage networks were destroyed, and hundreds of scholarly families were displaced. This situation led to 'a relative impoverishment and a decline in the influence of this group' of the *'ulama* class, and 'great numbers of clergymen and merchants fled Iran for the shrine cities of Ottoman Iraq'.[51] Migrant *'ulama* arrived at shrine cities as dislocated, penniless refugees with no social contacts and networks, and converted to Akhbarism.

The other section, which remained in the realm of Persia, sustained a social change. Their means of living were no longer sought at the royal court, or not solely in it. This segment now sought to foster links with the 'richer classes of the bazaar, seeking new forms of economic security'.[52] Some members of the *'ulama* families even tied themselves through intermarriage with the bazaar merchants and artisans with their powerful, autonomous guilds and social networks. They also took on new, non-clerical functions such as moneychangers, money coiners, landowners and administrators; others retained religious careers. Paradoxically, this change led the *'ulama* to create an independent financial base delivering them from state patronage and fostering their power and influence in later periods.[53]

The Resurgence of Neo-Usulism

Migrant Usuli elements in the shrine cities of Najaf, Karbala and Kazimain staged a comeback later in the century, first during the Zand period (1763–1779) and later in the Qajar period. Their revival is associated with the name of Muhammad Baqir Akmal al-Bihbahani (1704–1791). In Karbala, al-Bihbahani started his anti-Akhbari crusade with the utmost caution and secrecy. Usulism was not only excommunicated, but the Akhbari *'ulama* had the instruments of physical coercion to deal with any dissent, namely the Luti gangs.[54]

The first clandestine cells organized by al-Bihbahani were confined to his kin; his liaisons with merchant and artisan networks secured the needed resources.[55] The movement gained supporters and met favourable circumstances. Shrine cities in Iraq succumbed to a plague, which caused massive casualties among Arab Akhbari *'ulama* who, unlike their Persian peers, could not flee to Iran. The ensuing vacuum was soon filled in by the rising Usulis.[56] Political developments enhanced the group. The Mamluk rule grew weaker and could not control the emerging Shi'ite city-states in Najaf and Karbala which were inclined to assert their autonomy. A powerful social alliance of Arab landowners, merchants, artisans (mostly Iranians) and mixed Arab and Persian armed gangsters was the backbone of this autonomy. The formation of Shi'ite states in Qajar Iran and Oudh (India) furthered this trend. The Usuli school was a legitimizing force for both newly emerging Shi'ite dynasties.[57]

The 18th–19th-century neo-Usulism grew under novel circumstances. It was now in firm alliance with productive wealthy classes – the *bazaaris*, the artisans and landlords – with sources of income independent of state patronage and with vast social networks. The leading cores of the clerical class together with their *madrasas* were in the shrine cities of Ottoman Iraq. The new Shi'ite states, the Qajar and the Oudh, were either very weak or too remote to have any direct influence on the centres of *ijtihad*. And for the first time, the *'ulama* had an instrument of coercion, i.e. the Lutis, urban gangsters in the shrine cities who traded their security services for money, through their manipulation and organization of means of violence, with both the mercantile and clerical classes.

Tendencies to centralization developed in this period, leading to the emergence of the *marja' taqlid mutlaq* as the supreme source of religious authority. Neo-Usulism reasserted the categories of knowledge; the competence of reason, *'aql, ijtihad*; the probable knowledge, together with the power categories; the necessity of emulation of a living rather than a deceased scholar; the payment of *zakat* and *khums* to the *mujtahids* in their capacity as vice-regents of the Imam. This innovation redefined the inner structure of the Shi'ite world and laid the cornerstone for the emergence of *marja' taqlid* and the centralization of the latter.[58]

Tendencies Towards the Centralization of *Marja'ism*

There is a general view that the first *marja' taqlid mutlaq* was Murtadha al-Ansari (d.1864), or possibly his predecessor Muhammad Hassan Najafi (d. 1849).[59] Some informal arrangements to organize a leading core in the shrine cities gradually preceded the inception of al-Ansari as the supreme learned (*al-'alam*) *faqih*. It is presumed[60] that the oldest forms of such leadership arrangements dates back to Sayyid Muhammad Mahdi Bahr al-'Ulum (d. 1797), the disciple of al-Bihbihani. A division of labour was organized in which one *mujtahid* assumed prayer leadership (*salat*), another took over judiciary functions (*qadha'*), a third practised teaching (*tadris*) and a fourth issued *fatwas* and commanded emulation (*fatwa wa taqlid*). It is not clear whether this design was spontaneous, but it indicates one of the persistent features characterizing the elite core of the clerical class: division.[61] The single *marja' mutlaq* as we have come to know it today crystallized with al-Ansari. The term used to designate the *marja'* was clear and simple: *riyasat*, headship, that is leadership. Although the term conveys the meaning of power over subordinates, it nevertheless falls short of other terms of political power, such as *hakim* (ruler), *sultan* (monarch) and *amir* (prince).[62]

Unlike the institution of *mujtahid* of the age or *sadr* or *sheikh al-Islam* under the Safavid, the *marja' taqlid mutlaq* during the Qajar period was informally institutionalized separately from any state (Shi'ite or otherwise) by the clerical class in Najaf. This de-linkage freed the institution from direct bureaucratic control but deprived it of order. The process revealed two contradicting, in fact antagonistic, centrifugal and centripetal tendencies. The conflicting processes of integration and fragmentation kept *marja'ism* an informal, amorphous, structure-less institution.

Centralization was promoted by political, social and economic factors. To begin with, the second half of the 19th century was the era of political centralization generated by Western-influenced reforms of polities: reorganization of the military (standing armies), centralized bureaucracies, state-sponsored educational systems. It was also a period of hectic commercial activity, when telegraph lines, steamboats, and other modern communication systems gradually eroded the hitherto antediluvian segmentary borders. Centralization was a social tendency of which the religious class was only a part.

The *'ulama* class was ethnically and geographically divided: Arab, Turks, Indians and Persians. The latter were again split into two wings, one residing in the 'Atabat, the shrine cities in Mamluk-Ottoman Iraq, the other in Iran proper.

The *'ulama* in Iran wielded socioeconomic power in provincial towns. In addition to their control of the judiciary, they exploited the 'political vacuum'[63] and benefited from the flow of *sahm al-imam*, *zakat* and other religious payments to become directly involved in such economic activities of the market as investments, landowning or moneylending.[64] This caused tensions between the state and the local *mujtahids*.

The Qajar state, seeing diversity of the clerical centres of power as desirable, became in this situation more inclined to bypass local *mujtahids* and seek alliances with the 'Atabat-based supreme *mujtahids*. The latter were to inhibit the power of local *mujtahids*. Disputes between the local *mujtahids* and their clients – the merchants – over the registration of contracts and over injunctions by local *'ulama* who gave contradictory resolutions in financial and property-related disputes,[65] led the merchants and various owners of goods and property to seek higher authority for arbitration. The growing state-merchant tensions increased the need of the mercantile class to attract the support of the *'ulama* in the shrine cities as a counterweight to the absolute monarchy. These ingredients fed into a drive towards centralization.

The willingness of the pro-Shi'ite Mamluks of Iraq ... to extend their patronage to Usuli *'ulama*,[66] and the attacks by the Wahhabi desert warriors against Karbala also furthered the drive towards more centralization. The trend was so massive that the local *mujtahids* in Iran were turned into mere clients of the grand *mujtahid* at the centre.[67]

The Disorder of the *Marja'* System

The institution of the post of *marja' taqlid mutlaq* was a 'transformation of the *mujtahids*' 'function from mere teachers of the *madrasa* to powerful figures in the life of urban centres'.[68] This transformation did not, however, bring with it the creation of any sustained order of promotion, selection and appointment. Perhaps this is why Amanat calls the 'institution' of *marja'ism* an 'anarchic discipline', or says that 'the order of the clerical community ... is in its disorder'.[69]

The Process of Selection

The norms, procedure, method and routine of selecting the *marja'* have three major aspects:

(i)   *The subjectively unified normative self-definition of the* marja' *mutlaq as provided by the clerical class itself.* The idealized norms of the *marja' mutlaq* were subjectively defined by the clerical class. According to Shahid Thani the ability of *ijtihad* is based on

> ... comprehending the six premises which are: theology (*kalam*), methodology (*usul*), grammar (*nahwu*), syntax (*tasrif*), Arabic language (*lughat al-'arab*) and conditions of inference (*shara'it al-adilla*); and mastering the four sources which are: the holy book, the *sunna* (tradition), *ijma'* (consensus) and the evidence arrived at through reason.[70]

The person of the *mujtahid* is, however, restricted by ten major conditions. He should meet the following criteria:

(1)   adulthood (*bulugh*);
(2)   sanity (*'aql*);
(3)   belief (*iman*);
(4)   justice (*'adala*);
(5)   freedom (*hurriya*, i.e. not being slave);
(6)   being male (*rujulah*; women are allowed by only few scholars to be *mujtahids* and give *fatwas*);
(7)   being alive (no emulation of a deceased *mujtahids*);
(8)   being the most knowledgeable *mujtahid* (*al-'alamiyya*);
(9)   purity of birth (*taharat al-mawlid*, i.e. being of legitimate parenthood);

(10)   not being a lover of worldly wealth (*an la yakuna muqbilan 'ala al-duniya*).[71]

These ramified criteria are reduced by some contemporary scholars to three major conditions: being alive, being the most knowledgeable and justice.[72] Lacking an institution to measure knowledge or justice, the designation of the supreme *mujtahid* was marked by great uncertainties. A plurality or diversity of centres of clerical power was always there. Scholarly fame and with it the increased number of novices in the *madrasa* is another element influencing the choice. The subjective role of the *'ulama* has to do with their organizational skills and generosity in recruiting followers. In the words of one cleric, 'open-handedness' is the instrument of leadership [*al-jud alat al-riyasa*].

(ii)   *The segmentary nature of the clerical class.* With its divisions by family, city or ethnic descent, this is a highly segmented class. The organization of webs of *wukala'* and emulators starts from the family, the town and fellow students (who, again, are attracted by ethnic and town solidarities). For example, al-Ansari could assume the highest post thanks to the support of Arab, Persian and Turkish lay emulators. Shirazi of the Tobacco Revolt fame suffered a split between Azeri and Persian emulators and could not command the obedience of both Shi'ite communities until the death of his Azeri clerical rival.
Recognizing this reality, most *mujtahids* defined their tribal, familial, city and ethnic origins in their names.[73] This ethnic division would develop into nationalism proper with the creation of nation-states in the 20th century. Indeed, the masses of followers are, relatively, divided in their loyalties along national lines; at the very least there is a general Arab-Persian divide.

(iii) *The actual selection process as effected by the electoral college, such as mercantile and other urban classes or state functionaries.* Lay emulators, above all those with wealth and influence, such as merchants and landowners, are decisive in the selection of a grand *marja'*. Channelling the *sahm al-imam*, *zakat* and other taxes, towards a certain *mujtahid*, in the event of the death of the previous *marja' mutlaq*, is tantamount to a *popular vote*. State patronage, when and if translated into financial backing, can contribute to the choice. The uncontrollable preference of lay emulators, however, remains a decisive factor.

Leadership Ambiguities

The informal institution of *marja'ism* charted a zigzag course along which it was in constant attraction and repulsion between institutionalized centralization and fractured decentralization – between integration and fragmentation. It remained bereft of structures of power (apart from the employment and deployment of the Lutis for brief moments here and there) and was chronically unable to contain divisive tendencies. The integration we may witness in this class in certain periods is the result of pressures and forces acting from without the class itself.

Table 9.1: Marja' Taqlid, *mid-1845–1995. Plurality versus Single Headship*

Name	Date of accession	Died	City of residence or burial	Status	Remarks
Single headship 1845–64					
Muhammad Hassan Najafi	possibly 1845	1850[a]	Najaf	*sheikh*	author of *Jawahar al-Kalam*
Murtadha al-Ansari	1850	1864[b]	Najaf	*sheikh*	
First period of plurality, 1864–74;[c] diversified centres, among which:					
Muhammad Mahdi Qazwini	?	1882	Najaf	*sayyid*	
Muhammad al-Irwani	?	1888	Najaf	*sheikh*	
Single headship 1874–95					
Mirza Hassan Shirazi	1874	1895[d]	Najaf/ Samara	*sayyid*	Tobacco Revolt
Second period of plurality, 1895–1908;[e] diversified centres on the eve of the constitutional revolution					
Muhammad Fadhlulah Sharibyani	1884(5)	1904	?	*sheikh*	
Muhammad Hassan Abdullah Mamaqani	1895[f]	1905	Najaf	*sheikh*	
Mirza Hassan Khalil Tehrani	1905	1908	Najaf	*sheikh*	

Name	Date of accession	Died	City of residence or burial	Status	Remarks
Single headship, 1908–20					
Muhammad Kazim Khurasani	1908	1911	Najaf	*sheikh*	
Muhammad Kazim Yazdi	1911	1919[g]	Najaf	*sayyid*	under British Mandate
Muhammad Taqi Ha'iri	1919	1920	Karbala	*sayyid*	
Fathallah Isfahani (Sheikh al-Shari'a)	1920	1920	Najaf	*sheikh*	
Third period of plurality, 1920–35[h]					
Abdullah Hassan Mamaqani	?	1932		*sheikh*	
Mirza Hassan Na'ini	?	1935	Najaf/Qum	*sheikh*	
Aqa Dhiaudin 'Iraqi	?	1945		*sheikh*	
Hussein Qumi	?	1945		*sheikh*	
Single headship, 1935–70					
Abu Hassan al-Isfahani	1935[i]	1945	Najaf	*sayyid*	Iraq
Hussein Burujerdi	1945	1961	Qum	*sayyid*	Iran
Muhsin al-Hakim	1961	1970	Najaf	*sayyid*	Iraqi Republic
Permanent multiple centres 1970–95 *A: 1970–79*					
M. Abu al-Qassim Kho'i	1971	1992	Najaf	*sayyid*	
Kazim Shari'atmadari[j]	?	1986	Qum	*sayyid*	stripped of rank in 1982
Muhammad Hadi Milani	?	1975	Mashhad	*sayyid*	

174

Name	Date of accession	Died	City of residence or burial	Status	Remarks
Abdullah Shirazi	?	1984	Mashhad	*sayyid*	
Ahmad Khwansari	?	1985	Qum	*sayyid*	
Shihab Din Mar'ashi Najafi	?	1991	Qum	*sayyid*	
Muhammad Ridha Gulpaykani	?	1993	Qum/Najaf/ Tehran	*sayyid*	
Ruhollah Khomeini	1979	1989	Qum/Najaf	*sayyid*	accorded his rank in 1963
Mahmud Taliqani	?	1979	Tehran/Qum	*sayyid*	
B: After the Iranian Revolution, 1979–88					
Kho'i					
Khomeini					
Muhammad Baqir al-Sadr		1980	Najaf	*sayyid*	executed
Muhammad Muntaziri			Qum	*sheikh*	dismissed from office as deputy leader
C: Post-Khomeini, 1988–92					
Kho'i					
Muhammad Ali Araqi		1994	Qum	*sayyid*	
D: Post-Kho'i					
Muhammad Ali Sistani	1992		Najaf/Tehran	*sayyid*	
Ali Khamenei	1989		Tehran	*sayyid*	Supreme Leader
Muhammad Shirazi	?		Qum	*sayyid*	
Muhammad Ruhani			Qum	*sayyid*	

Name	Date of accession	Died	City of residence or burial	Status	Remarks
Muhammad al-Sadr[k]	1992	1999	Najaf	*sayyid*	allegedly nominated by Iraq; assassinated in Najaf

Remarks:
a. Or 1849 (al-Ha'iri and Kedourie).
b. Or 1865 (al-Ha'iri).
c. Kedourie, al-Ha'iri and Joyce give no details to fill in the ten-year gap between the death of al-Ansari in 1864(5) and the rise of Shirazi to *marja'* in 1874 (Kedourie). Fischer lists both Qazwini and al-Irwani without further details. Most probably it was a period of collective leadership.
d. 1894, according to al-Ha'iri.
e. This was a period of turmoil and internal struggle among the *'ulama*, when they split into two opposing camps: pro- and anti-constitutionalism. Among the names of prominent religious leaders are: Mazanderani, Fadhlullah Nuri, Khurasani, Na'ini, Yazdi and others.
f. Fischer gives the year 1895, a year or so after Shirazi's death.
g. Kedourie gives April 1919, Fischer, 1918.
h. The names of Kashani, Muhammad al-Sadr, al-Khalisi and others are prominent in this period.
i. Basri contends that Isfahani enjoyed his higher status for twenty years. This would modify his date of accession to the year 1925 when has returned from exile in Iran.
j. Shar'iatmadari was the first *ayatollah uzma* to be stripped of his title, in April 1982, by the Islamic Republic of Iran.
k. Al-Sadr was allegedly nominated by the Iraqi government in its bid for an Arab *marja'* based in Iraq. A student of martyr Muhammad Baqir al-Sadr, also his relative, al-Sadr's nomination by quarters supported by the Iraqi government may indicate the latter had realized the mistake it had committed by the execution of the first al-Sadr in 1980.

This table has been compiled from:
al-Ha'iri, A.Hadi, *Shiism and Constitutionalism* (Leiden, 1977), ch.2, pp. 62–64.
Fischer, Michael J. L., *Iran From Religious Dispute to Revolution* (1980), pp. 242–2.
Amanat, 'Abbas, 'In Between the Madrasa and the Market Place', in, Arjomand, S. A. (ed.), *Authority and Political Culture in Shiism* (Albany, 1988), pp. 98–132.
Momen, Moojan, *An Introduction to Shii Islam* (Yale University Press, New Haven, 1985), pp. 310–23.
Kedourie, Elie, 'The Iraqi Shi'is and their Fate', in Kramer, Martin (ed.), *Shi'ism, Resistence and Revolution* (Westview Press, Boulder, 1987), pp. 136–55.
Basri, Mir, *'Alam al-Adab fil 'Iraq al-Hadith* (Dar al-Hikma, London, 1994, V.2., pp. 313–48.
Wiley, Joyce N., *The Islamic Movement of Iraqi Shi'as* (Lynne Reinner Publishers, Boulder, 1992, p. 123).

Table 9.1, which covers the period from 1845 to 1995, sheds light on these contradictory tendencies. The period needs to be politically divided into three major phases. The first extends from 1845 to 1920. It is a pre-modern period in which Iran was under absolute monarchy and Iraq under the Ottoman and British occupation. The second extends from 1920 to 1960, and is the phase in which modernized central states were built in Iran and Iraq with a drive to solve the agrarian crisis as well as a rise in anti-colonialism. In Iraq, the monarchy was toppled; in Iran, the White Revolution was looming. The third phase extends from 1960 to the present. This is the era of authoritarian, single party or military regimes, culminating in the advent of the totalitarian Ba'th regime in Iraq and the Iranian Revolution. In each phase, *marja'ism* was sustaining mounting pressures and constraints.

While the state encouraged the centralization of *marja'ism* in the 19th century, a reverse process was developing as a result of the constant clash between the centralized state and centralized *marja'ism*. This trend was set off under the authoritarian, modernizing Reza Shah in the 1920s and under the newly Sunni-secularizing Iraq monarchy. Both regimes tried to check or mute the clerical class. The state, it seems, abhorred any autonomous centre of power. The two regimes in Iran and Iraq were interlocked in a bitter rivalry. The Iranian Pahlavi regime was bent on 'Iran-izing' rituals and religious teaching: *marja'ism* was returned to Qum to bring it under tight state control; pilgrimages were re-channelled from Najaf and Karbala to Mashhad and Qum.[74] Under Muhammad Reza Shah Pahlavi, just after the Shah's bitter controversy with the *marja' mutlaq* Burujerdi over agrarian reform issues, *marja'ism* was distanced back to Arab Najaf in the hope of rendering it weaker and ineffective.[75]

In all these cases, *marja'ism* was not tolerated by the state. This trend has intensified rather than receded under the Islamic republic. Ayatollahs Shari'atmadari and Muntaziri are cases in point. The first was stripped of his religious status as a Grand Ayatollah, the latter dismissed from his office as successor Khomeini to return to his pious lecturing in his *madrasa* in Qum. The political institutionalization of the post of the *marja' taqlid mutlaq* under the Islamic republic did not end the age-old segmentary, multiple nature of the Shi'ite religious establishment. Nor could it surmount the boundaries created by nation-states. The national rivalries among regimes weakened the 19th-century drive towards centralization of the religious establishment.

Political turmoil took its toll. There were four intervals of ambiguity (Table 9.1). The first coincided with the Tobacco Revolt; the second, with the Iranian constitutional revolution; the third, with the early decade or so of the monarchal era in Iraq when the *mujtahids* first took part in the 1920 anti-British rebellion, led the anti-referendum agitation and opposed the British-Iraq treaty. The Iraqi government under Premier Muhsin al-Sa'dun deported Na'ini, Kashani, Muhammad al-Sadr and al-Khalisi as a punishment for their agitation.[76] The causes of division among the clerical class were ideological (as in the case of pro-and anti-constitutional debate), social pressures (by their lay emulators-financiers) and state intervention (repressive and/or regulatory measures).

Table 9.2: General Ratio of the Period of Headship Ambiguity

Duration of ambiguity	67 years (44.7 percent)
Duration of sole *marja'ism*	83 years (55.3 percent)
Total period	150 years (100 percent)

Table 9.3: Periodic Ratio of Headship Ambiguity

Phase	Duration	Single headship	Multiple headship	Percent of multiplicity
1845–1920	75 years	51 years	25 years	32.9
1921–60	39 years	23 years	16 years	41
1960–95	35 years	9 years	26 years	74.2

Tendencies to centralization in the religious establishment produced counter-tendencies, by their own dynamic. As the revenues accruing to the supreme *mujtahid* mounted, a clerical career became all the more attractive and intensified competition among various contenders. The more the numbers of high- or medium-ranking *mujtahids*, the greater the competition among them. The competitive access to wealth and power structured the clerical class into different lower, medium and upper strata. Urban interests and urban-based solidarities were also forceful ingredients. Becoming a seat of *marja'ism* meant that a city would have a larger student population, increased religious tourism and better welfare. Noble clerical families promoted such solidarities and thrived on them. Karbala, Najaf and Kazimain families not only competed against Qum, Mashhad and other Iranian centres of learning and pilgrimage, but also rivalled each other. Between 1845, the time of the first recognized supreme *marja'*, and 1945, Najaf (77 years), Samara (twenty-one years) and Karbala (two years) held sway as the centre of *ijtihad* and, by extension, learning. Only in the 1920s did Qum manage to revive its *madrasa* system thanks to the deportation and migration of Persian *mujtahids* from Iraq. Between 1945 and 1961 (seventeen years), Qum was the seat of supreme *marja'ism* under Burujerdi. Najaf regained its former status for only ten years under al-Hakim (1961–70). Thereafter, the collective centres of *ijtihad* and authority were spread over Najaf, Qum, Mashhad and Tehran.

Another segmentary feature is status. Whereas the proportion of sheikhs, i.e. non-*sayyid* figures, was overwhelming between 1845–1920 (twelve out of sixteen *marjaʿ*), the opposite trend was visible in the period between 1920–95, when there was only one *sheikh* among twenty prominent *marjaʿ*'s. This may reveal the crucial role the noble status class of *sayyids*, played as a status group in controlling and preserving hierocratic centres and structures.

Attempts at the Institutionalization of *Marjaʿism*: Musa al-Sadr, Baqir al-Sadr, Taliqani and Khomeini

Marjaʿiya revolved around influential figures rather than institutions. Allegiance was based on local, mechanical solidarities of the guild, city quarter, clan or tribe. Under these social forms, Shiʿis had a dual traditional leadership, that of the guild master, quarter leaders and notables or tribal chieftains on one hand and the *sayyid*, cleric or local mullah on the other. The gradual dissolution of primordial solidarities created novel conditions under which the structure-less religious establishment seemed an anachronism. Different groups saw the reformation of this traditional institution as an imperative.

Modern lay Shiʿis argued for institutionalization to establish a procedure for accountability, planning and budgetary affairs in order to end the present chaos and illegal manipulation of assets.[77] Sensing these pressures, several initiatives came from leading religious dignitaries.[78] Other clerics also felt this need to avoid the squandering of resources.[79]

Several attempts at modernization were theoretically and/or in practice made by Musa al-Sadr of Lebanon or Muhammad Baqir al-Sadr of Iraq. But only in post-1979 Iran was the institutionalization of *marjaʿism* implemented.

Musa al-Sadr (1928–78) launched his project to organize the Shiʿite community on a national (Lebanese) basis. His first modernizing move was to establish a vocational institute in the southern town of Burj al-Shamali.[80] Originally al-Sadr's education was mixed, half-modern, half-clerical. A driving force in his modernizing attempt was his desire to unite the three distinct Shiʿite regions in Lebanon: the tribal Biqa valley with its clientele system and leading families of notables, the Jabal ʿAmil in the south with its landlord-peasant based society, and the poor southern suburbs of Beirut.[81] Under a circumstance of dual centres of Shiʿite leadership, the lay, notable families of *multazims* (property administrators) and landlords (al-ʾAsʿad, Himada and others), and a weak, local clerical leadership, al-Sadr's attempts at modernization and unification culminated with the institution of the Supreme Shiʿite Council (al-Majlis al-Shiʿi al-ʿAla) and the formation of a social movement, Harakat al-Mahrumin (The Movement of the Deprived).[82]

The assembly, the first modern Shiʿite institution of its kind, acquired legal status when the Lebanese parliament endorsed it in 1967, but it was actually functioning in 1969.[83] The organization aimed at the creation of an administrative-bureaucratic structure with a pan-communal assembly in which every male holder of an academic certificate, from secondary high school upwards, would be included.[84] The Supreme Shi'ite Council also had its bureaucratic apparatus: an administration, accountancy, official records, specialized committees, all with a clear set of disciplinary regulations and accountability. This modern formation combined bureaucratic structures and electoral representation in one.

The second attempt by Baqir al-Sadr was purely theoretical. He envisaged the creation of an organized structure to supervise the various functions traditional *marja'* usually administer through a group of protégés (*hashiya* or *atba'*) and next of kin.[85] In his treatise, *al-Marja'iya al-Saliha wa al-Marja'iya al-Mawdhu'iya* (The Righteous and Objective Religious Authority)[86] al-Sadr differentiates *marja'ism* in two ways – one by purpose, the other by form.

In terms of purpose, *marja'iya* is either *saliha*, righteous, or not, depending on the course it takes. It is *saliha* if it:

(i)   propagates Islam and educates Muslims;
(ii)   creates a wide current believing in Islam as the universal, all-valid system;
(iii)   promotes Islamic research in different economic, social and philosophical realms and expands the areas of jurisprudence;
(iv)   supervises and appreciates Islamic intellectual and practical works to support good and rectify wrong;
(v)   enhances the leading role of the *mujtahids* from highest to lowest ranks.

In form, *marja'ism* could be subjective and dependent on the person of the *marja'* and his entourage,[87] or objective and dependent on the institution.
The latter form should seek 'the creation of an operative, planning executive apparatus based on efficiency, specialization, division of labour, encompassing all areas of rational *marja'* work in the light of the designed targets'.[88] This apparatus should be formed of various standing pedagogical, educational, research, administrative, public relations, pan-Islamic and financial committees,[89] and should develop

> ... a code of religious authority practice. Historically the *marja'* practices his duties in an *individual* manner, hence the forces which are loyal to him do not feel they truly share his responsibilities. If the *marja'* practices his duties through a council which contains the *Shi'i 'ulama* and the *forces which represent him*, and if the *marja'* links himself [probably indicating some sort of consultation and accountability] *to this council*, the practice of religious authority would be *objective*.[90] (Italics added.)

With a collegiate council, the subject (the person) and object (the impersonal institution) are united to preserve continuity:

The person of the *mujtahid* is the element which *dies whereas the object, the council, remains constant* and provides a guarantee to fill in the vacuum.[91] (Italics added.)

Hence the new *marja'* would 'not start from zero, but continue the work already commenced by his predecessor'.[92]

It is not clear whether the institution functioned with a sole authority at the helm, whether selection was to be based on ballot or whether this institution was to be national or supra-national.

The communal balance and political conditions in Lebanon helped Musa al-Sadr achieve his aims; the situation in Iraq kept Baqir al-Sadr's scheme in the realm of mere intellectual practice. In his last years, Baqir al-Sadr formed the nucleus of such an apparatus comprising three of his disciples, Kazim Hai'iri, Muhammad Baqir al-Hakim and Mahmud al-Hashimi, to fill in the vacuum that would result if he were eliminated.[93]

It was, however, in Iran that such a structural re-organization of religious authority could fully take place. Centralization without state authority is difficult. Two factors formed the cornerstone of this mutation: Khomeini's version of *wilayat al-faqih* and the Iranian Revolution. Khomeini's version of *wilayat* is 'simple and novel' in Shi'ite thought.[94] First it constitutes a break with the original concept, as it was elaborated by Naraqi in the 19th century, in that the *marja' taqlid* is no longer seen as a counterbalance to monarchy but as its substitute.[95]

Second 'is the idea of the *people* as a political force which can effect revolution and transformation'.[96] In other words, with Khomeini's theory, the concept was expanded beyond the legal-religious to the political sphere within the context of the modern nation-state.

Thus the *marja' taqlid*, the very subject of the doctrine of *wilayat al-faqih*, sustained a radical change in conceptualization, function and setting. For the first time in modern Shi'ite history, the post was constitutionalized and institutionalized within the context of the Iranian state. Previously the supervisory role over legislation had been assigned to the *mujtahids* in the 1905–09 Mashruta/Constitutional Revolution. A 'guardian council' of five *mujtahids*, elected by the parliament, was stipulated in the Fundamental Law to carry out this task. Moderate *'ulama* like Shari'atmadari were calling, in 1979, for the re-institution of this constitutional right.[97]

After the revolution, the *wali-e faqih* was given a pivotal leading role (Articles 2 and 5 of the Islamic constitution). It was endowed with vast legislative, executive and judicial powers (Articles 57 and 110) to endorse the election or dismiss from office the president of the republic and the supreme national security council, and to appoint six of the twelve clerics who sit on the guardian council. The other six were to be elected by the *shura* assembly/parliament (Article 110).[98]

The post of *wali faqih* (Supreme Leader) was organized on an electoral-bureaucratic basis. Article 107 of the constitution stipulated that either one perfect *faqih* is recognized by the people or by an 'assembly of experts' elected by the people, which would recognize the person or persons of the *wali faqih*(s) and declare them for the people.

The concept of the *marja'* also radically changed. Unlike the old *marja' taqlid*, the *faqih* was both a *marja'* (religious authority) and *wali al-amr* (leader). The terminology used to designate Khomeini was different from the old one: he was the *wali al-faqih* rather than a mere *marja' taqlid*.[99] The term *uli al-amr*, as has been noted earlier in discussion of the al-Tusi debate, referred to the infallible Imams and was never applied to *mujtahids* before 1979. Article 5 of the Iranian constitution reasserts this meaning: '*Wilayat al-amr* and the imamate of the *umma* is upon the just and pious ... jurist.'[100]

The supreme *mujtahid* was now declared the *imam* of the *umma*, the *marja'* and the leader (*rahbar*). His expertise transcended theological-juristic matters to political, administrative leadership (Article 101).

The change was a step towards modernization, indeed; but it never ended the traditional informal hierarchies. Instead it created a conflicting duality, whether in theological or theo-political terms. Non-political *ayatollahs* like Gulpaykani, Mar'ashi Najafi and others had no political influence; political *ayatollahs* like Shari'atmadari and Muntaziri were either destroyed as a religious and political centre of power or, as was the case with Muntazari, driven out of power.[101] Khomeini's followers were well aware of the implications of this duality of their own making and demanded full political compliance by all clerics:

> The maintenance of order in society necessitates that when the Leader or Leadership Council is accepted, *all should obey a single authority* in the social and general problems of the country within the framework of the Islamic constitution. Such *obedience* is implied in the title of '*vali-ye amr*' [wali al-amr] and the 'imamate of the *umma*' and applies to *all members of society without exception, and in this respect the* mojtahid *and the non*-mojtahid, *the* marja' *and the non*-marja' *are in an equal situation.*[102] (Italics added.)

The mood prevailing among *mujtahids* outside the realm of the *wilayat al-faqih* is best seen in the words of Ayatollah Sadeq Ruhani: 'My duty is to say that I see Islam in danger, the *marja'iyyat* is in danger.'[103]

Amanat contends that the doctrine of *wilayat al-faqih* was both an 'innovation as much in revolt against the authority of the secular ruler as it is against the hegemony of the emulator' who determines the *marja'* by voting through payment of religious taxes.[104] If this had been envisaged by the author of the doctrine, then the attempt had scored success on the political rather than theological level. The doctrine of *wilayat al-faqih* is held and supported by a minority of *'ulama*. It derives much of its influence from mass politics rather than from theological potency. The political division of the Shi'ite world among various nation-states renders the institution of the *wali faqih* limited in scope and character. The Iranian proponents of the *wilayat al-faqih* were able to gain little influence in either Iraqi or Lebanese circles, and resistance to their influence is continually growing.

The multiplicity of religious centres was attacked inside Iran; beyond it, however, various autonomous leading authorities continued. Kho'i was one, Sistani another. After Kho'i's death in August 1992, several centres of religious authority emerged, sharing popularity and income. Their proportionate popularity is estimated as follows: Sistani (Najaf) 40 percent, Ruhani (Qum) 40 percent, Khamenei (Tehran) 10 percent and Shirazi (Qum) 10 percent.[105]
This mainstream view among Shi'is abroad does not take into account the emergence, popularity and influence of the late Ayatollah Muhammad Sadiq al-Sadr, who was assassinated together with his two elder sons in Najaf in 1999. The case of Sadiq al-Sadr, or al-Sadr II, merits consideration.

In the wake of the execution of Muhammad Baqir al-Sadr in 1980, a cousin of his, Muhammad Sadiq al-Sadr, was claimed to have been 'appointed' by the government as an Iraqi *marja'*. Between 1980–90, al-Sadr II was very active in recruiting emulators and building webs of deputies and helpers. While his activities, at first, were pedagogical, at a later stage he took on organizational, charitable tasks with a militant tone.

This may have created a fifth militant centre in Najaf. Not only did al-Sadr II constitute during his life a formidable rival centre *vis-à-vis* militant Iraqi groups based in and patronized by Iran, but he continued to pale their influence even after his death.

His rise during the 1980s and 1990s has been controversial. Keen on preserving and aggravating the ethnic divide within the clerical class, the Ba'th government was in favour of an Arab line of *marja'ism*. In their eyes, Kho'i and his successor Sistani were both Persians. The Ba'th government may well have made proxy efforts to create a rival Arab Shi'ite centre. But al-Sadr II could, practically, neither oppose nor endorse such attempts.

His attitude, however, proved hostile to the government in the long run. In his first years of clerical headship, which coincided with a nation devastated by war and sanctions, he seemed much more inclined to otherworldliness. He reinstated the Friday prayers, a heresy by mainstream Shi'ite standards. But he was acting in a totally new situation where and when the Ba'th socialist-hegemonic ideology was in a shambles, the ruling regime itself having lost both its uncontested hegemony and its oil wealth, in order to ensure both submission and buy out consent. Much of the state-provided free services were suspended or commercialized; heavy taxes were also reintroduced for the first time in thirty years; inflation soared to around 24,000 percent(between 1991–96). The modern-educated middle strata, which constituted some 56 percent of the urban population, suffered heavily. Their salaried sections were virtually reduced to pauperism.

In an atmosphere of uncertainty, religious sentiments grew sharper. Stronger still was the need for sources of material support. Al-Sadr II managed to reconnect the Najaf clerical world with urban *milieux* and rural tribal domains. His networks of deputies and emulators fared wide and deep. His charitable services served scores of townships and large city quarters. In few years, he could muster tens of thousands of followers, admirers and sympathizers. Photographs and eyewitness accounts of his Friday sermons show massive crowds of a quarter of a million, a scene reminiscent of the Tehran Friday prayers during the first years of the 1979 Revolution. With the growth of his followers, he discarded his cautious and timid stand. Sensing the new menace, the Ba'th government cracked down on his vast networks – notably those in tribal domains – as well as curtailing the scope of his freedom, finally liquidating him together with his two sons.

Grieved by the loss, great masses of the Iraqi diaspora observed his memory. Perhaps the greatest and most emotive mass grief was evident among Iraqis in Iran, much to the dismay of SAIRI chairman Muhammad Baqir al-Hakim and his entourage, who were physically assaulted by angry crowds when they made infamous remarks against al-Sadr II, reiterating their old claim that he had been a government agent.

The assassination of al-Sadr II brought the Iraqi government back to square one in their tense relation with autonomous, institutionalized and popular, Shi'ite religiosity. If the government allegedly supported al-Sadr II as a calculated measure to mend fences with the Iraqi Shi'is in general and the al-Sadr family in particular in order to harness religion in their service, then this measure proved disastrous.

The legacy of al-Sadr II is embedded inside Iraq; it may vigorously outlive that of others.

TEN

'Ashura and the Arba'in: Popular Culture and the Politicizing of Redemptive Suffering

In the previous chapters we have seen that Shi'ite clerical culture is based on the text, sacred laws, canonical norms, methodological niceties and noble lineage of an elitist literate stratum akin, *mutatis mutandis*, to the Weberian typology of ethical religion. This class has been in constant decline; it produces militancy and its autonomy has potentially militant tendencies and divisive impact.[1]

Popular forms of religiosity, by contrast, present a Durkheimian model of community self-reflection, a cultural discourse imbued with powerful meta-historical narratives, paradigms and symbols.[2] Their major forms are ritual and rite, which play various social, spiritual, salvational, ethical, aesthetic and political roles in which the community reflects itself, reasserts its group solidarity and collective memory and mirrors its reality and the tensions it encounters in the Durkheimian sense of the term.[3]

Both the clerical class with its canonical-textual culture and the urban Shi'ite middle classes with their modern ideologies and structures may utilize these rituals as conduits of mass politics. Under the current Ba'th regime, the earliest mass popular opposition in the Arab urban areas flowed from the Arba'in pilgrimage to Karbala in 1977 (see Part Four). Secularization notwithstanding, participation in the Arba'in never waned. Contrary to many predictions,[4] participation in the pilgrimages massively increased. In 1913, the number of visitors to Karbala for the Arba'in commemoration reached 200,000.[5] Less than half were Iraqis. That is to say, the pilgrims were around 5 percent of a population of 2 million. By contrast, in 1995 the number of pilgrims was reportedly[6] 2.5 million, with no foreign participation, or 12 percent of the population (rounded to 20 million).

Shi'is mark a host of different occasions which are centred primarily on the first and third Imams, Ali and Hussain: the 'Ashura ritual, the Arba'in pilgrimage, Ali's birthday pilgrimage, Id al-Ghadir, Id al-Zahara. The most important are 'Ashura ('Ten Days') and the Arba'in pilgrimage to Karbala. Compared to Iran, the religious calendar in Iraq is relatively small and the level of participation and social organization is slight.

Below, we shall study the structure of two major rituals, 'Ashura and Arba'in, to examine the roles of different social actors involved in two towns, Twaireej and Daghara.[7]

The Example of Twaireej

The town of Twaireej, it seems, originated in the second half of the 19th century, possibly in 1869. A clan called the Zahhaf, allied through marriage to the Qazwini noble family (*sayyids*), settled there. The 19th century was a period of increased settlement of nomadic tribes across the Euphrates valley. The fertile soil and wealth of tributaries and canals turned the area into a garden of fruits, fields for cereals and tobacco crops.[8]

As the name indicates, Twaireej is the diminutive form of *tarij*, a rural pronunciation of the classical word: *tariq*, i.e. route. Indeed, Twaireej has been a trade route of vital importance for the countryside of the southwest, linking it with Baghdad via Hilla, or with Karbala and even beyond. It became the storehouse of agricultural products produced by its rural surroundings. In 1950, for example, the town had more than thirty flour mills with 1,500 seasonal workers. Tobacco was the other important item on its trading list. With commercial advance, the population grew from 6,800 in 1946 to 30,000 in the early 1960s, that of its mayoralty from 100,000 to 180,000.[9]

Government administration and services were gradually introduced, and with them the town acquired a new element in its social structure: the administrators' quarter, as opposed to the quarters of the traditional folk (artisans of all sorts). Unlike other small provincial towns or villages, the rural peasants' mud huts on its outskirts have long disappeared (compare with Daghara).[10]

Local Solidarities, Social Actors

Twaireej is situated on both banks of the original Euphrates. On the east bank there is one quarter, called the Sub Saghir (Smaller Side) or Tunbi. The western side is called the Sub Kabir (Large Side). It is divided into four quarters (*mahallas*): Sayyid Hussain, Sheikh Hamza, Mahram Aisha and Gass. The first three *mahallas* are named after notable patron families. The last is impersonal and indicates that the quarter is newly built.

The 'Ashura ten-day ritual commences on the first *hijra* year in the Sub Kabir. There are four assemblies or *majlis 'aza'* unevenly shared by these four neighbourhoods. The first is in the Sayyid Hussain quarter at the house of Aziz Wali; the second is 'Aza' al-Anbar in the Gass quarter; the third is 'Aza' Sayyid Hamza in the Sheikh Hamza quarter and the fourth is 'Aza' albu Abud in the

186

same neighbourhood. In the early 1960s there had been a fifth *majlis* organized by leftists in the Gass quarter. Each *'aza'* is named after the patron of the quarter or the quarter itself, a symbol of the communitarian nature of the ritual.[11]

The actors in the ritual are, first, the patrons. They are *wujaha*, notables or *sayyids* who by dint of status, wealth or both organize and supervise the assembly, *majlis*. By assuming these roles, they reinforce their leadership status in the community, implement their pledges towards their Imams (often their ancestors), enhance their trade and commerce and win the consent and respect of their community.

In Twaireej, as in other places, the patrons have traditional occupations practised by their families for generations. The Sayyid Hussain assembly was sponsored by Wa'li, a barber; the Anbar *majlis*, by a mercantile extended family trading in meat. The third *majlis* was organized by Hajj Mahmud, a coffeehouse owner; the fourth, by a small trader.

Latent competition among the sponsors surfaces only when there are two different *majlis* in one and the same quarter, reflecting conflicting tribal origins or trade interests.

The sponsor provides a space for the assembly, a pulpit for reciting. In summer or spring, the majlis is held in the open; in winter, a large tent is usually erected. The furniture and other logistics are provided by the sponsor.

The second group involved is the reciters, *rawzakhan* (a Persian term) and the chanter, *radud*. Their crucial role in popular religiosity notwithstanding, this group has seldom been studied. The forerunners of the reciters and chanters are the wandering poets who roamed marketplaces from the time of Buyids (11th century) to chant their verse praising the Imams, thronged by random audiences who would toss coins at them by way of reward.[12] The present-day reciters and chanters are generally but not exclusively professional. The reciter, *rawzakhan*, is usually a *sayyid* or a mullah of lower rank called *momen* (believer), an idiom linking them to the lower stratum of clerics. This class of reciters resides in the shrine cities, the 'Atabat. Their main function is to relate historical narratives of the Imams, preach their ethical and moral lessons and evoke grief and sadness over their tragic fate. Their services are sought after in the Muharram period, or even on other occasions, and Shi'ite communities vie with each other to command the presence of Najafi and Karbala figures.

The reciter's calling is an artistic one inherited through the family, which accumulates expertise, texts and traditions. Reciters descend from traditional families and some who are not *sayyids* take traditional occupations: tailors, cloth traders coffeeshop owners. They form an informal caste-like social group. Some enjoy great fame and their success ensures greater demand. Al-Wa'ili, a renowned reciter, is sought after by patrons from Kuwait and other oil-rich Gulf countries.

In the case of Twaireej, Sayyid Qassim al-Khatib was a reciter who enjoyed semi-monopoly status in the 1960s. In addition to the *khums* accruing to him as a *sayyid*, al-Khatib gained much from his religious services in Muharram. Like his father and elder brother, he inherited this profession and was schooled at home, where he acquired a wealth of texts, oral narratives and agitation techniques.

The *rawzakhan* is an agitator/propagandist of the first order, an agent who integrates historical narratives with present traumas, weaving them in a web of communal grievances. His capacity for mass agitation extends his social and political roles. Reciters are more often than not warned against playing with double metaphors in any potential anti-government agitation. Secret agents deliver such warnings and keep a watchful eye on the performance. At one event, the reciter advised the audience of such threats, much to the embarrassment of pro-government figures.

The reciter is potentially instrumental in conveying sociopolitical grievances.[13] He is held in high esteem by the traditional segments of the community, as the example of Twaireej shows, simply because poor traditional folk conceive of him as a symbol and agent relating them to the ideal worlds of the Imam. Yet he never escapes the sarcastic humour of the newly educated groups, notably high school and university students or modern-educated, middle-class intellectuals to whom he is a thing of the past, a symbol of parasitic living and a social anachronism. Such disdain may also be harboured and, at times, implicitly or explicitly expressed by doctors of religion who belittle the false or exaggerated historical accounts delivered by the reciter or his assistant, the chanter. This dual criticism shows the tension between popular religiosity and high religious culture on one hand, and popular and modern culture on the other, despite the fact that the religious culture of the three segments overlaps in many aspects.[14]

The second actor is the chanter (*radud*). The reciter mixes historical accounts and ethical preaching of scriptural Islam with expressive religiosity; but the chanter is a representative of popular culture in a pure form. He is not concerned with preaching ethics, deriving moral lessons or matters of legitimacy. He is a singer who functions to evoke and regulate grief. His instruments are his fine voice, folkloric verse and mourning techniques. Unlike reciters, chanters charge higher fees, ID100 per performance compared with ID20–30 for reciters. (The examples are from Twaireej in the early 1960s and 1970s, and may have local significance only.) The *radud* is neither a *sayyid* nor a resident of the shrine cities, but is from the same town. *sayyids* disdain chanters (and their occupation) as men of low social rank: their only talent is a melodic voice.

Among the best chanters in Twaireej area was Khidhir al-Sa'dawi, whose son Yas Khidhir is one of the celebrities of Iraqi song today. Jasim Abu Zerida is another. Both traded, like the rest of their group, on traditional occupations; the former was an owner of a wheat store, the other a shopkeeper.

The last actor in the ritual is the community itself. The part it plays will be discussed in the context of the performance of the ritual.

Structure of the Muharram Ritual

The Muharram ritual is a cultural discourse in which various visual symbols, sounds, narratives, performances, smells and food are integrated in a complex whole. The ritual builds a spiritual edifice from bricks of mundane objects and cultural paradigms. In the ritual, participants 'encounter the symbolic universe that underpins and gives shape to their deeply held beliefs'.[15]

The ritual of Muharram as practised in Twaireej is analytically divisible into various elements:

(i)   visual manifestations of the ceremony;
(ii)   the assembly (*majlis 'aza*'), with reciting, chanting and chest-beating;
(iii)   processions (*mawakib*);
(iv)   self-flagellation and head-cutting;
(v)   performance of passion plays (*tashabih*);
(vi)   pilgrimage to the shrine of the Imam.

Each aspect has a symbolic function to fulfill the three moments of the ritual:[16]

(i)   The separation of participants from their social structure;
(ii)   The creation of a transformative phase, a realm removed from actual time and space in which the social status of the participants is thrown into ambiguity and they are transferred to a state of 'collective obedience to a higher authority'.[17] This state produces a sense of equality and comradeship, a *communitas*, transcending social schisms and differentiation of rank, position, age, kinship, gender and the like;
(iii)   A re-aggregation of the participants, or the return from the liminal space back to normalcy.

Through this emotional journey change is effected. By their flight to the meta-historical realm of Karbala, where the battle of Imam Hussain took place some fourteen centuries ago, or by their direct performance of this episode, participants reassert their loyalty to the sacred house of the Prophet. Through it they reconfirm their communal solidarity; achieve what they believe to be forgiveness for their lapses; feel morally improved; and gain more confidence in acquiring powerful support for their worldly callings. We shall now discuss some of these aspects and the actors involved in them.

Visual Manifestations

The Muharram ritual is observed by raising the colours and banner bearing the name of the sponsor's family. Green, black and red flags are hoisted on the roofs. The green banner is the symbol of *sayyids*, those of noble lineage. They not only denote descent but also assert kinship with the saintly Imams, the continuity of this lineage and the cause they represent as cherished and kept alive. Black is the symbol of sorrow and grief; it denotes allegiance and belonging. Red is the sign of the blood of their slain Imam, a coded sense of the injustice, which fell on the household of the Prophet; it also signifies the murderous brutality of the Umayyad army.

This visual appearance of banners and flags is accompanied by the community members themselves putting on long black shirts in a general display of grief. Another visual symbol of great importance is water pots or water tanks. These are covered with black cloth and carry mottoes referring to Hussain and thirst. Water in Middle Eastern civilization, in the words of A. Exupéry, is 'not just necessary for life but is life itself.' The meta-historical accounts of the battle of Hussain stress the theme of water as part of the episode. Hussain and his family were denied access to water in the battle. Providing water free in the streets is a reminder of the ordeal of the Imam, which accentuates the sense of injustice and helps set the scene for the pending meta-historical journey. This is the major visual prelude of the ritual.

The Majlis *(Assembly)*

The second part is the *majlis*, which forms a daily gathering of the small community of quarter members. This assembly is the focal point of successively integrated elements: the narratives (reciting) of the episode, featuring the reciter, the *rawzakhan*; the *radud*, who usually chants mournful hymns; and a group of young male adults performing chest-beating and/or self-flagellation in accompaniment to the *radud*'s chanting. These three elements of the *majlis* have the major function of creating the meta-historical realm of Karbala for the audience, who comprise the mourning community of the elderly and young plus segregated females, all witnesses to the looming calamity. The narratives and chanting create this meta-historical space by employing and deploying such terms as symbolic cultural paradigms which relate to social relations, cultural goals, outlooks, values or patterns of belief.[18]

The *majlis* begins with a patterned structure: the stage is a rectangular shape. The pulpit at the centre is the token of the sacred history. Opposite to it, the elderly with higher status are seated on benches; in their capacity as the leaders of the community they display their allegiance to the sacred figures. Poorer individuals are located on both sides of the notables. The former usually sit cross-legged on the carpet. Youngsters stand on both sides. Females are kept at a distance, either standing in a remote corner with their bodies veiled, or viewing the scene from more convenient places, the roofs of their nearby houses.

The arrangement has also another significance and aim: to focus collective attention on the drama so as to dissolve all segmentary borders and create a whole body of mourners, a *communitas* unified in pain if not in social reality.

The *majlis* starts at sunset and continues for two to three hours during the first nine days. On the ninth day, the ceremony goes on until the following morning. The *rawzakhan* employs narratives to retell the mythological history of the Imams to reinforce the community's devotion by evoking their tears. The narrative appeals to the imagination of the audience with the assistance of the visual symbols surrounding the *majlis*, and through the employment of the community's cultural paradigms. The stories are known to every individual taking part in the ritual, whether as performer or spectator. It is the journey of Hussain to Karbala to regain his deserved caliphate. He is betrayed by supporters; outflanked and outnumbered by a brutal enemy; cut off from water; left almost alone with a few loyal supporters, a stranger in a hostile land with his children and sister. Opposite to the themes of thirst, loneliness, betrayal and the fragility of the women and children, there stand in bold relief courage, knightly manhood, defiance, adherence to rightful principles and martyrdom. With the themes of justice, imamate, sacred rights, acceptance of God's ordained fate and purity of soul, there are intertwined themes from everyday life, motives of thirst, brotherhood, fatherly and daughterly devotion, love, death and marriage.

As part of the complex of the ritual, narratives build human contact between the present and the past. History is fused the reality of the here and now. The border is crossed, superseded, and the holy figures are encountered.

The reciter mixes his classical Arabic presentation with local dialect and employs grief-evoking melodies called *nawa'i* or the melodic quartet known as *abuthiya*. The classical prose is the symbol of history; the sad tunes, of the present; they are joined together in emotive moments in which sorrow, grief and the shedding of tears are concentrated on the fate of Imam Hussain. More often than not, the reciter consciously includes events from the real life of the community to weave his version of historical narratives. The end result sought by the narratives is the extraction of real tears from real anguish. Tears indicate that the phase of liminal transformation has commenced; they function as an Aristotelian catharsis, a purifying salvation. In the words of Fischer: 'One wishes to weep for the martyr of Karbala so that on the Judgement Day he will intercede and one's sins will be weighed more lightly and with compassion.'[19] The more one is able 'to weep with repentance, humility and regard for Hussain', the greater the return.[20]

The transformative phase is reinforced by the chanting of the *radud*. His main function is to lead and direct the act of chest-beating, that self-inflicted pain which stresses the sense of repentance, injustice and readiness to sacrifice for the Imam, and carries the state of collective sorrow to its highest emotive point. The chanter uses only folkloric verse in local dialect. His performance is done in two phases. The first is called the *ga'da*, i.e. sitting still. The rhythm of the chanting is slow and melancholic. This phase is a sort of warmup, a prelude to the chest-beating or *latmiya*. As the tempo increases, a point is reached when the chanter gives a signal to a group of young men, adolescents and even young boys to start. Stripped to the waist, they stand in a circle and start beating their chests with the open palms of their hands. The elderly audience and the women symbolically emulate the act. Their participation generally takes the form of weeping. The chest-beating reaches its climax with the rising tempo of the chanter. The end of this act marks the end of the daily ritual.

The drama is divided into sub-themes and sub-plots covering the first nine days. Parts of the themes delineate the individual fate of Imam Hussain's kin. Episodes involving Hussain's daughter Sukaina, his sister Zainab, his son Muhammad Qassim and his half-brother 'Abbas permeate the narratives. The crossing of the border between the sacred and the mundane, the sublime universe of the Imams and the here and now of the community, is manifestly displayed in these episodes.

The seventh day of the Muharram ritual in Twaireej is focused on the fate of Qassim. This day is named the Day of Qassim (Yaum Qassim) or Qassim's Wedding. To heighten the dramatic sense of the pending battle and near-collective massacre of the male members of Hussain's household, the wedding of his elder son Qassim has been constructed by popular imagination and incorporated into the body of various narratives. In contrast to other days, the wedding is performed rather than told: a handsome young actor is dressed in white, in the best of traditional fashions, mounts a beautiful horse and is flanked by two rows of silent boys each holding a tray with lit candles and adorned with myrtle. The ornamented dress, horse, candles and myrtle are all visual signs of joy, usually seen in the community's weddings themselves. Yet, these symbols of bliss and joy are mixed with antithetical signs. The white dress is both a symbol of purity and of death, since it resembles the shroud of the dead, whereas the darkness which envelops the chorus and the knight-bridegroom, conveys the sense of uncertainty, doom and gloom.

The knight rides through the alleys of the quarter, beaming with happiness. The public greets him with cheers, with women sounding a cheerful trill. In the performance, the bridegroom is not aware of the bloody fate awaiting him – unlike the community of spectators. The coming tragedy of the bloody Lorcan wedding catches the audience in its grip. They toss candy and sugar-coated nuts at the bridegroom (sometimes even coins), as they usually do in marriage ceremonies; but this time they sob and weep at what they know will be a short-lived, unfulfilled happiness. This accentuates the sense of injustice. Members of the community identify in this drama their own ordeal: incarcerated young activists, the death of others under torture or even the premature loss of babies or infants. Thus the performance not only brings the holy family to life but also emotionally and physically makes the community part of this noble household. The reality of the community is incorporated into the fantasy of the drama. The imagined realm serves to reproduce the reality of the community. Both the sacred past and the worldly present intermingle and unite into one.

On the eighth evening the episode of 'Abbas is presented. Narrative is the medium for relating the story of 'Abbas, the courageous warrior, and conveying miraculous, ethical and moral themes. In the narratives observed in Twaireej and other localities, 'Abbas takes the image of a bold, dashing knight. Facing thousands of Umayyad troops, he insists on fighting though he is given the choice of safety by his brother. This loyalty is emphasized time and again to remind the community of the importance of blood belonging and solidarity.

Another theme is the drive of 'Abbas to get water to thirsty children in the besieged camp of Hussain. For their sake he risks his life. Thirst is employed also as a symbol of cruelty on part of the attacking troops who torture children, including infants. Water is a symbol of life itself. Nomads, peasants and provincial towns in their vicinity have a long history of devastation caused by drought, changing river courses, inter-tribal fighting over access to water sources, clashes between poor sharecropping peasants and their greedy sheikhly landlords over water. Due to its geographical situation, Najaf itself was deprived of water for centuries. All these collective memories are centred on this theme. Abbas's attempts to secure water for the children become a fight for the sake of life itself. His horsemanship and selfless endeavours bear much resemblance to the Bedouin values of courage and knighthood. His supernatural powers are also demonstrated. Miraculously, he fights with his left hand when his right hand has been severed. His sword fights for him, at his command, when his left arm receives a fatal blow.

'Abbas is a central figure in Shi'ite popular religiosity. His tomb, adjacent to that of his brother, Hussain, is venerated and visited. 'Abbas is not an Imam, and so not infallible like one. He has no power to intercede in the hereafter, but can inflict punishment on sinners – notably those who betray a trust or an oath.[21] 'Abbas is depicted as a hot-tempered guardian of oaths. His name is used for oaths by peasants in courts of law (criminal or otherwise).

Social Interaction

The audience is divided into the respectable elderly, younger spectators and segregated female viewers. Although they are all detached during the ritual into a unifying space, they soon re-aggregate the moment it is over. Indeed, when the *majlis* concludes, members of the community chat, smile or discuss family and business affairs. An atmosphere of social openness prevails.

The sponsor's social status is enhanced and his prestige augmented as more people from the community pay their respects to him in recognition of his rank. His business, whatever that might be, is also bolstered. The social and economic rewards he enjoys may, at times, surpass those sought in the hereafter. But social prestige also brings a degree of envy. The donation campaign launched at the end of the ritual is meant to share with the others the social prestige the sponsor derives from the occasion and, of course, spread the financial burden across the community. A member of the patron's family, his elder son, calls loud and clear for contributions. A tray is offered to collect notes, coins or even gold and silver ornaments. Contributions are made either as votive offerings or to express social standing through this display of public generosity. Payments are severely scrutinized by the public. As the name and amount are publicly given, the community reacts favourably or unfavourably. Unwillingness on the part of a well-to-do family to give a eater amount is frowned upon as a sign of tight-fistedness. A donation that is greater than that expected is regarded as a sign of pomposity. Reactions are direct and sincere. Differences aside, the donation is an assertion of the collective finances and catharsis.

When the collection is completed, the company relaxes. Rigid restrictions on male-female encounters or conversation weaken or dissolve. Girls move out and about. Young men may approach any house for a drink (water, tea) and liaise with the women. The limits expand each day until the last, ninth night, when women enjoy an unwritten right to move about freely all night long until morning. The occasion provides a space for young men and women to have brief, undetected or unpunished romantic encounters.

Chest-beaters represent the active part of the community. Their participation in the ritual is a symbol of local solidarity, a display of courage or votive offering on behalf of the family, besides interest in female attraction.

'Ashura is a local rite and Twaireej has its own distinct tradition. On the ninth night, the local ceremonies unite together in one body to assert the identity of the town as a whole. Total darkness prevails. Red lanterns appear in rows, their carriers chanting with a theatrical soft, sad melody: '*Ya Hussain, ya mazlum*' ('O Hussain, o the victim'). Lamenters march from different quarters to greet each other. Crowds with banners and lanterns dotting darkness march to the house of Qazwini, the founder of the town. The congregation pays tribute to the living saints, then marches to the tomb of Sayyid Hashim, the symbol of sainthood for the town. Banners are fixed at his grave and the crowd returns to the living saints, the Qazwinis, who provide the leadership for the mass delegation of pilgrims to Karbala at dawn.

The tenth of Muharram is the final day of 'Ashura for all Shi'ite communities. It is generally observed with processions (*mawakib*) of groups practising self-flagellation or head-cutting. As soon as the *mawakib* are over, another expressive ceremony takes place: the passion play. All this takes place locally.

Twaireej is the exception. The Twaireej pilgrims are called 'jugglers' because they go to Karbala on foot, some 24 km. Organized in contingents from each quarter, a great many people proceed with banners and flags to Karbala and then regroup behind a *sayyid* from the Qazwini family. After saying the noon prayers, the *sayyid* gives the signal for the charge, and the pilgrims run to the centre of the shrine.

The *mawakib* and the *tashabih* (passion plays) are based on visual representations: banners, marching contingents, chanting teams, beating drums, groups of men lashing their backs with chains or wounding their heads with machetes, the image of horses with arrows fixed on the saddle, the cries of children, the burning tents of the Hussain camp – all these scenes present a visual drama for the wailing crowds.

The Twaireej pilgrims are hosted by Karbala families. Food and tea are served. The meal is a speciality: crushed meat and cooked chickpeas, a dish desired by one of the women from Hussain's family. City and quarter borders dissolve. Random grouping is indicative of a unique collective spirit prevailing at these moments of re-aggregation.

Cultural Cleavage: the Daghara Example

Daghara, a large village or small rural-urban town some 18 km north of Diwaniya, presents a unique example of how Shi'ite culture – while shared by different segments – is differently conceived. Attitudes towards the symbolic, visual narratives and performances of the 'Ashura ritual vary greatly.

Originally, Daghara was a centre for pastoral nomadic tribes who adopted a sedentary way of life. They settled on the east bank of the river. On the west bank, a government quarter was built with a town hall, police station, schools, an administrators' residential quarter and a few other, modern buildings. The transformation of the village from pastoral to sedentary conditions, coupled with the effective presence of the central state authority, produced three different yet interrelated segments living in a state of quasi-equilibrium. As observed by Robert Fernea[22] these are, first of all, the civil servants and *effendis* (administrators) the newly rising and expanding modern middle classes. They live in a separate quarter, have their own social realm.

The second segment is *ahl al-suq*, the market people, who consist of traditional middle and lower strata, small traders, merchants, craftsmen of various types, shopkeepers, coffeehouse owners, butchers, pedlars and the like. They reside in a *mahalla* (quarter) of their own, separated from the *effendis*. In fact, the marketplace itself separates the two quarters. The third quarter is on the east bank of the river and is the tribesmen's quarter.

Each segment has its focal point of association. For the administrators it is their club; for the market people, their coffeehouse. The tribesmen have their *mudhif* (collective guesthouse). The cultural differences between these segments are not only invisible cultural modes of thinking and values, but also visible ones, apparent in their dress and lifestyles. Each group has its kinship and/or occupational bonds.

As Fernea observes, 'intragroup relations are not based on economic self-interest alone': the people of Daghara, despite their socioeconomic differences, 'share a background of belief in the traditional culture of Islam'.[23] This shared belief is seen in the 'manner in which religious ritual is organized and expressed. The entire community is involved'.[24] But group differences are too large to ignore, and Fernea points out that 'at the same time, the *independence* and *identity* of each group ... is preserved and even *reinforced*'.[25]

This is apparent in the different modes of observation of the 'Ashura ritual. Fernea remarks that the effendis, the administrators, neither organize nor observe the ritual. The tribesmen dedicate their religious zeal not to 'Ashura but to Ramadhan, the holy month of fasting. Only the market people organize and observe the 'Ashura ritual. Other observations in Shi'ite neighbourhoods in Baghdad, such as Karrada Sharqiya, Thawra and Kamp Silaikh, demonstrate a similar pattern, namely that the ritual emanates from traditional segments.

These differences are elaborated as follows: ' ... The people of Daghara by no means take full advantage of the opportunities of expressive ceremonialism; certain Shi'a ceremonies are observed'.[26] The *sheikh* of the al-Shabana tribe in Daghara

> ... used to engage the service of a reader [for the *karaya*] for the entire month of Ramadan who would proceed to tell one episode after the other from the lives of the Imams ... These readings were attended primarily by tribesmen, but every night or so, men from the market and effendis from the government would stop by, perhaps exchanging a few words with the shaykh after the proceedings were over.[27]

Administrators do not sponsor any such religious services or recitals, but their wives might entertain other women of the community by hosting a recital assembly, *karaya*. The 'Ashura ceremony is *entirely organized and promoted by the market people*. The details:

> 'Ashura, the tenth of Muharram ... is in Daghara the occasion for the most dramatic public religious ceremony of the year. At this time, several hundred men and boys, *largely from the market families*, participate in the *ta'ziya* (also called *subaya*), mourning of the death the religious hero which takes the form of public self-flagellation. Groups of men stripped to the waist or wearing black robes cut open in back, march in procession, rhythmically chanting and beating themselves with lengths of chain and leather whips. Comparably arranged groups of young boys often follow behind the groups of men, learning the chants and imitating the actions.[28] (Italics added.)

Although a segment of their own, they are subdivided on the basis of the quarter: 'The individual teams who make up the *ta'ziya* usually come from the same neighbourhood or street within the residential area occupied by the market families of Daghara.'[29]Tribesmen, on the other hand, have a different attitude. They 'were not observed to participate in either the local *ta'ziya* or in the Daghara *'aza'*, the delegation teams participating in the grand *ta'ziya* in Karbala.'[30] The sheikhs would have supported such ritual 'if this were considered quite in keeping with the public demeanour of a proper tribesman'.[31]

The market people nevertheless try to engage the whole community in their ritual. Their 'Ashura procession tours Daghara, passing along the main streets in both the market and *effendis*' neighbourhoods, crossing the Daghara canal to the tribal settlement and ending in the tribal guesthouse where they are served tea.

The administrators take part only in the 'rather formal occasion of 'Id el Fitr at the end of Ramadan fast'.[32]

The Arba'in Pilgrimage: Pan-Shi'ite Identity

The Angel Gabriel had advised Muhammad and Muhammad advised his daughter Fatima that one of her sons would be slain the way Hussain was slain and that his tomb, around which a city of great fame would be built, would gain world repute. Events did occur as in the prophecy. One of the companions of the apostle, Jabir [Ibn Abdulah al-Ansari], came forty days after the horrific massacre to dignify the grave of the martyred Imam. That is because Muhammad had told him: Hussain will be killed and buried in Karbala; after forty days of his burial the visitation to his tomb should begin. Jabir's was the first visitation to this soil. The history of Karbala began from that moment.[33]

The pilgrimage to the shrine city of Karbala occurs forty days from the conclusion of the 'Ashura ritual. Like other rituals, this pilgrimage has transformative effects. It is believed to be instrumental in evoking the Imam's mediating powers to improve the well-being of the pilgrims in this world, forgive their lapses and grant them rewards in the hereafter. Pilgrims seek cures, protection of their property and children and fulfilment of their personal wishes in general. The personal status of the pilgrim is also enhanced among his or her peers and in his or her own community; he or she is called *zayir* (pilgrim; literally, 'visitor to the shrine city'). Votive offerings, supplicants, prayers and blessings are part of the pilgrimage. In this experience, pilgrims can only cross the borders to the supra-natural realm of the saintly Imams by means of special recitations and prayers.[34]

197

Liaisons with the saintly universe are monopolized by the shrine city and its various strata of religious functionaries. The direct ritual of the pilgrimage is the monopoly of a low stratum of mullahs who guide the participants. Shi'ite religious education encourages pilgrimage and raises it to equal footing with the pilgrimage to Mecca. One prayer in the shrine mosque is said to equal one thousand prayers elsewhere. The soil itself is sacred, considered to produce magical and miraculous effects; to touch the soil is to affect a physical contact with dust trodden on by saints. It is as if the heavenly potency and protective powers of the Imams can penetrate the body of pilgrims through this contact with soil, the shrine itself or even the gates of the tomb.

The pilgrimage is also an event of social, economic and political importance. Unlike Muharram, the Arba'in pilgrimage is centred on Karbala as the seat of the Imam. Shi'is at large organize themselves in teams and contingents (delegations) and travel to Karbala to assert a collective cause. They go beyond the limits of their localities into the wider universe of the shrine city as a focus of pan-Shi'ite allegiance. Local communities become peripheries, so to speak, whereas Karbala (on other occasions, Najaf) is the command centre. Hence the pilgrimage is instrumental in building an all-Shi'ite identity going beyond the local solidarities of the rural areas and provincial towns.[35] The unifying effect is enhanced by the collective experience of mourning.

The pilgrimage reflects 'the tension of the people with their social reality'.[36] Through the sacralization of the Imams, pilgrims search for 'ideal relations with ideal figures' and this experience enables people to 'examine the relation between power and justice'.[37]

In social and political terms, pilgrimages are potentially explosive. It has been observed that the less institutional politics, the more mass mobilization through rituals (pilgrimage included); the weaker modern social identities, the stronger communal ones, the more militant these rituals become. Oscillations in the number of pilgrims may reflect changing circumstances, which may encourage or inhibit participation in these rituals.

Since the early 1970s, pilgrimage rituals have been heavily regulated by the security service. Delegates are tightly scrutinized: a head of delegation must be elected. His registration includes family and residence details. The whereabouts of all visiting delegates is fixed and controlled by the security forces. Apart from pilgrimage permits, video and other types of camera are installed to record all visitors to the shrine cities, Karbala and Najaf, on these occasions. During the Iraqi uprising in March 1991, the rebels in Karbala confiscated hundreds of videotapes recording every move by pilgrims.[38]

It was during the Marad al-Ras pilgrimage in February 1977 that the delegations travelling from Najaf to Karbala, running into tens of thousands, were agitated by a group of young organizers of popular rituals to stage the largest and, until then, the most powerful anti-Ba'th mass protest. This movement will be analysed in the coming chapters.

PART FOUR

Shi'ite Islamism and the Ba'th

ELEVEN

From Peaceful Protest to Bloody Confrontation

The First Phase: 1968–78

The era of the Ba'th, which began in 1968, was decisively new in many respects for Shi'ite activism. The tensions building up between the two led to a series of confrontations, in which the three circles of Shi'ism participated – the supreme *marja'*, the *qiyadat husayniya* of popular rituals and the Da'wa Party in between, as a bridge uniting and transcending the two.

The strongest defiance, however, came neither from the *marja'iya* (the religious authority), nor the Da'wa (the political movement), but surprisingly from young Najafi apprentice organizers of the popular ritual. Although their defiance was spontaneous, structurally fragile and lacking self-sustained continuity, it surprised the Da'wa as much as it shook the Ba'th regime. In this chapter we shall examine the circumstances of this incident.

Four major areas of conflict developed under the Ba'th. First, the secularization drive by the state was mainly directed at the autonomous Shi'ite religious establishment. Second, the totalitarian Ba'th state reproduced the ethnic, religious and communal disequilibrium in terms of political representation and participation and the uneven distribution and allocation of economic benefits. Third was the ideo-cultural clash between the *étatiste*, pan-Arab, social-nationalist ideology of the ruling Ba'th and the universalist or particularist Islamic discourse developed by Shi'ite Islamic groups in the manner of the Da'wa model. The fourth area was regional politics, that is, relations between Iraq and Iran which – except for a brief interval of cooperation (1975–88) – were tense, and led eventually to a protracted eight-year war.[1]

Totalitarian pressures, secularization, coerced Ba'thization, the command economy and other factors hit various lower, middle and upper Shi'ite classes, lay groups and clerics alike. Under such circumstances, a common base for rapprochement among sundry Shi'ite groups was created. As they were alienated from the Communist and Ba'th parties either because of a clash of social interests (the mercantile) or for ideological or political reasons (rejection of secular ideologies), pressures re-channelled all actual and potential social and political activism among different Shi'ite groups, mainly but not exclusively towards the grand *marja'* Muhsin al-Hakim and the Da'wa.

But al-Hakim was too cautious and hesitant, while the Da'wa had major flaws in the inner, subjective sense. First, the Da'wa had neither a vision of the political battles it should wage nor the solid and tested organizational structures to match such tasks. Its second defect was its proxy or implicit involvement in the Iran-Iraq struggle. Indeed, Batatu contends that the Da'wa was 'tainted' by collaboration with the Shah's regime and that some of its leaders had links with the Iran of the Shah.[2] Thirdly, the Da'wa was facing, as has been shown in Part One, a new and formidable Ba'th Party Leviathan, backed by handsome oil revenues, strong security and military apparatuses and mass party and popular welfare programmes.

To compensate for these weaknesses, the Da'wa tried, without success, to involve the *marja'ism* of Muhsin al-Hakim in its cause and to harness the potential for agitation offered by the Shi'ite popular rituals to its ends. But each component – al-Hakim, the Da'wa and the ritual organizers – fought separately.

We will look in detail at the three circles in turn:

(i)   the al-Hakim/Ba'th tension and collision (1968–70);
(ii)   the anti-Ba'th Da'wa agitation and the subsequent execution of Da'wa leading figures (1974–75);
(iii)   the eruption of the February 1977 Marad al-Ras demonstrations in Najaf and Karbala, known as the Intifadat Sufar.

Ayatollah al-Hakim versus the Ba'th

The totalitarian Ba'th state preyed on every autonomous component of society. The religious Shi'ite establishment, that is, the loose networks of Shi'ite centres of learning, *khums* networks and local community organizations, were no exception. The Shi'ite religious leadership, which in 1963 had some access to national leadership, in this period had none. The Ba'th leadership had fallen into predominantly Sunni hands. Inaccessibility exacerbated mutual mistrust. The regional struggle between Iraq and Iran, which also had a global East-West colouring, was crucial. Pan-Arabism in Iraq was always a source of alarm for Iran. From the early 1960s, the Shah had spared no effort in attempting to alienate Iraq from Egypt under Nasser.[3] Iranian hostility was aggravated by domestic changes in Iraq: the inclusion of the communists in the cabinet and the declaration of the March 1970 agreement for Kurdish autonomy. Both developments made uneasy reading in Tehran. The conclusion of the Soviet-Iraq treaty was another factor exacerbating Iraq-Iran tensions.[4]

While these developments were still in the making, Iran tried first to establish economic and political cooperation and discuss territorial disputes with the visiting Iraqi delegation in March 1969.[5] The failure of these attempts led to heightened tensions which were centred on border issues, the Shatt al-Arab waterway in particular. In the wake of three successive Iranian ultimatums, the Iranian embassy in Baghdad was notified that no Iranian navy personnel would be allowed on board vessels in this waterway. On 19 April Iran abolished the 1937 treaty, declaring that the tolls agreed under its terms would not be paid to Iraq and the Iraqi flag would not be raised on vessels sailing in the waters of the Shatt al-Arab. The situation was so tense that the two sides put their armed forces on full alert. Tehran, Abadan and other major Iranian cities were sandbagged.[6]

Border disputes had always been a proxy method of pursuing other, undeclared ends.[7] The escalation was a source of deep concern to the fragile Ba'th regime, which in retaliation unleashed a propaganda war against Iran. A decision was taken to 'comb out' all Iranian nationals in Iraq and deport them. As the official propaganda put the numbers of this group at half a million (a highly inflated figure) the flood of refugees would, the regime thought, put pressure on the Iranian economy and bring the Ba'th a wealth of confiscated property and assets.[8] The arrests and deportations began on 18 Sufar (7 May 1969), two days before the Arba'in pilgrimage to Karbala. Reaction to the measure in the shrine cities was severe and widespread. In protest, al-Hakim cut short his visit to Karbala and returned to Najaf, thereby fuelling mass protests.

To moderate the situation Hardan Tikriti, the minister of defence, was despatched to Najaf to meet al-Hakim and soften his position, or even enlist his mediation in the Iraq-Iran dispute. Tikriti reported the following:

> Instructions from the president were to negotiate with the *sheikh* [al-Hakim] on the Shatt al-Arab on the following basis: That Sheikh Muhsin al-Hakim should ask the Iranian government to withdraw its military units from Shatt al-Arab, adhere to the old treaty on the waterway; in exchange Iranian detainees would be released and deportation would be halted. We hoped that should the Iranian side decline we would launch a new, more successful propaganda campaign utilizing al-Hakim's great spiritual influence on the Iranian people.[9]

The mediating role requested of him was a sensitive issue for a clerical dignitary of al-Hakim's status. In the closed meeting which took place with the Ba'th Party's envoy in Najaf, al-Hakim offered a different vision. He is quoted as saying:

> No war can be won without a strong internal front; if such a condition is met, any government can fight the strongest of other nations. The Iranians in Iraq are not simply a migrant community; they are Iraqis by birth and

lineage but deprived of their Iraqi nationality by previous administrations. To deport them is not only a measure running contrary to any human principles but may also weaken the internal front.

On mediation with Iran, al-Hakim asked for an official letter signed by the president empowering him to undertake such a task. The demand was linked to other issues like the release of detainees, some 25,000 at that point. '... The president [al-Bakr], however, categorically declined to give the *sheikh* the authorization he asked for."[10] The demand the government made of al-Hakim was definitely provocative.[11]

Al-Hakim-Ba'th tensions were intensified by the uncovering of an Iranian-inspired plot to unseat the Ba'th. Methat al-Haj Sirri, an anti-Ba'th, pro-Western nationalist, appeared on television to 'confess' his involvement with the Shah. Some of his alleged accomplices were notable Shi'i figures. Mahdi al-Hakim, the son of Muhsin al-Hakim, was implicated and accused of collaborating with the Kurds who, according to the official point of view, were spying for the CIA.[12]

The disclosure of the alleged plot came on 20 January 1970, and dozens of individuals were sentenced to death and executed, including some Da'wa sympathizers – Mahdi al-Timimi, the director of the Shi'ite schools in Baghdad, retired general Muhsin al-Janabi, Muhammad Faraj and others.[13]

The Ministry of the Interior was then under the Ba'th military officer Salih Mahdi Ammash, a staunch sectarian and a person of limited horizon and tolerance; the security services were under Saddam Hussein. Both men vigorously resumed the anti-al-Hakim crusade.

Before as after the aborted al-Hakim mediation a host of measures aggravated the situation. First, the project to establish Kufa University, a scheme laid down by prominent Shi'i scholars and notables and backed by al-Hakim himself[14] was suspended. The funds raised for it, some ID 4.5 million, were confiscated.[15] Second, the deportation of persons officially designated as Iranian subjects – Kurdi Failis, i.e. Shi'i Kurds, or Arabs of Iranian origin residing in and around the holy cities – dislocated some 40,000 people. Since the officially recognized total number of Iranian nationals resident in Iraq at the time was 22,860,[16] the banishment must have included Iraqi Shi'is of Arab origin. Third, restrictions imposed on the centres of learning and the closure of the borders with Iran reduced the flow of pilgrims and seminarians thereby damaging the welfare of the shrine cities and weakening the position of the *ulama*. Fourth, the *hawza* in Najaf suffered a further blow when an old act exempting religious students from military service was abolished, removing an attraction which for decades had compensated these schools for their loss of appeal in other spheres.[17] Finally, Shi'i merchants suffered. The Ba'th imposed tight controls on foreign and domestic trade,[18] bringing the share of the state sector in the value added produced in retail and wholesale trades from 12.1 percent in 1968 to 51 percent in 1974.[19] By 1973 the state controlled 82 percent of foreign trade, compared to 42 percent before the Ba'th takeover.[20] In less than two years this proportion increased to 90 percent.[21]

A confrontational mood persisted in Najaf and beyond. Al-Hakim, it seemed, heeded the advice of his junior disciples, al-Sadr included, to organize a popular tour to put counter-pressure on the Ba'th. His first procession, from Najaf to Kazimiya in Baghdad, was interrupted by the authorities.[22] Delegates and crowds from different parts of the country visited al-Hakim to express allegiance. A special delegation representing the Da'wa Party included Sahib al-Dakhil, the actual leader of the Iraqi branch of the now pan-Islamic organization; Hassan Shubbar, Fakhrul Din Shustari and others recommended that Ayatollah al-Hakim take the initiative and issue a statement critical of the Ba'th policies.[23] They handed al-Hakim a list of demands among which were:

(i)   restoration of political freedom;
(ii)   freedom of the press;
(iii)   the lifting of restrictions imposed on the *hawza*s, the religious centres of learning in Najaf;
(iv)   the inclusion of the Ja'fari (Twelver) Shi'ite jurisprudence in the curriculum of state-run religious academies;
(v)   that opportunities for Shi'ite participation in the government be opened.[24]

These demands were partially echoed in a confidential letter, rather than a public statement, despatched by a group of *'ulama* to the Ba'th government. This was in line with the tactful, subtle style of al-Hakim. The letter demands:

1. Censorship imposed on *Islamic publications* should be withdrawn.
2. Permission to launch a daily newspaper to uphold Islamic view of life and Islamic belief [must be granted].
3. There should be no confiscation of property [the reference is unclear], no false accusations of espionage [the charge levelled against Mahdi al-Hakim] against persons because they have different political views ... No confessions may be forcibly extracted and used to label such accusations. [The reference here is to the confession by Methat al-Haj Sirri on television.]
4. The law should guarantee that every Muslim, irrespective of sect, would be permitted to reside in the holy places in accordance with his religious belief. [Reference is made here to Persian seminarians and pilgrims.][25] (Italics added.)

Obviously al-Hakim was keen on avoiding any political colouring, such as participation in the government, or general freedom of the press. The wording of the demands was carefully confined to the interests of the *'ulama* in Najaf. It was requested that censorship be removed from Islamic publications rather than publications in general. The other demands, relating to espionage and confession and the residence of co-religionists in the holy shrine cities, were al-Hakim's. The item against the confiscation of property may refer to land appropriations under new land reforms promulgated in 1970, and the nationalization of big mercantile capital, or the confiscated Kufa university funds. This is the only political demand. Al-Hakim had been crusading for the abolition of 'socialist acts' since 1964.[26]

Whereas the demands proposed by the Da'wa were manifestly political and express grievances over group-discrimination against the Shi'a, those in the al-Hakim-inspired letter had a narrow, self-interested, *'ulama* appeal. The Da'wa failed to engage al-Hakim in its battle. The divergence of the idiom of the Da'wa from that of the al-Hakim suggests they were worlds apart in matters of methods of action. Muhsin al-Hakim died on 2 June 1970, at the height of the first almost open clash with the Ba'th. Huge masses of people attended his funeral, chanting anti-Ba'th *husa* (glorifying verse).[27]

The Execution of Da'wa Leaders

The al-Hakim example of mild, behind-the-scenes but thinly veiled opposition to the Ba'th benefited the Da'wa just as his death may have served their cause. The allegiance (*taqlid*) of the lay Shi'is now shifted to two figures: the pacifist, apolitical but Persian Grand Ayatollah Abu Qassim al-Kho'i and the younger, still junior but vigorous and staunch Arab radical reformer, Muhammad Baqir al-Sadr, their old comrade.

The Da'wa inflated its ranks during this period to such an extent that the district committees in Baghdad ran into the hundreds; it also expanded its membership in the southern cities.[28] The Fifth Branch (al-Shu'ba al-Khamisa) of the General Directorate of Security Services, in charge of the surveillance of dissident religious groups, sensed this growth and the connections the Da'wa was forging with the *hawza*, the Shurja Suk, the universities and beyond.[29] One indication of this was the arrest of Sahib al-Dakhil on 28 September 1971, of Muhammad Baqir al-Sadr in 1972 and of others. Al-Sadr was incarcerated at the Kufa Hospital because of his ill health. Sahib al-Dakhil was never seen again.[30]

In December 1974, five leading members of the Da'wa Party were executed[31] (see Table 11.1).

Table 11.1: Da'wa Leaders and Cadres Executed in 1972–74

Name	City	Birth	Profession	Party	Locality of activity
'Arif Basri	Basra	1930[a]	cleric[b]	leader*	Karrada, Baghdad
Sahib al-Dakhil	Najaf	1932	merchant	leader	Najaf & Baghdad
Hussein Jalakhan	Najaf	1942	postgrad. economics	leadership**	Najaf
Izil Din Qabanji	Najaf	1951	cleric[b]	member***	Najaf
Imad Tabrizi	Najaf	1945[c]	cleric[b]	unspecified	Najaf
Nuri Tu'ma	Karbala	1943	engineer	unspecified	Najaf and Karbala

Names are in alphabetical order.
This table has been compiled on the basis of interviews with three leading members of the Da'wa Party (*Da'wa Doctrine*, vol. 1, and Joyce Wiley, op.cit.).

a. Born in Najaf.
b. Referred to as Hujjat al-Islam (*Da'wa Doctrine*, vol.1, p. 83).
c. Another source gives the year 1951 (*The Information Bulletin of the Islamic League in the USA*, p. 8).

*   Referred to as member of the Da'wa leadership.
**   Referred to as *sayyid* and member of the central organization of Iraq, formed after the general leadership (*al-qiyada al-amma*) suffered difficulties.
***   Referred to as *sayyid* and from the Du'at Mujahidin, i.e militant missionaries, that is an advanced cadre below the central leadership.
****   Referred to as the planner (*mukhatit*), thinker, tutor and member of the general leadership.

The year 1974 also witnessed the offered, but not delivered, '11 March Agreement' concluded between the Ba'th government and the Kurds under their legendary leader Mullah Mustafa Barzani. Relations between the Kurds and the central government were highly tense, and conflict was looming, as with relations between Iran and Iraq. In mid-February that year, skirmishes on the Iraq-Iran borders claimed 100 casualties on both sides.[32]

The support Iran was extending to the Kurds was an open secret. Heavy artillery and equipment poured from Iran into Iraqi Kurdistan.[33] Units of the Iranian army gave support to the Peshmerga, the Kurdish fighting partisans. The Iraqi army sustained heavy human losses which, by some estimates, were more than 10 percent of an army of 90,000, and the number of casualties (killed or wounded) was put at 9,543 up to March 1975.[34] Another estimate put the number at 15,000 by the end of the war against the Kurds.[35]

With the flow of Shi'i soldiers for burial, the war against the Kurds was severely felt in shrine cities. In two successive 'Ashura rituals in 1974 and 1975, popular discontent was evident. 'Ashura coincided with 25 January 1974, two months before the eruption of the Kurdish war. The following 'Ashura (1395 AH) fell on 14 January 1975, four months before the end of the same war. Mass discontent was apparent on both occasions, with Da'wa militants active in them.[36]

Arrests of Shi'i figures and cadres occurred in July 1974. They were soon put on summary trial and five of them were sentenced to death. Others received heavy sentences ranging from ten to twenty years.

Again, in order to silence the criticism of the Kurdish war and the casualties it was causing, 'the authorities executed as recently as last December [1974] five Shi'i notables in Najaf. It may be that agitation among Shi'is was secretly instigated by the Iranian government.'[37]

In Baghdad a crowd of some 200 friends and acquaintances of the executed gathered at the entrance of the morgue to mourn.[38]

The executions led the bulk of the Da'wa leadership and scores of cadres to flee the country to the Gulf, Lebanon, Iran or Jordan. The exodus weakened the Da'wa Party in organizational and political terms. Structures which were only just beginning to crystallize were dissolved. Passivity also surfaced in different party localities.[39]

The political nature of the confrontation was veiled: the Da'wa did not disclose what it had suffered and the ruling Ba'th was unaware of the latter's real nature.[40] Both sides would correct this error some five years later. This silence may have preserved the party inasmuch as it deceived the Ba'th security services.[41]

The Marad al-Ras Upheaval, February 1977: Ritual as an Instrument of Mass Politics

The February 1977 upheaval in Najaf and Karbala during the Arba'in procession was perhaps the first urban-based mass political demonstration. In fact, it sharply contrasts with the barren landscape of popular street politics from the mid-1960s to the mid-1970s just as much as it is a unique reminder of the richness of street politics in the 1940s and 1950s. The 1977 upheaval has no precedent as a massive challenge to the Ba'th regime. It came long before the name of Khomeini was ever in circulation.

The episode is known in popular jargon as the Marad al-Ras or the Arba'in pilgrimage (see Part Three on popular rituals); in Da'wa jargon it is the Sufar

Intifada. The movement was totally spontaneous with no organized leadership or political vision.

Sufar is the second month of the lunar year; on its twentieth day Shi'is commemorate the fortieth day of the death of the Third Imam Hussain in the historical battle of Karbala. It is a highly emotive, regular ritual, widely observed.[42] As noted in Part Three, the pilgrimage is multi-vocal and multi-functional, involving various social groups who relate to different levels of the ritual. Pilgrims expect redemption, salvation from their sins and deliverance from social pressures. The occasion also involves a quest for social prestige, fulfilment of collective responsibilities, an emphasis of cultural identity, expression of political grievances and protest.

The commemoration is organized along fixed temporal and spatial lines. This structure is not in and of itself political, but is a ready-made instrument capable of functioning in that direction. Islamist or other activists realize they have the benefit of these mobilizing tools dense with emotive signs, agitating symbols and intensive participation. This is one of the sources of the paradox that although the Da'wa Party was severely hit in 1974, lacking, as it were, sufficient field leadership and networks, colossal demonstrations against the Ba'th nevertheless erupted.

In 1977, a host of issues and circumstances triggered resentment in Shi'ite localities among various groups. Harsh measures were taken against the clerical class,[43] targeting their autonomous financial and social power base.[44]

In the mid-1970s, a severe drought plagued vast areas of the Euphrates valley in Iraq and hit peasants hard. The construction of a dam at Tabaqa by Syria was the main cause.[45] In the countryside, the low level of the water supply was viewed with anger by the disadvantaged peasants who form the bulk of the *zuwar* (pilgrims) to the holy shrines.[46] Another source of discontent was the Kurdish war in 1974–75 which claimed 15,000, mostly Shi'i, soldiers. As for the student population, in the academic year 1976–77 the campaign to Ba'thize universities was at its height. The process was coercive and counterproductive.[47]

The rigid controls imposed on the pilgrimage to the holy shrines caused economic damage. The ban was humiliating to the *qiyadat husayniya* (ritual headship) families notably in Najaf. In 1977 the ban on the pilgrimage was made on the grounds that an alleged Syrian agent had been arrested and supposedly confessed to a conspiracy to plant a time bomb at the holy shrine of 'Abbas in Karbala.[48] The *mawakib* leaders and pilgrims were cautioned by security services against any defiance.[49] Admission permits were denied by the mayoralty. Secret police personnel with loudspeakers toured Ali's holy shrine to warn pilgrims of the alleged Syrian conspiracy, obviously to frighten and persuade them into retreat.

A sense of defiance was in the air among the pilgrims as a body as among the *qiyadat husayniya* families in Najaf who took the lead.

Pilgrims usually take two major routes: one from Basra, Nasiriya or Diwaniya to Twaireej; the other from Baghdad, Kut or Omara through Hilla

to Karbala. Twaireej and Hilla became thermometers for measuring anti-
government feeling among pilgrims.[50] One indication of defiance is the level
of local solidarity and hospitality shown to pilgrims en route to Karbala:
villagers erected tents as temporary guesthouses, offered pilgrims soft drinks,
water or tea and even shelter in contingencies. Twaireej people, for example,
hailed the pilgrims with *husa*.

Another indication of defiance was the *husa* chanted on the occasion:

Ghasban 'Ala Khushoom-l 'Ida
Rayatna Manshoora
Ansar Jayna-l Karbala
L-Qabr-l Shaheed Inzorah.

Defying the foes in the eye
Our banners are hoisted aloft
Advocates we came to Karbala
The Tomb of the Martyr [Hussain] to visit.[51]

Pilgrims are organized along primordial lines in the village or the quarter, often
involving extended families. But their collective behaviour would soon be
controlled and oriented by the Najaf ritual leaders. In Najaf, as has been
pointed out, rituals are organized by fixed, almost hereditary bodies who regard
their task as a sacred obligation and take pride in its fulfilment. These bodies
are known as *hay'at husayniya*. Some of them descend from the old, traditional
guilds of *qasabin* (butchers), *khayatin* (tailors) or even new professions such as
teachers, and include students as well.[52] They are based in the quarters and
involve notable families who mobilize volunteers through kinship networks
and quarter solidarity structures. The actual implementation of various tasks
is usually left to the younger members. It is these Najafi *hay'at husayniya*, and
more specifically their younger members, which escalated the confrontation in
1977 and lent it leadership and purpose.[53]

The actual agitators all came from Najaf. Led by a Najafi youth,
Muhammad al-Balaghi, the group contained some dozen angry Shi'i young
men (see Table 11.2) mainly from Buraq and Umara quarters. Most were
students and servicemen in their twenties from petty merchant families. Linked
by neighbourhood, family alliance and, in certain cases, shared school
experiences, the group formed a spontaneous leading and agitating centre
projecting and amplifying the mood prevailing in Najaf and among the
pilgrims. Some petty wheeler-dealers may have also taken part in the episode.

Table 11.2: Najafis who Initiated the Arba'in 1977 Upheaval

Name	Quarter	Education	Profession	Family	Age	Remarks
Abu Yusra Balaghi	Buraq	secondary school	student	merchant	b. 1958	in exile, London
Yousif Satar Asadi	Buraq	secondary school	merchant	merchant	b. 1950	executed*
Kamil Naji Malo	Hananat	secondary school	conscript	merchant	b. 1951	executed*
Muh. Sa'id al-Balaghi	Buraq	secondary school	student	merchant; ritual headship	b. 1959	executed*
Naji Muh. Karim	Buraq	secondary school	conscript	merchant	b. 1956	executed*
Ghazi Judi Khuwayir	?	?	?	?	?	executed*
Muh. Ali Ni'na'	?	?	?	?	?	executed*
'Abbas Hadi 'Ajina	Buraq	?	dealer	merchant	b. 1940	executed*
Sahib Rahim Abu Gulal	Umara	none	dealer	merchant	b. 1948	executed*
Wahab Taliqani	Umara	secondary school	cloth trader	merchant	b. 1948	killed under torture
Jassim al-Irwani	Umara	?	?	merchant	b. 1937	killed under torture

* Those marked with (*) were officially tried by a special tribunal and sentenced to death. The names of the executed were published officially (see *al-Jumhuriya* daily, Baghdad, 25 February 1977). The last two names are not included in any official document, but remembrance literature issued by various Iraqi Islamist groups mentions these and other names such as Muhammad Mayyali, a teenage Najafi student shot dead by security forces during the confrontation at Khan al-Nus; his death is believed to have driven angry crowds and masses to break into the police station there and ransack weapons and ammunition.

This table is compiled on the basis of documents provided by Akram al-Hakim of SAIRI, *al-Shahada* weekly, 16 Sufar 1404 ah; *al-Jumhuriya*, 25 February 1977.
These executions were also reported in a very brief manner by Amnesty International (AM report, *The Death Penalty Survey by Country*, 26 September 1979, p. 175).

On Friday 15 Sufar, i.e. five days before the Arba'in anniversary, the group distributed handwritten leaflets which appeared on the walls of al-Suq al-Kabir encouraging Najafis and pilgrims to take part in the procession from Arba'in to Karbala.[54] Agitated gatherings appeared in the neighbourhoods of Mishraq, Huwaish, Umara and Buraq as well as in the Suq al-Kabir. The commotion soon developed into spontaneous massive unrest. Police and security forces encircled the throng but no clashes or arrests occurred. Sporadic groups chanted:

Ahl al-Najaf Ya Amjad
Rayatkum Irfa'uha.

Noble Najafis
Hoist aloft your banners.

Najaf, then, took the initiative and played the decisive, leading role.[55] Sensing the gravity of the situation, the Najaf notables held meetings to discuss ways of persuading officials to change their prohibitive position. Contacts with the city mayor took place, but some of the notables were arrested.[56] Crowds were enraged rather than inhibited. Contingents of pilgrims proceeded from Najaf on their way to Karbala, heedless of the warnings. On the first day the procession reached Khan al-Rub' (the first quarter of the distance from Karbala to Najaf). Armed police and security vehicles challenged the march but could not stop the human flow of 30,000 or so.[57] Clashes were very limited.[58]

On the second day, crowds neared the halfway mark of Khan al-Nus before dusk; security forces and police units opened fire, killing some demonstrators. As a result, the police station at Khan al-Nus was attacked and ransacked by the angry masses. This was perhaps the source of the firearms used by some demonstrators, not 'the Kurds who had been exiled to the south after the collapse of their rebellion in March 1975' who were said to have 'also participated in arming and inciting the Shi'is'.[59] Another possible source of firearms was the rural areas. Tribal peasants are usually armed, and their participation in the pilgrimage was exceptionally large in that year; some must have carried guns.

Outnumbered by the crowd, police units withdrew to reorganize themselves and

... pilgrims resumed their procession to Karbala next morning when they were attacked by armoured police vehicles and several people were killed and injured. Drawing towards the Nakhila village, the procession was about to disperse when new contingents of pilgrims joined them from various nearby villages.[60]

Muhammad Baqir al-Hakim was despatched by al-Sadr from Najaf to caution what had by this time become the leading committee of the procession to avoid direct political slogans against Saddam Hussein and Ahmad Hassan al-Bakr which, however, had already been voiced. Demonstrators chanted different couplets expressing a challenge to the Ba'th and a commitment to their Shi'ite identity:[61]

Ya Saddam sheel eedak
Jaish wa Sha'b may reedek.

Saddam take your hands off
Neither our army nor our people want you.[62]

Armoured vehicles backed by helicopter gunships were despatched under 'Adnan Khairullah Tilfah, Saddam's maternal cousin and al-Bakr's son-in-law,[63] to quell the demonstrators. Two thousand or so were rounded up and transferred to the military prison at the Rasheed military camp in Baghdad. Of this number only 500 were kept for thorough interrogation.[64] Karbala was, in fact, virtually under army occupation in order to prevent demonstrators from entering the city. Sixteen demonstrators were reportedly killed and an unspecified number wounded.[65]

The bloody Marad al-Ras or Sufar Uprising in 1977 marked a turning point in the Shi'i-state relationship. It shook the Ba'th regime and caused conflict within Saddam Hussein's Revolutionary Command Council (RCC) and the Ba'th party. It generated political differences, created ideological rifts and brought home to the ruling Ba'th the impact of religion and the religious Shi'ite establishment in political and social life. The differences revolved around the role of religion and methods of crisis management.

A special court was formed by the RCC which included Dr Izzat Mustafa, Minister of Municipal and Provincial Affairs, Flayih Hassan al-Jassim, Minister of State and Hassan Ali al-Amiri, Minister of Commerce, to try the 'plotters'. Eight men were sentenced to death and executed; two others were killed under torture. The ten were part of the spontaneous leading committee which emerged during the episode. None was affiliated with any Islamist group, including the Da'wa. Fifteen others were given life sentences, including Muhammad Baqir al-Hakim (then chairman of SAIRI) on account of his mediating mission.[66]

The verdict arrived at by Mustafa was extremely lenient in the eyes of the RCC vice-president Saddam Hussein.[67] Although the Ba'th organ *al-Thawra* on 25 February 1977 claimed that, contrary to the laws which demanded capital punishment the RCC showed mercy,[68] Mustafa was in fact cautioned by some of his kin to avoid having Shi'ite blood on his hands;[69] his close relations with al-Bakr may have been the source of his defiance of Saddam Hussein's orders. A behind-the-scenes power-ideology struggle ensued, and two members of the special court, Izzat Mustafa and Flayih Hassan al-Jassim, were relieved of party and government duties on 25 March. Both were accused of defeatism, weakness, inability to shoulder party duties and responsibilities and a lack of faith in the 'principles of the revolution'. *Al-Thawra* explained that the expulsion was necessary to protect the 'revolutionary purity of the party'.[70]

In response, Saddam Hussein delivered a speech titled '*Nazra Fil Din Wal Turath*' (A View of Religion and Traditional Heritage), in which he defined a secular/pragmatic line towards religion and politics. The Ba'th party, Hussein asserted, was not a religious party, but on the other hand it was not neutral between belief and disbelief: it was on the side of belief. This point may well serve to draw a dividing line separating the Ba'th from the materialist-atheist view; but it also set the Ba'th ideology into secularist parameters. The importance of this point rests also on the fact that there were voices calling for 'changes in the party ideology … to adopt a religious stance'.[71]

Hussein attempted to subsume religion and religious symbols under state control. In addition to extending funds to the holy shrines, he made various visits to Najaf and Karbala in May 1977, and claimed noble descent.[72] His maternal uncle Khairullah Tilfah manufactured a noble lineage for al-Bakr.[73] Years later, a similar attempt produced a family tree linking Hussein to the same noble ancestry.[74]

The second point asserted in Saddam Hussein's talk on religion was that the Ba'th party was against unprincipled or erroneous interference in religious matters; the party should not be provoked into 'undisciplined and insensible' behaviour which would 'isolate it from its masses'. The third point specified in clear terms that while the party respected religion and safeguarded the right to conduct rituals and religious ceremonies, it was categorically against the 'politicizing of religion' and hence against 'interpenetrating trenches where religious or sectarian affiliation would be the social divide'. Those who indulged in such politicization of religion would receive 'stern punishment' under the 'iron fist of the revolution'.[75]

The ruling Ba'th then changed direction. For the first time Shi'i members were introduced into the RCC, which was expanded in September 1977.[76] In 1977 the representation of Arab Shi'is at the upper and lower levels of the regime's ruling elite underwent a visible increase compared to the early years of the Ba'th rule.[77] Yet the increase still fell short of the levels of representation during the military period, 1958–68, in its entirety.[78] During the military phase, the Shi'is accounted for 16 and 35 percent of posts at higher and lower levels respectively; the average for both levels was 30 percent. In 1977 these proportions were 24 percent and 17.6 percent respectively; the general average was 21 percent.[79]

The improvement in Shi'ite representation was counterbalanced with new acts making double affiliation punishable by death:

[T]wo additional laws were introduced providing the death penalty as a mandatory punishment for ... Arab Socialist Ba'th Party members who deliberately conceal previous political membership or affiliation, or become affiliated to other political organizations or parties or work in their interests (Second Amendment to the Penal Code).[80]

According to Da'wa sources, restrictions on participation in Shi'ite rituals were imposed by the general directorate of the security service, including a prohibition on the collection of contributions for rituals. If not instructed to do so, Ba'th members and civil servants were not permitted to take part in the pilgrimage; they were also denied leave on these occasions. Party and administrative apparatuses were instructed to educate citizens and advise them to distance themselves from such practices, and instill into them patriotic and nationalist principles (*wataniya wa qawmiya*). Security and police organs in Najaf and Karbala were directed to avoid friction and act in accordance with a special plan set by the RCC. The *'ulama* were also advised to steer clear of politics and assured that the state would respect their adherence to rituals and spiritual activity – otherwise, they would be held liable.[81]

Despite the general secular line adopted by the Ba'th party it nevertheless began, pragmatically, to employ religious symbols in general and Shi'ite symbols in particular. The birthday of Imam Ali ibn Abu Talib was declared a national holiday. Hussein began to make further trips to the holy shrines, which became permanent items on his agenda.

Official ideology, already in a process of reconfiguration, could not escape mutation. With the growing and uneasy awareness of the ethnic and religious divide, the ruling Ba'th charted a new course of reconstructing an Iraqi identity that reflected and encompassed this cultural pluralism. A cultural Mesopotamian identity was manufactured to include pan-Iraq rather than pan-Arab identity. Islamic, Shi'ite symbols were also used to the same end. This reconstruction was undoubtedly reinforced by the 1975 and 1977 events.[82]

The religious establishment and the sources of Shi'ite power independent of the state were now put under the watchful eyes of a growing and ruthless security apparatus equipped with a new strategy: to divide and weaken these groups by splitting them on ethnic basis (Arab against Persian), further deprive them of their financial sources and destroying, if need be, the power of social wealth controlled by Shi'ite propertied groups should these autonomous centres of social power oppose or seem to defy the state.[83] On 7 March 1978, a year after the episode, Shi'ite shrine money was put under government control.[84] A detailed survey of the industrial, mercantile and propertied Shi'ite groups and individuals was conducted by the security service under General Fadhil Barak.[85]

It was not only the ruling Ba'th Party that underwent mutation in the aftermath of the Marad al-Ras clashes; Shi'i militants themselves began to change.[86]

TWELVE

The Particularist-Political Model: The Origins and Structure of the MAI

Whereas the rise of the Da'wa was triggered in 1959 by a general decline of the clerical class, the crystallization of the Islamic Action Organization – Munazamat al-'Amal al-Islami (MAI), formed in the 1970s – was a response to a different threat, namely the secular-nationalist Ba'th regime. The MAI had its local roots in the strife within the clerical class between the Karbala and Najaf groups, embedded in doctrinal differences and familial and regional competition.

The actual crystallization of the movement, however, had much to do with the clash between the Shi'ite clerical class on one hand and, on the other, the nationalistic military regimes of the 'Arif brothers first and the ruling Ba'th Party second. Under the latter regime, Shi'i *mujtahids* in general, and the group behind the MAI in particular, were the main targets of state-sponsored secularization measures aggravated by political persecution related to the regional power struggle with Iran. So the group started its activity as a staunch advocate of tradition, developed into a Karbala-versus-Najaf configuration then mutated into a politically militant and radical Shi'ite organization defying an atheist and 'Sunni' regime.

These mutations were occasioned by various factors which were consecutively but cumulatively at play across three different and clearly defined periods: 1960–63, 1964–68, 1968–79.

The formation of the MAI in the mid-1970s constituted the second Shi'ite Islamist response to the Ba'th. It was a communal-political organization from its very inception. It emerged to defend Shi'ite identity, or an ideal projection of it, from the constant and always aggravating encroachment of the secular Ba'th regime on the autonomous power structures of the clerical class and its allies.

The prosecution of the Shirazis and al-Mudarisi, together with the executions of clerical figures and seminarians in 1974, and the bloody confrontation in 1977, led the core group into direct involvement in political rather than doctrinal and educational activity. The present leaders of the MAI take pride in asserting that they had been on the move against a sectarian, violent state (the 'Arif and Ba'th regimes) rather than the threat of communism as such. While the group envisaged armed struggle as a strategic choice, it consciously retained the traditional structures of *marja'ism/muqallidin* (religious authority/emulators) as the legitimate form of organization. Only in 1979 did the MAI opt for a modern, cell-structured, clandestine organization.

The emergence and development of the MAI was first connected with the names of Hassan Shirazi (killed in 1980 at the hands of the Iraqi security service in Beirut), his elder brother Muhammad Hussain Shirazi, their younger nephew Muhammad Taqi al-Mudarisi and his younger brother, Hadi al-Mudarisi. We shall now review these background developments in their sequence.[1]

The Shirazi-Karbala group, as mentioned in Part Two, was invited by Najafi initiators of the Da'wa Party during 1959–60 to discuss ways and means of combating the rise of communism and reversing the decline of the religious class. In the meeting, the young Najaf circle was in favour of innovation while the Shirazi-Karbala circle showed a highly traditional stance, rejecting any change in practice, let alone in long-accepted Shi'ite political thought. The controversial doctrinal issues were starkly and lucidly debated by Hassan Shirazi, whose political instincts and quick eye for differences in Islamic political ideologies gave the doctrinal schism a clear-cut, thesis-antithesis polarization. Hassan Shirazi is said to have been a natural-born politician in terms of practice, thought and leadership qualities. It was he who first raised the question of who should assume leadership – the proposed political party for the Shi'is or *marja*'s (religious authority or authorities)? His question was: who would decide for whom and how?

Outwardly, this was a practical question shrouded in theological idiom; actually, it was a theological question presented in administrative jargon. Hassan Shirazi was of the mind that Islam had declined after the demise of the Ottoman Empire and been on a continuous downward slide ever since. In his view, three solutions or forms of response had been tried.

First there had been individual attempts at reform or militancy, such as that of Jamal al-Din al-Afghani, who had initiated Islamic reform in late 19th century. This kind of reform was doomed to be limited because it withered away the moment its initiator left this world.

Second, his argument went, there had been the movements led by modern Islamic parties such as the Muslim Brotherhood, Hizb al-Tahrir al-Islami (Islamic Liberation) or the proposed Da'wa Party. Shirazi argued that parties which adopted Western methods in their work and movement led to un-Islamic forms of practice. Islam, in his interpretation, abhors parties, and there have been no parties in Islam.

Third, there were in the history of (Shi'i) Islam movements of the *fuqaha* and *maraji'* who inspired and guided the political action of laymen. He had in mind his forefather Mirza Shirazi, who led the Tobacco Revolt in Qajar Iran towards the end of last century from his seat of religious power in Samara. For

Hassan Shirazi, this was not only the ready-made but also the feasible and legitimate Islamic form, a well-defined structure with a religious authority at the helm, the *muqallidin*, emulators and followers at the base and the *wukala'*, agents who collect the *khums* and lead on a local basis, in between. To him this was the authentic, true, tried and rightful organization.

Shirazi sums up his argument as follows: 'The Islamic modern parties in their present form ... are a copy of the democratic party movements in the 'Free World' (i.e. the West) ... We reject this.'[2] On the other hand, 'Individual alternatives ... are invalid.'[3] The only solution is a movement led by the *fuqaha*: 'This [*fuqaha*] movement consists of three elements: top [*qumma*], apparatus [*jihaz*] and base [*qa'ida*].'[4]

Elaborating on these three elements, Shirazi says the 'top' is the grand or supreme *marja'*. Interestingly, whereas he uses the plural form for the leadership in general, here he uses the singular. The second element, the apparatus, is a high administrative body of *wukala'* who should meet at the *marja*°s headquarters to receive directives and instructions relative to their specified tasks. They act like a 'ministerial cabinet'. The 'base' or constituency is the Islamic nation in its entirety.[5]

These ideas, seemingly derived from practical, clerical experience, represent the traditionally accepted Shi'ite doctrinal positions which formed the intellectual framework of the Shirazi family in Karbala and were injected into the minds of the militant individuals and groups who revolved around the Shirazis. Hassan Shirazi elaborated these themes in his lectures and indoctrination lectures which were widely published and reprinted.[6]

These notions governed the activity of his group: whatever organization, movement or grouping might be needed for the Shi'is to defend their cause, it should not be structured in the form of a cell-party, nor even called a party, because this was a Western concept alien to Shi'ite thought. *Marja'ism* had always to be the supreme arbiter, source of legitimacy and spring of knowledge; it is the Imam incarnated. And the *'ulama* 'received authority of leadership by specific and direct will of God, hence they have the right to lead humans'.[7]

Unlike the traditional, apolitical position of the Najafi *'ulama* (say, that of Kho'i), Shirazi's was not an apolitical case. His argument reflected the stance of a group of *'ulama* who, on one hand, realized the need for militant activism but, on the other, abhorred the prospect of losing command and control over to a new form of militancy (a political party) they were asked to legitimize. His position also differs radically from that of other *'ulama* (like the followers of Muhsin al-Hakim) who endorsed activism but restricted it to pious educational endeavour. He was for Shi'ite politics but only under the direct supervision of the *'ulama*. This was, perhaps, an early call for a version of the theory which would later be given the name of *wilayat al-faqih* by Khomeini.

A possible Khomeini influence in Shirazi's argument is difficult to dismiss. Khomeini was in Iraq from 1963 and was first welcomed in Najaf by the Shirazi family. The family itself had connections with some of Khomeini's novices and associates like Mutahhari. Among the anecdotes in circulation in the MAI milieu is that, upon his arrival in Iraq, Khomeini visited Muhammad Shirazi at his residence in Karbala, although usually such a social call would have been regarded as inappropriate because the latter was younger than the former. Khomeini's modesty was indicative of his gratitude for the Shirazis' anti-Shah agitation in his defence in 1963. In response to the gesture, Shirazi stepped aside to give Khomeini leadership of prayer at the former's centre, Masjid al-Imam al-Hussain in Karbala.

This Shirazi-Khomeini connection was also enhanced by the fact that there was no language or ethnic barrier between the two. Even in the 1980s, Muhammad Shirazi had a clear Persian accent in his Arabic speech.[8] Khomeini, for his part, lived in relative isolation from his Arabic surroundings. Mallat, for example, mentions that hardly any encounter had occurred between him and Muhammad Baqir al-Sadr during Khomeini's stay in Najaf for almost a decade and a half.[9]

Both Hassan Shirazi and Muhammad Shirazi distanced themselves from the Najaf group which was agitating during the early 1960s for the initiation of the Da'wa Party and renewal of Islamic thought, and they resumed their own religious-ritualistic duties and activities in Karbala.

Emulators of the Shirazis were recruited in the traditional manner: attending prayer, collecting *khums* and expressing personal allegiance to the *faqih*. The groups or clusters they formed were loose in nature and more in the traditional spirit of sporadic gatherings of relatives and neighbourhood mates revolving around a pivotal clerical figure in direct personal bond. These groupings were far short of any attempt at organizing any political or social movements in the sense of having a clear-cut political forum or programme and a disciplined group dedicated to a cause. They were local groupings in reaction to the Najaf initiative, a sort of assertion of local community spirit so well-known among families and *mujtahids* competing for fame, followers and power. The rivalry with Najaf sustained the potentiality of a Karbala-based social movement.

In the mid-1960s another factor was at play to help push potentiality nearer towards actualization: the rise of the 'Arif brothers' regime on one hand, and on the other, the new air breathed into the body of the Da'wa Party which spread its influence in a vacuum of political opposition. It was only then that the milieu around the Shirazi family took some initiative to express self-readiness in the wake of a local but decisive incident.[10]

Muhammad Shirazi had founded *al-Jam'iya al-Khairiya al-Islamiya* (The Islamic Charity Society) in Karbala in 1962. As the name indicated, the society was mainly concerned with charity and the promotion of Islamic education, but was instrumental in building networks of clients. Sayyid Murtadha Qazwini was in charge of the society on behalf of the Shirazis. Da'wa supporters and sympathizers, expanding their bases at the time, felt confident enough to challenge the Shirazi influence over the society. At a gathering to renew the society's leadership in the mid-1960s, Sadr al-Din Shahrastani, presumably a Da'wa supporter, won a majority backing and became the chairman of the society much to the discomfort of the Shirazi family and their client Qazwini. A split erupted and was aggravated by bitter agitation. Intellectuals and activists in Karbala were divided into two massive rival camps, that of the Shirazi and that of the Da'wa. Street fights and heated debates, partly reminiscent of the 19th-century Usuli-Akhbari clashes, erupted.

The Shirazi camp was defined by the slogan: *La lil hizbiya! na'am lil marja'iya!* ('No to partisanship, yes to the *marja*'!') The Da'wa agitated under the banner of partisanship in the service of *marja'ism*. The ideological/doctrinal/familial split was expanded to the realm of rituals, with the Shirazis accusing the Da'wa *effendis* of opposing the popular practice of self-flagellation and head cutting in the 'Ashura ceremonies. Inflamed by Shirazi's incitement, sections of the Karbalais responded positively.

The old jealousies between Karbala and Najaf were essential ingredients in the anti-Da'wa drive. Old anti-Najaf accusations were revived and thrown into the battle. Some neighbouring cities and towns in Iraq have long histories of open rivalries, such as the case of the Kurdish cities of Arbil and Sulaymaniya, or the Sunni provincial towns of Ana, Rawa and Heet.

These old *'asabiyas* (solidarities) have been designated by the Iraqi sociologist Ali al-Wardi as town-solidarity. He attributes the local *'asabiyas* to external danger, the need to defend the city from the military incursions or assault by Bedouin tribes.[11] The *'asabiyas* of the town is further fostered by the different tribal origins of each town, or by competition in trade. In the case of Najaf, Kazimain and Karbala there have always been strong contests and rivalries in a number of fields – over the seat of *marja'ism*, corpse traffic, religious tourism [pilgrimages], religious learning and the like. Al-Wardi confirms that Shi'is in Kazimain used to call themselves the 'sons of Musa', that is Imam Musa al-Kazim who is buried there, whereas the Najafis would call themselves 'the sons of Ali'. The battles between the two groups were described by both as 'a fight between the sons of Ali and the sons of Musa', using tribal-patriarchal idiom to denote local-city antagonistic solidarities.[12]

In the new contest, Karbalais were reminded by their Shirazi leaders of the fact that it was Karbala, not Najaf, that had been attacked by the Wahhabi desert warriors in the 19th century because, in the words of pro-Shirazi agitators, Najaf had been no challenge to Wahhabism. Karbala rather than Najaf had defied the British, and was revolutionary while Najaf was conciliatory. The example of Ayatollah Kazim Yazdi of Najaf and his collaboration with the British in 1918 was cited. Najaf, the propaganda campaign claimed, was immersed in theological and jurisprudential niceties, paying no attention to politics or the daily concerns of the people; and Najaf always concealed its weakness and pacifist stand under a barrage of criticism of Karbala over its alleged superficial knowledge of theology and jurisprudence or its limited intellectual horizons. Karbala's theology, the argument boasted, had always approached issues and problems felt or suffered by the *umma* rather than meddle with the irrelevant sophistries that were the style of Najaf.

In these and other arguments, the local spirit was thrown into the service of a thinly veiled, family- or city-based clerical power struggle. The campaign created a very strong movement indeed. During the 'Ashura of 1965 (which fell in mid-May), a group of pro-Shirazi devotees and zealots carrying machetes was roused to attack the premises of a charitable society, the leadership of which they had lost to rivals. The attackers smashed furniture and destroyed whatever they could lay hands on. The Shirazi-incited movement overwhelmed the Da'wa enclave in Karbala to the point that the supremacy of the Shirazi family was reinstalled. Muhammad Shirazi and Hassan Shirazi emerged as the leaders of the clerical circles in Karbala on the heels of their late, renowned father Sayyid Mahdi Shirazi, who had been the spiritual leader of the city, or their forefather Muhammad Taqi Shirazi, who assumed the highest position of *marja' mutlaq* for a brief span before his death in 1920.

The anti-Da'wa drive produced sporadic groups of dedicated yet united followers. From their meetings in the *husayniyas* or mosques, an elementary form of unnamed organization began to crystallize. To lend them a sustained character they were named *hay'at* (committees). They were not, however, traditional entities, but more like patterned and sustained party cells. Indoctrination was confined to general Islamic education in a particularist Shi'ite spirit.

Towards the end of 1968, a new figure emerged to lend these vague nuclei a more solid character: Muhammad Taqi al-Mudarisi, whose advent symbolized the rise of a new generation, more open to new ideas, new problems and new horizons. The shift from a traditional configuration of allegiance to an organized machine called al-Haraka (The Movement) is attributable to al-Mudarisi's organizational talents, political instincts and ambitions. Born in 1945 to a *sayyid* family on the side of both parents, al-Mudarisi relied on the patronage of Shirazi as his maternal uncle, a case similar to that of al-Sadr in 1960. He was twenty years old at the time of the Da'wa-Shirazi clash in Karbala and, it seems, he sensed the strengths that could be derived both from a sustained, organized machine of dedicated followers and his uncle's rejection of the concept rather than the reality of partisanship. Having more contact with colleagues of his own generation, he was more prone to political action and organization.

The *hay'at* revolving around Shirazi were to a large extent his invention. These cell-like circles were now directed to meet regularly, discuss general matters and read the Islamic literature of the Shirazis and others. The groups remained unnamed until the early 1970s when pressures from different members brought the issue to constant debate. Several names were used: al-Haraka al-Marja'iya, Harakat al-Risaliyin, or al-Tala'i (The *Marja'ism* Movement, The Movement of the Messianic, The Vanguard). As these names show, the word 'party' was consciously avoided. Al-Mudarisi in the end chose al-Haraka, both to satisfy his need for a sustained effort and to observe the imperative of avoiding the unacceptable connotations of the term 'party'. Politically, however, the group was still aimless, and its command structure still shapeless.

During the 'Arif era, the Shirazis were harshly treated as aliens, i.e. Persians. In a lengthy polemic against Arab nationalism, which he describes as a 'Western tool transplanted to divide Muslims', Muhammad Shirazi recalls how he was denied a residence visa by the 'nationalists'.[13] But the group had no recorded clash with the 'Arif regime. With the advent of the Ba'th Party in 1968, a new situation developed. We have already identified two interacting factors: secularization and the Iraq-Iran regional struggle, both reacting against the clerical class and shrine cities. Leading figures of al-Haraka were prosecuted. Hassan Shirazi was incarcerated for seven months in Qasr al-Nihaya (The Palace of Death) in 1969–70, then transferred to Ba'quba prison and later expelled from the country. His arrest was part of a wider crackdown on al-Hakim's family and the religious leadership of the Shi'is in general. He settled in Lebanon. His brother Muhammad Shirazi, under pressure to acquiesce in exchange for naturalization in Iraq, chose to leave Karbala for Kuwait, where he made the mosque of Junaid al-Qar his *hawza* and headquarters.

The arrest and departure of Hassan and Muhammad Shirazi gave Muhammad Taqi al-Mudarisi a wider and freer scope in which to work and organize. Al-Haraka spread its networks beyond Iraq to Saudi Arabia, Bahrain, Kuwait, Oman, Lebanon, Iran and even Africa, where Lebanese Shi'is prosper and their mullahs win African converts to Shi'i Islam.[14] The nature of al-Haraka was still dual in the sense that it was for both political and religious ends. The prosecution of Shi'i *mujtahids*, together with the execution of the Da'wa leaders in 1974, shifted the thrust of al-Haraka from general indoctrination to themes of political militancy such as armed struggle. Certain circumstances helped promote this new tendency. As al-Haraka had links with Iranian radicals in Lebanon such as Muhammad Muntaziri,[15] or with the Lebanese Shi'i radicals of Amal (who themselves were gradually being radicalized)[16] they came into contact with the well-organized, well-armed Shi'i activists of Lebanon.

The example and influence of the Palestinian radical organizations operating in Lebanon was also powerful. The Muntaziri and Amal organizations had close links with the Yasser Arafat-led Fatah movement, which extended help to the militants of al-Haraka. Apart from receiving shelter, the militants were introduced to the various Latin American guerrilla warfare tactics of Cuba and Bolivia or those of Vietnam. The number of trainees was small: eighteen to twenty in each course. The quality of the members was high in terms of dedication and allegiance. The military training project had no tactical or strategic policy but was embedded in a vague idea of somehow, somewhere putting up some form of resistance to the Ba'th regime in Iraq and perhaps beyond. A gradual new turn was also visible in the field of indoctrination. Militants were introduced to Sayyid Qutb (author of *Ma'alim fil tariq* [Signposts on the Road]) and Muhammad al-Ghazali, who were both from the radical wing of the Egyptian Muslim Brotherhood and had at least one thing in common: the rejection, excommunication of and fight against ruling radical nationalists.[17] It seems that from these Islamist ideological sources the leading cadres of al-Haraka derived new energy and borrowed ideas supportive of their early, Shi'i-embedded rejection and refusal of the Ba'th regime and its secular ideology. Al-Haraka made important steps in the direction of Shi'ite political activism in Iraq and other countries.

It is interesting to note the differences between al-Haraka and the Da'wa in terms of ideology, organization and orientation. The Da'wa Party achieved ideological-intellectual modernization before it actually built a modern organization. This process took almost two decades. By contrast al-Haraka, which later became the MAI, revolutionized traditional organizational structures before it embarked upon any ideological innovation. By contrast to al-Sadr's writings, for example, al-Haraka publications of the 1970s were anchored in traditional Shi'ite tenets, as will be seen in the chapter on ideology below.

While the Da'wa intellectual effort was meant to produce a sort of universal Islamic thought, al-Haraka's conception was strictly Shi'ite and traditional. The former was generally directed against the West but particularly against communism. Al-Haraka's was directed against pan-Arab national thought. And while the Da'wa started as an educational-pedagogic movement to change ideas and keep aloof from political action, al-Haraka or MAI was, right from the start, for political action. Finally, whereas the Da'wa was healing the wounds inflicted upon it by the Ba'th regime, al-Haraka was almost intact. Thus, when in 1978–79 the Da'wa and al-Sadr were enthused by the Iranian upheaval into a premature challenge of the Ba'th regime, al-Haraka was the only group ready to stage violent political acts such as the attempt on the life of the ex-foreign minister Tariq Aziz. It was only after the Iranian Revolution that the main body of al-Haraka assumed the name Munazamat al-'Amal al-Islami. But by then it had become a modern political party in the strict sense of the word.[18]

We shall now consider the process of this ultimate radicalization which shifted the old groups and created new ones.

Table 12.1: The Composition of the Political Bureau (PB) of the MAI in the 1980s

Name	Date of birth	City	Education	Profession	Remarks
Muhammad Taqi al-Mudarisi	1945	Karbala	cleric	*mujtahid*	leader
Muhsin al-Husaini	1944	Karbala	cleric	party cadre	deputy
Nizar Haidar	c. 1950*	Karbala	BA	economist	PB
Nuri al-Amin	c. 1950*	Karbala	secondary school	merchant	PB
Abdullah al-Musawi	c. 1950*	Baghdad	BA	engineer	PB
Ibrahim al-Mutairi	c. 1950*	Karbala	BA	agricultural engineer	PB
Jawad al-'Attar	c. 1950*	Karbala	BA	economist	PB
Ridha Jawad Taqi	1955	Karbala	BA	chemical engineer	PB

Dates of birth marked with * are between 1950–55, as estimated by informants who could not give accurate details.

The data in this table is mainly based on information provided by the PB member Ridha Jawad Taqi, who resides now in London. Some details were derived from *al-Sahafa Tuhawir al-Mudarisi* (The Press Interviews of al-Mudarisi, the Doctor of Religious Sciences, al-Basa'ir printing house, Tehran, 1985, first edition, pp. 33–97).

THIRTEEN

Radicalization: 1979–82

The Iranian Factor

The revolutionary upheaval in Iran during 1978 and the phenomenal success of the Iranian Revolution in February 1979 radically changed the political landscape in the Middle East, and had a profound impact on regional relations and the internal development of neighbouring countries. Iraq was among those most affected.[1] At this juncture Iraqi Islamic Shi'ite social movements emerged as the new challenger to a formidable regime. They hastily shifted from clandestine educational activities to open mass political struggle and urban guerilla warfare. The demonstration effect of the Iranian Revolution was decisive in this shift.

The revolutionary upheaval took Shi'ite opposition as well as the regime in Iraq by surprise.[2] The chain reactions starting from the Faydhiya school incident in the spring of 1978, strikes by the bazaar and oil workers and mass street demonstrations seemed to the ruling Ba'th leaders temporary, futile unrest.[3] Reassuring party members and the general public, the Ba'th official organ *al-Thawra* ran an editorial together with an internal circular in late September 1978 belittling the strikes and professing that they would fail to effect change. The 'masses would get tired' of strikes, whether by the bazaar workers or civil servants, the organ predicted, and the restoration of normality was only a matter of time.[4] This view questioned the sustainability of the mass movement against a well-organized military and state control machine,[5] and reflected the mentality and experience of its authors, who held a firm belief in conspiratorial palace coups rather than spontaneous mass agitation. For them, elitist (military or otherwise) initiatives were the decisive but missing factor. When the mass movement – the first of its kind in a developing nation[6] – eventually triumphed, the Ba'th leadership shifted to the opposite extreme. They feared that the Iranian scenario was reproducible in Iraq itself. This was clearly stated by Saddam Hussein on various occasions. In February 1980, he stressed these concerns:

[U]nless the inhabitants of Iraq demonstrated their loyalty to a specifically Iraqi state, the country would be divided into three 'mini-states': one Arab Sunni, one Arab Shi'i and one Kurdish.[7]

In a conversation with President Mubarak of Egypt, Hussein admitted that Islamic Iran posed a greater threat to his regime than Israel, since unlike Israel, Iran possessed an ideological weapon capable of destroying Iraq both as a political system and nation-state.[8] Some parallels between the two regimes may have strengthened this conception. Both were based on single party system (Rastakhiz and the Ba'th); both had a command-oil rentier economy; both had a mutinous religious establishment and actually or potentially rebellious Kurdish and leftist movements. Of course these similarities do not take account of the structural differences between the two sociopolitical systems.[9]

Thus Iraq was caught in the fear of an Iranian demonstration effect and acquiesced to the Shah's pressures to control and remove Ayatollah Khomeini from his residence in Najaf.

Up to that moment Khomeini had hardly ever been recognized in Iraq beyond a narrow circle of clergymen in the holy shrines. His relations with the Iraqi government had been cool. Hosted in 1964 under the 'Arif regime, he led a seemingly quiet life. The Ba'th government co-opted some of his aides during the tense period of the Iraq-Iran relations in early 1970. One of them, Sheikh Mahmud, served at Persian Radio in Baghdad.[10] After the conclusion of the Algiers Agreement in 1975, cooperation with Khomeini's assistants was suspended and Iranian clerical dissidents kept under tight surveillance. Similar favours were extended to Iraq by the Iranian government, which scrutinized or even incarcerated Da'wa leaders (like Muhammad al-Asifi)[11] who had to leave their customary haven in Iran and take refuge in Kuwait.

This must have already soured Khomeini's relations with the Ba'th. His harsh deportation from Iraq at the request of the Shah in October 1978 was part of the Iraq-Iran security treaty. The Iranian ambassador relayed the Shah's request to Hamid Juburi, who notified the vice-chairman of the RCC. Khomeini was escorted to the Kuwait border when another request from the Shah to keep him under tight control in Baghdad was relayed, but the request was denied.[12] Khomeini had to return to Baghdad, and the surrounding publicity drew the attention of sections of the Iraqi public to his presence and status. When he spent the night at the holy shrine of Kazimain, hundreds of Shi'i militants and ordinary people flocked to try to see him and wish him a safe journey to France on 6 October 1978. Da'wa activists and leading figures were among them.

Growing Militancy

The lay leaders of the Iraqi branch of the Da'wa Party, mostly based in Baghdad, sensed there was a historical moment in the making and decided, sometime in December 1978, to probe the situation of the *'ulama* in Najaf. A delegation of prominent activists and intellectuals (Dr Hassan Raja'i, Dr Hussein Shahristani, Mahdi Salih al-Adib and possibly others)[13] visited Baqir al-Sadr in Najaf. Reflecting a search for prominent and pan-Shi'ite leadership, this choice was made for several reasons. First, al-Sadr was an ex-founding member of the Da'wa and second, he was the only Arab – and hence Iraqi – leading figure in the hierocracy. Third, Kho'i, the supreme *marja' taqlid*, was traditional, apolitical and did not have a solid Iraqi lineage.[14] Both sides, the Da'wa delegation and al-Sadr himself, were for caution, self-restraint and vigilance. Al-Sadr even voiced reservations in view of his admitted 'medium rank' in the clerical world of Najaf in terms of influence and revenues. The potency and readiness of the Da'wa Party was also questioned by al-Sadr. According to one Da'wa leader, al-Sadr explained he needed at least two to three years before he could complete the 'building up of his religious standing' (*istikmal bina' al-marja'iya*).[15] The meeting ended with a recommendation to meet and consult regularly every three months.

The delegation did not represent the general leadership (*al-qiyada al-'ama*) of the Da'wa but of the Iraq Branch (*iqlim*). The members of the general leadership were scattered in different countries in the region: Suabayti was in Jordan, Korani in Lebanon or Kuwait, al-Asifi in Kuwait, al-'Askari in Iran. (See Table 14.6 on Da'wa leadership.) Only Hassan Shubbar, presumably in charge of the Da'wa in Iraq after the execution of 'Arif al-Basri in December 1974, was available.

The party-*marja'* (or layoclerical) meeting, the first of its kind in almost two decades, would have been inconceivable had not the role of the clergy been so manifestly asserted in the Iranian upheaval. Long before a second meeting was due, events took a rapid turn as Khomeini was already, in Tehran, a triumphant leader of a revolution.

It seems it was al-Sadr rather than the Da'wa who was first to cast some of the caution aside. To celebrate the triumph of Ayatollah Khomeini, al-Sadr declared a three-day holiday from 11 February 1979 at the Najaf *hawza* (religious university). On the same day a peaceful procession was organized from Masjid al-Khadhra after the evening prayer and Khomeini's images were hoisted aloft. The march was forcibly dispersed by security police, who arrested seminarians. On the following day the al-Khadhra mosque was encircled by security forces to prevent any movement. The al-Khadra demonstration produced what might be figuratively called a 'tragedy of errors'. The Da'wa saw it as a deliberate act of escalation by al-Sadr; al-Sadr himself thought it was the making of the Da'wa

Party; the reality was neither. It was a spontaneous initiative by individuals who were both Da'wa members and students at the *hawza* seminaries. The demonstration was, in the words of one of these men, Ahmad Kubba, contrary to party instructions.[16]

Al-Khadhra was the seat of the collective prayer service conducted by Ayatollah Kho'i. The tactic was to camouflage the origins of the march and lend it a general clerical significance. The Jihaz Marja'iya, a loose entourage of Kho'i, distanced themselves from the march to avoid liability.[17]

Although not of his making, al-Sadr's mediation for the release of detained seminarians further implicated him. Public pressure was also put on Kho'i to intervene.[18]

The demonstration and open expression of support for the Iranian Revolution was, by all accounts, an alarming challenge to the Ba'th regime. A sequence of interlinked events then led to what has come to be known as the Rajab Uprising.

Successive moves by al-Sadr revealed not only his enthusiastic support for Iran's revolution but also his assertion of the leading role of the *'ulama* in politics. His telegram of support for Khomeini in the aftermath of the official declaration of the Islamic Republic in March 1979 is one example:

> While we look forward to more decisive victories, we put our whole being [literally *wujuduna*, i.e. life or effort] at the service of your great prominence, may the sublime Lord preserve your shadow to achieve our expectations under your authority [*marja'iyatikum*] and leadership.[19]

By contrast, Kho'i's cable was formal and without exaltation of rank and status. Whereas Khomeini was addressed by al-Sadr as the supreme *marja'*, he was addressed by Kho'i as '*hujjat al-Islam*', a much inferior rank by clerical standards.[20]

On 1 May 1979, Ayatollah Mutahhari, a prominent militant mullah in the Iranian Revolution, was assassinated. Mutahhari was known in Najaf circles in the old clandestine days of anti-Shah agitation, and al-Sadr marked his death with a religious ceremony (*fatiha*) at the al-Tusi mosque. The official reaction was harsh and al-Sadr was asked to stop the ceremony on the grounds that Mutahhari was an Iranian official rather than a religious colleague.[21]

Earlier, during March and April, al-Sadr wrote and published six booklets titled *al-Islam yaqud al-hayat* (Islam Guides Life) as a theoretical contribution to the construction of a new Islamic state and society.[22]

These were dangerous liaisons with Iran. To lend relations with Khomeini and the Iranian Revolution a more systematic character, al-Sadr despatched a permanent envoy to Tehran – his disciple Sayyid Mahmud al-Hashimi.[23] Al-Sadr's plan to visit Tehran at the helm of a religious and popular delegation was made public. Numbering around 100 or so, al-Sadr's *wukala'* were very active and held permanent contacts to keep up manifestations of popular support for the Iranian Revolution in Shi'ite localities. The authorities intervened to stop these attempts and prevent al-Sadr from visiting Iran.[24]

Al-Sadr's real intention at this point is obscure. Whether or not he planned to leave Iraq for good to avoid looming hazards is unclear. Certain Najafi and Da'wa Party circles asserted that he did consider the idea, while others dismissed it. The former tend to stress the Ba'th threats to the radical *ayatollah*, the latter to underline the bold challenge he mounted.[25]

The Iranian leadership, Khomeini in particular, was advised of al-Sadr's thoughts on departure. Towards the end of May 1979 (possibly on 18 or 19 May), the Arabic Service in Radio Tehran broadcast a short, concise telegram from Khomeini addressed openly to al-Sadr:

> Samahat [your Grace] Hujjat al-Islam al-Hajj Sayyid Muhammad Baqir al-Sadr: we have been informed that your holiness has decided to leave Iraq because of some events [*hawadith*, i.e. disturbances]. I do not see good [*min al-saleh*] coming from your leaving the holy city of Najaf, the centre of Islamic learning, and I am worried about this matter. I hope, God willing, that the concerns of your holiness shall vanish. May peace and God's mercy be upon you.[26]

The cable was a little short on instruction and placed al-Sadr in the inferior status of *hujjat al-Islam*. In his analyses of this cable, Mallat says the title formalities denoted the rivalries among the *'ulama* over who is more knowledgeable.[27] The minimal title and the cable itself may indeed have been the result of clerical rivalries, but not on Khomeini's part. He was victorious and at the helm of power and there was hardly any need on his part to assert his supremacy. Al-Sadr himself had addressed Khomeini not only as 'Ayatollah 'Uzma', but also as 'Imam'. The MAI was perhaps the initiator of the episode. At that point, MAI cadres and leaders were in Tehran representing their branches in Iraq, the Gulf and elsewhere under various names to gain control and receive benefits. Prominent figures of the MAI, Ahmad al-Katib (*nom de guerre*) and others, were in charge of the Arabic Service in Radio Tehran. Receiving unconfirmed reports from Iraq on al-Sadr's intentions to depart, they not only advised the Iranians but recommended he not leave lest the so-called Iraqi Islamic revolution collapse. Najaf-Karbala rather than Najaf-Qum rivalries were present.[28]

The Da'wa leadership, which had been advised to be cautious in December, saw in the series of developments from February down to mid-May 1979 a clear change of direction on the part of al-Sadr. He had been appealing for caution, but now he seemed to them to be ready for confrontation.

Da'wa leaders saw in this change a *taklif shar'i* (religious imperative) to go into action. Plans to stage mass demonstrations in various Baghdad quarters and beyond were discussed in late February. The issue proved controversial.[29] After the Iranian Revolution another meeting between a Da'wa delegation and al-Sadr took place. Both were in dire need of each other: al-Sadr for organization and followers (or simply hands), and the Da'wa for leadership of high status and calibre akin to the Khomeini model. According to Da'wa leaders, al-Sadr agreed to cooperate provided he be the centre of decision-making, i.e. the undisputed leader.[30] Al-Sadr had his own traditional organization, a set of *wukala'*, mostly low-ranking sheikhs and *sayyids* or some devout laypeople who act as mediators for the collection of *khums*, the organization of pilgrimages and the like. It is estimated they numbered 100 or so operating in at least twelve towns, including Baghdad.[31]

Al-Sadr's *wukala'* were already agitating their local followers for the very thing the Ba'th government dreaded most: an exhibition of support for the Islamic revolution. Although al-Sadr had taken measures since 1974 to separate the *hawza*, i.e. the religious school and establishment, from the party organization[32] to assert his independence and avoid unnecessary and detrimental overlapping, a degree of intersection existed. Obviously, the *wukala'*'s activities were visible and detectable; those of the Da'wa organization were more subtle and better cloaked. The overlap produced a duality of directing centres, the so-called *ithnainiya* (double, duplicate, duality) which lend their action a somewhat contradictory line. This was clearly noticeable in the Mubaya'a (Allegiance) movement, the portent of the Rajab Intifada which started after the telegram Khomeini sent to al-Sadr urging him to stay in Najaf. It continued for nine days, from 22 May 1979 and was the first real and intentional show of force. The Mubaya'a movement was wholly initiated by the Da'wa and al-Sadr's *wukala'* networks had to follow suit. Contingents of emulators and supporters were instructed to go to Najaf, visit al-Sadr's residence in the Umara neighbourhood and pledge allegiance to him as leader. Hundreds of supporters, disciples and devout followers poured into Najaf. The geographical setting these delegations represented was extensive: al-Thawra, Baya', Kazimain, Shu'la and Karrada (all Baghdad neighbourhoods), Kut, 'Aziziya, Nu'maniya, Imara, Basra, Hilla, Nasiriya, Diwaniya, Karbala, Simawa and other places.[33] Some delegates were chanting:

Bism al-Khomeini wil Sadr
al-Islam dawman mintisir.

In the name of Khomeini and al-Sadr
Islam will always be victorious.[34]

The other verse was in classical style:

Ya faqiha al-'asr ya sayidana
Ya Aba Ja'far Ya qa'idana
Nahnu junudun laka dawman umana
Wa satabqa 'abqariyan ra'ida.

O our Lord the faqih of our time,
O the father of Ja'far, our leader
We always are your faithful soldiers
And you shall remain a pioneering genius.[35]

Both the *wukala'* networks and the Da'wa Party committees were now vying with each other to bring out the largest crowds they could. This rivalry contributed to the uncovering of hitherto well-cloaked networks. The verses and mottoes were spontaneously fiery and threatening. Realizing the gravity of the situation, al-Sadr, in order to protect emulators and stop further escalation, pleaded with supporters to stop flocking to his home. According to his disciple, Sheikh Muhammad Ridha al-Nu'mani, al-Sadr was irritated by the Mubaya'a movement itself, considering it unnecessary and detrimental.[36]

At the height of the Mubaya'a movement, on 1 June 1979, al-Sadr replied to Khomeini. Although the cable stressed the 'scholarly nature' of Najaf, it nevertheless carried Arabist political themes. It read:

> Samahat Ayatollah al-'Uzma al-Imam al-Mujahid Sayyid Ruhalla al-Khomeini, I have received your kind telegram, which embodied your parenthood (*ubowatumukm*) and spiritual patronage for the Holy Najaf that has been living your great victories since parting with you; I draw from your honouring guidance a spiritual breath, as I also feel the depth of responsibility for the protection of the scholarly existence of Holy Najaf. I would like to express to you on this occasion the salutations of millions of Muslims and believers in our dear Iran, which found in the light of Islam, now shining again thanks to you, a guiding beacon for the whole world, and a spiritual energy to strike the atheist colonialists (*al-musta'mir al-kafir*), and American colonialism in particular, and to free the world from all forms of its crimes, foremost among which the crime of the usurpation of our holy land Palestine; we ask God Almighty to grant us the perenniality of your precious presence, peace on you and God's blessing and mercy.[37]

Crackdown

Al-Sadr's worries were not unfounded. Shrewdly, the Ba'th security organs, notorious for their fast and tough measures, let the Mubaya'a procession continue without interruption. The smooth running was deceptive. From the first to last moment, the delegates were kept under constant surveillance: names were registered, and all visitors were photographed and filmed. Vast intelligence was gathered, it seems, in a very short time. The crackdown was planned for 12 June 1979, when around 200 or so security and police agents arrested al-Sadr at dawn (5.00 am) and escorted him to the general directorate of the security service in Baghdad, then under Fadhil al-Barrak. No further arrests were made. From that day onwards, a series of demonstrations and mass unrest spread across Shi'ite towns, quarters and even villages. Da'wa organizations were mobilized into action. Apart from Najaf and Karbala, demonstrations took place in several predominantly Shi'ite suburbs in Baghdad, mainly in al-Thawra city and Kazimain. Similar commotions swept Kut and Nu'maniya (Wasit province); al-Khalis, Jedaidat al-Shat and Jizan al-Chol (Diyala province); Kufa (Najaf governorate); Simawa and Rumaitha (Muthana province); Fuhood (Nasiriya or Thi Qar province). Other towns witnessed limited or unsuccessful attempts to act (Basra, Diwaniya and other cities). This was the 17 Rajab (12 June) Intifada. The defence of the Shi'i *marji'*, i.e. al-Sadr, on such a massive level was the first *organized* popular movement of its kind in decades. Agitation abroad was no less evident, especially in the United Arab Emirates, Lebanon, Britain and France, where pro-al-Sadr and pro-Da'wa activists were strong.[38] It proved effective in bringing public pressure to bear and was successful as far as its immediate aim was concerned, namely the release of al-Sadr.[39]

Attempts to persuade al-Sadr to suspend and bring to an end his pro-Iran agitation were made. Zaid Haider, a Lebanese member of the national command of the Ba'th party, was entrusted with a mediating mission to this end. His attempts, according to Da'wa sources, were to no avail.[40]

These diplomatic attempts were alien to the nature of the Ba'th regime and were, in point of fact, the outcome of an acute power struggle within the Ba'th leadership. In retrospect, an al-Bakr wing supported by Shi'i RL and RCC members was in the making. The power struggle revolved around various issues, including the position towards Iran, the Syria-Iraq conciliation and unity and the unification of the Ba'th parties of Syria and Iraq. The power struggle was also driven by inter-generational, clan-Party and even al-Bakr-Saddam clashes.[41] Negotiations with al-Sadr had been recommended by the flexible wing who, however, had no influence in the security apparatuses and military bureau. The failure of this flexible wing and its ultimate elimination put Saddam Hussein in an undisputed position to pursue his tough domestic and regional policies. Al-Bakr was ousted in June 1979 and twenty-two leading Ba'th figures were executed on charges of conspiring with Syria.[42] The advent of Hussein to the first position of the state was a portent of the looming confrontation.

Building on the collapse of the previous conciliatory efforts with al-Sadr, both the government and the Shi'i militants were speedily embarking on a collision course. The security crackdown was now reversed. Earlier, the campaign targeted the head, al-Sadr himself, not the grassroots. Now al-Sadr was left intact at his residence in Najaf while his grassroots organizations were attacked. Most of his *wukala'* were arrested and nineteen of them were reportedly executed.[43] Some 4,000–5,000 Da'wa activists and sympathizers were rounded up *en masse*, of whom between 200–260 were killed under torture or executed.[44]

Al-Sadr was put under house arrest. Nevertheless he was officially approached with two intriguing and politically costly demands: to religiously prohibit (*tahrim*) the Da'wa Party and to show support to the Ba'th regime in any 'flexible' way. A press interview was proposed in which al-Sadr would give a general talk, though of course his appearance would seem to be a gesture of goodwill towards the government. These demands were obviously rejected.[45]

The destruction of the *wukala'* and the Da'wa networks created a drastic vacuum. Mass agitation came to a standstill. A new medium was deployed: individual violence or acts of terror. Unlike mass agitation, terror needs loners or small groups who can act with a high degree of secrecy and have a wide margin of operational freedom. Even if such groups were discovered or destroyed, the damage would be limited. And there was no shortage of suicidal loners.

The Da'wa Party had invested and spent much of its human capital in the pro-al-Hakim campaign in 1969–70, or in 1974–75 or in the Mubaya'a movement and pro-al-Sadr release demonstrations. The blows it sustained were so extensive that the party was unable to respond further. Even its determination to resort to violent attacks was more the decision of desperate loners than a clear strategic choice. Hence when the RCC issued Resolution No. 461 on 31 March 1980, which made Da'wa membership punishable by death, the party was actually disorganized to the point that it could not operate.

The bombing campaign which followed was carried out by different loners as a strategy of revenge rather than a political tactic of destabilization. The leadership of the MAI and some other pro-al-Hakim family supporters assumed the new role. The latter operated briefly under the name of the Mujahidin.[46] The MAI was in better shape, with cadres trained between 1976–79 in Beirut, intact organizational links and regional support from both Tehran and Syria.[47] In late November of 1979, a student of the MAI, Talib al-Alili from Hamza town, attacked a number of Ba'th members and security agents who were parading the processions of mourners in 'Ashura on its way to the Hussain mosque. A Ba'th figure was killed and the attacker was shot dead. The incident did not, perhaps, draw much security attention. The major turn came on 1 April 1980 with an attempt on the life of the deputy premier and foreign minister Tariq Aziz, a member of the RCC and the Ba'th Party. At a rally in Mustansiriya University, Baghdad, an Islamist loner and member of the MAI, Samir Nuri Ali, hurled a grenade at Aziz and pulled his gun to fire a few shots into the crowd before he was killed in the crossfire with Aziz's bodyguards. Some students were also killed in the incident.

Four days later, the funeral of the victims organized by the NUIS, the Ba'th official student's union, was assaulted near Waziriya with a spray of bullets and a hand grenade. Some mourners were killed and the president of NUIS, Muhammad Dabdab, was injured.

The MAI field operators in Iraq were authorized by their leadership to launch attacks, but the assailants in these two incidents acted on their own although in line with directives.[48]

This chain of events led to two major and perhaps final developments: On 31 March 1980 a decree issued by the RCC made membership of the Da'wa punishable by death; on 4 April, al-Sadr was arrested for the second and last time. Some Da'wa sources have claimed that al-Sadr had issued two important *fatwas*, one prohibiting affiliation to the Ba'th party, another endorsing armed struggle.[49] Other claims maintain that he also issued three successive political appeals to the Iraqi people to rise up against the Ba'th. These appeals were alleged by the Da'wa to have been recorded and circulated; but al-Sadr's attendants admit that they were published posthumously.[50] The final arrest of al-Sadr was shrewdly effected. This time he was secretly escorted with his sister to Baghdad. On the dawn of 9 April the body of al-Sadr, but not of his sister Bint al-Huda, was brought for burial at the Salam Cemetery in Najaf. Presumably he was executed the previous day.[51] This was the first execution of a Grand Ayatollah in the modern history of the Middle East.

With the elimination of al-Sadr, the Iraqi Shi'i militants – above all the Da'wa Party – lost a unifying symbol and a centre of political and social gravity. Al-Sadr himself met his death as a result of a premature violent confrontation in which he was entangled.

Islamic Shi'ite militancy in Iraq paid dearly for its euphoria at the success of the Iranian Revolution. The militants had suddenly discovered the decisive importance of mass agitation in the street and jumped at an overestimated conception of their ability to reproduce it. They were driven into exile under the Iranian umbrella or into sporadic, limited clandestine activity. Paradoxically, this accelerated their transformation into political parties proper, but detached them from their political habitat.

The Ba'th state had itself miscalculated. It had overestimated the potency of Iraqi organized Shi'i Islam – a fact which, among other factors, had far-reaching consequences: a change of hands at the helm, a severe and bloody crackdown on Shi'i militants and even Shi'is at large with mass deportation and a regional war which lasted some eight years.

Ba'th-Shi'ite Islamist relations shifted from limited cultural opposition to massive, political bloody confrontation.

FOURTEEN

The Formation and Development of SAIRI: Coercive Unification, War and Schisms, 1982–90

The Formation of SAIRI

On 17 November 1982, Muhammad Baqir al-Hakim announced the establishment in Tehran of the Supreme Assembly of the Islamic Revolution in Iraq [SAIRI] (al-Majlis al-A'la lil Thawra al-Islamiya fil Iraq), a scheme providing an all-encompassing structure for Islamist activism in Iraq.

The announcement came two years after the execution of al-Sadr and the outbreak of the Iraq-Iran war. In this period, all Iraqi Shi'ite groups transferred their headquarters and the bulk of their human resources to Tehran, where they sustained a radical change in organization and ideology – entering, thereby, the third, new, Islamist phase of their development. From the moment of its inception, SAIRI represented the ideological-Islamist model proper in contradistinction to both earlier models presented thus far: the *modernizing-universalist-cultural* model of 1959–60 and the *particularist* model of the 1960s and 1970s.

The formation of SAIRI was envisaged as a result of Iranian impact and intervention. The Iranian effort to unseat the Iraqi regime was in dire need of an all-representative Iraqi body of which Iraqi Shi'ite militant Islam fell short. Iraqi Shi'ite groups were extremely divided; they lacked any mechanisms for pan-Shi'ite, let alone pan-Iraqi, cooperation and representation; they were mostly led on a pan-Islamic rather than an Iraqi national basis. The Da'wa, for example, was an international structure including Lebanon, the Gulf and beyond. The MAI had similar pretensions. On the other hand, both organizations were confined to the sectarian divide in the context of the Iraqi nation-state. In addition, the MAI was more in line with Ayatollah Shirazi than Khomeini; the Da'wa was conceived with the customary clerical suspicion of any 'party' outside the realm of the *marja'*-masses dichotomy.

The Iranian endeavours for the formation of SAIRI were plagued by chronic contradictions. Divisions among these groups were ramified: political, ideological, ethnic, local and even familial. The leadership vacuum caused by the execution of al-Sadr also aggravated differences. Shi'ite militant Islam was represented by the Da'wa, the MAI, the Mujahidin' and the independent Shi'i *'ulama*. Each group was associated either with a Karbala, Najaf or certain family centre of gravity. Each jealously guarded its own positions and boundaries. The previous ideological differences were all the more exacerbated by new political and ideological issues: the nature and limits of *wilayat al-faqih* or who would assume leadership in the Iraqi field; what forms of cooperation among different groups, what methods of political struggle and the like.

From May 1980 (when al-Sadr was executed) to November 1982 (when SAIRI was proclaimed) several Iranian-sponsored attempts to unify Iraqi groups were not only unsuccessful but also more divisive.[2] In 1979, the first attempt to organize the Iraqi *'ulama* in Assembly of *'Ulama* for the Islamic Revolution in Iraq (The Majlis al-'Ulama Lil Thawra al-Islamiya fil Iraq), presided over by Murtadha al-'Askari, ended with the disintegration of this group. Possibly the ethnic and ideological factors were crucial because al-'Askari was of Iranian origin and a founding member of the Da'wa. A second attempt, the creation of The Revolutionary Army for the Liberation of Iraq (al-Jaish al-Islami Li Tahrir al-Iraq), crumbled under the impact of factional struggles over shares in the leadership. Another new plan to assemble the Iraqi *'ulama* in the The Society of Militant *'Ulama* in Iraq (Jama'at al-'Ulama al-Mujahidin fil Iraq) under Muhammad Baqir al-Hakim also had an organizational problem. It was the first elected body (from among 80 clerics) but its general secretary was an appointee.[3] Those who could not survive elections protested against both their exclusion and the appointment of Baqir al-Hakim. The new organization of *'ulama* had no power over any of the different organizations represented by its leading figures; for these were directed, financed and controlled by independent centres. The Society of *'Ulama* enjoyed but a moral influence with no real apparatuses or networks to formulate policy or execute it.

The crisis indicated a gulf between the *'ulama* and the political organizations acting independently. The balance of power within the *'ulama* group did not coincide with the actual power relations among political groups. These contradictions rendered the Jama'at inoperative. The ensuing political impotence of the Jama'at paved the way to the creation of The Bureau of the Islamic Revolution in Iraq (Maktab al-Thawra al-Islamiya fil Iraq) headed by Muhammad Baqir al-Hakim. The Bureau was set up to provide administrative and logistic support for Iraqi militants, deportees and refugees residing in Iran (issuing residence permits, identity cards, providing lodging, arms and the like). But it was soon transformed into a political framework in which to assemble different Shi'ite organizations and to include some Kurdish and Turkoman Sunni Islamists in order to overcome both the supra-national and sub-national tendencies inherently built in the Shi'ite Islamist groups.[4] The Maktab was modelled in harmony with the Iranian conception of mass politics. Its aversion to any form of party politics was anchored in its firm belief in the charismatic powers of the *mujtahids*, their ability to move mountains of mass followers with a twinkle of an eye. Iranian clerical officials kept reprimanding and reminding their Iraqi counterpart of the *muzaharat milioniya* (millions of demonstrators) and the *madad ghaibi* (divine intervention) which the Imam could create. To this the MAI had responded with harsh criticism:

> The Islamic revolution in Iran was not made by the Imam [Khomeini] but by the people [*sha'ab*] ... The Imam could never trigger the revolution or topple the Shah's regime had the Iranian people been idle and quiet.[5]

Different disadvantaged clerical or partisan groups extended several proposals to the Iranians. One bid offered rehabilitation of al-Sadr's plan to establish a collective leadership known as *al-qiyada al-na'iba*, which included in its original version Muhammad Baqir al-Hakim, Kazim al-Ha'iri, Mahmud al-Hashimi and possibly one or two other figures. In opposition to this, al-Hakim's supporters advanced the concept of 'single leadership'. Seeking a midway solution, a third proposal envisaged the submission of the Iraqi movements to the direct leadership of Khomeini. Two delegations visited Ayatollahs Muntaziri and Khomeini successively to address the problem, but were advised to seek an Iraqi solution to an Iraqi question. In this instance we may observe to what extent Shi'ism in Iran was integrated with Iranian nationalism while Iraqi Shi'ite clerical groups were more immersed in Islamist internationalism.

The concepts of leadership revolved, as is obvious, on the given leading role of the *'ulama*, in itself a contradictory notion inconsistent with the reality of partisan life. Islamist parties advanced a totally contrasting view: the leading role should be assigned to a leading party; a second variant was to form a front of parties and personalities.[6]

These objections were unheeded. Khamene'i (the present 'leader' of the revolution in Iran), then Khomeini's representative in the Higher Defence Council and the Leader of Friday Prayers in Tehran, was supportive of al-Hakim. As he was in charge of liaison with Iraqi groups, he was bent on developing the Maktab and completing its transformation into what became known as SAIRI. Muhammad Baqir al-Hakim was appointed speaker of SAIRI, Mahmud al-Hashimi as president. Both were disciples of al-Sadr, and both were among the four or five clerical figures named by al-Sadr to form what he presumably had envisaged as the 'vice-leadership' (*al-qiyada al-na'iba*). Al-Hashimi was a Najafi of Iranian origin; al-Hakim was an Arab.[7]

As the concept of 'vice-leadership' had been a measure to appoint a collective leadership to assume responsibility should al-Sadr himself face a hazard, the Iranian patrons made utmost use of it in their own way to resolve the sundry pressures from different groups. To avoid any negative reactions, the leading figures and the composition of SAIRI committees were kept secret. The only exception was the name of the speaker, Muhammad Baqir al-Hakim. It was only after the fourth session of SAIRI that the name of the chairman, al-Hashimi, was declared.

By mere titles, the status of Speaker is lower or second in the hierarchy to that of Chairman. The arrangement, it seems, was to please and appease clerical opponents who attacked al-Hakim's appointment on the grounds that he was less versed in matters of jurisprudence than other contenders such as al-Hashimi himself. Mahmud al-Hashimi, a disciple and close aide of al-Sadr, was of a much higher calibre in terms of theological, intellectual production. Al-Hashimi rose to prominence in jurisprudence in the 1970s when he co-authored, with al-Sadr. a number of works including a multi-volume treatise on legal methodology (*'usul*) titled *Buhuth fi Sharh al-'Urwa al-Wuthqa (Studies on the Interpretation of* al-'Urwa al-Wuthqa), published in Najaf in 1971.[8] And it was al-Hashimi who was entrusted with the task of liaising with the Iranians shortly after the 1979 revolution.[9] Unlike al-Hakim, al-Hashimi had no political record. Al-Hakim was among the early individuals who had joined the Da'wa. His name also figured on the list of the junior or apprentice *'ulama* in 1959. He was arrested several times in the 1970s, and emerged as an influential Najafi cleric who negotiated peace with the organizers of the Marad al-Ras episode in February 1977. He was arrested in its aftermath and received a life sentence. In 1979 he was granted amnesty and managed to flee the country to Syria shortly after the execution of his patron al-Sadr. After a brief stay of a few months, he went to Iran. To the Iran-based Iraqi Islamist group, al-Hakim was a latecomer and an alien. His rise would have been inconceivable without Iranian patronage and pressures on other groups.

The establishment of SAIRI was accelerated by the apparent Iranian successes in the war. In April 1982, Iraqi forces had been driven from the Iranian territory they had occupied, and plans were then made to invade Iraq. A possible scenario was to seize the port city of Basra in the south and proclaim and Iraqi Islamic government in the 'liberated' city.[10]

The duet, al-Hakim and al-Hashimi, played different roles in the animation of SAIRI. Al-Hakim actively filled the leadership role, conducting day-to-day tasks and building the apparatuses SAIRI needed. He so surpassed al-Hashimi in this realm that the two changed position in 1986. Al-Hashimi became spokesman of SAIRI, al-Hakim its influential and supreme chairman. The former left for Qum and kept a very low political profile. Al-Hashimi's eclipse was the fate of so many prominent clergy. Their diminishing weight was attributable to their lack of family repute (as with al-Hakim) and of lay support networks and, of course, of Iranian patronage. Perhaps that is why al-Hakim left his leading position in the *Jama'at al-'Ulama al-Mujahidin* in the elections of 1985. He was replaced by Muhammad Baqir al-Nasiri.[11] In a word, religious knowledge was not conducive to political significance, a reality which contradicts Shi'ite theological norms of clerical leadership, including perhaps some interpretations of the *wilayat al-faqih* concept.

SAIRI's Structure

SAIRI went through various phases of development. At its beginning in 1982 it was more of an Iranian-sponsored bureaucratic structure to effect an administrative unification of fragmented Iraqi Islamist groups. As is shown in Table 14.1, influence has been divided among the Da'wa (five members, i.e. one third), the MAI (one member) and SAIRI, that is, al-Hakim's clients. The latter had three direct representatives. The number of independents was five, but at least three of them were pro-al-Hakim; the other two independents were obviously pro-SAIRI as an umbrella organization, but not necessarily pro-al-Hakim as a person. Other features of the table are also interesting: the overwhelming weight of Najaf: seven out of fifteen representatives (almost half); Karbala had four; Kazimain, one (two by origin rather than residence); Baghdad proper, one (but of Najafi origin); Nasiriya, one and Basra, one. The regional distribution is very narrow and almost entirely concentrated in Najaf and Karbala due to the weight of the clerical category. It is also interesting to note that six of the members (just under half) were laymen with modern education, and only eight were clerics. This was at a time when the primacy and leadership of the jurisprudents were held supreme. But three of the laymen were of noble descent (*sayyids*). Lastly, there were only four members of Persian origin, compared to ten Iraqi Arabs.

Table 14.1: The Composition of the First SAIRI Council (1982)

Name	City	Occupation in 1982	Age	Party	Based	Ethnic origin
Muhammad Baqir al-Hakim	Najaf	cleric*	41–50	SAIRI	Tehran	Arab
Mahmud al-Hashimi	Najaf	cleric*	51–60	Independent	Qum	Persian
Hussein al-Sadr	Najaf/ Kazimiya	lawyer*	41–50	Independent	London	Arab
Muhammad Baqir al-Nasiri	Nasiriya	cleric*	61–70	Da'wa	Qum	Arab
Kazim al-Ha'iri	Najaf	cleric*	41–50	Da'wa	Qum	Persian
Aziz al-Hakim	Najaf	cleric*	41–50	SAIRI	Tehran	Arab

Name	City	Occupation in 1982	Age	Party	Based	Ethnic origin
Muhammad Taqi al-Mudarisi	Karbala	cleric*	41–50	MAI	Tehran	Persian
Muhammad M. Asifi	Najaf	cleric	51–60	Da'wa speaker	Tehran	Persian
Jawad al-Khalisi	Kazimiya	engineer	31–40	Independent	Damascus	Arab
Akram al-Hakim	Karbala	university lecturer	31–40	SAIRI	London	Arab
Ali Musawi	Najaf/ Baghdad	engineer	31–40	Independent	London	Arab
Abu Ahmad Ja'fari**	Karbala	Doctor of medicine*	31–40	Da'wa PB member	London	Ara
Salih Adib	Karbala	engineer***	51–60	Da'wa	Tehran	Arab
Hasan Faraj Allah	Basra	cleric	51–60	Independent	Khuzestan	Arab
Shihab Abu Haidar	Omara	engineer	31–40	ex-Da'wa	?	Arab

This table is based on information provided by Akram al-Hakim, director of the Maktab al-Thawra al-Islamiya (Tehran) and a close aide of SAIRI's chairman, Baqir al-Hakim. Akram al-Hakim is at present head of SAIRI's office in London. He descends from a Karbala 'al-Hakim' family and should not be confused with the Najaf *mujtahid* al-Hakim family. The table has been enriched by details and amendments suggested by Abu Ahmad al-Ja'fari. The table was also verified by Muhammad Baqir al-Nasiri, chairman of the Jama'at al-'Ulama al-Mujahidin. All individuals described as 'independent' have patronage relations with al-Hakim.With the exception of al-Nasiri, all membes have been verified by al-Hakim and Ja'fari.

* All individuals marked with * are *sayyids*.
** This is a *nom de guerre*, and was kept as provided by the informant according to the official announcement of SAIRI. The real name of Abu Ahmad is Ibrahim al-Ushaiqir (see tables on the Da'wa leaders in the 1980s).
*** Actually holder of an MA degree in agriculture.

In a second step, SAIRI's leading body was enlarged to encompass Kurds and other Sunni Islamic or allied groups to lend the structure a pan-Iraqi character. SAIRI was reorganized time and again. Its leading body, the Majlis Shura – which is the equivalent of the central committee in Leninist cell-parties – was increased to seventeen members in the second annual session, then to thirty-two in the fourth annual session. In 1986 (the sixth session) a two-tier governing body was established: The Majlis Shura, or central committee, was restricted now to fifteen members, renewable every year. Below it there was a General Assembly (al-Hay'a al-'Amma). Actual power and decision making rested only partly in the hands of the Majlis Shura. Real power was in the hands of the executive committee. This body was an administrative and managing bureaucracy with client functionaries handpicked by al-Hakim.

SAIRI was administratively arranged on modern lines. Five sections were set up: the Information Unit, Military Unit, Administrative and Financial Unit, Social Welfare Unit and Intelligence Unit. All these units were answerable to al-Hakim's bureau. The individuals in charge of the management and administration of the five units, including al-Hakim's bureau, constituted the Executive Committee. It is this committee which held real power in SAIRI. In its turn the executive committee was almost totally under the direct control of al-Hakim. Inasmuch as SAIRI could act on its own, the units, the Executive Committee and their functionaries, formed al-Hakim's own organization and his active political instrument.[12] Thus SAIRI had the reality of being both an Iranian apparatus and a political instrument of al-Hakim.

However, it should also be mentioned that SAIRI's military and intelligence units were both actually managed by the Iranians. With the creation of the Faylaq Badr (the Badr Army), intelligence and military affairs were taken from these units and conveyed to Badr. The jurisdiction of SAIRI's military unit was thus restricted to the administrative affairs of the military: salaries, budget and recruitment.

A second Majlis Shura was formed in 1986, which totalled eleven members. The council was later expanded with the addition of two to three new members. According to Table 14.2, the council sustained considerable changes in many ways. The new list shows that six of the previous members were dropped. Three of them were influential clerical figures: Hussein al-Sadr, Muhammad al-Nasiri and Kazim al-Ha'iri, who commanded a higher religious status than al-Hakim, if not by dint of intellectual production then by age; all three were older than al-Hakim. This aspect of the reshuffling suggests the new list was aimed at curbing the influence of strong clerics and replacing them with more convenient figures.

With the exception of SAIRI, the influence of different parties changed in quantity or quality. SAIRI retained the largest share. It had three direct members and three pro-al-Hakim independent representatives: six voices under its control. The Da'wa sustained a significant loss. Four of the six dropped were from the Da'wa, which commanded three seats compared to five in the previous formation. The MAI still held one voice but the level of its representation was lowered. There were fewer newcomers in the Majlis Shura: a Da'wa splinter group was allocated one seat (sponsored by al-Hakim and the Iranians); the Haraka al-Islamiya (a Kurdish organization), two; another Arab Sunni group is represented by one.

Table 14.2: Composition of the Second SAIRI Council (Majlis Shura), Sixth Session, 1986–90

	Name	City	Occupation	Age	Party	Base	Ethnic origin
1	Muhammad Baqir al-Hakim*(now Chairman)						
2	Mahmud al-Hashimi*(now Spokesman)						
3	Aziz al-Hakim*						
4	Muh. Taqi al-Mudarisi**						
5	Muh. al-Asifi*						
6	Akram al-Hakim*						
7	Abu Ahmad Ja'fari*						
8	Ali Adib Abu Bilal***	Karbala	teacher	40–49	Da'wa	Tehran	Arab
9	Muh. Najib Barzanji	Halabja	cleric[a]	50–59	Haraka	London	Kurd
10	Muh. Haidari	Baghdad	cleric[b]	40–49	Independent	Tehran	Arab
11	Representative of Badr Army (anonymous)[c]			40–49	Independent	Tehran	Arab
12	Abdul Zahra Uthman	Basra	teacher	40–49	Da'wa (split)[d]	Tehran	Arab
13	Muh. Taqi Mawla (Abu Ali)	Kirkuk	cleric[e]		Haraka		Turkoman
14	Sami al-Badri	Baghdad	cleric[f]				Arab

This table has been compiled based on information provided by Akram al-Hakim. A few amendments have also been provided by Abu Ahmad al-Ja'fari (*nom de guerre*). The table has also been verified by Muhammad Baqir al-Nasiri, Chairman of the Jama'at al-'Ulama.

*   Retained their membership in the Majlis Shura or Central Committee. For details see Table 14.1.

**   After a few months, al-Mudarisi withdrew in protest and was replaced by his deputy in the MAI, Muhsin al-Husayni.

***   No. 8 is a *nom de guerre*. Adib is a member of the Da'wa Political Bureau and was a secondary school teacher in the 1950s.

a   No. 9 is a Sunni Kurd of the Kurdish Islamic Movement, a graduate of the Fiqh School in Baghdad.

b   No. 10 is a science graduate, but is now 'turbaned'. He was one of al-Sadr's disciples and has, presumably, close links with al-Hakim who, in turn, was a novice of al-Sadr.

c   No. 11, the representative of the Badr Army, is said to have been an ex-member of the Da'wa who defected to SAIRI. He is described as an Arab from the south, either from Umara or Massiriya. In 1988, the representative of Badr was specified as being Haitham Mahfuz, aka Abu Ibrahim.

d.   No. 12 represents a splinter group which defected from the Da'wa mother party. The group was mainly formed of Basrite members. The group identifies itself as 'Da'wa Islamiya', without the term 'party'.

e   No. 13 is from Tuz Khurmato, a small town south of Kirkuk. He was entrusted with the military unit which administered logistics and finances of the armed wing.

f   No. 14, Badri, is originally from Samara.

Regional representation was modified. True, Najafis and Karbalais still commanded the largest share: eight out of fourteen (compared with virtually eleven out of fourteen in the previous configuration), yet Baghdad increased its share from one to two, and two Kurdish cities from the north appeared in the forum for the first time. Basra and Nasiriya did not change their respective positions.

The clerical/lay ratio also changed. The number of clerics increased to nine (compared with eight) while the number of lay persons decreased to five (compared with six). The status of the newcomers was less prominent than their previous counterparts.

The proportionate presence of different ethnic groups was also significantly changed: the number of Arabs decreased from ten to nine, although they were still the largest single group. The number of Persians decreased from four to three and concomitantly the Kurdish and Turkoman presence (two for both) increased. Finally, Sunnis made their appearance for the first time: three out of fourteen compared with none in the previous list. The list shows a general tendency towards wider regional, ethnic and communal inclusion. But it also shows a tendency to weaken the Da'wa and to retain an al-Hakim monopoly on the organization. Another apparent inclination is the fostering of the presence of clerics at the expense of laymen, but also a leaning towards younger, less experienced or well-versed clerical figures.

Some of these tendencies were more visible in the constitution of the General Assembly (al-Hay'a al-'Amma). It included 80–82 members. Theoretically, the general assembly acted as a monitoring body to check and balance the activities of the Majlis Shura (the leading body). But this assembly was, in point of fact, a symbol of a pan-Iraqi Islamist parliament. Clear evidence supporting this conclusion is the regional, ethnic, sectarian and occupational profile of the general assembly. According to biographical details of an incomplete list of 65 members, the following observations may be established:[13]

The ethnic profile is more assertive of the Arab character. Fifty-four members were Iraqi Arabs; only four were of Persian origin, i.e. persons who have by law the right to acquire, or may have obtained, Iranian nationality. The weight of Arabs in SAIRI's assembly far surpasses their actual weight in the leadership of the Da'wa, the MAI or even the Majlis Shura of SAIRI itself. Five are Kurds and two are Turkomans. The inclusion of both the Kurds and Turkomans is symbolic but not without significance. They come from two groups: the pro-Iran Hizbollah Kurdish Party, led by Khalid Barzani (the maternal uncle of Mas'ud Barzani, leader of the KDP), a configuration organized according to the tribal following of Sheikh Khalid himself; and al-Haraka al-Islamiya, led by Sheikh Uthman. This group relies on the Jaf tribe and their tribal kin in the Halabja town and its surroundings.

Table 14.3: Regional Origins of Members of the General Assembly of SAIRI

District	Number	Percent
North	7	10.00
Middle	21	30.00
Baghdad	16	22.80
South	18	25.80
Unspecified origin	3	4.30
No available details	5	7.10
Total	70	100.00

The overall membership of the General Assembly was 70. The present calculation is based on information mainly provided by Akram al-Hakim. Minor corrections were added according to information given by Muhammad Baqir al-Nasiri, Chairman of the Jama'at al-'Ulama, and details given by Abu Ahmad al-Ja'fari, PB Da'wa and SAIRI council member. The ratio of representation would alter if details on the five anonymous members were obtained.

The sectarian profile of the general assembly is overwhelmingly Shi'ite (57 members) as opposed to only eight Sunnis of whom seven were non-Arabs. Arab Sunni representation thus only comprised one member.

The regional distribution of the delegates is more varied than that of the Majlis Shura or the executive committee. It is as follows: The northern provinces (Anbar, Salahudin, Kirkuk, Sulaimaniya, Arbil and Mosul), which are mainly Sunni but with pockets of Shi'i Turkomans, are thinly represented. The middle provinces (Karbala, Najaf, Hilla, Diyala) have a large share because of the influence of the clerical class of the holy shrine cities. This region is predominantly Shi'ite; only Diyala is a mixed province. The southern provinces are mostly Shi'ite (with the exception of mixed Basra and Nasiriya, which has Sunni pockets) and have shown growing political activism and furnished many leading cadres to all Islamist groups.

The regional spread may provide a clearer picture when the list is broken into individual cities and towns. Measured against the whole population of a province (urban and rural), the proportion of known delegates from each province in the general assembly not only varies but reveals an over- or under-representation. Only Baghdad proper has a representation which matches its demographic size. A number of provinces have a higher ratio. Karbala is the highest with 5:1; Najaf has 3:1; Basra, more than 2:1; Umara, more than 2:1; Sulaimaniya, 1.5:1; and Kirkuk, almost 1:1.

These ratios assert the leading roles played by Karbala and Najaf as the holy shrine cities and the seat of the clerical class. Basra and Umara come next in their relative activism for the rising role of the 'ulama from these provinces. The eminence of Sulaimaniya is explained by the advance and growth of al-Haraka in the Kurdish region together with the rehabilitation of the Kurdish armed guerrilla movement in general. The low ratios are observable in some southern and middle Shi'ite or mixed provinces where the percentage of urban population is relatively low. This is an indication that the Islamist movements are situated in densely urban provinces. It also reveals how thin the presence and influence of the clerical class in the countryside is, and how far these classes and strata are removed from the demands of the peasantry.

Table 14.4: The Composition of SAIRI's General Assembly According to City or Province

City	No. of delegates	Percent of total	Pop. of province	Percent of urbans in prov.	Percent of prov. to tot. pop.	Ratio of delegates to prov.
	1	2	3	4	5	2 to 5
Baghdad**	13 (+2)	23.00	3,841,268	23.50		1 to 1
Karbala	10	15.40	469,282	71.00	2.80	5 to 1
Najaf	9	13.80	590,078	72.00	3.60	4 to 1
Basra***	8	12.30	872,176	72.30	5.30	1.5 to 1
Umara	4	6.10	487,448	61.60	2.90	2 to 1
Sulaimaniya	5	7.10	951,723	71.50	5.80	1.4 to 1

City	No. of delegates	Percent of total	Pop. of province	Percent of urbans in prov.	Percent of prov. to tot. pop.	Ratio of delegates to prov.
	1	*2*	*3*	*4*	*5*	*2 to 5*
Nasiriya****	2	3.00	921,106	53.30	5.60	1 to 3
Kirkuk	2	3.00	601,219	75.40	3.60	1 to 1
Kazimiya****	1	calculated within Baghdad				
The South (unspecified)	2	3.00				
Diwaniya	1	1.50	559,805	56.40	3.40	1 to 3
Kut	1	1.50	364,670	52.00	2.40	1 to 2
Hilla	1	1.50	1,109,574	46.00	6.80	1 to 7
Diyala***	1	1.50	961,073	46.10	5.80	1 to 6
Samara***	1	1.50	726,138	40.20	4.40	1 to 4*****
Unknown	3	4.60				
Total	65	5 are not included in the calculation for lack of information				

*   Based on census for the year 1987 (Republic of Iraq, Ministry of Planning, Central Statistical Organization, *Annual Abstract of Statistics*, 1992, pp. 40, 64–5).
**   The size of population is for the city of Baghdad.
***   These are mixed cities in terms of Shi'i-Sunni composition.
****   Kazimiya is a northern suburb of Baghdad. Being exclusively Shi'ite in character and residence, it merits a special mention. This is to contrast it with Najaf and Karbala in view of the historical rivalries among their clerical families and possible alliances.
***** The city and its rural surroundings.

Occupational features of the 65 members of the general assembly are unique indeed. Contrary to the structure of the Majlis Shura where the *'ulama* rank high, the general assembly has the following features (see Table 14.5, Categories A, B, C, D).

Table 14.5: The Composition of the General Assembly According to Education and Profession

A. Nature of education			
Category	Number	Percent	Remarks
Clerical learning	18	27.7	
Secular learning	31	47.7	
Mixed	15	23.00	Individuals who have secular and clerical academic training.
Other	1	1.5	Tribal chieftain with no formal education.
B. Secular educated group by profession and/or academic degree			
Postgraduates	7		
MAs	2		
PhDs	4		
Physicians	5*		
Lawyers	1*		
Pharmacists	1*		
Engineers	4*		
Secondary school teachers	4*		
Accountants	1*		
Teachers	2		
Total	31		
C. Mixed education category			
MA	1		
BA	13		
Secondary schools	1		
Total	15		
D. Mixed category by profession			
Engineers	2		
Scientists	1		
Lawyers	1		
Teachers	1 (secular school)		

Category	Number	Percent	Remarks
Pharmacists	1		
Clerical functions	9		
Total	15		

*   All categories marked with * are postgraduates.

Modern professionals constitute a larger group than ever before (47.7 percent), an indication of the growing role of the ever-expanding, urban-based middle and lower middle classes whose political activism has been steadily increasing. By contrast, the *'ulama* occupy the second rank, almost half the size of the first category. What is more interesting in the list of 65 members is the existence of a mixed category, namely individuals who have religious and secular learning, hold higher degrees (PhDs, MAs, Bas; only one has a lower grade) and enjoy high standing in both disciplines. Some were originally clerics (nine out of fifteen) who yearned for academic rank because of the diminishing importance of religious learning and religious academies (*hawza*). Such a trend had been going on for decades, at least until 1979. Others (six out of fifteen) present the direct opposite pattern: lay persons with scientific, secular education yearning for theological and jurisprudential learning to satisfy a new need for religious rank.

This tendency was triggered by the Iranian Revolution and the general Islamist critique of secular Westernized education. On the basis of this differentiation, we may increase the number of modern educated members from thirty-one to thirty-seven (from 47.7 to 56.9 percent), and the number of clerics from eighteen to twenty-seven (from 27.7 to 41.5 percent). The result would retain the overwhelming weight of the first category of modern educated elements.

Lastly, there is only one tribal *sheikh*, a Kurd, which in itself is self-evident. Arab tribal sheikhs in the Shi'ite south have lost their power as a social class. Their Sunni counterparts have been ascending the social ladder under the Ba'th. Traditional Kurdish clan chieftains have different fortunes: some have thrived on handsome state contracts, as did the Surjis and Herkis; others were involved in anti-government guerilla wars.[14]

The General Assembly, the prototype of an Iran-sponsored Islamic parliament, could have played a crucial role had the Iranian war effort been victorious. With the end of the war, the general assembly lost much of its importance and has virtually fallen into oblivion.

The actual and enduring aspect of SAIRI is its reality as an organization of the al-Hakim group. With Iranian logistics and assistance, al-Hakim built both institutions and supportive popular bases. The former consist of the Al-Sadr Foundation in Tehran, a social agency to extend welfare services to deportees, the Markaz al-Tawthiq (Documentation Centre) and, in addition, networks of offices in various towns or Arab and foreign capitals such as Damascus or London.

Al-Hakim did not build a Leninist-type party with cells and vertically arranged committees and sub-committees, but instead combined both the small but effective bureaucracy he had (the executive apparatuses of SAIRI) with traditional recruitment and mobilization methods: agitation of mass followers through a system of young *wukala'* (deputies or agents), both lay and clerical, active in mosques. His *wukala'* organized loosely held *hay'at* (bodies) of sympathizers and clients who would attend public meetings, demonstrations, ceremonies and ritual services.

The *wukala'* who supervise these *hay'at* form the so-called Body of Preachers (Hay'at al-Mubalighin). In the words of one of his aides, al-Hakim wished to fuse both modern institutions with traditional networks of Shi'i emulators[15] – the former to ensure day-to-day functioning, the latter to uphold his religious standing for a forthcoming elevation to Grand Ayatollah status. The former consists of departments and offices, the latter of mosque-based popular bodies of sympathizers. No longer is SAIRI looked upon as a unified Islamic front or an all-encompassing umbrella; rather it is merely perceived as another Shi'ite Islamist party existing side by side with other, similar groups. In different events or political negotiations, Da'wa, MAI and SAIRI send their respective delegates as independent organizations.

SAIRI's function as an Islamic front for Shi'i militants, or its capacity as a pan-Iraqi Islamist forum was indeed formal. But its reality as an al-Hakim project also explains its other facet as an Iranian-managed institution.

Strategy and Tactics

The formation of SAIRI signalled an Iranian-encouraged change of strategy and tactics. For the first time in their history, the Iraqi Islamic groups adopted the establishment of an Islamic state as their immediate political goal and the only way to build an Islamic society.[16] The groups also embraced, or claimed to embrace, the Khomeinists' version of the absolute guardianship of the jurisconsult. This new political strategy, however, required new thinking and practice in terms of methods and action.[17] All sorts of conceptualized 'revolutionary violence' were debated.[18] Pressures were applied on the Iraqi organizations by different centres of power in Iran, with different conceptions of Islamic action. These may be divided into three major themes:

(i)   the concept of mass street movements – the so-called multi-million marches under the auspices of clerics – which was advocated by

Muntaziri, Khomeini's deputy at the time, as well as by the ideological Khomeinists;

(ii)   the concept of clandestine, elite armed action, bombing and assassination tactics, which was advocated by Mahdi al-Hashimi and Muhammad Muntaziri;[19]

(iii)   the concept of including the army of Iraqi fighters into the Iranian war effort. This was the vision of the administration.

In conceptual terms, the first theme was debated in 1980–82 while the second and third were used as temporary practical solutions.

During the phase of debate, multi-million-man street demonstrations were the slogan in every clerical mouth in Tehran. This concept appeared as the magical, mystical source of defeating not only the Shah, but also any regime anywhere in the world. In the eyes of clerical actors, it was a 'divine intervention' (*madad ilahi*) of universal occurrence. In early April 1982, Ayatollah Muntaziri delivered a speech advising the Palestinians to deploy the multi-million tactic to destroy the Israeli army and Israel itself.[20] The advice was directed to other Islamic groups, and clearly implied Iraqi groups, but accusations of inactivity were also thrown at them.

Against such accusations the Iraqi Shi'ite Islamic groups reacted by asserting their autonomy in the definition and management of their own action in accordance with their national realities, Islamic internationalism notwithstanding. Three responses surfaced.

Muhammad Taqi al-Mudarisi, leader of the MAI, opposed Iranian pressures for immediate mass and public action, i.e. to take to the streets and raise the slogan '*Allah Akbar*' ('God is Great') to agitate the masses of the people into defiance. This tactic of activating 'divine intervention', al-Mudarisi says, would be too costly and doomed to failure. In his many lectures delivered in 1981–82, al-Mudarisi maintained that clandestine, organizational work to educate and prepare the people was the most important thing to do at that time, and no mass politics should ever be envisaged, let alone started, before such education and mass preparation had already reached a mature level. It was then and only then that the 'zero hour', in the words of al-Mudarisi, would materialize.[21] In a booklet by the MAI, we read a fierce criticism against the 'divine intervention' attributed to direct, mass street politics:

The Imam could not have ignited the revolution to unseat the Shah had the Iranian people been calm and passive.

The booklet gives the following projection of the right revolutionary tactics, which are phased out into three different moments:

The option is ... mass *popular revolution* ... this term means that we have to [first] mobilize the masses, all classes, all strata of the people in order to topple the ruling [Ba'th] regime. The popular revolution would [secondly] materialize if and when all popular strata and classes, from workers, toilers, intellectuals, civil servants, to honest army officers, enter the arena of struggle, of hot confrontation, taking to the streets in brave marches and massive demonstrations.[22]

A few lines later, there is a bit of romantic agitation:

With bare hands but with hearts full of belief [in God], we shall face the [Ba'th] regime's agents, thugs, mercenaries, tanks, cannons and jet fighters.[23]

This is how the mass movement, the second phase, would begin and end. As the confrontation escalated, it would enter the third phase:

... The movement reaches a boiling point where streets would be dotted by barricades, burning tires ... And the masses would arm themselves with whatever is available, sticks, bricks and Molotovs to attack the security and intelligence headquarters, occupy prisons and detention camps [to liberate militants], banks [to provide cash] and military barracks.[24]

This armed insurrection would be synchronized with

... a general strike by pupils, students, workers, civil servants, merchants, in addition to a mutiny by [some army and other] officers who decline to obey official orders.[25]

The MAI envisages that such a co-ordinated series of peaceful to violent mass street and armed, military-civilian tactics would culminate in the collapse of state control and lead to

... the total paralysis of the economy, of the regime, of crucial state departments ... The regime verges on the end, takes its last breath and perishes trampled underfoot.[26]

While written in defence of the Iraqi Islamic movement, this text is also a literal idealization and paraphrasing of the events that erupted, grew and culminated in the Iranian Revolution between 1978–79. The text, however, is meant to deploy the Iranian past experience against present Iranian pressures.

The defence against Iranian criticism and pressures urged another leader, Baqir al-Hakim of SAIRI, to contrive a method and tactic of his own. This was the second response.

Muhammad Baqir al-Hakim, then Speaker of SAIRI, adopted and circulated the well-known Maoist 'popular war' tactic.[27] He also used another term, *jihad musallah* (armed holy struggle).[28] Armed struggle is a broad general term; the popular war is a definite form of the former. Whether or not SAIRI's speaker was aware of this difference is unclear. What is clear, however, is that both were meant as a counter-criticism of the Iranian attempts to impose certain tactics on SAIRI. Al-Hakim says:

> It is true that we agree with the Islamic Revolution [in Iran], ... but we differ from the Islamic revolution in our methods and organization ... because the circumstances under which the Iraqi people live [are different] ... In many areas there are many other differences between Iran and Iraq, especially the nature of the regime in Iraq which is more repressive compared to that of the Shah.[29]

Another, third response, came from Ayatollah Shirazi. He disapproved of both multi-million street politics and single-handed car-bombing. The shortest and safest method of action, Shirazi maintains, is to arm the Arab, Shi'ite tribes of Iraq. In his view, Iraqi tribes are a vital, even crucial social organization imbued with powerful political clout. If the tribes were won over, according to Shirazi, a hostile, popular insulating belt could easily strangle the Ba'th regime.[30]

This tactic, it should noted, was successful in annoying the British colonial forces in 1920 just as it was fruitless in 1924 when *mujtahids* allied themselves with some Shi'ite tribes, financed them and enthused them into rebellion. But that happened in an agrarian society in which the rural population exceeded 70 percent of the nation.

These three different Iraqi responses have been defensive; the inactivity of these groups in 1981–82 was in fact the result of their over-activity during the period 1979–80. And in the former period they had already tried, to no avail, the Iranian tactic of street, mass politics and other armed forms like assassination and bombing campaigns.

From pedagogical, ritual-anchored local spirit and organization in the 1960s, they shifted, in thinking or practice, to all kinds of 'revolutionary violence': rural guerilla warfare, urban guerilla action, civilian, armed insurrection and armed uprising – themes and practices which occur in Maoist, Guevaran and Leninist literature. But far from executing their own professed line of long-term action, Iraqi organizations worked hand in glove with the Iranian establishment, the armed forces and the security service in two directions: the Iranian war front and a clandestine destabilizing campaign.

The reality of the Iraq-Iran war and the fact that the logistic base and constituencies (Iraqi deportees and POWs) of these movements were largely based in Iran itself, explains why and to what extent they were tied to the Iranian war-effort.

The Badr Army

The formation and functioning of the Badr Army (Faylaq Badr, named after the first battle fought by early Muslims against the polytheistic Meccan merchants) serves as a good example. The soldiery of this unit was drawn from among the Iraqi deportees and Shi'i POWs. Volunteers were sent by SAIRI and other Iraqi Islamist organizations. POWs had to have an amnesty from al-Hakim or any other religious authority. Absolved of their 'sin' as ex-Ba'thists, the Shi'i captives would join Badr as *tawabin* (penitents). Apart from a *tazkiya* (recommendation) given to individuals, and keeping records of recruitment, soldiers were actually part of the Iranian Revolutionary Guard, the second wing of the armed forces in Iran. Badr forces were trained, armed and deployed by Iranian authorities.[31]

At the beginning, some 200 volunteers were organized in 'The Forces of Imam al-Sadr'. From 1979–83 a few thousand Iraqi volunteers were trained by this unit, of whom around 1,000 were on permanent duty serving on the frontlines at in Dahleran, Ilam, Bakhtaran and in Iraqi Kurdistan. When SAIRI was established in 1982 it renamed this unit 'Liwa' al-Sadr' (The al-Sadr Regiment). The force was renamed: Regiment Badr Nine. It appeared partly at the front in Haj Omran (a village in northeast Iraq, north of Sulaimaniya), which had been captured by the Iranians in 1983. Haj Omran was declared a 'liberated' area, and al-Hakim visited the 'Iraqi' units there and said his prayers on 'freed' Iraqi soil. Badr Regiment Nine received a boost in 1987 when the Iranian Revolutionary Guard announced plans to expand its size and role. It was promoted to a full regular division.[32] Some estimates put the force at a few thousand.

Despite SAIRI's talk of the Badr Army as an Iraqi organization, the force was under Iranian command.[33] The commander of the force was an Iranian colonel, although there were some Iraqi officers on the general staff of the unit. Badr soldiers who fell on the battlefield were mourned by the Hay'at Ta'bi'at Mustaz'afin (Body for Popular Recruitment, an Iranian institution for the formation of the so-called Basij volunteer units). This Iranian body would send telegrams of condolences either to Iraqi families or Islamist groups advising them of the 'martyrdom of their son[s]'. The telegrams were neither sent to Faylaq Badr nor despatched by it. One example is the text of one of these telegrams published in *Tariq al-Thawra*. It read:

> We congratulate you [Harakat Jamahir Muslima] for the martyrdom of four heroic brothers from your political, military movement ... in the battle to retrieve the hills of Bazi Draza.[34]

In addition, SAIRI and other groups were also engaged in a destabilizing campaign of bombings inside Iraq as part of their strategy to topple the regime. These operations were also backed by Syrians to counter a similar crusade unleashed by the Iraqi Ba'th. While the web of regional power politics provided the Islamic groups with logistics and flexible bases for mobilization and operation, it also tied their strategies and tactics to these regional powers.

Various reported attempts on the life of the Iraqi president Saddam Hussein were claimed by these groups, including one by SAIRI's front organization, Al-Mujahidin.[35] The published list of bombings and would-be attempts is lengthy. It shows how far SAIRI, as well as other groups, were absorbed into the Iranian war effort on one hand, and how little attention they paid to political work inside Iraq on the other.[36]

Repercussions

All this had negative effects on the Islamic groups, weakening them. First, the collaboration with the Iranian war machine assumed an anti-national character, notably so after the withdrawal of Iraqi troops from Iranian soil in the spring of 1982. Both the Iraqi retreat and the Iranian incursions into Iraqi territories shifted the nature of the war. Prior to that point, it was a defensive war on part of Iran; now it became defensive on part of Iraq.[37] The repeated Iranian attempts to occupy major cities, or their seizure of the Iraqi village of Haj Omran in 1983 and the Fao peninsula in 1986, enhanced this shift of roles.

Prioritizing religious identity over national allegiance, SAIRI and its allies could not reach out to their co-religionists in Iraq. Among the results of the eight-year Iraq-Iran war was the rise of popular Iraqi patriotism and its momentary merger with *étatiste* nationalism. This development formed a relatively strong protective shield, which sheltered the Ba'th regime and alienated Islamist groups from the mainstream of popular sentiment.

Thus, while Iranian Islam appeared as a national force with a secondary international dimension, the Iraqi Islamic movement acted as an international movement with a secondary national dimension. The surge of Iraqi nationalism was one factor among others explaining how and why Iraq could sustain an eight-year war with an army in which 80 percent of the soldiers and 20 percent of the officers were Shi'is,[38] against a Shi'ite nation led by an *ayatollah* of noble descent from the Shi'i Imams.

Second, as the political strategy for the Islamic revolution in Iraq was pinned entirely on Iran's military campaign, Iraqi groups were minor players in their own affairs.

Third, the belief that an Iranian victory was pending kept Iraqi Islamic groups aloof from any political or even logistical cooperation or understanding with powerful secular nationalist or Marxist groups. This self-imposed alienation had ideological anti-secular overtones.

Fourth, the Iraqi Islamic groups were severed from their national habitat and locked in a few locations in Iran and Syria, where most Shi'i deportees and militants found temporary lodging. The separation from Iraq was not merely physical but also cultural and political.

The moment the war effort came to a halt in 1988, the Islamic movement lost direction and confidence and entered a rapid phase of rethinking and reorganization conducive to internal schisms and divisions, an aspect we shall deal with below.

One indication of the disillusionment is that while the Iraqi Shi'ite migrant masses used to prepare their luggage to return home in the aftermath of each and any Iranian assault on Iraq during 1982–88, during 1988–90 they carried their bags to Europe. In fact, the years 1988–90 witnessed a high and rapid exodus of Shi'is, notably from Syria, seeking political asylum in Western Europe.

Fracture Lines

The modernization of Shi'ite militancy was paradoxical. It helped shape an active social movement with the union of three Shi'ite social components: the clerics, middle class intellectuals and urban poor. But the very rapprochement of these three elements in a new configuration caused tensions to flare, triggering a host of schisms. Two types of split developed: one traditional, the other modern.

The traditional split was produced by the clerical class. As has been shown, the clerical class had its power base in the family-city solidarities. Families like al-Sadr, al-Hakim, Shirazi, Khalisi, Bahr al-'Ulum, Kho'i and others constitute through direct descent, intermarriage or alliance (patronage) a crucial factor in the rise and prominence of individuals.[39] Al-Sadrs, Shirazis and al-Hakims are classic examples of the workings of this regularity. The cases of Khomeini and al-Mudarisi are indicative of the intermarriage pattern. The former was related to Burujerdi, the latter to the Shirazis, through intermarriage and patronage. Shams al-Din of Lebanon is a case of an achievement-oriented rise.

The traditional fracture lines have, it seems, been too rigid to be overcome by the new needs and demands of ideological cooperation. Under various norms, prominent clerical families retained their actual or potential autonomous power base. This factor fragmented social authority and produced multiple political centres within the militant Shi'ite realm in Iraq.

With the exception of the Da'wa party, Iraqi Shi'ite organizations, movements or establishments have some family basis. The MAI, as has been clearly demonstrated in previous chapters, revolved around the Shirazi and al-

Mudarisi families and the Karbala local power base. Under Iranian pressures, the differences between the Shirazi and the al-Mudarisi families led to the temporary creation of the Harakat Jamahir Muslima (The Movement of Muslim Masses) supervised by Abu Ibrahim, a novice of the Qum-based Shirazi in 1982.[40] SAIRI, on the other hand, is based on the powerful al-Hakim family. Bahr al-'Ulum, who appeared on the list of Da'wa leaders and cadres in 1959, withdrew in early 1960s to lead his family. He presides over the Al al-Bait Foundation in London and was active for a few years in the INC's presidency as an independent political figure.[41]

The Kazimain-based al-Khalisi family, an active agent of political opposition during the early stages of the formation of the Iraqi state in the 1920s and a staunch anti-communist force in 1959–63, also appeared on the list of initiators of the Da'wa movement, but later dropped out to reappear in London at the head of a London-based alHaraka, a small group of rather limited influence.[42] Some members of the al-Sadr family made efforts in recent years to invest the family political assets and establish the Ma'had Islami (Islamic Institution) in London.[43]

Of course, mention should be made of the most powerful centre: the Kho'i Foundation, which is still in operation under the sons and grandsons of the late Grand Ayatollah Kho'i (d.1992). The Kho'i organization wielded vast revenues and wide informal networks of followers inside and outside the region.[44] The influence of the Kho'i trend may be demonstrated by the fact that in the aftermath of the Iranian Revolution, the militant Shi'is of Iraq were labeled Khomeinists; those advocating quietism were labeled Kho'ists. Segmentary definitions were used to denote a modern ideological divide. Although the Kho'i trend had been largely apolitical as far as Iraqi politics was concerned, it gained a powerful political potential after the March 1991 Intifada in Iraq with the active role Kho'i played in his two *fatwas* before and during the Intifada – the one prohibiting the purchase and sale in Iraq of any item brought over from occupied Kuwait between August 1990 and February 1991 (implying that the invasion was illegal) and the other calling for the preservation of peace and order during the March uprising.[45]

With the exception of SAIRI, the emergence, existence and continuation of these groups would have been inconceivable without an independent source of religious taxes, *khums*, either directly from followers or by proxy means, i.e. an authorization to collect *khums* on behalf of another powerful patron of higher clerical standing. The segmentary universe of the clerical class is nowhere more evident than in the Iraqi case, at home or in exile.

These *traditional* divisions had been in existence earlier but were activated after the drive to the politicization of Shi'ite milieux.

Another set of divisions, the modern type, plagued these movements from the mid-1970s down to the early 1990s. Five such splits occurred – four within the Da'wa party, and one in the MAI. In these factional cleavages, ideological, organizational, national and political factors were at play.

The Da'wa party gave birth to four splinter groups: the Jund Imam (Soldiers of the Imam) in 1977; the Da'wa Islamiya (without the noun 'Party') in 1982; the Da'wa Party -Majlis Fiqhi 1988 and the Kawadir (Cadres) of Da'wa Party in 1990.

The Jund Imam faction began to crystallize in 1971–72 at the hands of Sami al-Badri, who had been in charge of the Karrada Sharqiya district organization (Baghdad) of the Da'wa. Badri was greatly influenced by Sayyid Qutb's doctrine of *jahiliya*.[46] Assisted by a group of devout followers such as Sheikh Latif Khafaji (now the leader of the Jund Imam, based in Damascus), Izzat Shabender (based in Damascus), Sa'ad Jawad (based in London) and Abu Zaid (*nom du guerre*, based in Holland), al-Badri broke away from the Da'wa but never declared a new movement. It seems he reinterpreted the Qutb *jahiliya* concept in a unique way. Originally Qutb's ideas were borrowed from Abu 'Ala Madududi, the Pakistani Islamist (d. 1973).[47] Qutb's concept denounces all modern nationalist regimes as barbarian and to be toppled and replaced by an Islamic government (*hukum Islami*).[48] Qutb's notion of *jahiliya* was reinterpreted by al-Badri in the Shi'ite idiom. His conception was that Shi'is should launch a campaign to destroy Sunnism, wipe out the Sunni sources of jurisprudence (*Sihah Sitta*, the six compendiums of Sunni jurisprudence) and pave the way for the coming of the long-awaited Shi'ite polity.

This polity, however, was not to be achieved through gradual political organization, indoctrination and political action against the state itself but through the re-emergence of Mahdi, the Twelfth Hidden Imam. The strategic thrust, according to this formula, is not directed to establish an Islamic state but to pave the way for the Imam to return. In al-Badri's view, this was to be the true Shi'ite path, which should distinguish the Da'wa from the Sunni Tahrir party. The latter point may have implied an accusation against 'Arif Basri, who was then the main figure in the Da'wa to whom al-Badri was answerable. And al-Badri must have been aware of Basri's previous liaisons with the Sunni Tahrir party. Murtadha al-'Askari, the oldest figure in the Da'wa, supported al-Badri's challenge. The messianic communal tendency of the group was markedly expressed when it decided to identify itself as the Jund Imam. *Jund*, a superlative form of *junud*, soldiery, denoted the combative spirit of the group. That of the Imam, referring to the Hidden Twelfth Imam, the Mahdi, strongly expressed the ethos of Shi'ite messianic activism.[49]

The second schism had matured during 1980–82. A combination of organizational differences, national and local factors were at work here. It should be remembered at this point that the Da'wa was still an international organization with a general leadership supervising national branches. A mixture of Lebanese and Iraqi leading cadre led by Ali Korani (a Lebanese) and Abu Yasin (an Iraqi from Basra) formed a rebellious faction opposing the introduction of elections in the party. What joined them together was that the Lebanese presence in the leadership was weak and the cadres from Basra were short of representation at the top. Leadership, they argued, should be *appointed* according to achievement and militancy. Votes did not count and elections could be easily manipulated.

The Basra group was seeking ascendancy in the organization; the Lebanese, by contrast, had the achievement of autonomy in mind. The faction as a whole split from the main body of the mother party and took on a new name: Da'wa Islamiya, dropping the 'party' from their insignia. The Lebanese group under Ali Korani, again, broke away from the faction, returned to Lebanon and took part in the formation of Hizbullah. The Basra leftovers continued their activities under the same name and issued their mouthpiece *I'tisam* in Iran. The group received warm support from the Iranians and the officials of SAIRI in which it was represented.

The third breach occurred in 1988, centring on the Majlis Fiqhi (Jurisprudence Council) which, theoretically represented the symbolic power of the *'ulama*. Theoretically the council was empowered to give advice on actions, ideas and programmes. They had a hold over the interpretation of the creed, and presumably stood over the leadership: they could veto any party decision. The *faqih* of the party, Kazim Ha'iri and the Council of Fuqaha were not an elected body. In day-to-day work they virtually had no place and no say. In an attempt to reassert their leading role, they conducted a campaign of restoration. Two organizational and political points were raised: first, what is the role of the *faqih*? Does he constitute the real leadership or is he simply a cover-up to lend superficial legitimacy? Second, what is the nature of the relation of the Da'wa with Iran?

Ha'iri's view was that the *faqih* should not and could not be a mere facade and, in point of fact, should have a key role rather than an advisory duty in decision-making. On the second, more sensitive point, Ha'iri conceived of the Iranian state as the legitimate source of authority over Shi'is at large, commanding their loyalty, and believed that the Da'wa party should 'merge with it'.[50]

The clash between the elected body, party leadership and self-appointed clerics is nowhere more apparent than in this case. The second point had different connotations. Strong Iraqi leanings and sentiments were visible on various levels in the Da'wa party. This was intensified by the collapse of Iranian plans to invade Iraq and the mounting Iranian pressures on Iraqi groups after Khomeini had to take, in his own words, the 'cup of poison'.[51] Ha'iri had a clear interest in taking the first point in defence of his position. He might have taken the second point, regarding the relationship with Iran, as a tactic to pressure the Da'wa leadership and win Iranian backing to consolidate his position within his own party. The tactic, however, did not work. The congress voted against their own *faqih* and discharged him. Paradoxically, party rules required that the decision to remove the *faqih* of the party be endorsed by this *faqih* himself. Ha'iri left the party together with scores of supporters. They launched a new organization named The Da'wa Party (Jurisprudent Council).[52]

The outcome of this factional struggle set a precedent of successful challenge to the authority of the clerics and of an assertion of national Iraqi spirit. These two factors, among other catalysts, were explicitly at the root of the fourth and most important split in the Daʿwa in 1990.

A number of intellectuals had left the Daʿwa at different points and for different reasons. Some resented what they termed 'the merger' (*indimaj*) with Iran, revealing sensitivity towards the need to express an exclusive Iraqi identity. Others were skeptical of Khomeini's *wilayat al-faqih* and of the whole idea of giving the *ʿulama* a leading role in government. Other elements rejected the Iranian and single-party models in general, opting for a democratic, pluralistic system. For political or tactical reasons, certain individuals were more inclined to an open attitude towards secular parties in Iraq, or the so-called *infitah siyasi* (political openness and cooperation). As their social profiles show, they descended from solid, urban, well-to-do, middle-class families, holding high academic degrees (MAs and PhDs), and were of two age groups: 30–39 and 40–49. This group had resented their blocked upward mobility in the party and the growing Iranian influence over the Iraqi Shiʿis. Unlike the clerics, they had neither previous liaisons with the Iranians nor any interest in forging them; they had also been more exposed to modern influences. The group got together and formed Kawadir Hizb Daʿwa (The Daʿwa Party Cadres), and started a semi-clandestine weekly, *Badil Islami* (The Islamic Alternative), in Damascus. The new offshoot stressed Iraqi nationalism, the renewal and modernization of Islamic thought, the adoption of democracy and the sacralization of party politics.[53]

The MAI had a similar fate. It was led by two strong figures: the *mujtahid* Muhammad Taqi al-Mudarisi, and the ex-sheikh but now *effendi*, Muhsin al-Husaini. As a result of the monopoly imposed by al-Mudarisi over revenues and party apparatuses, tensions built up between him and other leading figures in the Political Bureau of the MAI – above all al-Husaini, who had been systematically bypassed in decision-making and had no control over finances.[54] Internal debates in the MAI took a direction similar to what had flared up in the Daʿwa ranks over the limits of the *mujtahid*. Whereas the *mujtahids* in the Daʿwa were set apart from the actual leading body in a separate council, in the MAI it was the first leader who assumed both roles. Arguments were voiced that the *mujtahid* should withdraw to ecclesiastical scholarly work, leaving political matters to the experts. The MAI ended with a splinter group emerging under al- Husaini.

Table 14.6: Known Leaders and Political Bureau (PB) Members of the Da'wa, 1990

Name	Base	Class	Education or profession	City	Age group	Remarks
Muhammad Mahdi Asifi	Tehran	middle	religious	Najaf	51–60	Speaker
Kazim al-Ha'iri	Tehran	middle	religious	Najaf	51–60	leadership
M. Salih al-Adib	Tehran	middle	engineer	Karbala	51–60	leadership
Hussein Shubbar	Tehran	middle	lawyer	Najaf	51–60	leadership
Jawad Maliki	Damascus	middle	engineer	Twaireej	41–50	PB
Ibrahim al-Ushaiqir	London	middle	physician	Karbala	41–50	PB
Abdul Zahra al-Bander	Tehran	middle	PhD (philosophy)	Chibayish	41–50	PB
Muwafaq al-Rubai'i	London	middle	Physician	Mosul	41–50	PB
Hamza Fawzi		middle			41–50	PB
Abu Yasin	Tehran					PB
'Adil al-Adib	Tehran	middle	teacher	Karbala	41–50	PB
Sami al-'Askari	London	middle	engineer	Suq al-Shuyukh	31–40	PB

This table has been constructed on the basis of information provided by Muhammad A. Jabar, Muwataq al-Rubai'i and Sami al-'Askari.

Table 14.7: List of Leaders of the Kawadr Da'wa, a Da'wa Party Splinter Group, 1994–95

Name	Social origin	Education	Occupation	Date of birth	City	Rank
Jalil Khairallah	middle class	graduate	military	1950	Nasiriya	secretary
Husam Muh. Ali	middle class			1951	Hilla	
Salim Mashkur	middle class	graduate	journalist	1954	Najaf	
Adib Tabataba'i	middle class	BA	physician	1958	Baghdad	
Ali al-Haidari	middle class	BA	naval engineer	1949	Baghdad*	
Muh. A. Jabar	middle class	BA	journalist	1949	Baghdad**	editor of al-Mu'tamar
Mahmud al-Husayni	middle class	BA	engineer	1947	Hilla/ Baghdad	
Dhiya' Shakarchi	middle class	PhD	academic	1948	Baghdad*	
Mustafa Habib	middle class	BA	academic	1950	Basra	
Hazim Nu'aimi	middle class	BA	civil servant	1956		
Madani al-Musawi	middle class		writer	1958	Najaf	

This table is based on information provided by Muhammad A. Jabar who has been an active leading cadre in Da'wa and editor-in-chief of the London-based INC organ, al-Mu'tamar.

*   In Karrada Sharqiya, a predominantly Shi'ite suburb.
**   Originally from Kut.

Table 14.8: List of Jama'at 'Ulama Mujahidin fil 'Iraq (Tehran-based) the Elected Leading Committee, 1982

Name	City	Age group in 1992	Position or affiliation	Ethnic origin
Muhammad Baqir al-Nasiri	Nasiriya	61–70	General Secretary	Arab
Kazim al-Ha'iri	Najaf	61–70	Da'wa	Persian
Mahmud al-Hashimi	Najaf	51–60	SAIRI	Arab
Muhammad Mahdi al-Asifi	Najaf	61–70	Da'wa	Persian
Hasan Faraj Allah	Basra	61–70		Arab
Muhammad Baqir al-Hakim	Najaf	41–50	SAIRI	Arab
Muh. Hasan al-Jawahiri	Najaf	d. 1992		Arab
Muh. Taqi al-Tabataba'i al-Tabrizi	Najaf	51–60		Iranian Turk
Alternate members				
Abdul Rahim al-Shawki	Basra	d. 1993		Arab
Hussein al-Sadr	Kazimiya/ Baghdad	51–60		Arab
Composition of the Jama'a in 1992				
Muhammad Baqir al-Nasiri*				
Muhammad al-Asifi*				
Hasan Faraj Allah*				
Abdul Rahim al-Shawki*				
Hussein al-Sadr*				
Mahdi al-'Attar	Najaf	51–60		Arab

Name	City	Age group in 1992	Position or affiliation	Ethnic origin
Hussein al-Bashiri	Kirkuk	61–70		Turkoman

This table is based on information provided by the general secretary of the Jama'a. The names are listed according to the official sequence based on the number of votes each member received in a secret ballot. The Electoral College numbered 70 *mujtahids*. The general secretary won 69 votes.

*   Members marked with * remained in the body since its foundation.

FIFTEEN

Wartime, the Diaspora and the 1991 Uprisings

The Iraq-Iran war came to a halt when Grand Ayatollah Khomeini had, in his own words, to 'drink the cup of poison' and end his dream of invading Iraq. On 18 July 1988, UN General Secretary Javier Perez de Cuellar received Iran's official acceptance of the UN Resolution 598 stipulating an immediate ceasefire and withdrawal of the belligerents to internationally recognized borders. Cessation of hostilities came as an unpleasant surprise both to the Iraqi Shi'ite movements based mostly but not exclusively in Tehran, and to their 2 million or so migrant constituencies across the Middle East – notably in Iran and Syria. Their leaders' hopes had been pinned on a full-scale Iranian invasion, in which they took part as troopers in the Basij forces, fighters destabilizing Iraq's war effort in the Kurdish mountains where they had established guerrilla bases[1] or as clandestine activists in their bombing campaign.[2]

Iran's Failure

The nine successive Iranian Wal-Fajr campaigns, codenamed after a Qur'anic verse, were launched between 6 February 1983 and 3 March 1986 in the hope of capturing Basra in the south and Haj Omran in the north. They scored a phenomenal success by occupying the Fao peninsula at the mouth of the Gulf, south of Basra, on 11 Feb 1986, and Haj Omran, a small resort village north of Sulaimaniya, on 4 March 1987.

Wal-Fajr operations were followed by another series of campaigns named Karbala, after the Shi'ite holy shrine in Iraq. Between 20 June 1986 and 9 April 1987, Karbala 1 to Karbala 9 were launched but failed to achieve their objectives. Iranian troops were dislodged from Haj Omran, Basra, the Majnoon Islands, the Fao peninsula and from other territorial pockets gained in previous battles.[3] What was achieved in the Wal-Fajr operations was lost in the Karbala ones. US military pressure added to the Iranian ordeal. On several occasions the American warships operating in the Persian Gulf made several attacks on Iranian shipping and oil installations. In early July 1988, American vessels shot down an Iranian airliner, signalling a stern warning that was clearly and correctly read in Tehran. Both the Soviet Union and the US had already responded positively to a Kuwaiti appeal to lease flags to protect Kuwaiti tankers. Bereft of global support, Iran was left in no position to continue its war effort successfully. Iranian national security was at stake, and Islamic internationalist idealistic expansionism had to be forsaken.[4]

The depth of bitterness felt by the Iraqi Islamists in the Diaspora was evident. Iraqi Shi'is, who used to pack their bags during any Iranian offensive in order to return to Baghdad, had to unpack again and wait. In the wake of the ceasefire, however, they took what was left of their worldly goods, packed for the last time and flooded asylum havens in Europe. Tens of thousands of Iraqi exiles made for the West. Tourist agencies, human traffickers, smugglers, visa-forgers and passport-fakers of every kind flourished in Damascus, Beirut, Amman and beyond. One popular exit route was Russian tourism; travel agencies in Syria specializing in Soviet tourism thrived beyond the dreams of Soviet officials. However, hotels in Moscow – where these would-be tourists were to be accommodated – waited for their guests in vain. The moment Iraqi 'tourists' touched down in Moscow, they continued their journey to Sweden, London, Amsterdam, Brussels or Copenhagen. The majority were Shi'i laypersons who, like the members of Islamist groups, lost faith and direction. It was the end of an overdue stay in what now looked like permanent exile. On the heels of poor Shi'ite families, staunch Islamist activists followed. The exodus soon overwhelmed opposition groups from all ideological strands. Their ranks swelled with newcomers from the Kurdish mountains, who fled the wrath of the nine Anfal campaigns launched successively by the Iraqi army. The massive onslaught by the Iraqi troops drove thousands of Kurds, communists and Islamists (mostly from the Da'wa Party), out of their bases in the mountains of Suran and Bahdinan. Crossing the Syrian borders, they flocked to Damascus and from there joined the steady flow of asylum seekers reaching out to the West.

War and Nationalism

The years 1988–90 were bleak indeed. The Ba'th regime emerged from the Iraq-Iran war victorious but not unscathed. How could it survive?

During the eight years of the first Gulf war, most opposition groups – Kurds, communists and Shi'i Islamists – developed a belief that war and revolution were inseparably linked.[5]

War demands the unity of the nation; rebellion reflects its discord. The logic of war, if so prevailing, buries all schisms under a thick, even monolithic, layer of union of purpose and action and channels energies outwards. The logic of revolt hoists aloft the principle of dissent and directs fury inwards.

This model is complex. In early 20th-century Europe, certain cases seem to endorse it: the two Russian revolutions (1917–18), the 1918 German revolt, the first Hungarian rebellion in 1919 and the Italian workers' insurrection in the 1920s. In all these episodes domestic dissent rather than cohesion was paramount. One interpretation is that official nationalism was seen to have failed, and loyalty was placed elsewhere – on class, internationalism or social revolution. But was it? Eric Hobsbawm suggests a slightly different reading: during World War One, nationalism rather than internationalism was a factor in soldiers' rebellion against their own beleaguered governments and official nationalism.[6] If these European examples have anything to tell, they suggest a more accurate formula: for rebellion to succeed, Iraqi nationalism (also dubbed patriotism) had to stand against the Arab nationalist discourse of the ruling Ba'th elite. A union between the two may well explain how a country with a vast Shi'ite majority could fight Shi'ite Iran and prioritise national defence over religious brotherhood. Religious and national identities have often been misunderstood in the Middle East. Scholars seem to conceive of them as diametrically opposed rather than two complementary spaces. Nationalism may or may not use religion as a marker. As cultural artefacts, nationalism and religion may lead to a peaceful symbiosis or take other trajectories. Persian nationalism was interwoven with Twelver Shi'ism. Iraqi nationalism was a common Sunni-Shi'i creation, as the Iraqi sociologist Ali al-Wardi has amply shown.[7] It was the Shi'i *'ulama* in Najaf who called for, agitated and legitimised the drive for 'Iraqi' nationhood in the 1920s.[8] They were complemented by Iraqi Ottoman officers, who had dual Iraqi and Arab nationalist feelings and tendencies. Liberal Arabists who cooperated with Britain to structure the monarchy in 1921 were also Iraqi nationalists. In the 1950s, for example, it was Shi'i middle-class students such as Fuad Rikabi, Hamid Khilkhal, Hani Fukaiki and others who initiated radical Ba'th Arabism.[9] Shi'is from Iraq joined the Ba'th Party *en masse* during the oil-boom years of the early 1970s. This is clear evidence that Shi'ism, as I argue throughout this volume, is neither a sociological nor a political category. It is also a reminder that nationalism and religious culture are not alien to each other.[10]

One of the startling features of the eight-year-long Iraq-Iran war was Saddam Hussein's ability to re-fashion his regime's ideology, incorporating widely varied appeals to the many social groups and forces that might support him.

During that war this ideology became a new synthesis of Arabism, Islamism and Iraqi patriotism. This new invention reached deep into history for heroes like the Babylonian king-warrior Nebuchadnezzar, who invaded ancient Palestine, or Salah al-Din al-Ayobi, the Kurd who challenged the Crusaders in Jerusalem. In these examples ancient Iraqi and Kurdish motifs intermingle with anti-West and anti-Israel themes.[11]

On the regional and global fronts, the Ba'th Party's pan-Arab, secular ideology helped bolster Hussein's image as a defender of both the Arab nation and of secularism against the Persian fundamentalist threat.

Among organized opposition groups three positions crystallized in response to the war-dominated society: pro-Iran (some Kurds and all Shiʿi te groups); pro-Iraq (chiefly the pro-Syrian Baʿth splinter party, an insignificant political outfit based in Damascus); and against both Iran and Iraq (the main body of the Iraqi Communist Party).

Shiʿite Islamist organizations had traditionally prioritised religious identity, or an ideal projection of it, over national identity – mistakenly assuming they possessed a religious legitimacy in the eyes of the majority of the Shiʿis, which would justify such an anti-Iraq alliance. An interesting debate was triggered by this problem among Iraqi Shiʿi leaders in exile: whether or not to obey the injunctions of Ayatollah Khomeini. Some argued he was 'Imam', a term denoting both religious and political status and implying total obedience. Others responded that the principle of emulation allows for a free choice of any living religious authority to be emulated.[12] At any rate, none of the Islamist groups involved called for a union between Iran and Iraq. The nation-state remained a basic point of reference in their general discourse, but not in their attitude towards the war.

In that sense, nationalism was a missing factor in their calculations of war and revolution. They failed to assess the extent to which the Islamic Revolution in Iran arose from a sense of national indignation and bitterness towards the Shah's fealty to Washington, and forgot that the Iranian leader, Ayatollah Khomeini, initiated his own political career as an advocate of Iranian nationalism. Even in 1988, the leader of SAIRI (Supreme Assembly for the Islamic Revolution in Iraq), Muhammad Baqir al-Hakim, rejected the use of terms like *watan* (homeland) in the communiqués he was negotiating with other secular groups. According to al-Hakim such terms never existed in Islam.[13]

Iraqi nationalism or patriotism, then, was taken more as an ideological discourse than a national space or political unit of the modern world. This confusion stems partly from ideological choices and partly from Iranian patronage.

The Invasion of Kuwait

During much of the war (1980–88), the opposition in general and the Islamists in particular were cut off from the major urban centres of Baghdad, Basra and Mosul – which contained half the population. Their organizational networks were physically destroyed. In the inter-war period, the opposition was in disarray, and so was the Baʿth system. Iraq emerged as a formidable military giant but an economic dwarf. Social tensions were high, and keeping a 1 million-man army was problematic. The nation teetered on the verge of two options: reform and rehabilitation, or another military adventure.[14]

Economic hardships were accentuated by global and regional political change. Transformations in Eastern Europe took the ruling elite by surprise and triggered deep concerns. The Soviet totalitarian model, from whose arsenal much of Ba'th dogma was drawn, collapsed. It dealt a fatal blow to the very ideological pillars of Ba'th rule: the command economy, single-party system and self-tailored legitimacy. The bloody street uprisings in neighbouring Jordan and Algeria in 1989 ushered democratic reform into these two Arab countries. The Iraqi president offered a similar package of reforms: economic liberalization, a new constitution (which envisaged political pluralism), a free press and other democratic freedoms. An offer of genuine peace was made to the Iranian president, Ali-Akbar Hashemi-Rafsanjani. Both the reform package and the conciliatory move towards Iran endeavoured to ease domestic and regional tensions, as a precondition to expand and exploit the Majnoon oilfields (in the southern Amarah province, bordering Iran).

Another option was to seek quick and easy access to resources. The reform package was offered but never delivered, and the invasion of Kuwait followed. On 2 August 1990, Iraqi troops crossed the border into Kuwait; a domestic puppet government was installed and 'union' between the two countries announced, all in a matter of weeks. The second Gulf or Kuwait War will go down in history as the first war fought over oil in modern times.[15]

The invasion and annexation of Kuwait aimed, among other things, to secure enough oil wealth to relieve Iraqi economic burdens, rekindle the flames of popular patriotism among Iraqis so as to go hand in glove with *étatiste* nationalism and, last but not least, win the consent of the war generation. To ensure wider support, Arab unity and just distribution of Arab wealth were upheld as the motives behind the annexation of Kuwait, and withdrawal from Kuwait was conditional upon Israeli withdrawal from the West Bank and Gaza. These demands exploited genuine Arab issues but covered self-interested Iraqi ends.[16]

Islamic and other opposition groups looked at the invasion of Kuwait and shuddered at the prospect of renewed Iraqi patriotism, not realizing this time it would be inward-oriented. Actually, the war generation was drained of its sense of loyalty to the 'state', as defined by its ruling class, and took to arms. They longed for peace but ended up in a beleaguered *cul-de-sac*.

When opposition leaders hoped that Iraqi nationalism would detach from the Ba'th's official nationalism, these two united during the Iraq-Iran war; when they feared these two would unite again in the Gulf War, they went separate ways. The leaders made this double, tragicomic error.

In a communiqué from Beirut dated 19 January 1991, two days into the war, Muhammad Baqir al-Hakim ordered his followers in SAIRI to join 'recruitment forces' and instructed those based near the Iraq-Iran borders to stand firm against 'the United States aggression'. The Iraqi Communist Party denounced the war, and the Kurdish Democratic Party (KDP) leader Mas'ud Barzani took a similar position.[17]

However, their adversary, Saddam Hussein, had an inkling of the unfavourable popular mood inside his country. His ideological campaign revealed a shift from nationalistic to religious themes. In the run-up to the Gulf War, a sense of *angst* took hold amongst a majority of the war generation, now veterans in the strict sense of the word. All attempts by the ruling elite to contaminate this generation with Arab and Third World pro-Saddam enthusiasm were fruitless. Such anxiety, which appears in military jargon as 'low morale', could easily lead to passivity, which in turn might result in abstention or inaction. But passivity and inaction could develop into anti-government action if a final break with an *étatiste*, jingoistic form of nationalism occurred.

Such a break was in the making for a decade or so, but the final blow was brought about by the combined effect of defeat, disorganized retreat and destruction in January–February 1991. Indeed, as a result of the massive US-led air campaign and ground war, early estimates put the number of casualties at a horrendous level: perhaps around 50,000 military personnel and 10–15,000 civilians were believed to have perished. Later estimates were much lower: some 25–30,000.[18] Soldiers in the Kuwaiti theatre voted with their legs; more than 70,000 surrendered in less than 100 hours. Saddam Hussein's strategy of winning the war was a total blunder. Withdrawal of his soldiers from the Kuwaiti theatre without air cover was a great folly. The air campaign, which he predicted would last three days, went on for more than a month. The Israelis did not attack. No oil famine occurred. The Europeans stood fast behind the Bush administration. The ground battle Saddam so confidently awaited never materialized. And the havoc wreaked upon the nation surpassed imagination.

The Uprisings

Angry, retreating soldiers with heavy armour swarmed the southern Sunni towns of Abu al-Khasib and al-Zubair, firing at Saddam's murals and triggering what has come to be known in opposition jargon as the 'Popular Uprising', and in the government idiom as 'the demagogic mob' (*ghawgha'iya*).[19]

The first sparks of rebellion came from retreating soldiers in Zubair on the last day of February, three days before the formal Iraqi surrender to General Norman Schwarzkopf at Safwan. The revolt gained momentum immediately. Basra, March 1; Suq al-Shuyukh, March 2; Nasiriya, Najaf, March 4; Karbala, March 7; and then Amara, Hillah, Kut and on throughout the south.[20]

A detailed account of what happened in each city and township is impossible, but media reports and eyewitness accounts speak of a series of events remarkably similar, with differences in some details.

Apart from the input of retreating soldiers, a mass of urban rebels gathered at the city centre and marched to seize the symbols of power: the mayor's office; the ruling party headquarters; the secret police building; the prison; and the city garrison, where applicable.

Ba'th and government high-ranking officials were butchered, in some cases mutilated. The violence was horrific.

The forces that took part in the uprising were different. Army defectors and deserters swelled their ranks with angry civilians, mostly from the Ba'th Party grassroots. In certain cases tribal groups such as the Marsh tribes of Albu Hicham and Albu Gassed, who attacked Suq al-Shuyukh, joined them. Sleeping, sporadic leftists and Islamist cells, however small, took active part. A few thousand of SAIRI's Badr Army combatants poured in through the porous borders with Iran. They headed mainly for Najaf and Karbala and partly for Basra.

In the north, it was a different scene. Paradoxically, the rebellion was initiated by the Mezouri-Doski tribal chieftains who had served as Jash, i.e. pro-government mercenaries. Army units capitulated and rendered their weapons non-operational. Soldiers simply deserted chaotically. Urban masses took to the streets to be followed by the well-organized eight parties of the Kurdistan Front.[21]

In Baghdad, passivity prevailed. More than 2 million citizens were evacuated. The capital was under tight security control. Rebels in other cities promised but could not deliver a march to Baghdad. The silence at the heart of the nation was fatalistic.

The rebellion, however, signalled a new turn in Iraq's history. First, the final divorce between Iraqi patriotism and official Arab nationalism was the result of a national defeat caused by a political folly. It was the political manifesto of the war generation who were now disillusioned. Second, the 'regular' format of civilian uprising was stood on its head: armed mutiny was the first, not the last, link in the chain of agitation, demonstration and mass mobilization, a fact that reflects the extent to which organized effort had been weakened, but how deep rooted the feelings of the opposition were. Third, the military establishment partly disintegrated and split into three facets: rebellion in the south, capitulation in the north and cohesion in the middle. Lastly, institutional forces such as Ba'th members, pro-government paramilitary chiefs and army units turned against their own government. This was an urban phenomenon spearheaded by the young war generation.

The uprisings lacked command and control systems. SAIRI and other groups could not lend it a sustained character. On the contrary, they raised disastrous, divisive slogans and hoisted aloft Khomeini 's image, alienating potential allies. Unnecessary killings added to the problems. The army itself seemed bereft of any political instincts. With their heavy armour, communications systems and skills, revolting formations could have initiated a march on Baghdad. They simply revolted for the sake of revolt, a protest of sorts. Military professionalism bred apolitical attitudes.

For only two brief weeks the uprisings were phenomenally successful. The saviours of the Ba'th, i.e. loyal units, carried out their mission as a killing machine almost to perfection. The uprisings, which were regionally and globally isolated, were soon drowned in blood. Government forces shelled holy shrines and promoted communal slogans like 'No Shi'is anymore'. The symbol of Shi'ism, Grand Ayatollah Abu al-Qassim al-Kho'i – who had formed a committee to fill the vacuum during the upheaval – was summoned to Baghdad and shown on TV with Saddam.[22] The Ba'th party mouthpiece, *the* daily *al-Thawra*, ran a series of editorials degrading the Shi'is and calling the rebels 'mob demagogues'.[23]

Iraq Under Sanctions: Tribes and Religion

The nation that emerged from the 1991 Gulf War hardly resembled the one that entered it. The country was bombed back to the Stone Age. A new era was ushered in, one of deprivation and the further destruction of what remained of already fading civility.

The sanctions period, stretching on for thirteen bleak years, weakened the state as a system of governance, devastated the economy, launched hyperinflation and reduced the bulk of salaried, modern middle classes to paupers. Per capita income, for example, went down from US$4083 in 1980 to $485 in 1980. It then declined further to around $300. More than sixty percent of the population sank below the poverty line. Even after the introduction of the oil-for-food programme in 1996, society became more dependent on the state for their livelihood. The politics of starvation turned out to be the best weapon of mass mobilization the government could have dreamt of.[24] The systematic destruction of civil association and vital civil forces created a vacuum that was filled by spontaneous or manufactured rehabilitation of traditional tribal networks.

The ruling elite shifted from mass party politics to clan politics, from top to bottom. Statesmanship became a family business. Modern party systems were partly replaced by loyal tribalism; nationalism, by lineage; Arabism, by religion.

The official policy towards religion merits examination.

Out of pragmatism, the once-secular Ba'th began to deploy religious symbols to combat Ayatollah Khomeini's Charismatic fundamentalism. The president contrived a sacred family tree, linking himself to the Prophet Muhammad and his house in order to match Khomeini's noble descent. The discourse of lineage was thus politicised. Scud missiles launched at Iranian cities were named after the third Imam Hussain and his venerated half brother, 'Abbas, believed in popular culture to be wrathful and vindictive towards disbelievers. These moves remained within the realm of religious symbolism. Another symbolic step came in the aftermath of the invasion of Kuwait.

Hanbalite Riyadh was now the foe. On the eve of the Gulf War, *Allahu Akhbar* ('God is great') was inscribed on the Iraqi flag; and the motto 'the Believer strides forward' replaced the old slogan 'The Ba'th Strides Forward'. A host of Islamic gatherings took place in Baghdad.[25] Yet Iraq appeared to retain much of its secular character throughout the eight-year war with Iran. Social and cultural undercurrents, however, were eroding this secularism. An upsurge in popular religiosity was observed, but it was yet mild. The quantum leap came in the wake of the 1991 defeat and failure of the uprisings. A steep rise in popular piety and religious symbolism spread nationwide.

The government launched faith campaigns to harness the new sentiments and make good for their discredited Arab ideology. In Baghdad alone, more than 100 grand mosques were built for a starving nation under sanctions.[26] Women were both encouraged and pressured back into the veil. Even middle-class females in the capital had to acquiesce. They did not want to be seen morally lax as marriage opportunities would be hampered or jeopardized. As unemployment surged, the president personally advised Iraqis to keep women at home, triggering male chauvinism among the unemployed.

The government also shuttered bars along the Abu Nu'as street, an avenue named after the medieval poet, notorious for his love of wine and sexual poetry. Encouraged by the new atmosphere, mosque-goers trebled. More than 50,000 pilgrims turned daily to the Kazimiya shrine in Baghdad, roughly three times over pre-war levels of visitation, according to its custodian.[27]

Fear, dislocation, destitution, uncertainty and social ills drove masses to the warmth of religious charities and fraternities. The steep rise in prostitution and crime strengthened this bent. Violent crimes doubled by the season. Religious charities provided food, medical care, and more importantly, certainty in a world of macabre arbitrariness. Porridge-seeking Iraqis figured in the thousands on the front pages of Arab dailies. More than 2 million pilgrims (almost 10–12 per cent of the population and 20 per cent of the Shi'is) travelled to Karbala in 1999 to commemorate the martyrdom of Imam Hussain. In 2001, the figure reached 2.4 million. These figures should be read against the activist background of Ayatollah Muhammad Sadiq al-Sadr, usually called Sadr II.[28]

Al-Sadr had begun his activity in a gradual manner, focusing on recruitment, charities and sermons. He seemed apolitical and in line with the government's pious activity. Rising in prominence after the death of Grand Ayatollah al-Kho'i, Sadr II established an apparatus of novices and seminarians to fill in the gap left by the destruction of the first al-Sadr's network of disciplined novices. Clerics of lower rank and students usually form what in the Iraqi jargon is called *jihaz al-marji'iya*, the apparatus of *marja*'ism – the core of leadership and functionaries who lead local communities, benefiting from an expanding infrastructure comprising mosques, *husayniyas* and local assemblies for mourning. This core, working in utmost caution, extended its influence through networks of *khums* collectors. Together, the core and the *wukala*, the Imam's agents, liaised with communities and administered their daily affairs.

Sadr II succeeded, for the first time in a generation, in building vast networks of followers among the peasantry and urban lower classes, notably in shantytowns in Baghdad and Nasiriya, forging some alliances with influential segments of urban middle classes. Large constituencies soon took shape in Najaf, Baghdad, Nasiriya, Basra and other townships. Authorizing Friday prayers, Sadr II could mobilize hundreds of thousands of people for his sermons, which grew critical of the government.

Najaf was now a bipolar centre of Shi'ite leadership, poised between the apolitical Grand Ayatollah Ali Sistani and Sadr II. Friction was manifest but diplomatic. Followers hardly concealed their feelings of pride to have a homegrown, Iraqi Arab leading clerical authority. The authoritarian Ba'th rule could not tolerate a rival centre of popular power; the assassination of Sadr II in February 1999, together with his two sons, was a tragic turn. His photograph, which depicts him grooming a long, silver, untrimmed beard and wearing a white shroud – a signal of readiness for martyrdom – has become a household icon. His followers dubbed him the 'White Lion', *al-layth al-abyadh*. As a rule, physical elimination augments the potency of symbolic influence beyond the grave.

Sadr II had succeeded in materializing Shi'ite identity by creating massive infrastructures and organized constituencies that, by dint of their sheer numbers, poverty and humiliation, will play an important, radical role in the years to come.[29] In an assessment written in September 2002, I stressed that

Sadr's extended family, along with other leading Najaf and Karbala families, will again undoubtedly supply new leaders of prominence ... Such new centres of religious authority, born in the period since 1991, may well surpass the influence of any or all Shi'ite Islamic groups working against the Ba'th from Iranian exile.

The Da'wa party and SAIRI ideologized Shi'i te identity during the Iraq-Iran war, a circumstance that severed this ideological conception from its national habitat; Sadr II institutionalised this identity during the period of sanctions, a situation that helped blend religion, charity and communal identity all in one; yet Sadr II never embedded this identity in a fundamentalist ideological system. These are two divergent trends, parallel communal overtones notwithstanding. The trajectories of the two may well be further accentuated by the regular Najafi competition for rank and primacy.

PART FIVE

Ideology: Sociopolitical and Economic Doctrines

SIXTEEN

Political Theory

Before the advent of the 20th century, both Shi'i and Sunni Islam kept their traditional political systems – the Shi'ite doctrine of the Imamate and the Sunni dogma of the Caliphate – both in theory and practice. The classical doctrine of the Imamate confines legitimacy to the Twelfth Imam, the Mahdi.[1] The doctrine of the Caliphate, by contrast, fixes the legality of rulership in the hands of an Arab from Quraish, the Prophet's tribe, rather than a definite segment of it.[2] As a normative concept, the Imamate and Caliphate doctrines were challenged by a small minority, the Kharijites, who advocated the right of all Muslims to the post of Caliph or Imam, irrespective of whether or not they were Quraishis. To some extent, these divergences of opinion reflected the tensions inherent in the transition from pre-political tribal authority to supra-tribal political power. In itself, this transition was fraught with infighting. Various examples of accommodation by the 'ulama and mujtahids with the de facto rulers who did not meet such criteria, however, dotted the Sunni and Shi'ite political histories from the mediaeval epoch down to late 19th or early 20th centuries.[3]

Reformation: Two Trends

The classical political theory in Shi'ite jurisprudence was debated, interpreted and re-interpreted during and after the constitutional movement in the late 19th and early 20th centuries. This debate produced two trends: *pro-constitutional* and *traditional-authoritarian*. These two trends, which overwhelmed the beginning of this century, developed in the second half of the 20th century into different authoritarian and democratic currents of thought. We shall examine the genealogy of this debate and the clash on one hand between the early constitutional current represented by the *mujtahid* Mirza Muhammad Hussein Na'ini and on the other hand the traditional-authoritarian trend represented by Fadlullah Nuri, which developed into authoritarian (Khomeinist) and democratic trends in the second half of the 20th century.

The late 19th- and early 20th-century ideological battles fought between the constitutional and anti-constitutional clerical camps, whether in Shi'ite Qajar Iran or the Sunni Ottoman lands (Egypt and Turkey), provide an instructive way to understand contemporary trends.

The constitutionalism of the 19th century was not initiated by the clerics, but rather by reforming Ottoman and Qajari functionaries.[4] In the process, constitutionalism gained supporters as well as staunch enemies among the clerics. The two most prominent figures on each ideological side of the battle were Nuri, who was a strong supporter of absolutism, and Na'ini, a champion of restricted monarchy.[5]

Nuri expounded his anti-constitutionalist ideas and positions in two renowned works, one a pamphlet titled 'Tadhkirat al-Ghafil wa Irshad al-Jahil' ('Admonition of the Forgetful and Guidance for the Ignorant'); the other is a *fatwa*. Both were presumably written between February 1908 and January 1909 amidst the battle between the monarchist and the constitutionalist movements. Nuri's arguments were purely juristic, revolving around the right to legislation and the imposition of divine law.[6]

In Nuri's view, Islam rested on two supplementary authorities. The first was the 'deputyship in the affairs of prophecy', that is, the *'ulama* in the chain of authority running from the prophet to the Imams down to the *mujtahids*, the Imam's deputies. The second was 'kingship, defined as the power that executes Islamic provisions'.[7] If the assembly of deputies elected by the people was commendable in his view, it was because they usurp the power of legislation reserved for the *mujtahids*. The sacred, exclusive nature of legislation is not only defended against the denunciations of lay Muslims but also against non-Muslims who, by dint of equal vote, would gain equality with Muslims together with the right to legislate.[8] In Nuri's words:

> Participation in the affairs of the community by anyone other than the Imam amounts to denigrating the authority of the Prophet and the Imam.[9]

The concept of a constitutional/representative system was also attacked by him on ethical and contractual bases. Nuri criticized representation on the grounds of possible deviations on the part of laypeople from the tenets of Islam when given a free hand to legislate, and that deputation or mandate (*wikala*), while permissible in certain contractual dealings, does not apply to political matters.[10] Hence the whole argument rested on the idea of the Imam as leader of the community and on the idea of the Muslim community in contradistinction to the nation-state.

By contrast Na'ini, another *mujtahid*, took up several issues in defence of constitutionalism. In his *Tanbih al-Umma wa Tanzih al-Milla* ('The Admonition and Refinement of the People'), written in 1909 in Najaf,[11] he moulded his pro-constitutional attacks on absolute monarchists on a novel reinterpretation of the jurisdiction of the *Shari'a*, the scope and feasibility of the *'ulama*'s authority, as well as on the old principle of de-legitimizing the secular ruler.

Na'ini saw the concept of usurpation of the power of the Imam as applying to kingship. Kingship 'was usurped authority and liable to become tyrannical, to which constitutionalism was ... preferable.'[12] Secondly, Na'ini argued that where Islamic provisions have not covered political and social matters, there was a need for legislation. Constitutionalism and the right of the assembly to give legislation were supported by the need to cope with changing developments and by the principle of expediency (*maslaha*).

This view is in fact a major breakthrough in Islamic political culture, elaborating, as it were, on the division of law into *Shari'a* (sacred) and *'urf* (customs) on one hand, and on the other the division of law or statutes into state statutes and community laws. These two domains, splitting the area of jurisdiction as a reality, would help promote the concept of secular laws (in politics) versus sacred law.[13] Thirdly, Na'ini argued for the right to deputation, i.e. to authorize others to act on one's behalf, i.e. the election of deputies as an act of *wikala* already endorsed by the *Shari'a*.

It is interesting to cast a comparative glance at the late 19th-century Sunni argument for constitutionalism, which was already a strong movement in Istanbul at the hands of state reformers and radical students societies.

In the words of Muhammad 'Abdo of Egypt, echoing the ideas of his master Jamal al-Din al-Afghani:

The Prince or ruler is a layman in every respect ... His selection or unseating are two questions to be decided by human beings and do not depend on divine right which this ruler may enjoy by way of his religion.[14]

Like Na'ini's Shi'ite traditions, 'Abdo and al-Afghani stripped the ruler of any divine sanctity, but they did so in absolute terms, directly with no reference to a superseding, legitimized caliphate. The 'Abdo and al-Afghani version of constitutionalism was, as a matter of course, an echo of the constitutional movement that matured in Ottoman Turkey. Like their Persian counterparts, they based themselves on a reinterpretation of Islamic concepts with a 19th-century evolutionist-rational reading of mediaeval Mu'tazilite rationalism. Thus they reinterpreted prophecy as *reason* and prophets as being 'mind' (or reason). The Qur'anic *shura* was reinterpreted as democracy, *bay'a* (oath of allegiance to a caliph or prince) as the ballot and *ahl al-hal wal 'aqd* (the people who bind and loose) as the parliament.[15]

This was a cultural, though elitist, revolution both in the Ottoman domains and in Qajar Iran. But whereas al-Afghani's innovation was a portent to the Ottoman Union and Progress takeover in 1909,[16] Na'ini and the others in the Shi'ite renewal trend were the result of the 1906 constitutional revolution.

In these two cases, the Qajar shahs and the Ottoman sultans tried to deploy clerical traditionalism in favour of unrestricted monarchy against the constitutional camp. Both camps, however, pro and con, engaged Islamic idiom, symbols and paradigms in the battle. One interesting feature is that when the Qajar Shah called for an 'Islamic assembly', the radical clergy raised the motto of 'national (*milli*) assembly', a national rather than a religious institution.[17]

This battle was a major breakthrough in the process of secularization of politics and legislation. It was fully achieved in the Ottoman case but only partially in the Iranian. This is perhaps why Kawakibi, years after al-Afghani's death, presented for the first time in Islamic history the idea of a 'constitutional caliphate'. The caliph, in Kawakibi's works, should reside in Mecca, with no powers to appoint any Muslim ruler. He himself should be elected by a council and could be removed by vote.[18]

This conception, while contrary to al-Afghani and 'Abdo, established a separation of worldly rule from religious matters in direct contradiction to the classical concept of the caliphate, reducing the latter to a mere symbol and even making it dependent on the will of the people as the source of its legitimacy. Similarly, if in a somewhat different fashion, this example of subsuming religious figures (here the *mujtahids*, as representatives of the Hidden Imam) to an elected assembly was attempted in Iran. An amendment to the Fundamental Law in June 1907 set up a permanent council of no less than five *mujtahids* or jurists who were to be well-versed in Islamic law and who would distinguish whether or not the laws of the assembly were in accordance with Islam. The leading *'ulama* would submit 20 names of learned *mujtahids* to the assembly of which five or more 'shall be *appointed* by *agreement or ballot* of the National Consultative Assembly'.[19] (Italics added.)

The clerical establishment was part of the bureaucracy in the Ottoman Sunni domains; in Qajar Iran, by contrast, the clerics had already developed autonomous, informal institutions, multiple centres and independent power bases of their own. Under these circumstances, they retained *de facto* legislative and social powers. It was necessary, then, to accommodate this influential class. Yet, the accommodation process made the supervisory *'ulama* dependent on the assembly and constitutionally restricted their freedom of action in this sphere in the same way, as Kawakibi's caliph was electable and dismissible.

Al-Sadr: Liberal Hierocracy

In the second half of the 20th century, Shi'ite political thought took yet another turn, producing a multitude of trends.

Contemporary Shi'i Islamist activists began to legitimize their own quest for power in different ways. Various *mujtahids* and activists circumvented, debated or reinterpreted the classical dogma of the Hidden Imam to whom alone legitimacy is reserved. These attempts have carried Shi'ite political thinking along different trajectories, departing from the traditional framework towards new systems: the 'populist-authoritarian' (*à la* Khomeini, Shirazi and al-Mudarisi), 'populist-semi-liberal' (al-Sadr) or 'democratic' (Bahr al-'Ulum, Shams al-Din or Muhammad A. Jabar).

On one hand, these modern systems differ radically from that based on standards of traditional rulership, lineage, community, the necessity of order versus chaos and the *Shari'a*, divine law. On the other hand, they also differ from the early 20th-century Shi'ite innovative political thought based on the European evolutionist, constitutional, liberal thinking inherited from the 19th century.

The political theory of the 19th century was constitutional, monarchal, elitist and pan-Islamic, stripping the government of any divine pretence.[20] By contrast, the major trend in modern Islamist theories is republican, authoritarian, populist and nationalistic.[21]

Khomeini's *wilayat al-faqih* doctrine, for example, confined the right to legislation and rule, in theory, to the *wali faqih* in absolute terms. Al-Sadr, by contrast, took a different line. His theory separates the right to govern from the juristic functions of the *faqih*, subsuming both to constitutional mechanisms.

This entire conception is not only novel but also daringly innovative. It elaborates on secular views of human evolution as much as a new interpretation of the role of the Imams and their human deputies, the *mujtahids*, and it introduces the classical European notion of the division of powers – basing it on the traditional functioning of the Imam as ruler and lawgiver. This novelty merits detailed review. Al-Sadr expounds his political, economic and philosophical thinking on the state, constitution, division of powers, the economic role of the state, the institutional and constitutional roles of the *mujtahid mutlaq* or *mujtahids* as a collectivity if and when the sole *marja'* is wanting. These writings of the late 1970s have a practical trait and differ greatly from the dry, abstract roaming which had marked his 1960s political writings on the Islamic state.[22]

The new series of *al-Islam yaqud al-hayat* (Islam Guides Life)[23] was started on 6 Rabi' Awal 1399 AH (4 February 1979) and completed on 15 Rabi' Thani 1399 AH (14 March 1979).

In this work, al-Sadr presents his conception of the origins of the state. Then he proceeds to structure his version of the Islamic political system. The first conception is meant to support the second.

In explaining the origins of the state as an agency of governance, al-Sadr takes an anthropological-philosophical starting point: man and his contradictory freedom:

> Man is free; no other man, class, or group has supremacy (literally sovereignty, *siyada*) over him.[24]

Like Rousseau's, al-Sadr's man is born free but threatened by shackles; this man is thrown into direct clash, along Hobbesian lines, against sovereignty imposed upon him by other men, classes or groups. But, according to al-Sadr: 'Sovereignty (*siyada*) belongs to God.'[25] This duality would re-emerge in his explanation of the genesis of the state as a human tool to introduce harmony in chaotic, man-made society. Al-Sadr says:

> The state is a genuine social phenomenon in the life of man ... Humans were, at one stage, one community united by primitive conceptions, limited concerns and simple needs.[26]

In this primitive period, according to al-Sadr, there was no need for the state. But

> ... through social practice, talents and capabilities developed. Differences arose, and the contradiction between the weak and the strong emerged. Social life reached a point where it became in need of a criterion defining what is right [*haq*] ... and maintains unity among people ... rather than allowing [society at large to continue to be] a source of contradiction, clashes and exploitation.[27]

Sadr's presentation is replete with spontaneous Rousseau-ian but preconceived Marxian concepts. At this stage of evolution the 'idea of the state emerged' in order to restore the old unity, the reconciliation of all, so that 'all energies [of men] would be positively put in the service of all [members of society] much to their good and well-being'.[28] In this line of argument al-Sadr ascends from man versus God to man versus man, reaching out for a new duality: society versus the state.

His dichotomies run as follows: God versus Man; Sovereignty versus Freedom; Good versus Evil; Order versus Chaos; State versus society.

The state, as an agency of governance, says al-Sadr, returning to his traditional history, 'was established at the hands of prophets and divine revelations [meaning religions]'. The ideal state is the one established by the Prophet Muhammad. But the 'purest' state was soon adulterated

> ... because it was led, after the death of the greatest messenger of God, by leaders who could not live up to its ideals and now there is a need to rectify the deviation of this state.[29]

The state, or, actually, the political system al-Sadr advocates, is far from the old, traditional Imamate or Caliphate systems based on the Muslim community:

> Islamic theory *rejects monarchy* as well as the various forms of *dictatorial* [*fardiya*] government, it also rejects the *aristocratic regimes* and proposes a

form of government, which contains all the *positive aspects* of the *democratic system* but with additions, which would render the form more solidly objective and protected against deviation.[30] (Italics added.)

This new government would be based on 'the rule of law [*qanuniya*] that is supremely restricted by the law, because the *Shari'a* controls the ruler and the ruled alike'.[31]

Now al-Sadr needed to deduce the rule of law and constitutionalism from the classical Shi'ite dogma of the Imamate. He had two obstacles: one, how to legitimize the governance of humans by humans in a creed which is grounded in the rule of the sacred, infallible, God-chosen Imam. Two, how to define, in fact restrict, the role of *mujtahids* in this ultimately human arrangement in a social system anchored in the doctrine of emulation which presupposes the subsuming of the lay community to clerics. He had to achieve this double task within the confines of Shi'ite jurisprudence and theology.

Tract Four of *al-Islam Yaqud al-Hay'at* is dedicated to solving these two problems. It is titled 'Khilafat al-Insan wa Shahadat al-Anbiya' ('Man as Deputy of God and Prophets as Witnesses'). The tract, in the words of Mallat, is 'one of the most sophisticated texts in the modern literature of Islam on the connection between the Qur'an and the structure of an Islamic state'.[32]

Al-Sadr's text is structured on two basic concepts: *khilafat al-insan* and *shahadat al-anbiya*. He posits two categories, or in his words,

> ... two lines (*khattan*). Man's line and the Prophets' line. The former is the *khalifa* (heir, trustee or fiduciary) who inherits earth from God; the latter is the *shahid*, witness.[33]

In support of this dichotomy, al-Sadr presents, in the opening paragraph, two sets of Qur'anic verses. The first is composed of five verses from different chapters relating to the concept of *khilafa* (government of the Muslim state) or *istikhlaf* (choosing one's successor). The second contains eight verses from various chapters and deals with the *shahada* (testimony) of prophets. These two concepts are pivotal in the theoretical structure of al-Sadr's constitutionalism.

Relying on the first set of pro-*khilafa* verses, al-Sadr interprets these as signifying that the *khilafa* 'is meant for the whole of the human race'[34] and *khilafa* means 'that the agent who enjoys it is the lord of every wealth, of man, of animal, of cattle, of literally everything ... hence the *khilafa* in the Qur'an is the basis of government.' And 'since the human species is given – in the person of Adam – the right to *khilafa*, it is this human race then that is obliged [*mukalaf*] to tend the globe and administer human affairs.'[35]

This is al-Sadr's exegesis of the Qur'anic concept of *istikhlaf* or *khilafa* as an authorization from God to humanity in general to govern nature (*kawn* in his wording, i.e. universe or globe) and society. There is no caliph from Quraish, no Imam from Ali's household, no *mujtahid*, but only humanity and man in the Absolute.

The other pole in the dichotomy, the *shahada* of prophets, is a parallel line to that of human *khilafa*:

> ... it represents the *divine intervention* to safeguard *human khilafa* from going astray and re-orient the latter towards *rational khilafa* of the divine nature. That is because God has knowledge of how the human soul is pregnant with passions, temptations and worldly desires, or to what extent this soul is liable to all sorts of weakness and degradation should the human *khilafa* be left to act without guidance or direction.[36] (Italics added.)

At this point al-Sadr deploys the Ma'ida Sura (5:44). His target is to explain the divine intervention, its nature, limits and changing figures. Below are two translations into English of this verse, one from a Sunni English text,[37] the other a Shi'ite translation.[38]

First version
It was We Who revealed
The Law (to Moses)[The Torah]:
therein was guidance and light
By its standards have been judged
The Jews, by prophets
Who bowed, as in Islam, and the doctors,*
To God's will, by the Rabbis [*rabaniyon*]
And the Doctors of Law [*ahbar*]:
For to them was entrusted
The protection of God's book
And they were witnesses [*shuhada*] thereto.

*Literally, *ahbar*, Jewish doctors of religion.

Second (Kho'i) version
Surely We revealed the *Turat*
in which was guidance and light;
with it the prophets who submitted themselves (to Allah)
judged (matters) for those who were Jews,
and the masters of Divine knowledge**
because they were required
to guard (part) of the Book of Allah, and
they were witness thereof.

** Literally, *rabaniyon*, i.e. rabbis.

The classical interpretation of this verse reads the text relative to the *asbab al-nuzul* (causes of revelation), the case of two Jews who had a dispute over adultery and referred themselves to the Prophet as an authority; but the Prophet referred them to the Jewish laws mentioned in the Torah and interpreted by the rabbis and *ahbar*, doctors of religion.[39] Al-Sadr takes the verse and links it to his divine-intervention theory.

There are three categories of sacred figures in this Qur'anic text, he says:

(i)   the prophets, *nabiyun*;
(ii)   rabbis, *rabaniyon*;
(iii)   doctors of religion, *ahbar*.

In al-Sadr's view, these three categories are *witnesses* [*shuhada*] on behalf of the Divine. The *prophets* are on the highest levels; the doctors of the *Shari'a*, who are the *'ulama*, are at the lowest; the rabbis are the Imams, who occupy a middle rank between the prophets and the *'ulama*. The line of divine witness or testimony runs thus from God to the prophets, down to the Imams, down to the *marja'iya*.

As Mallat has aptly shown, al-Sadr drops the Jewish connotations and mutates the rabbis and the *ahbar* into Imams and *marja'iya*.[40] Testimony (*shahada*) by these three categories consists of the following tasks:

(i)   to grasp and preserve the revelation;
(ii)   to supervise human practice in his *khilafa* duties;
(iii)   intervention to resist deviation and restore the right march.[41]

Or, in al-Sadr's words:

> The witness [*shahid*] is an *ideological and juristic authority* who supervises the progress of the community and sees to it that this community acts in harmony with the divine message. (Italics added.)[42]

The three categories of witnesses, however, are different in nature and in limitations. Al-Sadr distinguishes them thus::

1. The prophet is the bearer of the message and chosen by God.
2. The Imam is the repository of the divine message.
3. The *marja'* is a man who, through long, painful, arduous, human endeavours, can deeply and thoroughly grasp Islam and its sources; a man who is so pious that he has powerful self-control and self-restraint capable of controlling his conduct and activities ... [43]

While the prophets and the Imam are chosen by God, the appointment or selection of the *marja'* as having the necessary qualifications is *'determined by the nation'*.[44] (Italics added.)

Another feature which derives from this is that the first two categories are infallible while the third, the *marja'*, is not. Hence the *marja'* needs, in turn, a *shahid* against him, an objective criterion to judge his conduct.[45]

The prophet's *shahada*, in al-Sadr's view, assumes a revolutionary role in staging social revolutions when the human-controlled *khilafa* deviates. His wording is that of *kifah* (struggle) *thawra* (revolution) or *muqawama* (resistance) against *zulm* (injustice) *mustaz'afin* (the downtrodden), *istighlal* (exploitation) and the like. Prophecy, in al-Sadr's words

> ... is a divine phenomenon, which represents a *revolutionary mission (risala thawriya)* an action for change and mobilization of the community (*jama'a*) ...[46] (Italics added.)

So far, the concept of *khilafa* is human and the concept of *shahada* is divine. How do they relate? There are two kinds of relationship: one historical, dating back to the time of the prophet; the other contemporary.

At the time of the Prophet Muhammad, both lines of *khilafa* and *shahada* were *combined in one*, in his person. The Prophet was God-chosen, yet he was obliged to consult the community in order to *prepare* humans to assume *khilafa* on their own.

So far we have *khilafa*, preserved for man, and *shahada*, preserved for divine figures. When *khilafa* deviates, the divine *shahada* has to interfere and assume both functions. But this applies only to prophets and Imams, who are infallible. As for the *mujtahids*, they enjoy no such jurisdiction by dint of their fallibility.

In the occultation period, according to al-Sadr, the *khilafa* and *shahada* lines are no longer united as one. This union can in no way recur without the presence of an infallible Imam. The separation brings back the *khilafa* to the *umma* (nation) and the *shahada* to the *mujtahids*. This is the duality with which al-Sadr ends. It gives the nation constitutional rights while lending *mujtahids* supervisory ideological functions. The well-known *shura* verse is thrown into the field at this juncture. While *khilafa* is governance clear and simple, the *shahada* is given the ambiguous terms of *ishraf* (supervision) *raqib* (censorship) and the like.[47] *Khilafa* is the right of the *umma* on the basis of the *shura* verse, but with the supervision of the *marja'* – and the *marja'* has the divine right to guide and give advice, but under the control of the nation.

Interwoven, as it were, with the Shi'ite traditions of the infallibility of the Imams, and the ethical-social roles played by Shi'i *mujtahids*, the worldly constitutional thrust of al-Sadr's argument is crystal clear.

To sum up, al-Sadr's political theory envisages a division of powers between the nation and the clerical class *en masse*, retaining the *khilafa*, executive and legislative powers for the nation, while reserving judicial powers for the *mujtahids* – both accountable before the law and the constitution. To define this scheme as a liberal, constitutional hierocracy is not a contradiction in terms, as it may seem on the surface.

Al-Sadr's liberalism stands in contrast to Khomeini's authoritarian model. Both, however, employ Shi'ite traditions and Qur'anic texts, both shift from the traditional community to the modern nation-state and both are for militancy and the institutionalization of the clerical class.

But al-Sadr's thought differs form the various strands of the Shi'ite concept of *wilayat al-faqih* or the Sunni concept of the Islamic government (*hakimiyat Allah*) of Maududi of Pakistan or Qutb of Egypt that assail parliaments, constitutional or democratic governments as 'modern heathenism'.

To measure the extent of such difference, it is instructive to see how other contemporary Shi'i *mujtahids* advocated absolutist or authoritarian forms of hierocracy on the basis of the *wilayat al-faqih* dogma.

In his *Al-hukum fil Islam* (Governance in Islam),[48] Muhammad Hussaini Shirazi, the leader/*mujtahid* of Harakat Jamahir Muslima, proposes a draft constitution for this polity. He states:

> Article 7 [of the draft constitution]: Legislation is God's exclusive right; no one has the right to legislate on personal or public matters that which is contrary to the text of Islam. The *absolute ruler in the Islamic state is the qualified* mujtahid ...
> Article 9: Legislative power in Islam is *not separated* from the executive power, but the two [powers] are held in the hands of the *president of the state, the qualified* mujtahid' (Italics added.)[49]

And, lastly:

> [There is] no parliament in Islam to give laws, nor are there assemblies for lords and notables.[50]

Similar views are advocated by Muhammad Taqi al-Mudarisi, leader/*mujtahid* of the Munazamat 'Amal Islami (MAI). According to al-Mudarisi, God is the 'owner of human beings', hence it is He who legislates, leads and governs.[51] He attacks the institutional division of powers advocated by fellow *mujtahids* and presents the 'just jurisconsult' (*al-faqih al-'adil*) as the source of legislation, constitution, judicial and executive powers all in one. Both Shirazi and al-Mudarisi carry the authoritarian system envisaged by Khomeini to the extreme.[52]

Muhammad Bahr al-'Ulum: Liberal Islamism

Khomeini's vision on the *wali faqih* as the supreme arbiter has much to do with the specific history of Iran and its 1906 constitution; the unique nature of Shi'ism in Iran and its integration with Iranian nationalism; the autonomy of the clerical class and their strong alliance with the mercantile and landlord classes; the fusion of popular Shi'ism with the social organization of the guilds and city quarters; the dense presence of popular Shi'ism in everyday life (the religious calendar); and the role of Shi'ism as a legitimizing force and national (Persian) sociocultural marker.[53] In Iraq, by contrast, Shi'ism lacks this density, or socially integrative or nationally cohesive bonding, while it retains an Arab-Bedouin character that differs from the Sufist overtones of Persian Shi'ism.[54]

To begin with, secularization has weakened the clerical class, which has been unable to develop autonomous social or financial bases or alliances. Successive political regimes in Iraq have been controlled by Sunni elites, who drew on various secular ideologies to legitimize their supremacy. The weakness of the highly segmentary clerical class in Iraq and the deep social cleavages driving different Shi'ite social classes apart have been strongly felt by the Shi'i Islamist activists of Iraq.[55]

Iranians were at pains to impose the Khomeinist version of the *wilayat al-faqih* doctrine on their Iraqi refugee-guests-turned-protégés. In the 1980s, different Iraqi Shi'ite groups advocated different strands of political thought: Khomeinist, al-Sadrist or Shirazist. Others were outspoken liberals. These divergences were bred by and resulted in sharp debates and reciprocal attacks exacerbated by the ethnic (Iraqi versus Iranian) divide.

Among the most interesting shifts in the thinking of many Islamists are the discussions started by a group of Da'wa Party cadres who had grievances over the lack of upward mobility in the party hierarchy and over the clerical control of their partisan life. These elements had also been pressured by the Iraqi realities of the Sunni-Shi'i divide and the ethnic, social and ideological *de facto* pluralism in Iraqi opposition politics.

In its *Bayan Tafahum*, 1980, the Da'wa Party – while echoing the traditional rejection of democracy and parliaments as heathen constructions – presented an early pro-democracy platform with specific mention of freedom of the press, of political action, of belief, the rule of law, elections, parliament and the like. Iranian counter-pressures were evident in the attack directed against the Da'wa by Muhammad Baqir al-Hakim's SAIRI or Muhammad Taqi al-Mudarisi's MAI. In 1982, barely two years after *Bayan Tafahum*, Muhammad Mahdi Asifi, the official spokesman of the Da'wa, announced in several press interviews that the Da'wa was for the *wilayat al-faqih* guided by Khomeini.

Under these circumstances a democratic trend began to crystallize among the Iraqi Shi'ite Islamist groups which fed on the ethnic divide and generational, cleric-lay rivalries. This trend was started by the Kawadir Da'wa as can be seen in the writings of their leading figure, Muhammad A. Jabar, on democracy.[56]

Fragile and vulnerable, this offshoot gathered momentum as soon as Lebanese and Iraqi heavy weight clerical figures such as Ayatollah Sayyid Muhammad Hussein Fadlallah, Ayatollah Sayyid Dr Muhammad Bahr al-'Ulum and Sheikh Muhammad Mahdi Shams al-Din, chairman of the Higher Shi'ite Council of Lebanon,[57] supported these pro-democracy calls. This created a sort of Lebanese-Iraqi axis explicitly or implicitly challenging Khomeini's authoritarian conception of the 'governance of the jurisconsult' with a theoretical democratic alternative.

The argument supporting the democratic alternative is unique in Shi'ite theological and jurisprudent terms and merits consideration. The crux of this new concept rests on the conceptual division of the idea of democracy, or the reality of political systems, into the classical philosophical duality of form and content.

The form of the concept or system consists merely of mechanisms regulating the relations between government and nation, between different departments and powers of government, with the jurisdiction of governance and the methods of peaceful change of administration at the centre. These, the thinkers mentioned earlier argue, are not ideological but existential arrangements. They are neither Islamic nor heathen; they are nothing but mere instruments.

The content of the system is the concrete acts, statutes, social, economic and other policies implemented through the system by those who have the provisional mandate to govern. This content is determined by the philosophy of the group in power rather than by the mechanisms of the system. Islamists may thus, the argument goes, be able to provide the content they adopt and have it injected into the system. The mandate they should seek is obviously a popular one backed by the ballot rather than a pre-ordained, unquestionable, divine right.

There are four pro-democracy arguments in this respect. They attempt to solve various problems relevant to Shi'ite theology and jurisprudence, each in its own way.

For example, Bahr al-'Ulum considers democracy a non-ideological mechanism in harmony with the Islamic concepts of freedom, *shura, bay'a* and the like.

In his *Al-Islamiyun wa khiyar al-dimuqratiya*, Bahr al-'Ulum[58] breaks down democracy into two constituent elements: on one hand it is a set of mechanisms and procedures for the practice of politics; on the other, it is the product of a certain philosophical conception, liberal philosophical thinking. But the relationship between the two ceased to exist long ago. With this ideological break, democracy has become a mere mechanism of governance, the best alternative to dictatorship and monopoly of political power.[59] The mechanisms in question are

> ... the right of the citizen to freely choose the mode of government, the peaceful change of government, freedom of expression, respect for differing opinions, the political participation of the people, the rule of law, equality before the law, the restriction of the executive power with a constitution, and the like ...[60]

The same form/content argument is elaborated by Muhammad A. Jabar, in the following manner:

> Those who reject democracy consider it a system of ideology and law contrary to Islam; those who advocate it say it is a general framework or a set of mechanisms whose content is determined by the electorate, or their majority.
>
> On the newest juristic position towards this issue [of democracy], the prominent jurist and practising politician Muhammad Hussein Fadlallah said the following:

> We should differentiate between two things, on one hand, the democratic system which represents a framework for governance void of any specific ideology, because it is the majority who decide the picture inside this framework, and on the other hand, the committed system (*al-nizam al-multazim*) such as the Islamic or the socialist systems where both the framework and the picture are given. This passage is crystal clear ...

> The distinction made here between the system as a framework and the system as content differs radically from the views of so many Islamist jurists and thinkers such as Sayyid Kazim Ha'iri ... or Sheikh Muhammad Mahdi Asifi, who insist that 'democracy' is a system with specific ideological and legislative content, or that it is an ideology/political doctrine hostile to Islam. By contrast, the view advocated by Fadlallah ... supports the modern concept of democracy.[61]

Shams al-Din gives a more concise position with theological and juristic ramifications. His view is as follows:

> The position taken by the Islamists on democracy is conditioned by old theological constraints, the principle of the infallibility of the Imam and his right to rule (*wilaya*) according to the Shi'ite view; or the principle of the rule of the caliph as a person, according to the Sunni view ... The motto of establishing an Islamic state to administer all Muslims has no grounds

in [Islamic] jurisprudence at all. This is an old issue relevant to the Imamate and the Caliphate doctrines. But these two [the Imamate and the Caliphate] exist no more.[62]

He adds:

The Shi'i Imamate has ceased since the moment of occultation [of the Twelfth Imam]. No one has the *wilaya* over others. The jurist [*faqih*] has no *wilaya* [governance] over people [*nas*] ...[63]

To him,

Democracy or *shura* is an organizational tool of society and state, it is a method to engineer political power, a mechanism to practice political power, transfer it from one group to another peacefully.[64]

Shams al-Din, however, gives a warning over the limits of legislation, where he splits this sensitive area into secular and sacred domains. Democracy may

... legislate on organizational matters relating to the economy, development, foreign relations and the like. This has nothing to do with Islamic law (*Shari'a*), these were called justifications (*tabrirat*) and not sacred laws, justifications that are outdated and outmoded.[65]

There are, however, divine areas 'which should not be penetrated by democracy, such as the system of worshipping (*'ibadat*), the system of family ...'[66]

These conceptions create a solid foundation for democracy as for a peaceful symbiosis of secular and sacred laws and reduce the power of *mujtahids* almost to the level of citizenship, their lay emulators in theological terms. This trend represents a clear endeavour to revive the late 19th-century Afghani Reformation and the early 20th-century Na'ini pro-constitutional/parliamentary theology.

Though weak and fragile, the Iraqi branch of this trend has been gaining momentum. Two major factors influenced this line of development. The Lebanese circle of Shi'i Islam, where the first challenge to the doctrine of Khomeini emerged, developed a theological line of development advocating democracy as a system of mechanism rather than philosophy, a point which has been discussed earlier. In fact, this line was an attempt to accommodate the Lebanese realities, where the very concept of Islamic rule is incongruent with a multi-religious society. Without a pluralistic, liberal system, peaceful symbiosis is unattainable. The influence of the Lebanese Shi'i thinkers on the Iraqi militant circle is too obvious to dwell upon at length.

The other factor is the nature of the political system that has developed in Iran itself during the last two decades. The doctrine of *wilayat al-faqih* is authoritarian in itself. As we have seen, both Khomeini and al-Sadr agree on the supreme role of the *mujtahid*, but beyond that they are, theologically, worlds apart. Al-Sadr establishes the control of the jurisconsult over the state, but imposes control of the nation over the jurisconsult, and his argument is based on the fallibility of the latter. Hence the electoral mechanisms al-Sadr envisages enable the nation to override the power of the jurisconsult, and institute the right of community self-governance.

Paradoxically, both al-Sadr and Khomeini adopted the ballot system, the former in theory, the latter in practice. But whereas al-Sadr had a theological argument for his electoral procedure, namely the fallibility of the jurisconsult, Khomeini had a pragmatic need: the multiple centres of religious authority existing in the realm of Shi'i *'ulama*. The very electoral process needed or resorted to by Khomeini in order to prevail over other rival centres shook the foundations of the old traditional concept of *al-'alamiya* (the most-knowledgeable) as a criterion for headship.

The very segmentary and multiple nature of the clerical class and the specific circumstances of historical development of Iran paved the way gradually for a multi-institutional political system. The structure of the clerical class is characterized by a multiplicity of centres of authority, decentralized hierarchies and structure-less, informal methods of selection and succession, hence a system fraught with ambiguities. Under such conditions it was imperative to resort to the ballot box rather than theological conditions of knowledgeability, to enhance legitimacy. The inclusion of the clerical class in the modern state system in Iran led to the infusion of their traditional institutions with the modern institutions of the state. In addition to the executive, legislative and judicial branches, there emerged a host of other powers, such as the institution of supreme *marja'ism*, the council protecting the constitution and the council of expediency.

Under the charismatic Khomeini, the supreme *marja'* was the absolute centre of power; under the 'routinized' leadership of his successor, Khameini, the multiple centres of competing power weakened the authoritarian tendencies, or at least prevented absolute, totalitarian power. This feature contrasts with the patrimonial-totalitarian model in Iraq, where state power was not only centralized, but 'personalized' in the ego of 'leader-president'. By dint of the very cleavages of the clerical class, Iran enjoys this multitude of power.

Contending institutions may not be in themselves democratic, as Sami Zubaida has argued, but indeed their clash opens up spaces for democratic freedoms, albeit in a very limited sense. The paradox is that the fusions of both clerical and state institutions opened up the traditional theology to receive a fresh air of political modernity, or let this modernity, unintentionally, come out of the tradition. Division of power and electoral processes are only parts of a full-fledged democratic system, but no genuine democratic system is even thinkable without them.

In Lebanon as in Iran, the pragmatic accommodation with segmentary nature of society at large or the clerical class itself produced an antithesis of the authoritarian model *à la* Khomeini. Facing both sets of the Lebanese and Iranian problems, the Iraqi circle of Shi'ite militant Islam has to follow suit.

SEVENTEEN

Socioeconomic Doctrines

New Challenges

Islamic economics are new constructions dating back to the second half of the 20th century. Earlier examples may be seen in some older writings of Hassan El-Banna of Egypt in late 1930s, in Sayyid Qutb's *Islam and Capitalism* (published in the late 1940s) or Mahmud Taliqani's *Islam and Property* (1942).[1]

Solid economic writing came in the late 1950s and early 1960s with al-Sadr's *Iqtisaduna* and Siba'i's *Ishtrakiyat al-Islam* (The Socialism of Islam).[2] Yet pioneers remained but few.

From the late 1960s and early 1970s, a continued stream of Islamic economic studies, seminars, research and education endeavours was initiated and sustained by Islamic groups and institutions – centres like al-Azhar and King Abdul Aziz University, Islamabad, or Najaf and Qum. In 1978 it was reported that around 700 essays and books written by 406 authors dealt with Islamic economics.[3]

The spread of this intellectual trend was boosted by the rise of Islamism to power and/or the advance of Islamist social movements in the region. The establishment of Islamic banking systems gave an additional impetus to these tendencies.[4]

As such, Islamist thinkers (Sunni and Shi'i alike) endeavoured to create a new system of economic doctrine(s) to cope with the realities of modern economic life in a fashion which presents, on one hand, a break with the traditional Islamic jurisprudence of transactions (*fiqh al-mu'amalat*), which lost grounds in the face of populist-nationalist or Marxian challenges. On the other hand, however, this break was superficial or, at best, partial, because it tried to retain the old legal concepts and present them in a seemingly 'scientific', modern system of economics. This is what the works of modern Islamist economists do.[5] These classical basic concepts are five legal constraints of reward-punishment of human action:

(i)   imperatives (*fardh*);
(ii)   commendable (*mustahab*);

(iii)   permissible (*mubah*);
(iv)   reprehensible (*makruh* or *mabghudh*);
(v)   forbidden (*haram*).

These permissive or prohibitive limits are applied to modern economics to make room for their presumably 'eternal validity' as cultural markers of Islamic civilization.

The classical *fiqh* (jurisprudence) covered two major areas: the *usul* (methodology), which defined sources of legislation (the Qur'an, traditions, consensus, and reasoning), and the *furu'* (practices), which branched into *'ibadat* (worship rituals) and *mu'amalat* (contracts). In this sense, contracts were part and parcel of religious duties of worship.

This schema is as old as jurisprudence itself, and could be found reproduced, verbatim, in Khomeini's *Tahrir al-Wasila.*[6] The *mu'amalat* section treats various commercial activities (forms of purchase and selling), land tenure and usufruct rights, financial contracts (lending, usury) and the like: activities limited to agrarian, pre-industrial communities. In such societies, economic activities are confined to land possession and rent rights, artisan production and commercial and usury capital. These activities are centred in two areas, the *suq* (marketplace) regulated by the *hisba* (marketplace regulation) books and the *muhtasibs* (market overseers), or, as far as land is concerned, by the *kharaj* (property tax) books[7] and the rulers, the source of legitimation of land tenure rights. With the advance of various forms of modern capitalism, *fiqh mu'amalat* irreparably lost much of its relevance.

Modern Islamic economics, by contrast, tries to re-accommodate, modify and modernize the old *fiqh* of contracts so as to deal with problems of industrial societies – problems of property relations in ramified rural and urban settings; banking systems (interest, loans and credits); primary and secondary production; distribution; prices and wages; finance and monetary problems; securities, bonds and other forms of financial capital; development planning; state regulatory roles; industrial relations and wages; plus a polemic against Western theoretical systems, liberalism, *étatisme*, socialism and communism. Implicit in this novel approach and subject matter is the irrelevance of the traditional mode of 'transaction jurisprudence', although the renovation of Islamic thought in this field is meant to support the pertinence of this old jurisprudence itself as part and parcel of the 'eternal' *Shari'a* injunctions.

What jurists do is:

(i)   desert *'ibadat-mu'amalat* dichotomy as a system;
(ii)   retain, however, the classical ethical categories of imperatives (*fardh*), prohibition (*tahrim*), permissible (*mubah*), favourable (*mustahab*) and unfavourable (*mabghudh*);

(iii)   insert the old agrarian and commercial categories of contracts, such as *mudarabah*, *muzara'a*, *murabaha* and the like into the body of modern economics;

(iv)   inject into the body of old *fiqh* modern economic concepts of labour, value, exchange value, use value, capital, costs and the like;

(v)   dismember the organic correlations between different departments of production and different categories and concepts relevant thereto.

This method of inter-transplanting, this confusion of concepts, together with the removal of objectivity and the endowment of economic activities with a subjective-ethical character crystallized into an established method as soon as the monopoly of clerics in this field waned and modern-educated, academically-trained Islamist economists (notably from Pakistan) stepped in.[8]

Shi'ite Islamist economic theory in Iraq is part of this drive, covering some two decades or so. Three authors stand in bold relief in this area: Muhammad Baqir al-Sadr, Muhammad Hussaini Shirazi (together with his brother Hassan Shirazi) and Muhammad Taqi al-Mudarisi. These three thinkers produced three distinct conceptions. Al-Sadr's *non-capitalist path*; Shirazi's *free* halal/haram *enterprise* and al-Mudarisi's *cooperative economy*. The divergence between these conceptions reveals how wide the scope Islamic economics may be and the extent to which both different historical contexts and individual readings may well colour such intellectual constructions despite the fact that they are all rooted in one and the same legal school.

These three clerics, who were also spiritual and/or organizational leaders of social movements, monopolized theoretical economic writing, whereas their lay-followers/emulators contributed to moulding economic party platforms, as was the case with the Da'wa Party or SAIRI.

The economic writings of these *mujtahids* will be outlined in terms of their method, approach, basic categories, theoretical premise, historical context and line of development.

Al-Sadr : Non-capitalist, Rightful Islamic Distributionism

Economic Works

Following the demise of the monarchy in 1958, the young al-Sadr (then in his mid-twenties) embarked upon a cultural and intellectual challenge to produce an Islamic grand narrative. He fulfilled his promise by authoring *Falsafatuna* (Our Philosophy) and *Iqtisaduna* (Our Economics) but failed to produce his third projected volume, *Mujtma'una* (Our Society). The pronoun 'our' reveals a Weberian desire to establish a civilizational/cultural uniqueness of Islam.

In addition to the major work, *Iqtisaduna*,[9] economic writings by al-Sadr also include *al-Bank alla rabawi fil Islam*[10] ('The Non-Usurious Bank in Islam'), authored in the 1960s. Al-Sadr produced no further economic texts for some twenty years. In 1979, however, with the Iranian Revolution, a new impetus set in and al-Sadr returned to the issue and authored small economic pamphlets which were included in the already mentioned *al-Islam yaqud al-hayat*.[11]

The main thrust underlying the early writings *Iqtisaduna* and *al-Bank* was to construct a unique Islamic economic theory, juxtaposed with both capitalist and socialist doctrines, while the main drive of the latter pamphlets is more practical in the sense that it is more concerned with building a regulatory system ready for implementation.

The General Structure of Iqtisaduna

Iqtisaduna, a 783- page volume reprinted twenty-six times by 1990, presents a multitude of topics and themes relevant to method, approach, framework, basic principles, debate and construction.

The volume may generally be divided into two major sections. Section One, at 234 pages, is a critique of Marxism and capitalism based on readings in Marxist literature (Arabic translations of *Das Kapital* Volume I, works by Plekhanov, Lenin and others). The anti-Marxist polemic (200 pages) has a philosophical nature attempting to refute Marxist 'economic reductionism' and a critique of dialectics. A similar yet very short and meagre critique (34 pages) is directed against capitalist philosophical doctrines, the Benthamian and Darwinian included. The Marxist school is deployed against the liberals and vice versa.

Section Two presents Islamic economics. In it, a preliminary set of definitions relating to method, framework, subject matter and principles sets the stage for the conceived Islamic economic theory. As such, the theory has three wings:

(i)   the theory of distribution (both distribution prior to and after production);
(ii)   the theory of production;
(iii)   the state and state interventionism.[12]

The Basic Premise: Civilizational Essentialism

In the first section, a general framework is defined to emphasize the uniqueness of Islamic economic doctrine. There are two global trends between which humanity has been oscillating: one is the free, capitalist economy and the other is the planned, socialist economy. Both are Western products (pp. 8–9). *Iqtisaduna*, al-Sadr says, is a comparative study proving the superiority of Islamic economics (p. 10). The basic feature differentiating Islamic economics from the two wings of Western doctrines is ethical-religious (p. 16).

> The European's eyes are fixed on earth, not up to the heavens ... Even Christianity could not overcome this earthly propensity in European man ... This man, on the other hand, could bring Christianity's God down to earth, incarnating Him in a worldly being (p. 16).

Benthamian cynical pragmatism, individualism, Darwinian survival of the fittest are but products of this-worldliness. The Oriental, by contrast, is concerned, according to al-Sadr, more with the hereafter than with this-worldliness. Such a basic difference would hinder transplantation of alien economic systems and urge a turn to 'the internalized *ethical determinant* of the [Muslim] community'. (Italics added; see pp. 19–20 and *passim*.)

Al-Sadr expresses this civilizational confrontation in political, economic, religious and ethical idiom: two features of Islamic economy are derived from this premise: first, it is not a science and second, it is neither socialist nor capitalist (p. 29). Or, as he reiterates elsewhere:

> ... The Islamic [economic] doctrine (*mathhab*) does not pretend to have a scientific character. It is not a science, but, on the other hand, Islam is a non-capitalist economy ... We have the historical evidence ... to prove that Islamic economics are truly non-capitalist ... Projecting the non-capitalist nature of the Islamic economy does not mean we wish to lend it a socialist character (p. 404).

Basic Methods

Islamic economic theory, al-Sadr believes, is latent in Islamic jurisprudence and the latter is too rich with economic (*mu'amalat*) material to be ignored or displaced by Western literature. His work, he wrote, was only to 'extract' this unique Islamic economic doctrine. To this end, al-Sadr adopts a textual-logical analysis of Marxist and capitalist concepts of property rights with a comparative ethical-legal approach, viewing new industrial economies through the eyes of the old *fiqh* books, mainly of the two al-Hillis ('Allama and Muhaqqiq), al-Tusi and some other Sunni *fuqahas* such as al-Mawardi. Through inferences, deductions or inductions, al-Sadr reconstructs Islamic regulatory principles from the classical *mu'amalat* jurisprudence, moulds them in a new jargon of exploitation/non-exploitation and applies them to modern entrepreneurial activities of an industrial, commercial or financial nature.

As al-Sadr's conception of society and economy is anchored in an anthropological-ethical premise which conceives both as a random aggregate of unethical acts of individuals, the uniqueness he advocates is the ethical/cultural constraints imposed on man as an economic subject. In this context, religion would function both as a catalyst to the desired action and a hindrance against undesirable behaviour. And since economy is, again, a set of disconnected fields of distribution, circulation and production, the economic theory he creates is replete with an ethical-legalist spirit conducive to a regulatory body of principles. His theory revolves first and foremost on the definition of 'just' property rights and principles to effect 'just distribution', and endorses multiple forms of property existing in peaceful symbiosis together with a degree of state interventionism.

Basic Principles and Concepts

Al-Sadr specifies three basic principles of Islamic economics:

(i)   multiple ownership (*milkiya muzdawaja*);
(ii) limited economic freedom;
(iii) social justice (p. 279). These three principles combine in an individual's property rights on one hand and the ethical limits and constraints imposed on these rights to the benefit of the community on the other. Al-Sadr attempts to produce an individualistic/communitarian mix of an eclectic nature.

These three sets of principles are given in themselves before any analyses of actual economic processes. They seem rather 'the given', the non-derivative constants, although the method of their deduction implies that they are the negated form of capitalism and socialism. That is because the self-definition of Islam (e.g. Arab and Islamist essentialists: 'we are not like Westerners') is not direct. It is not presented in an affirmative mode, but rather in the negative, i.e. not what it is but what is not. Hence al-Sadr's negationist argument presents the first principle, that of recognizing multiple forms of property, as follows:

> Capitalist society believes in the private form of property as a general rule ... and recognizes public property only as an exception. Socialist society, by contrast, takes socialist property as the basic rule ... and private property ... is but an exception (p. 279).

Islamic society differs from both in that

> ... it recognizes all forms of ownership *simultaneously*, establishing thereby the principle of multiple [literally: *muzdawaj*, i.e. double or dual] property in its various forms: private, public ['*am*, i.e. common] and state property, giving each of these three modes a special field and never considers any of them as an aberration (p. 280). (Italics added.)

It is in this negative modality that the Islamic society is 'non-capitalist' (*lara 'ismali*) in al-Sadr's own wording (p. 404). Apart from this 'negation-ism', no other justification for the multiple forms of ownership is offered.

The second principle of Islamic economy is the

> *limitation of the freedom of individuals* by the gamut of *moral and ethical values of Islam* ... Individuals have the right to practise their freedom within the confines of the values and ideals which may civilize freedom [of individuals] and refine it (p. 282). (Italics added.)

Again, this is different from either unlimited or suppressed freedom under capitalism and socialism respectively.

The role of religion as an ethical regulator is introduced at this point to emphasize the singularity of 'our' economy. Moral ideals and values would be operable in economic space by two methods.

The first is subjective, namely spiritual education, to construct rather than limit the internal content of man so as to secure 'good and benefaction in Muslim society' (pp. 282–3). The other is objective, an external force defining and regulating social conduct; it is 'the force of *Shari'a*', the supervision by the Imam, state coercion (p. 284). If subjective, pedagogical means will infuse the required prohibitive/permissive ethics, state-administered law enforcement will seal off the prohibited areas such as usury, monopolization [*ihtikar*, i.e. of trade], gambling, alcohol and other forbidden activities (p. 284).

The third and last principle is social justice (p. 286). While al-Sadr is cautious in his definition of this concept, admitting that it is immeasurable – meaning it has no quantitative criterion – he nevertheless deduces two branches from his notion of justice: general solidarity (*takaful 'am*) and social equilibrium (*tawazun ijtima'i*) (p. 287).

Ultimate Objectives and Economic Problems Defined

Tied to a wider context in this manner, the three basic principles have a major function: to strike a balance between 'social interests and egoistic, selfish motives' (p. 303). Here al-Sadr wavers between three categories: the Western concept of the individual (*fard*); the religious concept of the Muslim and the anthropological notion of the human (*insan*) inasmuch as he oscillates between community (*jama'a*) and society (*mujtama'*); and between the *imam* (religious leader) and *dawla* (the state).

Because man (as a species, rather than Muslims alone) has natural as distinct from social interests, 'humanity' needs a 'catalyst operative in harmony with common social interests' (p. 303). In the contrast between egoistic individualism and communitarianism, al-Sadr's major concern is the 'natural' in man, his natural instincts (*al-fitra*), the source of all evils – above all the economic ones.

It is this Islamic version of the 'state of nature' which al-Sadr holds as the source of all problems: 'First and foremost, the problem is that of man (*insan*) himself; it is neither the problem of nature nor of forms of production' (p.

330). From this anthropological/ethical point of departure al-Sadr moves to the realm of the social without deducing one from the other. Social life has two processes – production and distribution – and Islam, in his opinion, 'rejects the determinant relation between the two' (p. 317).

The problem is 'that injustice (*zulm*) on the economic level is embodied in mal-distribution' (p. 330). What are simply required are 'Islamic solutions' to the 'problems of distribution and circulation' (p. 331). Just distribution is central to al-Sadr's thinking. As distribution, by definition, entails a quantitative aspect, al-Sadr is cautions and warns: 'Justice is neither a scientific notion in itself, nor a concrete, measurable and observable phenomena; it is in fact an ethical assessment and evaluation' (p. 361).

The Theory of Distribution

In this manner al-Sadr arrives at his economic theory, which we may term *rightful distributionism*:

> Distribution is unjust because here it is grounded on an individual basis [*asas fardi*], and there it is based on a non-individual basis [*asas la-fardi*]. The former encroaches upon the collective rights of community [*jama'a*], the latter upon the rights of the individual (p. 331).

Rights of distribution are constructed by al-Sadr on economic categories borrowed from Marxian political economy, namely concepts of *labour, need and property*.

He derives forms of distribution from the well-known Marxian definition of the differences between socialism and communism (*The Goethe Programme*).[13] 'Inequality' of distribution among producers is, in the first instance, anchored in labour (each expending a different quantity of it and receiving a different share of the product); in the second instance it is anchored in the volume of their varying needs.

Al-Sadr takes labour, need and property and links each to his system of distribution, as follows:

(i)   *Labour.* Al-Sadr defines *labour* almost in Marxist terms as general human activity and exchange between man and nature, a necessity for human existence and the like.[14] He (temporarily) recognizes labour as the sole source of property: 'Labour is the grounds of ownership by the worker of the product [*maadda*] of his labour …' (p. 335).

Using the notion that labour does not create everything and that nature is always there to provide objects to be processed, al-Sadr says, '[T]his labour is not the source of the product's value [*laisa sababan li qimatiha*]' (p. 335). The idea here is that while labour produces the right of ownership, it does not create the whole of the value of the product.

This differentiation allows al-Sadr to deduce ownership from labour as well as from sources other than labour. Hence he negates the very premise with which he started.

(ii)   *Need.* The second principle of distribution is need. Society has three major classes: the upper echelon, who have talents and great energies enabling them to live handsomely; those who can work but are unable to produce beyond basic needs; and those who cannot work because of physical weakness or mental impediments (p. 335). The first category gets its share of social product on the basis of *labour* as the grounds of property; the third derives its income and living from *need* alone because it is incapacitated; the second depends on *labour and need.* (p. 336)

    In this stratification labour, need and property enter the system of distribution. The notion of *need* must be discussed. As is clear from the previous paragraph, need is shifted away from its economic framework into that of ordinary connotation, namely deprivation or, simply put, poverty, rather than need in the economic sense as an objective relational bond stemming from the diversity and ramifications of the division of labour whereby producers need all they consume (in the production process or for their personal needs outside it) but cannot produce, hence the mutual need, reciprocity of circulation and exchange. Al-Sadr's need has a philanthropic rather than economic essence and is anchored in abnormalities of human physical structure: bodily or mental incapacitation.

(iii)   *Private property.* Lastly, his conception of private property or the rights of private ownership merits examination. We have seen how the principle of multiple ownership was thrown into the argument at the very beginning of the book; but that was void of any definition of property in itself; now, by contrast, property itself is inserted into the system of distribution; it is defined as a *product of labour.* This determination, if consistent, would destroy any claims of ownership outside the labour criterion. But this is not the case. Al-Sadr disentangles his defence of private property from the borrowed concept of labour/property rights by borrowing another: relations between labour and the value of product.

    According to the classical conception, the value of the product has one part derived from nature, another from the means of production (raw materials and tools of labour) and a third from labour itself, which is called 'living labour' as distinct from 'dead', i.e. stored or materialized, deposited, past labour.[15] Al-Sadr absorbs these parts into his own theories of private property to dismiss the labour theory of property and insert other elements. Hence he claims:

When Islam decided that labour is the cause (*sabab*) for property [al-Sadr's view], it reached two conclusions: first, it permits the emergence of private property and second, this private property should be confined to wealth in which labour can interfere to create or compose (p. 341).

On these grounds al-Sadr deduces two major forms of property (compared to three forms in his earlier discussion on the multiple forms of property). One is private wealth, which includes all wealth produced by human labour, that is, by producers. Another is public wealth (*milkiya 'amma*) in which labour has no hand (p. 343).

These two forms would have, in Sadr's argument, separate, independent aspects; that is, there are certain objects which are solely the product of labour while there are other objects, such as land, which are totally independent of man's labour. This independence of the two forms would constitute a demarcating line to prohibit private property in one case and endorse it in the other. In general, the prohibition of private property pertains to the domains of God (nature) or pre-production, whereas endorsing private property pertains to domains of human wealth, or the post-production sphere.

Yet there are objects in which two forms of property coincide, which means they have elements produced by labour and elements independent of labour. In this case, the labourer has the right to own the product but not the whole value of this product. This means that the labourer has to share the value of his rightly owned product with others.

In this context, al-Sadr proceeds to divide his distributive theory into two major departments, pre-production and post-production distribution to establish property rights in line with the old jurisprudence of *mu'amalat* but using modern categories of labour, value, distribution and the like.

Pre-production Distribution: Land, Minerals and Water Sources

Nature, according to al-Sadr, is the wealth given by God, and God's domains are (according to al-Sadr's own definition) independent of human labour. Hence no private property can be allowed in this field, and al-Sadr promises to allow such property rights only in the post-production sphere. He then proceeds to classify these sources.

Land is classified according to two different sets of standards: first, the method of seizing the land by Muslims, an old jurisprudential basis for determining land revenue and tenure; second, the natural condition of land itself. Methods of seizure are:

(i)   conquered land;

(ii)   land turned over voluntarily to Islam ('persuasion land' according to Mallat's translation);

(iii)   truce land (or 'land of agreement', as Mallat puts it), neither seized by war nor voluntarily converted to Islam but over which a truce was negotiated with pending or potential military threat.

Natural features of land are:

(i)   land cultivated by tillers [*'amira bashariyan*];
(ii)   wasteland [*mawat*];
(iii)   naturally cultivable land [*'amira tabi'iyan*]. This differentiation would give different rights to cultivators who would revive a wasteland or use unoccupied arable land and the like. This factor has to do with work or established property rights before the Muslim conquest.

Through the combination of these two sets, method of seizure and natural features and work done by tillers, a host of property rights have been deduced by classical Muslim jurists as al-Sadr does without any departure from these old standards, such as the rights of the conqueror or the right of the Imam (state) to change the titles of usufruct, possession or even ownership as they will. But al-Sadr would also include rights of possession and/or ownership of land before the conquest, or the work done by land revivers or first cultivators after this conquest.

Al-Sadr, who reiterated that no private property should arise in the domains of God, gives three forms of property rights in land:

(i)   public (common) property, that is, the land is the common property of the community of Muslims (not all humanity);
(ii)   state property;
(iii)   private property.

Both public and state property may be allocated to individuals giving rise to tenure rights; but whereas state property may be converted to private property upon decrees from the Imam (head of the state), public property is convertible to tenure or usufruct rights but not full property rights. The Imam, al-Sadr says, has the right to sell or give *gratis*, permanently or temporarily, even fiefdoms or feudal rights. The same ownership and/or possession rights apply to minerals, water and other natural resources.

Deducing land property rights from the method of seizure by early Muslims or from state (Imam's) rights limits al-Sadr's borrowed populist principle of 'no property without labour'.[16]

The principle of prohibiting private property in the domains of God has been destroyed throughout the detailed arguments in the pre-production sphere of distribution. And various forms of property, including feudal rights, are endorsed in the end.

Post-Production Distribution

In this second sphere al-Sadr authorizes private property on the basis of labour, because this is the field of human activity and exertion. But before we enter this second sphere, property rights have been established in the first sphere – usufruct, fiefdoms, private ownership of land – as the universal means and object of labour. These divine rights interfere with, modify and limit al-Sadr's principle of 'no property without labour', which he established earlier as the supreme ideal of his Islamic economy outside the domains of God. The conflict between the two is the very substance of his argument in this section of *Iqtisaduna* (pp. 545–650).

In the sphere of nature, al-Sadr relies on a wealth of material from classical jurisprudence, which was mainly but not exclusively concerned with land rent (*kharaj* and *'ushur*). But as soon as he enters the sphere of modern industrial relations, he has to restructure a host of classical Islamic concepts relating exclusively to agrarian and commercial relations in order to deduce what can or may be applied to modern enterprise. He begins this chapter (p. 545) with a number of citations from the two al-Hillis, al-Tusi and other jurists, and he later shifts to worker/employer, labour/capital, industrial/banking and industrial/commercial relations.

The examples he presents deal with the following activities (p. 545 and passim):

(i)   wood gathering (*ihtitab*) contracts (between wood gatherers and possibly an employer);
(ii)   grass gathering (*ihtishash*);
(iii)   hunting;
(iv)   fishing;
(v)   water peddling;
(vi)   *ijara* (tenancy of land) (pp. 558–60);
(vii)   *muzara'a* (sharecropping);
(viii) *musaqat* (contractual work in orchards);
(ix)   *mudharaba* (commercial partnership of capital and venture).

With the exception of (ix), all these activities are, according to al-Sadr's own conceptual framework, running in the domain of God. The common aspect to them is the contractual bond between the worker and a partner or between two partners, one who provides tools, pays wages or lends money or capital and the other who works or speculates. This intermediary link shifts the contract from the first sphere, the domains of God, to the second. All these examples are drawn from the two al-Hillis, al-Tusi and some Sunni jurists.

From these examples and the old injunctions arrived at by classical jurists, al-Sadr sets out to define a body of regulations of rights and distributive norms. In his customary method, these regulations contrast with the capitalist method of distribution. Capitalism, he says (p. 552 and passim), divides the product into four shares: interest, wages, rent and profit. Obviously this is the classical theory of political economy of Smith and Ricardo explaining the four sources of income (or revenue) as presented in Marx's *Capital*.[17] These modes of income or revenue are in money form, of course, and may be counted as portions of the aggregate of social product or as shares of a single commodity – as Marx counted them in his analyses of surplus value[18] or of industrial and commercial profit and rent.[19] Now we shall see how different ways of conceptualizing the components of the product function with al-Sadr.

Islam, according to al-Sadr, refuses the division of the product into interest, wages, rent and profit. In this rejection, there are two major problems. The first is methodological and the second is logical.

The methodological problem is that al-Sadr discards the distribution of the product into rent, wages, profit and interest, but endorses the payment by the producers to other parties for their services rendered in the form of land, raw materials, money or tools.

To grasp the contradiction in such a statement, it should be pointed out that the product, any product, might have different modes of representation. It may be represented in monetary categories of wages, rent, profit or interest, all measurable in *money* of account. Each of these categories has a *material* or physical representation:

rent = land;
wages = labour;
profit = capital = instruments of labour + raw materials.

These categories may also have a *subject* representation such as: worker, landowner, owner of machinery and owner of money or capital.

We may move from monetary to physical to subject categories. But such a shift only changes the mode of representation rather than anything else. What al-Sadr usually does in this and other areas is to shift from one mode to another, denying at first what he finally endorses. This method resembles the scholastic nominal approach, which conceives of things as names or concepts; hence any change in names is presumably conceived of as a change in the things themselves. This method fails to distinguish the different levels of monetary, physical or subject categorization of the components of the product of labour. Or if such a distinction is existent, then it is tantamount to a preconceived tautology.

Now to the logical problem. al-Sadr has denied the possibility of any private ownership arising in the domains of God, the first, pre-production sphere, inasmuch as he endorsed the rise of private property in the second, human labour-controlled post-production sphere. Yet, upon entering the second sphere, there had been a host of private and public property rights obtaining in the first sphere and determining and affecting, in advance, the property rights in the second sphere. The logical flaw derives from the inconsistencies in the concept of property, labour and value and the premise that the first sphere (nature) is separated from the second.

Paradoxically, al-Sadr arrives at endorsing modern economic relationships, industrial, commercial and banking inclusive, with the exception of a limited ban on certain types of credit-interest relations.

Solidly establishing private property rights in land and capital al-Sadr's theory endorses private, public and state property with a limited role for *étatiste* intervention to sustain a degree of social security and welfare.

Al-Mudarisi: Cooperative Islam

Works

Muhammad Taqi al-Mudarisi, leader of the Munazamat 'Amal Islami (MAI), produced a series of economic writings between 1975 and 1982 in which he charted a zigzag line of development from traditional positions and developmental thinking to cooperative schemes. His economic ideas are explicated in his *al-fikr al-Islami*,[20] and *al-Islam, thawra iqtisadiya*[21] [hereafter: *Thawra*] while he presented his cooperative conceptions in lectures delivered in 1982.[22]

In his starting point (*al-Fikr*, 1975), al-Mudarisi is totally within the traditional confines of classical, pre-modern jurisprudence; in his *Thawra* (1979), the *mujtahid* takes an abrupt turn to positivist, secular developmental theories and views; lastly, in *Interviews* (1982) the shadow of cooperative thinking overwhelms his intellectual horizon. These twists and turns occurred in a space of seven years, bearing witness to the colossal impact of changing circumstances – from the *hawza* in Najaf to Lebanon and the Gulf, down to the post-revolutionary period in Iran.

Traditional Thinking

In *al-Fikr*, a short, concise chapter is dedicated to Islamic economics (pp. 393–400). Al-Mudarisi takes human freedom (*huriyat al-insan*) as the given; this freedom constitutes the premise to deduce the rights of property, ownership contracts and economic activity. Almost all forms of private property are endorsed on *laissez-faire* grounds in the face of any populist or corporate *étatisme*. All justifications of property rights are supported by the sacred texts of the Qur'an, *hadith* and the traditions of the Imams.

In his words, 'commerce is virtuous' and 'land shall be the property of those who make it prosperous' with 'no limits set on the ownership of land'. The products of earth 'such as minerals and other riches shall be owned by those who extracted them'. Islam will 'endorse a credit system and encourage it'; it also 'sanctions economic speculation (*mudharaba*) but prohibits usury'.

All these ratified economic activities are attributed to free monads who move out and about in the domain of the economy, but the Islamic jurisprudence will chase these monads with taxes: *zakat* (alms tax); *khums* (religious tax); *kharaj* (rent of state land); *kaffarat* (redemptive payments to absolve sins); *nuthur* (votive offerings for desired ends); and others. With these financial levers al-Mudarisi's Islamic economy would ease and moderate social disparities and keep a certain level of communitarian welfare system. Unlike al-Sadr, al-Mudarisi at this point is far from any 'economics' in the strict sense of the word. His 'confrontational' drive with Western ideologies and schools is reserved to philosophical and social thinking, to which he devotes two different chapters totally unrelated to economics.

The Problem of Underdevelopment

After his flight to Lebanon and the Gulf in the mid-1970s, al-Mudarisi changed direction. Faced with the growing literature on development and hectic developmental projects and conferences in the Middle East, he took up the issue as an ideological challenge and dedicated his *Thawra* to the subject. Adopting the usual Islamic approach, he launches a fierce assault on both communism and capitalism, but from a developmental viewpoint.

Both approaches to development, he says, 'destroy human dignity' – but Islam, by contrast, provides 'the easiest and speediest methods for development rather than materialist regimes'.[23] He laments the backwardness of Muslim countries, which are short on progress by 'three civilizational generations than the rest of the world'.[24] He attributes this reality to the absence of an Islamic plan for development, but promises to fill this yawning gap, presenting what he terms his 'discoveries' in this field: the causes of backwardness and the remedies thereof.

The Islamic factors of underdevelopment are the weakness of the human factor; the absence of entrepreneurs; low savings; low investments; low productivity and the brain drain. He enumerates these factors, citing a few Western authors and UNESCO literature,[25] and stresses that they are the true scientific explanations of underdevelopment.

Cooperatives, the Islamic Way Out

In 1982 al-Mudarisi arrived at a new cooperative conception of the economy, postulating economic necessities and the ethical values of Islam. He begins with a liberal argument – the need to separate economic from political power – but ends with its opposite. Against the liberal argument supporting a private sector he deploys social justice, and against corporate and *étatiste* arguments he raises human freedom and then reinforces his double attack on liberalism and *étatisme*. He assaults state ownership (the public sector) from an ethical and social point of view and he attacks private property in the name of economic necessity, namely the need for gigantic projects rather than segmented and fragmented enterprises. When faced with ethics, he deploys economic objectivity, and when economic objectivity challenges him he raises ethics.

His arguments attempt to contrive or conjure up a 'third' alternative, a middle way between extremes. He equates private property with capitalism and state ownership with socialism.

Property can in no way, in his words, remain individual because of the gigantic investments required in industry and because the general, international and regional tendencies are towards more centralization and concentration, enhancing profitability and competitiveness.

As *étatisme* is rejected out of hand, he introduces his 'third', middle-of-the-road solution: cooperatives. In his elaboration of the cooperative project there is no mention of any previous history of the cooperative movement in 19th-century industrial Europe (e.g. Robert Owen in England or C. Fourier in France).[26]

The example he cites is the consumption and retail trade cooperative created in Iran in 1982. These had their precedent in some Middle Eastern countries, like Egypt under Nasser and Iraq under 'Arif.

But al-Mudarisi envisages a generalized form of cooperatives to cover wide economic activity. It is not clear, however, if such cooperatives would displace both public and private sectors or simply coexist with both.

The nature of these cooperatives is also ambiguous, whether or not they are productive, consumer or service cooperatives. Al-Mudarisi's cooperatives are conceptually indefinite.

It seems that the cooperatives, which replace both capitalists and the state in their capacity as owners and producers are as utopian as the imagined Islamic recipe for development. The trajectory along which al-Mudarisi's thought travels is interesting: from free, private economic activity in 1975 to developmental projects in 1979 and cooperativeness in 1982. In the first phase, he reflects both the traditional spirit of the *hawza* and the free market atmosphere of Lebanon where he wrote his first text. In 1979 he moved to Kuwait and Bahrain, where the problems of development in rich oil countries made an impression on his thinking. The populist turn to the cooperatives took place in Iran under the impact of Khomeini's pre-revolution populism. At the time, there were heated debates on land reform, cooperatives and the like.

Al-Mudarisi's frequent change of mind reveals a relentless endeavour to cope with modern realities outside the traditional fences of jurisprudence.[27]

Shirazi: Ethical *Laissez-Faire* Islam, *Halal* and *Haram*

Ayatollah Muhammad Hussaini Shirazi is a latecomer to debates on Islamic economics. His *Fiqh al-iqtisad* (Jurisprudence of Economy)[28] and *al-Iqtisad al-Islami al-muqaran*[29] (Islamic Comparative Economics), both appeared in 1980, some twenty years after al-Sadr's *Iqtisaduna* and Hassan Shirazi's *al-Wa'i al-Islami*[30] (Islamic Consciousness) and after Taliqani's writings. The works of his predecessors, it seems, had no palpable impact on Shirazi.

Works

Shirazi's *Fiqh al-iqtisad* appears to be more of a reaction against these earlier attempts at Islamization of economics than anything else. From beginning to end, Shirazi rejects all sorts of innovative thinking or constructions and adheres to the old body of jurisprudence, sticking to the dichotomy of *halal* (pure, pious, permissible, legal) and *haram* (impure, sinful, forbidden, illegal). This dichotomy permeates the whole book and acts as a regulator and classifier of all sorts of property, contracts or rights. His underlying premise is an essentialist cultural rejection of any non-Islamic economics, Marxist or capitalist, although in practical terms he adopts much of the liberal concept of the free market economy despite customary 'middle-of-the-road' claims.

The *Fiqh al-Iqtisad* tackles ramified issues and problems with no apparent methodological interrelations. It reminds its reader of the heap of undifferentiated issues jumbled together in classical jurisprudence where worship rituals, contracts, taxes and commerce overlap.

To chart a reasonable way through the book, we shall take the author's conception of

(i)   communism and capitalism;
(ii)   property rights;
(iii)   exploitation;
(iv)   the nature of the Islamic alternative he presents.

Communism and Capitalism

Shirazi criticizes both Western systems. Capitalism 'gives half bread and half freedom'; its counterpart communism 'gives one quarter of bread without freedom'. In these two systems, the 'East [Eastern Bloc] is state capitalism, where the government controls capital, and the West is commercial capitalism, where the rich hold money.'[31]

Both Eastern and Western systems deviate from the true path, he maintains, but capitalism deviates only slightly from right ethics and is more advanced than communist Russia:[32] 'Western capitalism is unrightful [*batil*] but is less evil that the truly unrightful communism.'[33]

Shirazi's criticism is focused on the polarization of wealth and poverty on national and international levels, and he denounces such disparities relentlessly: 'The wealth of the world has been concentrated in the hands of the few.'[34]

Private Property

With wealth, Shirazi takes the issue of private property. His position is twofold. On one hand, 'private property should not become an instrument of the exploitation of man by man'. On the other hand: 'In Islam men [as a species] are the commanders of their own private wealth.'[35] Between these two poles, Islam acts as a moderator to 'preserve the balance ordained by God ... so that every man is granted *full freedom* in his work and business'.[36] Private property, for him, is an anthropological given: 'Man owns because there is a possessive instinct in him'[37] which is created; any encroachment upon property is impermissible, which is why 'the so-called agrarian reforms, appropriation of factories and nationalization of forests and the like ... are groundless and unrightful (*batil*)'.[38]

Shirazi's defence of man's freedom goes beyond all limits, harking back to slavery: 'God has authorized man ... to own everything, even women slaves, but within the limits of Islam.'[39]

Unlike the populist limitations proposed by al-Sadr or al-Mudarisi on private property and free enterprise, Shirazi advocates free market norms. Profit on capital, Shirazi says, is permissible and legitimate and applies to commercial, industrial, agricultural and banking capital. Usury is, of course, prohibited in accordance with Qur'anic injunctions. But here too, Shirazi divides usury into two kinds: 'Usury is evil, forbidden and destructive,' but 'it is of two types, one extended for the consumption needs of the borrower, the other for profit-yielding production.' And, 'the lender has the right to receive a profit'.[40]

We notice here that the 'usurer' is given the name of 'lender' and the *riba* (usury) is given another name, *ribh* (profit), a method of endorsing both.

Whereas according to al-Sadr accumulated labour and risk-taking are the norms to legitimize or de-legitimize interest-bearing capital, for Shirazi the act of lending in itself constitutes 'labour' on part of the lender. Shirazi calls this labour 'thinking, which has rights because it moves the will to lend'.[41]

Sources of Exploitation

Contrary to al-Sadr and al-Mudarisi, Shirazi steers clear of the concept of equality and equal freedom for all so vital to his fellow jurists, yet he denounces exploitation. The notion of exploitation in Shirazi's work is less complex than in al-Sadr's but has similar distributive connotations relative to labour and property rights. Exploitation is any encroachment on these rights. According to Shirazi, 'exploitation exists whenever man appropriates a sum over and above his righteous share accrued to him by his thinking and labour.'[42] The term 'thinking' indicates intellectual as distinct from physical labour, and the term 'share' relates both to exertion of labour as well as to property rights. Since Shirazi had already denounced any encroachment (nationalization) against private property, he now goes into the contractual interrelations between various economic agents to build distributive, ethical *halal/haram* shares or profits.

Halal/Haram *Profits: Islamic Alternatives*

As every form of property or wealth is capital, and every revenue accruing from property, labour or thinking is profit, Shirazi introduces a system of contractual distribution of various shares (profits). Almost borrowing Sadr's argument of post-production distribution and Sadr's nominal/scholastic method, Shirazi compares three contesting systems of industrial relations. Profits, he says, should be not be distributed by communist, socialist or capitalist methods.[43]

Shirazi sets four norms of distribution based on labour, wages and need:

> The slogan of the capitalist distribution is: 'from the worker his labour and to him his *wages*'; the communist method is 'from the worker his labour and to him the equivalent of his *needs*'; the socialist, 'from the worker his labour and to him his *labour*'. The Islamic notion is 'from the worker his labour and to him his *share*'. (Italics added.)[44]

To sum up:

> capitalist method: labour/wages
> communist method: labour/needs
> socialist method: labour/labour
> Islamist method: labour/share

These four terms, as explained earlier, may be represented in physical, material or money forms; a share like wages or needs is calculable in money units, a quantity of products or as a percentage of the aggregate product. How Shirazi's 'share' differs, in quantitative terms, from capitalist wages or socialist needs is unclear; what is clear is that the Islamic concept of 'share' locates the thin line separating *halal* from *haram* profits. The very Islamic ethics of Shirazi is conditional on the quantitative determination of the legitimate share.

Shirazi explains that Islamic economics not only endorses private property but also 'distributes profits to management, capital, factory, land and workers'.[45] The quantitative norms defining the end point of the *halal* profit, which is also the starting point of the *haram* profit, are absent. Although the *halal/haram* profits are the cornerstone of his system, Shirazi departs from this notion if the parties involved voluntarily accept the breach.[46] The authority designated to control shares within the Islamic limits proposed by Shirazi is the state, which sees to it that 'neither the capitalist nor the feudal lord take more than their relative shares of profit'.[47]

The alienation of the modern economic concept from traditional religious morality is so glaring that the functioning of the economic system is reduced to purely ethical problems. Not only is Shirazi's thought bereft of any traces of populism, but he is an outright advocate of the ownership of slaves – old feudal and modern capitalist rights in one.

Remarks

Our examination of the idea of the Islamic economy suggests that the term can indicate varied populist, *étatiste* or *laissez-faire* notions. Diverging views have their roots in the different challenges facing various *mujtahids*. As this jurisprudence matured and expanded in pre-industrial societies, it contained vast, contradictory, flexible, even mercurial ideas capable of varied interpretations.

A common feature of these approaches is a responsive, cultural-essential tendency to preserve Islamic jurisprudence on an equal footing with the modern science of economics. This defensive shield was deployed to protect the clerical class as jurists, lend them an aura of modernity and defend various allied interest groups such as sheikhly landlords in 1958 (al-Sadr and Shirazi), or commercial interests in 1964 (Shirazi).

Another feature is the distributive character of the Islamic 'alternatives', a reflection of the absence of any organic understanding of production, circulation and exchange in modern, mass economies, a projection of the vast distributive functions of rentier states in the Middle East and a reproduction of communitarian ethics of agrarian societies whereby religious taxes are instrumental in the redistribution of wealth within communitarian welfare safety nets.

One of the unintended results of this response is the Islamization of industrial economics, although there remains a great deal of resistance and opposition among the *'ulama* to modern banking and other financial activities (stock exchange, bonds, securities and the like).[48]

Yet Islamic economists have hardly reached the threshold of science. Even the Pakistani-trained economists, who assumed the task of the so-called 'scientification' of 'Islamic economics', admit that theirs is merely 'ethical economics': no more, no less.

A new generation of Islamic economists is trying to analyse the economic system and scientifically prove the viability of ethical prohibitions such as that on usury and other activities.[49]

Perhaps the best way to describe the dilemma of Islamic economics in general and Iraqi contributions to it in particular is in the words of one of the organizers of Nadwat al-Iqtisad al-Islami (The Islamic Economics Seminar). Islamic economics, it is stressed, moves in 'a vicious circle' because 'technical economists lack deep insight into Islamic [jurisprudence] … whereas doctors of religion are alienated from technical economic studies.'[50]

Conclusion

Shi'ite Islamic activism in Iraq has been, and continues to be, a *sui generis* phenomenon. Various strands of fundamentalist or Islamist movements across the Middle East and even beyond have been typified as either populist, national or social movements of protest, or communal movements opposing group discrimination. The Iraqi case has been a combination of the two, hence it represents a new, unique pattern.

The Iraqi Islamic movements, which contained several currents and organizations, emerged in the aftermath of the demise of the monarchy in 1958. The Da'wa Party was the first group to be created. It developed according to a fundamentalist model, one characterized by cultural essentialism with a universal form of Islamic discourse. This model had no communitarian or sectarian character, but rather universal overtones. Its main thrust was to defend a creed, Islam, in the face of creeping secularization. The threat of secularism was acutely felt by the clerical class in Najaf, Karbala and Kazimiya, but was also shared by Sunni conservative and traditionalist groups such as the Muslim Brotherhood and the Tahrir Party. The processes which caused this response were in the making for decades, but were accentuated by the radical changes brought on and instituted by the post-monarchy military regime. The breakup of landlordism, the reform of family law and the rise of communism brought into sharp relief the decline of religion. The religious class has already lost much of its monopoly over the production and transmission of knowledge (the *madrasa*), over religious taxes (*khums* and *zakat*) or over the lay community. The decline of the clerical class and traditional status groups was projected in their minds as the decline of religion itself. Two responses were developed by the actors involved: a *pedagogical* trend (the senior conservative *'ulama*), and an *ideo-political* trend developed by junior *'ulama* and Najafi mercantile, ritual-leading groups. The project of renewal waned as soon as the direct threat of communism receded.

Shi'ite Islamic activism underwent three phases of development; it started as a fundamentalist movement in search of a universal Islam versus Western secular ideologies, a grand narrative which conserves the old tenets and dogmas together with the social interests they represent. Under the impact of the predominantly Sunni, military and authoritarian regime of the 'Arif brothers, the movement changed course towards a local politics of group protest against discrimination. It shifted to the second model, communal particularism. The third phase of radicalization came about during the Ba'th totalitarian secular regime under the impact of the Iranian Revolution, which was the culmination of a radical change in political culture across the Middle East – namely, the rise of populist Islamism. Of course the previous elements of universal Islam or Shi'ite communalism did not disappear, but were incorporated into the new movement with its new ideology and strategy.

The Iraqi movement was so over-radicalized that it fell into premature confrontation with a populist, rich and formidable regime. While the totalitarian, patrimonial regime of the Ba'th, like authoritarian regimes across the Middle East, destroyed mass movements and hegemonized an already feeble civil society, social protest was channelled through institutionalized and popular forms of religion: this is the case of Iran. When these spaces proved weak, a modern organization was created out of necessity: this is the case of Iraq.

Yet there has been an inherent weakness in the Iraqi Shi'ite Islamic movements in their various phases. The following may be observed:

(i) Shi'ite Islamic activism could not count in any important way on the clerical class, which was weak in numbers, had weak networks and was weak in financial power (*khums* and other sources of revenue). The conservative sections of the class opposed the creation of an Islamic party because it contradicted their interpretation of the tenets and structure of religious authority running from God to prophets, Imams and down to *mujtahids*, and because an Islamic party would compete with the religious class.

The activist sections of this class were split along theological lines, between reformers and traditionalists, i.e. those calling for modern organization, and those advocating the reinvigoration of *marja'*-emulator relations and networks. This class was also segmented along lineage, city and ethnic lines. The fractured nature of the institution of *marja'ism* has long been a decisive feature accounting for its weakness. This accentuated theological, ideological and political divisions, at least between Karbala, Najaf and Kazimiya, or Persian and Arab elements and families.

(ii) Rituals, as cultural spaces of Shi'ite identity and instruments of mass mobilization and agitation, are sparse, segmented and segmentary (i.e. not as dense as their counterpart in Iran). They are mainly based in the city quarter, with weak social networks anchored in traditional families. Only in Najaf and Karbala are they embedded in the local *hay'at*, the remnants of old artisan guilds. These rituals provided leadership in

Najaf for the anti-Ba'th agitation in 1977, but that was the first and last contribution during the period under consideration.

(iii)   The Da'wa Party tried to act as a bridge uniting both the *marja'* institution and ritual spaces; but it never managed to control these two, which retained much of their autonomy. The Iranian Revolution could rely on both the clerical networks and the ritual spaces as instruments of mobilization and recruitment. By contrast, in the Iraqi case, a modern, Leninist-type political organization attempted to compensate for this specific weakness. In a sense, the clerical class inhibited the creation and development of such a modern organization. Nowhere has the weakness of these three circles of Shi'ite activism been clearer than under the Ba'th regime. The supreme *marja'* (al-Hakim), the ritual leaders and, lastly, the Da'wa failed in their successive, single-handed challenge to the Ba'th.

(iv)   Another feature of Shi'ite Islamic activism is the absence of a strongly constituted Shi'ite identity. Different Shi'ite classes – clerical, sheikhly landlord, political (under the monarchy), mercantile, modern middle, working and peasant – all had different lifestyles, value systems, economic interests and political orientations. Primordial and modern social configurations were palpably stronger than pan-Shi'ite bonds, although a sense of being Shi'i was always existent. One such indication is that even in their religious culture, different Shi'ite segments had different forms of religiosity. The popular, ceremonial ritualism differed radically from the legalist-ethical theology of the clerical class or the ideological Islamism of populist middle-class groups. These forms also differed from the religious piety of tribal groups in rural areas, which disdained ceremonialism as 'un-manly'.

(v)   The Shi'ite Islamic movement in Iraq was initiated in the late 1950s by two groups, the junior generation of clerics in Najaf and Karbala and the Najafi middle and petty merchants. These two groups had different orientations: clerics moved towards the creation of ideology, merchants towards action and organization. With the flow of disadvantaged and disenfranchised middle and lower classes of rural migrant Shi'is during the 1960s and 1970s, the movement changed its social composition. It now contained wide sections of the Shi'ite lower and middle classes, along with poor migrant Shi'ite groups. These elements yearned for leadership. Generational, social and ideological rifts soon evolved out of these differences and rivalries. Paradoxically, the supremacy of the clerics was only preserved by dint of Iranian pressure.

(vi)   The alliance between the lay modern middle class and the clerics in the
         mature phase of the movement was contradictory; it was supportive and
         inhibitive. The clerical class brought to the movement its social
         networks of emulators, financial power as collector of religious taxes
         (*khums*) and, most importantly, legitimacy as holders of religious
         symbols and dogmas. But this class also brought its inhibiting and
         sundry impacts.

         First, the religious class was organized along primordial lines, and
         brought divisions to the movement within the national unit (Iraq).
         Second, it was organized in traditional sub- or supra-national networks
         of emulators and agents (*wukala'*). This mode of traditional
         organization collided with the need for nationally defined politics.
         Third, clerical authority competed with party politics as rival centres of
         power, creating an antagonistic duality. Fourth, the clerical class
         hegemonized the production of ideology and delayed the drive for
         renewal. Fifth, it also monopolized leadership posts or decision-making
         in the emerging modern organizations, hindering the upward political
         mobility of the new generation of educated, active lay Shi'is. This was
         paradoxical, since the clerical class was on the decline and the new,
         modern strata were on the ascent. So the powerful positions the clerical
         class held did not reflect the actual power relations between the two
         sections. The supremacy of the clerical class was artificially maintained
         by the Iranian ruling clerics.

(vii)   One of the crucial paradoxes in the development of these movements
         was that when they matured as modern social movements with
         disciplined organization and clear-cut blueprints, they were severed from
         their national habitat, thrown into exile and soon integrated, to a large
         extent, into the Iranian war effort.

         They conceived of the war as legitimate, in fact as the only way to
         obtain power in Iraq. Thus, while Iranian Shi'ite activism appeared as
         a national (Iranian) current with an Islamic international sidetrack, the
         Iraqi Shi'ite Islamic movements appeared as internationalist with a
         national sidetrack. This reality isolated them from the mainstream of
         Iraqi patriotism, which emerged during the Iraq-Iran war and was
         embraced by the majority of the Shi'is who fought Iran. When the
         Iranian war effort came to a halt, Shi'ite Islamic movements lost
         direction and fell into schisms. All previous cumulative fracture lines
         were accentuated and deepened, resulting in a series of divisions.
         Consequently, the currents in this movement may present a new
         example of what Olivier Roy had strongly called 'the failure of political
         Islam'; a better way of conceiving this case is as a pragmatic adjustment
         to the complex realities in Iraq, the region and the world at large.

In the aftermath of the failure of the 1991 uprisings, and the mass exodus of Islamist activists into exile, the Islamist movement sustained gradual but incessant change, which eroded the former, hard ideological crust and brought the Islamists a set of more realistic conceptions. If and when a rehabilitated Iraq embarked on a democratic process with the minimum standards of the rule of law, Iraqi Islamist trends might well take part in mainstream politics and abide by the rules such standards call for.

(viii) Under sanctions, new centres of clerical power emerged in Najaf (e.g. Muqtada al-Sadr) with full-fledged clerical and community networks that brought Shiʿite power back to segmentary and familial bases. Shiʿite ideological politics in exile seemed again outflanked by traditional segmentary politics at home.

(ix) The major outcome of this process is the politicisation of Shiʿite identity along sundry ideological non-ideological lines.

(x) Fragmented as ever, clerical pluralism remains the norm in the post-conflict, non-Baʿthi Iraq.

Notes

Introduction
1. See, for example, *The Washington Post*, Glenn Kessler, 'US Decision on Iraq Has Puzzling Past', 12 January 2002, p. A 01.
2. See my essay, 'Difficulties and Dangers of Regime Removal', MERIP, Winter 2002, No.225, pp.18–19.
3. The major theme in Adam Smith's *The Wealth of Nations* is the self-regulating commercial society that needs a minimal governance simply to administer justice, defence, and, perhaps, some public works. Even Smith's bureaucracy is under the thumb of demand and supply. Neo-liberals apply this theme to world politics in the aftermath of the end of the cold war, and give primacy to economics over politics.
4. Samuel Huntington, *The Clash of Civilizations and the Remaking of the World Order*, New York, Simon and Schuster, 1996. Consult his article, 'The Clash of Civilizations?', *Foreign Affairs*, Summer 1993.
5. Karl Clausewitz, *On War* (first published in 1832), Pelican Books, 1968.
6. ' Success in a new war against Iraq would be a defining moment in the evolution of the 'Bush doctrine ...[This] doctrine is an attempt to codify international relations in the post-Cold War era ...States in the Middle East and wider developing world will come under increasing pressure to conform to certain rules ...These [rules] concern suppression of all terrorist activity on their territory, the transparency of their banking and trade arrangements, and the disavowal of weapons of mass destruction.' Toby Dodge, IISS Paper, Dubai Conference, 15–17 February 2003.
   The rise in religion-embedded violence has been phenomenal since the 1980s. Organized violence targeting civilians, or terrorism, has been legitimated equally by secular and religious ideologies. All major religions contributed to this steep increase in political violence; but the notoriety was to stamp one small group: al-Qaeda, and one man. See, among other things. According to one authority, in 1980 the US scarcely registered one single religious organization involved in terrorism; in 1998 30 were registered, half of which were religious. The proportion of religious terrorist groups increased from 16 out of 49 in 1994, to26 out of 56 in 1995. See, among other authorities, Mark Juergensmeyer, *Terror in the Mind of God*, Berkley and Los Angeles, University of California Press, 2000, pp. 6–7; John Espositio, *Unholy War, Terror in the Name of Islam*, Oxford, Oxford University Press, 2002.
7. T. Dodge and S. Simon, 'Iraq at the Crossroads', IISS, *Adelphi Paper*, No.354, Oxford University Press, 2003, p.87.
8. On the threat to secularism in Iraq see my article 'Four-Headed Dragon', *The World Today*, London, March 2003. In this piece I argue that the state-sponsored 'faith campaign' – the steady trickle of Wahhabism through the porous Iraqi-Saudi borders and the anti-secular positions taken by SAIRI – pose a real threat to the future of secularism in Iraq. SAIRI may change course if met with a solid secular position by

Shi'i liberals. Thus far, the latter have taken no such position. On the other hand, Iran and Saudi Arabia have been and may well continue to be instrumental in this process of de-secularisation. Another ingredient in this process is the decline of Arab nationalism and the destruction of civil associations. On the importance of civil associations, see Alexis de Tocqueville, *Democracy in America*, 2 vols, New York, Random House, 1990. De Tocqueville considers voluntary civil associations the prime mover of modern society, in fact the essence of pluralism. These associations, having their roots in Montesquieu's 'intermediary' institutions, cushion the space between individuals and the powers that be, and are embedded in the separation of political from economic spaces.

9. This is not a Shi'ite rather an Iraqi phenomenon. A heated debate among Iraqis in exile and in Kurdistan suggest a deep cleavage over the US role, whether or not Iraqis should endorse an 'external' force to meddle with Iraqi politics or to remove the regime on their behalf. Even leftist views do not dismiss the US role altogether but call for a synchronization of internal and external factors.

10. In addition to SAIRI, these are: the Barzani-led KDP, the Talibani-led PUK, the Constitutional Monarchist Movement led by Sharif Ali, the Iraqi National Accord led by Iyad 'Allawi and the INC proper led by Ahmad Chalabi.

11. *al-Mutamar* weekly, London, 'Interview with Al-Ushaiqer', No. 334, 17–23 January 2003, p. 6).

12. Ibid.

13. It has been argued that the INC's liberal, pro-US politics may have much to do with the fact that many of its leaders owe their upward mobility and wealth to the monarchy; whereas the INA's quasi-national, quasi-liberal politics may well stem from owing their social and political prominence to the post-monarchy era, particularly the Ba'th period. This is a social rift that cuts across religious identities.

14. One example among many is Sandra McCay's *The Reckoning*, a book that warns the US not to indulge in nation-building in Iraq because there is no nation there to build, yet the author offers no concept as to what a nation is. In a word, it is bereft of the very premises that it claims to rely upon.

15. All are affiliates of SAIRI. In Arabic alphabetical order, they are:
    - (i)   Ibrahim Hammoodi;
    - (ii)   Colonel Ahmad Ali Muhsin
    - (iii)   Akram al-Hakim
    - (iv)   Bayan al-'Araji
    - (v)   Bayan Jabr
    - (vi)   Jawad al-'Attar
    - (vii)   Hajim al-Hasani
    - (viii)   Hamid al-Bayati
    - (ix)   Hussain al-Shami
    - (x)   Ridha Jawad Taqi
    - (xi)   Su'ad al-Krimawi
    - (xii)   'Adil Abdul Mahdi
    - (xiii)   'Abbas al-Bayati
    - (xiv)   Abdul-Aziz al-Hakim
    - (xv)   'Izz al-Din Salim
    - (xvi)   Muhammad Taqi al-Maula (a Shi'i Turkoman)
    - (xvii)   Muhammad al-Haidari

Non-SAIRI, moderate, pro-democracy Islamic figures are:

(i)   Abdul-Majid al-Kho'i (The Kho'i Foundation)
(ii)   Dr Muhammad Bahr al-'Ulum (al-Bayt Foundation)
(iii)   Muhammad Abdul-Jabar,(Kawadi al-Da'wa)
(iv)   Muwafaq al-Rubai' (the Shi'a Charter)

Liberal, nationalist, independent Shi'i figures are:
(i)   Ahmad Chalabi (INC)
(ii)   Iyad 'Allawi (INA)
(iii)   General Tawfiq al-Yasiri
(iv)   Hatam Sha'lan Abu al-Jon (tribal confederations)
(v)   Hussain al-Sha'lan (tribes)
(vi)   Sa'ad Jawad (Monarchists)
(vii)   Sa'ad Salih Jabr (Free Council)
(viii)   Sinan al-Shibibi (independent)
(ix)   Sadiq al-Musawi (monarchists)
(x)   Safiya al-Suhayl (independent)
(xi)   Ghassan al-Attiya (independent)
(xii)   Kanan Makiya (INC)

16. Interview with 'Adnan Pachechi, Abu Dhabi, 10 February 2003.
17. Abu Dhabi Network, 10 April 2003.
18. I am indebted to the Iraqi journalist Ma'ad Fayadh and other eyewitnesses who had been with Majid Kho'i in Najaf. For the record, see *al-Sharq al-Awsat*, 11 April 2003.
19. *Al-Mu'tamar*, London, no. 348, 2–8 May 2003. In London, Ayatollah Hussain al-Sadr categorically denounced assassination, a clear reference to his nephew in Najaf.
20. Ibid.
21. The Islamic London-based weekly *al-Mustaqbal* ran an editorial by Muhammad Jabbar which directly criticized Ahmad Kubaisi on this score. The newly published Shi'ite weekly ran two statements by three prominent clerics, Muhammad Baqir al-Hakim, Hussain al-Sadr and Muhammad Bahr al-'Ulum, in which they categorically opposed any religious injunction calling on Iraqis to fight US forces on Iraqi soil.

Chapter Two

1. Cole and Keddie (ed.) (1986), p. 3.
2. ACI (1997), pp. 44–5.
3. Cole and Keddie, op. cit., pp. 3–4.
4. Zubaida (1989), pp. 1–3; Azm (1993) in SAB, pp. 3–7; Watt (1988), p. 3; Lewis (1988), pp. 117–18.
5. Azm, ibid.; Roy (1992), pp. 75–7.
6. Zubaida, op. cit., p. 3; and Azm, op. cit., p. 7 and passim.
7. Mortimer (1982), pp. 60–4, 73–6 and 278; Jabar, F., in ACI, op. cit., p. 39
8. Zubaida, op. cit., pp. 13–20.
9. See tables in ACI, op.cit, pp.54–7.
10. Azm, op. cit.; Jericho and Simonsen (1997), pp. 3–11.
11. On such transformation and variety see Mortimer, op. cit.
12. Hoepp and Paetzold (1989), pp. 57–9 and Hourani (1962), pp. 51, 103–4, 110.
13. Holt (1966) and Lewis (1961).
14. Reetz, (1989), pp. 72–4.
15. Keddie (1983), pp. 37–8; Imara (1985), pp. 291–2 and Imara (1971, 1979), p. 145.
16. On Ahmad Khan see, Keddie (1983), pp. 54–5, Mortimer, op. cit., pp. 9–101; and Reetz, op. cit., pp. 71–2; On Pasha, see Hourani, op. cit., 67 and passim.

17. On al-Afghani's reformation, see Keddie, op. cit., p. 37 and passim; and Imara (1985) op. cit., 291; On 'Abdo and the unity of God, see Hourani, op. cit., p. 130 and passim.
18. Keddie, op. cit., pp. 42, 45, 82.
19. al-Afghani (1980), vol.2, pp. 329–31.
20. al-Afghani and 'Abdo (1957), pp. 13, 23 and al-Afghani (1980), vol.2., p. 55, 66; Also 'Abdo, op. cit., vol.3., pp. 282, 300, 443, 492–6.
21. 'Abdo, op. cit., vol.3., p. 355 and passim; Imara, op. cit., pp. 285–9; Iraqi, op. cit. (1995), p. 53 and passim.
22. Keddie, op. cit., pp. 3–4; and al-Afghani, op. cit., vol.3. pp. 315–21.
23. Keddie, ibid and al-Afghani, ibid.
24. QF, pp. 329–45.
25. Imara, op. cit., pp. 237–74; al-Khatib (1985), pp. 92, 96–104.
26. On the unity of God see Wahhab (1986). On the Salafiya movement see Imara (1985), pp. 253–8, 337–40; Mortimer, op. cit., pp. 77–9; Hourani (1962), pp. 37–8.
27. Watt (1962, 1987), pp. 142–8; Imara (1985) op. cit., pp. 135, 138–9, 145; Harbi (1987), pp. 129, 188, 248, 251 and 287; Ibn Taimiya (1991), pp. 99, 122–52, 158, 182.
28. Mortimer, op. cit., pp. 162–7; Cole and Keddie (1986), pp. 230–46.
29. Vassiliev (1986), p. 148 and passim.
30. Vassiliev, ibid. pp. 158–62; and Mortimer (1982), p. 163 and passim.
31. On al-Manar, Rashid Ridha and Hassan El-Banna, see: Mortimer, op. cit., pp. 243–50, 251–7 and passim; Enayat (1982), pp. 84, 94, 115; Hourani, op. cit., pp. 226–50, 360.
32. Gilsenan (1973), p. 5; Baldick (1989), ch. 4, pp. 132–68. On Sufism, see also Qassim (1989); Darniqa (n.d).
33. Mortimer (1982), pp. 70–9.
34. Eickelman (1976), p. 7; Gilsenan (1973), pp. 195–7.
35. Gilsenan, ibid. p. 19 and passim; Sidahmed (1997), pp. 6–7.
36. Hobsbawm, (1995), pp. 1–2.
37. On the abolition of the caliphate by Ataturk, see, among others, Enayat (1982), pp. 52–5; al-Ashmawi (1989), pp. 288–92; Desmond (1981) (Arabic) p. 238–43; Mortimer, op. cit., pp. 134–8, 159, 240; Hourani (1962), 183–4.
38. Batatu (1978), and Batatu (1977).
39. Hourani, op. cit., pp. 343–5, 349–61; Mitchell (1977) (Arabic), pp. 2–5. Sivan (1985), p. 64 and passim.
40. Mitchell, ibid.; Said (1977), pp. 52–8.
41. QF (1993), pp. 329–45.
42. Mitchell, op. cit., p. 5.
43. Taji-Farouki (1996), pp. 4–5.
44. Mortimer (1982), pp. 201–13; and Boulares, Habib (1990) pp. 75–9.
45. Roy (1994), pp. 75–6.
46. Azm (1969, 1982), p. 97 and passim.
47. Azm, ibid. pp. 7–11; Heikel (1982), pp. 192–3.
48. Boulares, op. cit., pp. 76–9, 87, 130; Sivan, op. cit., pp. 23–6, 66, 185; Kepel (1985), pp. 29–30.
49. Zubaida (1989) in his foreword to the second edition; Halliday (1995), pp. 11, 107; Burgat (1992), pp. 77–94.
50. Kepel, op. cit., pp. 215–18, and activists' profile, pp. 219–22; Roy, op. cit., pp. 48–59, 89–97; Kepel (1992), pp. 34–7 and Kepel and Richard (eds) (1994) (Arabic), pp. 15–7; Burgat, op. cit., p. 75 and passim.

51. Kepel and Richard, op. cit., pp. 25 and passim.
52. QF, op. cit., pp. 4–7–14.
53. Halliday, op. cit., pp. 11–41.
54. Kepel (1985), pp. 25–35; Matthee, in Cole and Keddie (1986), pp. 247–74; Mortimer, op. cit., pp. 353 and passim; Boulares (1990), pp. 1–11.
55. Sidahmed (1997), pp. 7, 191–3; Ali (1991) p. 45 and passim.
56. Ayashi (1993); Roberts, in JAS, vol.1, 1996, pp. 1–18, and Bozzo, JAS, vol.1, 1996, pp. 51–64.
57. Sivan 1989, in IJMES, vol.21, no.1, pp. 1–30; Sivan and Friedman (eds) (1990), pp. 11–38, 143–176.
58. Jericho and Simonsen (1997), pp. 1–12; and ACIal- 47–9.
59. Owen (1992), p. 13 and passim; Owen in Fernea and Louis (eds) (1991), pp. 155–71.
60. Gellner (1983), pp. 18, 28–9, 35–8.
61. Hegel, (1967), p. 155–216.
62. Mohamedou (1997), pp. 71–9; Salam (1994, 1996), pp. 13–6; Kienle (1990), pp. 16–24; Faleh A. Jabar (1995), p. 41 and passim.
63. Hobsbawm (1990), pp. 130, 131–4.
64. Slugletts (1990), p. 11; Longrigg (1953), p. 107 and passim; Cohen (1976), p. 256 and passim; al-Nafisi (1973), p. 127 and passim.
65. al-Kawakibi (1975), p. 229 and passim; Khalidi et al. (eds) (1991), pp. ix–x.
66. al-Ha'iri (1977), pp. 112–20, 124–38.
67. Slugletts, op. cit., p. 12; Shiblak (1986), pp. 37–8; Longrigg, op. cit., pp. 151, 191–200; and Owen (1992), pp. 166–9.
68. al-Hassani (1988), vol.3., p. 316.
69. Ibid., p. 316.
70. Ibid., p. 315.
71. Batatu (1978), p. 40 and Shiblak (1986), p. 19.
72. Batatu, ibid., pp. 58–61, 130–1, 276–281, 358–9. and al-Kazimi (1986), pp. 118, 178–80.
73. al-Hassani (1988), p. 317.
74. Batatu, ibid., pp. 17–20; al-Wardi (1991) on the *mahallah asabiya*, vol.1, pp. 21–9; Heine (1995), p. 7 and passim.
75. al-Kazimi, op. cit., pp. 113–5; Batatu, op. cit., pp. 75–7.
76. al-Hassani, op. cit., vol.1, pp. 111, 255, 27–1, vol.2, pp. 70, 129, 186; Marr (1985), pp. 55, 57, 862–5; Fuccaro in IJMES (1997), pp. 559–61; Batatu, op. cit., p. 27 and passim.
77. Marr, op. cit., pp. 127, 143–6; Batatu, op. cit., pp. 27, 32, 807.
78. Marr, op. cit., pp. 282–3; Marr in MEJ (1970), p. 284 and passim; Marr in Lenczowski (1975), pp. 118–21; Batatu, op. cit., pp. 40, 103, 176, 178–9, 180–4, 186–7, 313; Pool (1972), p. 203 and passim; Pool in Kelidar (ed.) (1979), p. 63 and passim.
79. Ibid.
80. Batatu (1978), p. 1126.
81. Ministry of Planning, Republic of Iraq, Statistical Handbook 1960–70, p. 31.
82. This view is shared by a number of writers among whom are Batatu, Marr, Owen, Khadduri and others.
83. Again there is a consensus on this score. See, Chartouni-Dubarry, in Hopwood et al. (1993), pp. 20–30; Khadduri (1969); Slugletts (1990), p. 108 and passim; Owen (1992), pp. 197–200, 206–12.
84. Batatu, op. cit., p. 807; Marr (1985), pp. 282–3; Marr in MEJ (1970), p. 284 and passim; Marr, in Lenczowski (1975), pp. 118–21.
85. Marr, ibid.
86. Chaudry (1991), in MERIP, No. 172, vol. 21, no. 3, pp. 14–23; Chaudry, vol.21, no. 31,

Sep. 1993, pp. 245–74; Beblawi and Lucciani (eds) (1987), vol.2, pp. 10–11, 18–20; Kienle (1990), p. 23; Slugletts (1990), pp. 229–31.

87. On middle class schisms in the Middle East, see al-Naqib and Haido (1988), pp. 39–47; Fadheel (1988), pp. 120–34.
88. Mohamedou (1998), p. 98.
89. Faleh A.Jabar (1995), pp. 53–62.
90. Chartouni-Dubarry, Heine and Tripp, in Hopwood et al. (1993), pp. 19–36, 37–50, 91–115.
91. Heine, ibid., p. 46; Baram in IJMES (1989), pp. 447–93; Iraq Gazette, July 1970, no. 1900, constitution of 1970, articles 38–45.
92. Baram, ibid.
93. Heine, op. cit., p. 46 and Baram, ibid.
94. Baram, in *Orient* (1981), pp. 391–412.
95. Iraq Ba'th Party, Ninth Congress (1982), pp. 83–6.
96. Slugletts, (1990), pp. 231, 223, 248–9.
97. Springborg in MEJ, (1986), pp. 33–5; Niblock and Murphy (eds), (1993), pp. 77–83; Chaudry in Harik and Sullivan, (1992), pp. 152–5.
98. Slugletts (1990), pp. 206–7; Clark (1994), pp. 35–6.
99. The ratios are calculated on the basis of figures drawn from al-Nasrawi (1994), pp. 92 and 93.
100. Ibid.
101. Ibid.
102. Ibid.
103. Batatu (1978), p. 1093; Slugletts (1990), pp. 114–636.
104. Chaudry, in Harik and Sullivan (1992), pp. 152–5; Chaudry, in MERIP, 1991, No. 172, vol. 21, no. 3, pp. 14–23.
105. Faleh A. Jabar (1995), pp. 233, 234; Fadheel (1988), pp. 120–34.
106. Ibid., p. 230 and passim.
107. Chaudry, in MERIP, op. cit., pp. 14–23.
108. Ibid., also, Clark (1994), pp. 32–5, 37–40.
109. Faleh A. Jabar (1995), p. 233 and passim.
110. Iraq Annual Abstract of Statistics, 1992, pp. 57, 108, 229–30.
111. al-Naqib and Haido (1988), p. 38; Fadheel, op. cit., pp. 140–1.
112. Iraq Annual Abstract of Statistics, 1992, pp. 37, 39, 41.
113. Soviet Ethnographic Studies, Moscow, 1986, no. 1, p. 90.
114. Iraq Annual Abstract of Statistics, 1992, pp. 74–94.
115. Slugletts in Hopwood et al. (1993), p. 81; Slugletts in BSMESB, 1978, vol. 5, no. 2, p. 80.
116. al-Nasrawi (1994), pp. 93–5.
117. Iraq Annual Abstract of Statistics, 1992, pp. 56–9.
118. El-Solh, in Hopwood et al, op. cit., p. 261.
119. Batatu, in Stowasser (ed.) (1986), pp. 211–2.
120. Ibid., p. 204.
121. Marr (1985), pp. 22–4.
122. al-Kazimi, p. 93 and passim; Batatu (1978), pp. 115, 119; al-Ruhaimi (1985), pp. 42, 72.
123. Nakash (1994), pp. 174–82; al-Wardi (1992), pp. 100–6; al-Ruhaimi, pp. 105–6; Hassan al-Alawi (1990), pp. 41–3.
124. Nakash, ibid., p. 176; al-Wardi, ibid.; al-Ruhaimi, ibid.
125. Nakash, ibid., pp. 100–1
126. Cole and Momen, in PP, 1986, no. 112, pp. 112–43; Heine (1995), pp. 7–17.

127. Heine, ibid.
128. Heine, ibid. and al-Wardi (1991), vol. 1, pp. 21–2.
129. Heine, ibid. Cole and Momen, op. cit., p. 126.
130. Batatu, in Stowasser (1986), p. 204.
131. al-Atiyya (1988) (Arabic), pp. 111–20; Nazmi (1984), pp. 125–8; al-Wardi (1991), vol. 4, pp. 127, 181, 188–199; al-Ruhaimi(1985), pp. 165, 175–7.
132. Ibid.
133. Batatu in Stowasser, op. cit., p. 205.
134. Al-Kazimi(1986), p. 84.
135. Ibid.
136. al-Wardi (1976), vol. 6, pp. 217–30; al-Hassan (1988), vol. 1, pp. 171–7; Nakash (1994), pp. 82–5.
137. al-Temimi, (1996), pp. 166, 314 and passim.
138. al-Temimi, pp. 166–70 and passim; Nakash, op. cit., pp. 115, 118 and passim.
139. Batatu, in Stowasser(1986), p. 208.
140. Shiblak (1986), pp. 30–6; Batatu, (1978), pp. 270–1.
141. Slugletts in Hopwood (1993), pp. 81–2.
142. *al-Mawsim*, 14, 1993, special issue on 'Sectarianism and Separatism'; al-Hassan, vol. 4, pp. 50–5, 91–7; al-Uzri (1991), pp. 62–71.
143. al-Uzri, ibid., pp. 5, 343 and passim; also *al-Mawsim*, ibid.
144. al-Hassan, op. cit., vol. 3, pp. 315–21.
145. On curbing Shi'i merchants and industrialists, see al-Barrak (1984), pp. 148–58, 192–3; On state control over trade sector, see: Ba'th Party, 8th Congress (1974), pp. 109–14.
146. al-Uzri (1991), pp. 33–5, 38; Nakash (1988), p. 229 and passim;Ministry of Awqaf , (1972), pp. 19, 23, 79 and passim.
147. Cleveland (1983) (Arabic), pp. 140–2, 144–5, 155, 201–3; Techonova (1987) (Arabic), pp. 15, 34–5, 45–50; QF, 1993, pp. 338–9.
148. Khalidi et al., op. cit., p. 151 and passim, pp. 189, 196–201; also: QF, pp. 339–40.
149. Tarabishi (1992), severely criticized what amounted to 'ethnic cleansing' in theArab heritage by such nationalist writers as Arsuzi, Imara or Muhammad 'Abid al-Jabiri.
150. On the Nusuli issue, see among others, Uzri, op. cit., pp. 215–30; Jamil (1987), pp. 183–202; Hassan al-Alawi (1988), pp. 142–60; al-Mallah (1980), pp. 64–9; Nakash, op. cit., p. 114.
151. Jamil, ibid., p. 185; al-Uzri, ibid., pp. 217–9.
152. For example, al-Jawahiri's *Memoirs*, pp. 167–72; al-Uzri, ibid., p. 210.
153. al-Duri, Aziz (1984), pp. 100–2. In defence of the Shi'a, by contrast, see al-Ghita (1994). Al-Ghita complains in the introduction of the Dulaim tribes' professed anti-Shi'ism, and complains of the Egyptians and Arabs in general of their misunderstanding of the Shi'is.
154. al-Uzri (1991), pp. 251–7; Hassan al-Alawi (1990), pp. 19, and passim; also: *al-Mawsim*, 1993, pp. 68, 105, 133, 151.
155. Shiblak (1986), p. 103 and passim; al-Barrak (1994), pp. 141–2; Uzri, op. cit, pp. 281–94.
156. al-Wardi, vol.1, p. 65 and passim, pp. 99–146.
157. Nakash (1988), pp. 81, 83 and al-Hassan (1988), vol. 1, pp. 175–7.
158. al-Hassan, op. cit., vol. 3, pp. 216–9.
159. Fattah Basha in his late eighties was interviewed by al-Uzri in Amman, Jordan, in 1975. al-Uzri (1991), p. 346.
160. Batatu in Cole and Keddie (1986), pp. 195–6; al-Uzri, op. cit., p. 287; UN High Commissioner for Refugees, Geneva, 1994, Nov., pp. 3–6; Makiyya (1993), pp. 218,

333, no. 7.; INC, 1993, p. 156.
161. *al-Hiyad* newspaper, Baghdad, 3 June 1960, no. 48; 9 June 1960, no. 49; 24 June, 1960, no. 60; 8 July 1960, no. 70; 24 July 1960, no. 81.

Part Two, Introduction
1. DF, no. 23, Summer 1995, pp. 93, 95 and passim; al-Sadr, *Risalatuna* (1982), pp. 9–10; Murtadha al-'Askari, interview in *Sawt al-Da'wa*, 15 April, 1993; *Sharara* (1966), pp. 32–3. Abdul Razzaq al-Safi, a Karbala lawyer and PB ICP member described how the shrine cities in the visitation season in 1959 seemed almost as deserted cities, a fact which enraged the clerics and stunned those who benefited from religious tourism. (Interview.)
2. Batatu (1978), p. 890 and passim; Slugletts (1990), pp. 62–71; Marr (1985) pp. 164–7.
3. Al-Ani, al-Safi and Ajina, interviews.
4. Fadlallah's introduction to al-Sadr's *Risalatuna*, op. cit., p. 10; Ferhad (1996), pp. 242–6.
5. On the agrarian reform in 1959 see al-Kazimi (1986), pp. 237–72; Dan (1989) pp. 76–81; Zubair, unpublished paper, introduction.
6. On *khums* paid by landlords, see Zubair (interview).
7. See Chapter Eight.
8. Akhavi (1980), p. 90 and passim.
9. Da'wa doctrine (DD), vol. 1, pp. 418–26; vol. 2, pp. 463–4, vol. 3. pp. 158, 163–6; vol. 4, pp. 5–19; also DD PS, vol. 1, pp. 14–9.

Chapter Three
1. Sivan and Friedman (eds) (1990), pp. 96–7.
2. Sharif (1995), pp. 28–30; Mitchell (1977) (Arabic), pp. 67–70.
3. DD, vol. 4, p. 48.
4. DD, vol. 1, p. 146.
5. DD, vol. 4, p. 48.
6. DD-PS, vol. 1, p. 80–1.
7. DD, vol. 4, p. 146.
8. Ibid., pp. 82–3.
9. DD PS, vol. 1, p. 79; DD, vol. 4, pp. 13–5.
10. DD, vol. 4, p. 13.
11. Ibid., p. 13–15.
12. DD, vol.1, Usus, pp. 130–52; vol. 4, pp. 14–5.
13. DD, vol. 1, pp. 160–72.
14. Ibid., p. 15.
15. Dickens (1968, 1992), pp. 36–7, 44. Hill (1972, 1991), pp. 154–5.
16. DD, vol.4, pp. 166–70.
17. We shall come to this point later on in much detail, see for example, DD, vol. 1, pp. 219–34, 249–54, also vol. 2, pp. 217–34, 240–8, 270–6, 296–311; also vol. 3, pp. 221–3; p. 259–63; p. 308; also vol. 4, pp. 56–8, p. 166–70; 171–6.
18. al-'Askari, Jabar, al-Rubai'i and Taqi, interviews.
19. Mitchell, op. cit., pp. 43–5.
20. For the stages of struggle as envisaged by Sayyid Qutb, later on, and the various periodizations by Takfir wal Hijra and other militant groups in Egypt, see Kepel (1985), pp. 54–5 and pp. 74–5.
21. DD, vol. 2, pp. 240–8; p. 296–311, p. 398–401.
22. DD, vol. 1, pp. 139–40.

23. Ibid., p. 130.
24. Ibid.
25. Ibid., p. 132.
26. Ibid., p. 130.
27. Ibid., p. 142
28. Ibid., p. 143.
29. Ibid., p. 144.
30. Ibid., p. 136–7.
31. Jamali, MW, vol. 1, no. 59, January 1960, p. 15.
32. See Chapter Four.
33. DD PS, vol. 1, pp. 16–7.
34. DD, vol. 3, p. 323.
35. Ibid., p. 324.
36. Ibid., pp. 323, 345.
37. Taqi and al-Katib, interviews.
38. Hassan Shirazi challenged the Da'wa in a direct polemic, see his *Kalimat al-Islam* (1964) and *al-Wa'i al-Islami* (1960).
39. al-Katib, interview.
40. Hadi al-Alawi, al-Nahj, 1987, no. 17, pp. 8–34.
41. Literally, religious schools, metaphorically, the establishment of grand *marja'*.
42. DD, vol. 1, p. 426, vol. 2, pp. 463–4; vol. 3, p. 158.
43. DD, vol. 4, p. 73; vol. 1, p. 420.
44. DD, vol. 1, p. 420.
45. Ibid.
46. Ibid.
47. DD, vol. 3, p. 347.
48. al-Sarraj (1993), p. 280; Ferhad, op. cit., pp. 247–8.
49. DD, vol. 1, p. 420.
50. DD, vol. 3, p. 350.
51. Ibid.
52. DD, vol. 3, pp. 223–5.
53. al-'Askari, interview.
54. al-Katib, interview.
55. DD, vol. 3, p. 225.
56. Ibid.
57. Ibid.
58. *Liwa' al-Sadr*, No. 144, Rijab, 1404 AH (1982).
59. *al-'Amal al-Islami*, No. 84, 9 Rijab 1404 AH (1982).
60. *al-Jihad*, No. 131, Monday, 7 Rijab 1404 AH (1982).
61. Ibid.
62. al-Rubai'i and al-'Askari, interviews.
63. Da'wa sources claimed that ten issues were published under the first logo between 1960–3. See DD, vol. 4, p. 216. In volume 3 it is said that the third issue of the new, i.e. renamed, publication, *Sawt al-Da'wa*, was published in 1380 AH, i.e. sometime between June 1960 and June 1961.
64. DD, vol. 4, p. 80.
65. The Qur'an, 1964, n.p. p. 1296 footnote.
66. DD, vol. 2, pp. 440–1.
67. Ibid.
68. Ibid.

69. DD, vol. 2, pp. 398–401. Italics added. The above article was dated Rabi' al-Awal 1383 AH (August 1963).

Chapter Four
1. DD PS, v. 1, p. 18.
2. DD, v. 3, p. 323 and passim.
3. *Sawt al-'Iraq*, 14 April, 1993; Ferhad, op. cit., p. 279, n. 46; Ja'far (1996), p. 511, n. 17 and 18.
4. Ja'far, ibid., p. 511; *al-Jihad*, No. 326, 1 February, 1988.
5. Batatu, in MEJ, 1981, no. 35, p. 578; and Batatu, in Cole and Keddie, (1986), p. 179.
6. Baram, (1991), p. 18; Baram in Piscatori, (1991), p. 29.
7. Slugletts, (1990), p. 195.
8. Marr (1985), pp. 236–7.
9. Wiley (1992) p. 31; Ferhad, op. cit., p. 243.
10. al-'Askari and al-Rubai'i, interviews.
11. al-Mu'min (1993), pp. 32–3.
12. Jabar, Taqi and al-Katib, interviews.
13. Ibid.
14. al-Mu'min, op. cit., pp. 32–3, Ja'far, op. cit., p. 511, n. 17 and 18; Ferhad, p. 244. The latter's list of founders excludes al-Sadr.
15. Ja'far, ibid., p. 511.
16. al-Mu'min, op. cit., p. 32, footnote.
17. Ibid, p. 32.
18. Ferhad, p. 244.
19. Jabar, al-'Askari and Bahr al-'Ulum, interviews.
20. Shubbar (1990), pp. 353, 358–61, 366–70.
21. Bahr al-'Ulum, Jabar, al-Rubai'i and al-'Askari, interviews.
22. al-Mu'min (1993), p. 32; Ja'far, Mulla (1996), p. 511, n.17 and 18.
23. Ibid.
24. al-Nazari (1991), p. 33.
25. al-Mu'min, op. cit., p. 33.
26. Shubbar (1989), p. 317.
27. Batatu, in MEJ, 1981, no. 35, pp. 586–7; Mallat (1993), p. 15.
28. See Part Three, Chapters Seven, Eight and Nine.
29. Akhavi (1980), p. 90 and passim.
30. DD, vol. 3, p. 157; DD, vol. 1, pp. 300–9.
31. Nazari, op. cit., p. 22; Shubbar, op. cit., pp. 307–17.
32. Nazari, ibid., p. 16; Bahr al-'Ulum, interview.
33. On Munatada al-Nashr, see *al-Najaf* (monthly), no. 2, March, 1968, pp. 80–4, and no. 4, May, 1968, pp. 35–8. Also, *al-Mawsim*, no. 16, 1993, pp. 305–7. Interviews, Bahr al-'Ulum, Taqi and al-'Askari.
34. See al-Ghita (Najaf, 1954, Beirut 1980) and idem (Najaf, 1953).
35. Jabar, interview; al-Nazari (1991), pp. 135–57.
36. al-Nazari, ibid., p. 27.
37. Bahr al-'Ulum, interview.
38. His date of birth is controversial.
39. Bahr al-'Ulum, interview.
40. al-Ha'iri, Kazim, part 1, vol. 2, pp. 11–5, 29–30. For other biographies see: al-Nu'mani (1997); al-Assadi (1997); al-Khalili, vol. 10, section on Kazimain.
41. al-Ha'iri, Kazim, op. cit., pp. 61, 67; Mallat (1993), p. 46 and passim.

42. Khomeini (1987), vol. 1, p. 6; Abrahamian (1993), pp. 8–10.
43. On Murtadha al-'Askari, see *al-Mawsim*, no. 16, 1993, pp. 305–10; Batatu in Cole and Keddie (1986), p. 180. Batatu mistakenly refers to al-'Askari as a 'layman'.
44. al-Khatib, interview.
45. Bahr al-'Ulum, interview.
46. Ibid.
47. al-Ruhaimi (1985), pp. 281–3; Hassan al-Alawi (1988), pp. 82–4.
48. Ibid.
49. Batatu, in Ibrahim and Hopkins (eds) (1977), p. 380.
50. For the influence of Shi'i merchants consult Batatu (1978), p. 245 and al-Barrak (1984), pp. 148–58.
51. Shubbar (1989), vol. 2, pp. 366–8.
52. DD, vol. 4, pp. 78–9.

Chapter Five
1. Bahr al-'Ulum, interview; Mallat (1993), p. 9; Wiley (1992), p. 34.
2. Akhavi (1980), p. 100.
3. Slugletts (1990), p. 196; Akhavi, ibid., p. 98; Batatu (1978), pp. 365, 705; Wiley, op. cit., p. 36.
4. Bahr al-'Ulum, Muhammad Baqir al-Nassiri, interviews.
5. Ibid. Also Wiley, op. cit., pp. 34, 41, 76–7; Uwe-Rahe (1993) pp. 23, 25.
6. Wiley (1992), p. 157.
7. al-Najaf (1982), al-Khatib, pp. 16–7.
8. al-Sadr, *Risalatuna* (1982), op. cit., p. 7.
9. al-Ha'iri (1977), p. 76.
10. Bahr al-'Ulum, interviews.
11. Ibid.
12. Muhammad Baqir al-Nassiri, interview. Al-Mu'min (1993), pp. 45–7; al-Hussaini, (1996), pp. 91–3.
13. Wiley, op. cit., pp. 34–5 and 157–9.
14. Ibid. The titles were found in different Shi'ite Islamist journals and interviews.
15. Ibid., pp. 158–9.
16. Al-Sadr, op. cit., p. 7.
17. The articles were posthumously published in separate collections under the same title: al-Sadr, *Risalatuna*, Beirut, second edition, 1981, [presumably prepared by Muhammad A. Jabar] and also: *Risalatuna*, Tehran, 3 edition, 1403 H, 1982, introduced by Muhammad Hussein Fadlallah, see also Rieck (1984).
18. Mallat (1993), p. 16.
19. Shams al-Din (1991, 1955), introduction; Sharara (1996), pp. 32–3, 40–1; Shubbar (1990), vol. 2, p. 352.
20. Ibid. Also Bahr al-'Ulum, interview.
21. The date of suspension is unclear; see Mallat, op. cit., pp. 16–7.
22. al-Sadr, *Risalatuna* (1982), p. 11.
23. Ibid., p. 18.
24. Ibid., p. 7.
25. Interview with Muhammad A. Jabar, who was in charge of the Kuwait branch of the Da'wa Party and later became member of the Information Bureau of the Da'wa.
26. Mallat, op. cit., p. 1.
27. al-Sadr, *Risalatuna*, op. cit., p. 21.
28. Ibid., p. 22.

29. Ibid., p. 22.
30. Ibid., p. 22–23.
31. Ibid., p. 22.
32. Ibid. pp. 27–32.
33. Ibid., p. 28.
34. Ibid., pp. 30–1.
35. Ibid., pp. 41–7.
36. Ibid., p. 41
37. Ibid., p. 42.
38. Ibid., p. 46.
39. Ibid., pp. 49–54.
40. Ibid., p. 49.
41. Ibid., p. 50.
42. Ibid., p. 51–2.
43. Ibid., p. 53.
44. See al-Ghita and his *Muhawarat* (1954).
45. Batatu (1978), pp. 295, 446; also Mallat (1993), p. 36; Mallat, however, reduces the call of Kashif al-Ghita to two points: a) reformation of Islam; and b) unless reformation is achieved, Zionism and communism, the two main threats, would go unchecked. The idea of reformation is barely argued. Islam, in these polemical texts, argued mainly against the Americans and the British, is taken for granted as solid and pure. The idea of adulteration of religion, usually recurrent in the discourse of reformers is wanting.
46. al-Ghita (1954, 1980), pp. 3–10.
47. Bahr al-ʿUlum, and Taqi, interviews.
48. Jabar, al-ʿAskari, interviews. Wiley (1992), pp. 34–5.
49. al-ʿAskari, interview.
50. al-Haʾiri, Kazim (1977) p. 74.
51. A lawyer and an ex-turbaned figure who was a Baʿthist. See al-Haʾiri, ibid., p. 74.
52. The letter is dated Sufar 1380, that is after 26 July 1960. It was addressed to Baqir al-Hakim who reprinted it in an essay by him published in *al-Jihad* (weekly), issue no.14, Jamadi Thani, 1401. See al-Haʾiri, ibid. p. 72.
53. The three mentioned in the last paragraph are presumably Ayatollahs Murtadha al-Yasin, Hussein al-Hamadani and Khidir al-Dujaili.
54. al-Haʾiri, op. cit., p. 76.
55. Ibid., p. 75.
56. Ibid., p. 74.
57. Enayat (1982), p. 48.
58. Ibid., p. 49.
59. Ibid., p. 49.
60. Ibid., p. 49; al-Ghita (1954, 1980), p. 123.
61. Enayat, op. cit., p. 49; On Azhar and Shiʿism, see, Bagley, in MW, vol. 50, 1960, pp. 122–9.
62. Enayat, ibid., p. 50.
63. al-ʿAskari, interview.
64. On Shams al-Din's position on the loss of Palestine see al-Sadr's, *Risalatuna* (1982), p. 60. For Fadlallah's position, see DF, no. 23, Summer 1995, pp. 93–121, notably p. 95.
65. DF, Ibid, p. 94.
66. al-ʿAskari, al-Rubaiʿi, interviews.

67. *Al-Hiyad* (daily), no. 87, 31 July 1960; al-Sarraj (1993), op. cit., pp. 286, 310–11; Hussaini (1996), p. 93.
68. Many writers, observers and Islamic leaders unconvincingly contend that the Jama'at al-'Ulama was a mere appendix of the Da'wa.
69. Bahr al-'Ulum, interview, London, 16–17 November 1995.
70. Kazemi (1980), pp. 33–4; Abrahamian (1982), pp. 422–3 Graham (1987), pp. 40–1; Akhavi (1980), p. 93.
71. Akhavi, ibid., pp. 92–3.
72. Ibid., p. 91.
73. Abrahamian, op. cit., pp. 424–3; Fischer (1980), p. 164; Akhavi, op. cit., p. 93.
74. Mortimer (1982), p. 361, Akhavi, op. cit., p. 100.
75. Wiley (1992), p. 33.
76. Slugletts (1990), p. 196; Akhavi, op. cit., p. 98, Mallat (1993), pp. 9–12 and p. 198.
77. Zubair, an expert on land reform, and al-Safi, member of ICP PB, interviews.
78. Batatu, (1978), p. 869 and passim.
79. *Hay'at e al-Hakim*, cited in Wiley, op. cit., p. 36; Slugletts (1990), p. 196; Akhavi, op. cit., p. 98; al-Sarraj, op. cit.
80. Batatu (1978) p. 954.
81. Batatu, ibid., p. 954.
82. Khadduri (1969), p. 145.
83. Ibid., p. 145.
84. Dan (1989) (Arabic), op. cit., p. 379; Khadduri, ibid., pp. 145–6.
85. Marr (1985), p. 168; Khadduri, p. 146.
86. For details on the law see, among others, Dan, op. cit., pp. 333–337).
87. Dan, p. 380; Marr, op. cit., p. 168, Khadduri, op. cit., p. 146.
88. Dan, p. 381.
89. Such is the assumption given by Wiley (1992), p. 36.
90. DD, vol. 1, pp. 241–4, vol. 2, p. 217–34.
91. For the text of these two memoranda, see *al-Hiyad*, no. 45, 31 May, 1960, and no. 81, 24 July 1960. The text reads as follows: The Jama'at al-*'Ulama* in holy Najaf believe that the demands set by the memorandum of the Islamic party envisaging the constitution in the country should be based on the pillars of the sacred *Shari'a* and should coincide with the system of Islam, are of vital importance without which the nation can not exist. Officials have no excuse to overlook it [the memorandum]. *Al-Hiyad*, no. 48, 3 June 1960.
92. Khadduri, op. cit., p. 146.
93. Dan, op. cit., pp. 381–2; Khadduri, op. cit., p. 146; *al-Hiyad*, no. 48, 3 June 1960.
94. Dan, ibid., p. 381.

Chapter Six
1. Khadduri (1969), pp. 211–7; Slugletts (1990), pp. 85, 92–4; Batatu (1978), pp. 1010, 1027 and passim; Marr (1985), pp. 188–90.
2. Batatu, ibid., pp. 700, 702, 703, 856, 960–3, 964.
3. These remarks are based on discussions with leading members and cadres from the ICP as well as from living experience of the writer and many of his generation. It is interesting to note how a similar popular sentiment prevailed in Syria in 1976 when the Syrian army invaded Lebanon in 1976 to attack both the Palestinians and the mostly Muslim/Durzi patriotic movement. People at large saw in the Syrian intervention an Alawite conspiracy to help Christians against non-Alawite Muslims.
4. al-Fukaiki, 1993, p. 269.

5. Ibid., p. 273.
6. Ibid., p. 273–4
7. Ibid., p. 274. Communist sources confirm the al-Hakim *fatwa* against the ICP in 1960 was reprinted by Ba'thists in 1963 after their coup. Copies were circulated in so many towns to legitimize the killings and that al-Hakim did nothing to stop them.
8. Ibid., p. 275.
9. Batatu (1978), pp. 806–7; and Batatu, in Stowasser (1986), pp. 206–12; Marr in MEJ, 1970, no. 24, pp. 283–301; idem, in Lenczowski, op. cit., p. 110 and passim; Pool (1972), pp. 203–13; Pool, in Kelidar (1979), ch. 4, pp. 63–87.
10. This observation is shared by all scholars of modern Iraq. A study on the Iraqi armed forces in the eighties and nineties showed the persistence of such tendencies. See Zaidi, Ahmad (staff colonel), 1990, pp. 211–43; Zaidi, A. (1993), p. 5 and passim.
11. Khadduri (1969) p. 18; Batatu (1978) pp. 784, 790–1.
12. Anecdotes on Tahir Yihya's position against the Shurja Shi'i merchants. Al-Uzri (1991), pp. 276–7. On the position president Abdul Salam 'Arif against the Shi'a, see al-Fukaiki (1993), pp. 73, 273, 280, 319, 350.
13. Batatu- p. 1,000 and passim.
14. Hasib now is now chairman of the Beirut-based Centre for Arab Unity Studies.
15. Khadduri, op. cit., pp. 233–6; Marr (1985), pp. 193–5; Slugletts (1990), pp. 95–6; Batatu, op. cit., p. 1031.
16. A Group of Researchers, Moscow, 1975, vol. 1, pp. 140–4; Wilson (1979), p. 101 and passim; Hudson, in Piscatori (1983), p. 826.
17. al-Durra (1977), pp. 22–3; Khadduri (1969), p. 235.
18. Faleh A. Jabar (1995) pp. 59–62 and 112–15.
19. Khadduri (1989), p. 233; al-Uzri (1991), p. 274.
20. Abdullah, interview.
21. Khadduri, op. cit., p. 236; al-Uzri, op. cit., p. 274 and passim.
22. This theme is reccurent in Shi'ite literature among secular and Islamic minded writers and activists. For example see al-Uzri, op. cit., p. 179 and passim; *al-Mawsim* (quarterly), (1993), n. 14, pp. 11–158.
23. Bahr al-'Ulum and al-Khatib, interviews. See also al-Hussaini al-Shirazi, *al-Qawmiyat*, Tehran (n.d), p. 5.
24. Batatu (1978), p. 1,000.
25. al-Duri (1962); Jalal al- Sayyid, *Hizb al-Ba'th*, Beirut, 1963; see al-Duri (1984), pp. 100–2.
26. al-Uzri, op. cit., pp. 271–2.
27. Hassan al-Alawi (1988), pp. 144–5.
28. Ibid., p. 156.
29. Cleveland, op. cit., pp. 200, 216–23; Techonova (1987), pp. 51–2; Hassan al-Alawi (1988), pp. 142–50, 168–9; Uwe-Rahe (ed.) (1993), pp. 67–82.
30. Zubaida, in Littlejohn (ed.) (1978), pp. 54–5; Haim (1962), presents illustrative excerpts from various Arab theoreticians, such as: Sati al-Husri, pp. 147–53, Michel Aflaq, pp. 242–9, or Iraqis, such as Abdul Rahman Bazzaz, pp. 172–88, Sami Shawkat, pp. 97–9; see also Gellner (1983), pp. 41, 44, 53–62; and Smith (1971), p. 22; Anderson (1983), p. 14.
31. Jamil (1987), pp. 183–97; Hassan al-Alawi (1988), pp. 118–25; al-Mallah (1980), pp. 68–9; al-Ghita (1994), pp. 18–9, 30–33; Gottlieb, in Curtis (ed.) (1981), pp. 154–5.
32. Interviews with a host of leading cadres and rank and file activists among whom are Khatib, 'Adil Abdul Mahdi, Akram al-Hakim, Taqi, Jabar, al-Ruhaimi, al-'Askari, Ghanim Jawad and others. All were unanimous that there was a fierce attack against

Shi'is and that discrimination in civil and military service was a major catalyst for their recruitment in the Da'wa, SAIRI, MAI or other Shi'i-Islamist activist groups.

33. Interviews with ex-ministers under the monarchy, al-Uzri, al-Dalli and others.
34. Interview with al-Nasiri (Abu Huda) who was active in the circulation of the memorandum.
35. al-Uzri (1991), pp. 180–1.
36. Ibid., pp. 180–5
37. On Shi'ite political activism in the 1930s, see, Hassan al-Alawi, (1988), pp. 125–6; al-Hassani (1988), vol. 4, pp. 63, 91–7; Nakash (1994), pp. 120–5.
38. For al-Shibibi's biography, see, Shnawa (1993). al-Sarraj (1993), p. 233 and passim. Family sources have also been helpful in this regard.
39. al-Sarraj, ibid., pp. 132–5 and 241–3.
40. This is based on personal experience.
41. Interviews with Jabar and al-Rubai'i.
42. This draws on my personal experience as an eyewitness of the march from the eastern gate to Bab al-Mu'azam. See also, FO 371/180809 November 1965, al-Bayati (1997), pp. 142–4. FO report reads in part: 'This has been an eventful week for the Shi'a. The first excitement was caused by the transiting through Baghdad, on 20/21 November, of a new gold and silver lattice-work cover, made in Isfahan to the order of Imam Muhsin al-Hakim, for the tomb of the martyr-hero 'Abbas at Karbala. This *chef d'oeuvre* took two years to make and cost the faithful in Iraq and Iran some ID100,000. In Baghdad the main streets on the way to Kazimain, where the procession was to stay the night, were packed for hours before the arrival (which was late), and the civil and military police turned out in force to try to control the mob and the traffic, which was at a standstill all afternoon.' Ibid., p. 142.
43. FO 371/170445, October 1963 and FO 371/180809, 26 November 1965, in al-Bayati (1997), pp. 154–6.
44. Marr, Slugletts and others quoted on this score FO reports which were based on informants conveying rumours rather than documented evidence.
45. Interviews with Jabar, al-Rubai'i and others.
46. Ibid.
47. Batatu in MEJ (1981), no. 35, p. 588.
48. The British Embassy reports covered this inactivity on the part of al-Hakim and the success of 'Arif in winning over some of the al-Ghita clerical family in Najaf: 'Tribal leaders and some *'ulama* are reportedly becoming more and more dissatisfied with the inactivity of Muhsin al-Hakim. They resent not only his continued refusal to issue a *fatwa* against the nationalization decrees and the war in Kurdistan, but also his complacency in the face of Government attempts to pass off their puppet, Ali Kashif al-Ghita as the true ayatullah.' FO 371/180807, May 1965. See also, FO 371/180813, 17 July 1965; FO 371/186743, January 1966; FO 371/186743, 18 March 1966. Al-Bayati, op. cit., pp. 113–7.
49. al-'Askari, Jabar and al-Rubai'i, interviews.

Part Three, Introduction
1. For a criticism of the monolithic concept see Zubaida (1989) pp. 64–81 and pp. 99–120; For the variety of forms of religiosity within one school see, Fischer, (1980), pp. 12, 133, 137, 140, 149, 170–7; Abrahamian (1982), p. 15.
2. A critique of this holistic categorization of Islam is found, among others, in Edward Said's two works, *Orientalism* and *Covering Islam*.
3. Cole and Keddie's *Shi'ism and Social Protest* (1986) contains various chapters on

different Shi'ite militant groups in different national settings which are far from being identical. A similar differentiation is apparent in Mortimer's *Faith and Power*, Keddie's (ed.) *Religion and Politics in Iran* (1983) and *Iran, Religion, Politics and Society* (1980); Abrahamian (ibid.) and Fischer (ibid.). On the other hand, Nakash's *The Shi'is of Iraq* provides ample evidence of how, in contrast to Iran, Shi'ism in Iraq forms a *sui generis*.

4. Weber (1968, 1978), vol. 1, pp. 447–51.
5. Durkheim (1915, 1971), pp. 10, 18, 206–13, 416–24; Lukes (1973), pp. 238–9; Robertson (ed.) (1969), p. 42 and passim: Robertson (1970), pp. 150–63.

Chapter Seven
1. Weber, op. cit., pp. 457–63, 50–1, 526–9; Bryan S. Turner (1983), 87–9, 98–102; Robertson (1970), pp. 89–90.
2. Bryan S. Turner, ibid., pp. 87–9; Calder, in BSOAS vol. 44, no. 3, 1981, pp. 468–80; Calder, 'Khums in Imami Shi'i Jurisprudence', in BSOAS, vol. 45, 1982, pp. 39–47.
3. Calder (1981), p. 480.
4. Khomeini (1987), vol. 1, p. 281.
5. al-Ghita (1994), p. 90.
6. al-Mawardi, *al-Ahkam al-sultaniya*, p. 145.
7. Calder (1981), p. 468; Hadi al-Alawi (1988), pp. 95–102.
8. Calder, ibid., p. 468.
9. Ibid.
10. Ibid., p. 469.
11. Ibid., p. 475
12. Ibid.
13. Ibid., pp. 469–70.
14. For a historical comparative view of *khums, fai', jiziya*, in early Islam and pre-Islamic civilizations see, Tahhan (1985), pp. 30–4, 41–4.
15. In the Hashr (Chapter 59, Verse 6) we read a slightly different version.
16. See al-Ghita (1994), pp. 91–2; Khomeini (1987), pp. 317–332; Momen, 1985, pp. 179–80, pp. 206–7.; Calder, (1982), pp. 39–47. For an extensive modern Shi'ite survey on *khums* see al-Hashimi, vol. 1 (Sha'ban 1409 AH.)
17. Al-Mawardi, op. cit., pp. 161–2; Ibn Taimiya (1991), pp. 251, 262.
18. See al-Ghita, op. cit., pp. 91–2 vb; Khomeini, op. cit., pp. 317, 328; and Calder (1982), p. 39.
19. This is al-Tusi's position. See Calder, ibid., p. 40.
20. Ibid., p. 43.
21. Ibid.
22. Calder (1981), p. 480; also Kohlberg, in Arjomand (ed.) (1988), pp. 25–52.
23. For the Indian money from the Oudh Shi'ite principality, see Cole, in MEJ, vol. 22, no. 4, Jan. 1986, pp. 461–80.
24. For the treasures pillaged see, Kotlov (1975), p. 330; On comparative revenues by Sunni Ashraf (noble) in Mecca, see Kotlov (1981), pp. 178–85. For further details on Shi'ite money see, Amanat, in Arjomand (ed.) (1988), pp. 98–130; Nakash (1994), pp. 206 and 208.
25. Arjomand (ed.) (1988), p. 9.
26. For details on this abolition, see Fischer (1980), p. 114; Arjomand (1989), pp. 82–3.
27. On financial resources in this period, see Nakash, op. cit., pp. 229–31.
28. Nakash, ibid., p. 230; Arjomand (1989), p. 84.
29. al-Wardi (1992), p. 246; also interview with the Agrarian Reform expert Zubair.

30. On the social roles and status of *sayyids* in rural settings, see al-Wardi, ibid., 246–8; Salim (1970), p. 125 and passim.
31. Cole and Keddie, (eds) (1986), pp. 14, 18, 21.
32. Kho'i Foundation, Interviews. Interviewees wished to remain anonymous.

Chapter Eight

1. On the organizational role of the *'ulama* and *'ulama* class with their networks in the Iranian Revolution, Zubaida (1989), pp. 59–60; Fischer (1980), says that the revolution of 1978–9 used the networks of preachers and the administrative structure already in place in alliance with people outside the *'ulama* hierarchy (p. 102). In a similar assessment, the mass movement received a ready-made, robust organizational tool made from tens of thousands of medium and poor clergy, hundreds of mosques. These mosques and *husayniyas* became centres of mobilization and recruitment which surpassed the best organized of modern political parties. In these centres people would gather at least three times a day to say their prayers; Faleh A. Jabar (1985), p. 198.
2. Makdisi (1981), p. 2; Fischer (1980), pp. 41–2
3. Makdisi, ibid., p. 28
4. Ibid.
5. Dodge (1961), pp. 4 and 10; Berkey, (1992), pp. 44 and 47. For Sunni institutions see, Haddad (1981), pp. 48–9, 50–1; Tibawi (1979), pp. 47–50; Berkey, op. cit. p. 50 and passim; Dodge, op. cit; Tritton (1957), p. 98 and passim.
6. Momen (1985), pp. 86–104.
7. Arjomand (ed.) (1988), p. 80. For the Shi'i *sadr* there has been a Sunni counterpart, the *sheikh al-islam*, under the Ottomans. The *sheikh al-islam*, the highest clerical post in the Ottoman administration, was appointed by the sultan. The clerical class under the *sheikh al-islam* consisted of; 1) judges (*qudhat*), classified into five grades in the formal judiciary; 2) *muftis*; 3) custodians of worship places (Friday prayer leaders, preachers, prayer leaders, those who call for prayer; mosque servants); 4) the *ashraf*, noble descendants of the prophet family who act as heads of noble guilds (*nuqaba' ashraf*); 5) Darwishs or Sufis, leaders of mystic orders. These categories were integrated into the administration. Their higher echelons formed part and parcel of the ruling elite and had important social and political role to play. See Keido (1992), pp. 9–37; 44–52 and 110–120.
8. On the Usuli-Akhbari conflict and its effects, see Chapter Ten.
9. Tibawi, op. cit., pp. 62–3 and 65.
10. Ibid., p. 50.
11. Ibid., p. 66
12. Arjomand (1989), pp. 29–33.
13. Fischer, op. cit., pp. 128–30
14. al-Khalili (1987), vol. 7, part 2, Najaf section, pp. 132–87.
15. Tibawi, op. cit., pp. 70–1.
16. al-Ruhaimi (1985), p. 101. Compared to 1200 students in secular schools the ratio is roughly 10:1.
17. Nakash (1994), pp. 250–4, and al-Ruhaimi, ibid., p. 101.
18. Jamali, MW, vol. 50, 1960, p. 15.
19. Figures (a) and (c), Fischer, op. cit., pp. 76–6, 135; figures in (b), Nakash, op. cit., p. 259 quoted from: Mottahedeh (1985), p 236. Fischer's figure suggest a lineal pattern of diminishing magnitude; Mottahedeh's and Nakash's figures for the thirties and fifties suggest a cyclical rather than linear pattern.

20. Shubbar (1990), vol. 2, pp. 143–5; al-Wardi (1991), vol. 3, pp. 262–5.
21. Shubbar, ibid., p. 137
22. Jamal al-Din (1995), pp. 37–41; Basri, vol. 2, p. 520; Shubbar, ibid., pp. 329–38.
23. Mottahedeh, op. cit., p. 11–2; Mallat (1993); Fischer (1980), pp. 78–83. Quchani (1992), pp. 196–8.
24. al-Quchani, op. cit., relates his story in Najaf, which exceeded 20 years in order to go up the clerical ladder, p. 147 and passim.

Chapter Nine
1. al-Ha'iri, A. Hadi (1977), p. 62.
2. Ja'far, in *A Group of Researchers* (1996), p. 516; al- Ha'iri (1977), pp. 90–4.
3. *al-Nur* (monthly), no. 69, Feb., 1997.
4. al-Ha'iri, op.cit., pp. 64–5.
5. Cole, in IS, vol. 18, no. 1, Winter, 1985, pp. 26–7; Cole, in Keddie (ed.) (1983), pp. 40–6., al-Ha'iri, op. cit., pp. 62–5; Arjomand (ed.) (1984), pp. 242–9; also Arjomand (ed.) (1988), pp. 8, 305 and passim; Moussavi, IS, vol. 18, no. 1, Winter, 1985, pp. 35, 44–6; Amanat, in Arjomand (ed.) (1988), pp. 101–9; Enayat (1982, 1988), pp. 162–3.
6. Arjomand (ed.) (1984), pp. 122–55; Akhavi (1980), pp. 10–11; Enayat, op. cit., pp. 167–8; Bayat, in Esposito (ed.) (1980), pp. 90–2.
7. On Mu'tazilite position on this score see, Muruwa (1979), pp. 661, 763 and passim; Fakhri (1983), pp. 43, 46–7, 49–50. On the Hidden Imam, see Sachedina (1981).
8. These are: 1) Al-Kafi fi Usul al-Din by Muhammad Ibn Ya'qub al-Kulaini (d.941 and buried in Baghdad); 2) Man La Yahdhuruhu al-Faqih, by Muhammad Ibn Babiwayh al-Razi al-Qumi, aka al-Sadduq (d.991); 3) Tahthib al-Ahkam by Muhammad Ibn al-Hassan al-Tusi, aka Sheikh al-Ta'ifa. (d.1067); 4) Al-Istibsar by al-Tusi.
9. Bahr al-'Ulum (1983), pp. 120–4.
10. Ibid., p. 123.
11. Ibid., pp. 124–5. See also Bahr al-'Ulum (1991); Arjomand (ed.) (1984), para 5.3.2.; Moussavi, IS, vol. 18, no. 1, Winter 1985, p. 37.
12. Arjomand, ibid. para 5.3.2.
13. Ibid.; and Moussavi, op. cit., p. 37.
14. Ibid.
15. Momen (1985), pp. 87, 89, 94–5.
16. Cooper, in Arjomand (ed.) (1988), p. 263. For conditions of *ijtihad* see also Chapter 10, pp. 240–9
17. Moussavi, op. cit., p. 39.
18. Ibid., p. 39.
19. Ibid.
20. Arjomand (ed.) (1984), pp. 242–3
21. Bahr al-'Ulum (1983), pp. 10–14; Enayat (1982, 1988), pp. 167–9.
22. The Qur'an (1946), p. 198.
23. Ibid.
24. Bahr al-'Ulum, op. cit., pp. 14–15.
25. Ibid., pp. 15–16.
26. Ibid.
27. Momen, op. cit., p. 189.
28. On al-Karki and Shahid Thani, vice-regency of the Imam, see, Arjomand, Momen, Newman and others.
29. Moussavi, op. cit., p. 40.
30. Bahr al-'Ulum (1991), pp. 251–2

31. Cole, IS (1985), op. cit., p. 2–32.
32. Newman, DWI, 33 (1993), pp. 60–112; also Arjomand (ed.) (1984), ch. 5, para, 5.3.1 and 5.3.2.
33. Newman, ibid., pp. 81–9; Arjomand, ibid.; also Arjomand (ed.) (1988), pp. 6–7.
34. Arjomand (ed.) (1984), ch. 5, para 5.3.1.
35. Ibid., para 5.3.3.
36. Ibid.
37. Ibid.
38. al-Qazwini, FJ, no. 1, January 1992, pp. 208–10.
39. Mallat (1993), gives the years 1617 and 1623, p. 29; Arjomand (1984), para 5.3.3.; Qazwini, ibid., pp. 209–10; Cole, IS (1985), op. cit.; Momen, op. cit., pp. 117–8, 222–31.
40. Momen, op. cit., p. 222.
41. Bahr al-'Ulum (1991), p. 169.
42. Cole, IS (1985), p. 13; Bahr al-'Ulum, in Khalili, op. cit., vol. 7, part 2, Najaf, pp. 64–71.
43. Momen, p. 222; Moussavi, in IS, vol. 18, no. 1, Winter 1985 p. 38.
44. Cole, op. cit., p. 19.
45. Arjomand (1984), para. 5.3.3; Momen, Ibid., p. 222 and passim; Cole, IS (1985), pp. 6, 13, 19, 21 and 23.
46. Bahr al-'Ulum (1991); Bahr al-'Ulum in Khalili, op. cit., vol. 7, part 2, pp. 67–8; Cole, IS, op. cit., p. 13; Arjomand (1984), pp. 145 and passim; Newman, DWI, 33, 1993, p p. 86–8.
47. Bahr al-'Ulum, MB (1991), pp. 175–81.
48. Arjomand (1984), p. 145, para 5.3.3.
49. Newman, op. cit., DWI, 33, 1993, pp. 86–91.
50. Ibid.
51. Cole, IS (1985), p. 5.
52. Ibid., p. 6.
53. Ibid., p. 9.
54. Cole and Momen, pp. 112, August, 1986, pp. 112–43.
55. Cole, IS, op. cit. (1985), p. 20.
56. Ibid., pp. 21–2.
57. Algar, Hamid (1980), pp. 33–44; Cole, ibid., pp. 26–7; Cole and Momen, PP, op. cit., pp. 117, 119–21 and passim; Cole, in Keddie (ed.) (1983), pp. 38–40.
58. Enayat 1982, p. 167 and passim; Momen (1985), pp. 223–5; J. Cole, IS (1985), pp. 3–33; Bahr al-'Ulum, in Khalili, op. cit., vol. 7, part 2, Najaf, pp. 64–71; 'Ulum (1991), pp. 175–83; Akhavi, op. cit., p. 7; Cole, in Keddie (ed.) (1983), pp. 33–47; Amanat, in Arjomand (ed.), 1988, p. 98–132.
59. Cole in Keddie (ed.), pp. 40–50; Moussavi, op. cit., p. 45, Amanat, 'Abbas, op. cit; Ha'iri (1977), p. 63 and passim.
60. Bahr al-'Ulum, interview.
61. This version provided by Bahr al-'Ulum is backed by the analyses presented by Moussavi who contends that under Bihbahani the time was ripe for the emergence of *marja' taqlid* but there were a multitude of powerful Shi'ite figures whose rivalry prevented and delayed the emergence of this post (Moussavi, pp. 45–6). The dates of the death of the prominent *mujtahids* he presents differ greatly from those dates given by Fischer and other sources which makes any scrutinizing of these developments all the more difficult.
62. Amanat, op. cit., p. 102; Arjomand (ed.) (1988), pp. 8–9; Moussavi op. cit., pp. 44–5.

63. Amanat, ibid., p. 106.

64. Ibid., p107.

65. Ibid., p. 118. Reaction against the wealth and power of hometown *mujtahids* in Iran took also another form: an anti-clerical Sufi and Babi tendencies.

66. Ibid., p. 103.

67. Ibid.

68. Ibid., p. 102.

69. Ibid., p. 98.

70. *Al-Rawdha al-Bahiyya fi Sharh al-Lum'a al-Dimashqiyya* (The Magnificent Garden in Explaining the Damascene Illumination), v. 1, p. 236, in *'Ulum* (1991), op. cit., p. 51.

71. Bahr al-'Ulum, ibid., pp. 230–50.

72. Ibid., p. 250

73. See for example the list of Shi'i supreme *mujtahids* from the time of Kulaini in the 10th century in Fischer, op. cit., pp. 252–4; see also Basri, Mir (1994).

74. Nakash, op. cit., p. 200; Akhavi, op. cit., pp. 30–8.

75. Akhavi, ibid., pp. 91–3.

76. Wardi (1976), v. 6, pp. 218, 221–30; Khalid Timimi, op. cit., pp. 194–5.

77. This view has been voiced systematically by modern secular and Shi'i lay writers and activists who look for a Vatican-type of institution.

78. For Musa al-Sadr, see, Cole and Keddie (eds) (1986) pp. 161–3. Also interview with Karim Muruwa.

79. Najaf, 'A. (nom de guerre), April (1981), pp. 32–3.

80. Cole and Keddie, op. cit., p. 161.

81. Ibid., pp. 162–3.

82. On Islamist Shi'is in Lebanon, see Picard (1993); Norton and Cobban in Cole and Keddie (eds) (1986), pp. 137–55 and 155–78 respectively.

83. Norton, Ibid., p. 165.

84. These details were relayed by Karim Muruwa, member of the Political Bureau of the Lebanese Communist Party, who was a member of the General Assembly by dint of being a Shi'i postgraduate.

85. For a detailed account of al-Sadr's scheme see, Najaf, *Dawr al-'ulama* (n.d), pp. 9–10; idem, April (n.p) (1981), pp. 32–3; al-Ha'iri, vol. 2, part 2, pp. 91–102; Ja'far, Mulla (1996), pp. 487–8.

86. The text of his treatise is reprinted in al-Ha'iri, op. cit., p. 92 and passim.

87. Ibid., p. 94.

88. Ibid.

89. Ibid., pp. 94–5.

90. Ibid., p. 96.

91. Ibid., pp. 96–7.

92. Ibid., p. 96.

93. Ibid.

94. Zubaida (1989), p. 18; Bayat, in Esposito (ed.) (1980), pp. 103 and passim; Enayat, in Piscatori (ed.) (1983), pp. 162–7.

95. Moussavi, op. cit., pp. 46–7.

96. Zubaida, Ibid., p. 18.

97. Abrahamian (1982), p. 474; Martin (1989), p. 120.

98. The Constitution of the Islamic Republic of Iran, Arabic Translation, 1043 AH.

99. For more details on the difference between the two concepts, see Arjomand (1988), p. 179 and passim.

100. The translation has been reproduced from Arjomand, Ibid., p. 179.

101. Arjomand, ibid.
102. Ibid., p. 181.
103. Ibid. (Underline added.)
104. Amanat, in Arjomand (ed.) (1988), p. 124.
105. Kho'i Foundation. Interviewees wish to remain anonymous.

Chapter Ten
1. See Chapters Seven, Eight and Nine.
2. Schubel (1993), pp. 2–3; Fischer (1980), analyses religious rituals as a cultural discourse and focuses on what he terms as the 'Karbala paradigm', pp. 4, 9, 12–19.
3. Durkheim (1915, 1971), pp. 10, 18, 206–13, 416–24; Lukes (1973), pp. 238–9; Robertson (ed.) (1969, 1976), p. 42 and passim; Robertson, Roland (1970), pp. 150–63. In his *The Elementary Forms of the Religious Life*, Durkheim analyses the duality of the world into profane and the sacred and sets society as the real object of religious veneration. See Parsons, in Robertson (ed.) (1976), pp. 42–54.
4. Nakash sees state-imposed secularization as a lineal process progressively reducing participation in rituals (Nakash, op. cit., pp. 160–2). Fischer, on the other hand, observes the opposite, namely an increase in pilgrimage participation under the secularizing Shah regime. The number of pilgrims increased from 12,000 in 1961 to 75,000 in 1972, that is almost 66 percent increase in tens years, with peasants accounting for 32.5 percent of pilgrims, while *ziyarat* (local pilgrims) showed greater popular participation (pp. 137–8).
5. Karmali, in LA, July 1912–June 1913, pp. 238 and 319. In the early decades of this century the number of pilgrims was estimated to reach 200,000 to Karbala and more than 300,000 to Najaf annually (Karmali, p. 238). As the average number of pilgrims of Iranian origin was 100,000 in the same period (Nakash, 1994, p. 164) it is safe to conclude that Iraqis accounted for half of the total number.
6. *al-'Iraq* daily, Baghdad, 20 July 1995. The flow of visitation and ritual participation seems to be affected by sociopolitical factors, mass oppression, war, economic hardships, demographic change, and social decline. This is true to Iraq in the post 1991 war period.
7. Twaireej is a small town while Daghara is a large village. The former exhibits the *mahalla* solidarity, the latter denotes the cultural cleavages among different social groups in terms of forms of religiosity.
8. al-Hassani (1948), pp. 120–1.
9. Ibid.
10. On Daghara and other Shi'ite villages see Robert Fernea (1970) and Elizabeth Fernea (1968).
11. From the interviews, Ridha al-Zahir and Siham al-Zahir; the former is a writer, the latter a language teacher from Twaireej.
12. Khalili, Ja'far, op. cit., vol. 8, Karbala section, p. 372; Karmali, L. A., op. cit., p. 236. On the origin of 'Ashura rituals, see also, Nakash, DWI, 33, 1993, pp. 161–81.
13. Apart from personal experience based on observation of rituals in Karrada, Kazimiya, Kamp Silaikh and Thawra districts in Baghdad, Karbala, Najaf and Nassiriya, I am indebted to various informants from Najaf, Karbala, Hilla and Baghdad. See also: Elizabeth Fernea,, op. cit., who provides descriptive accounts of rituals in Shi'ite villages in the south, pp. 151–66. On Kazimain in the 1930s see Stark (1938, 1992), pp. 143–7. For a general view see Wardi (1992), pp. 236–40.
14. The fact that tensions still exist between scriptural religiosity of the clergy and the ceremonial ritualism of the popular religiosity is verified by the debate on the

'irrational nature' of narratives and other practices in these rituals in *al-Nur*, a Shi'ite monthly published by the London-based Kho'i Charitable Foundation, see *al-Nur* monthly, no. 75, August, 1997, pp. 46–52. Clerical attempts at the reformation of the popular rituals have been going on since the 1920s of this century (Nakash, 1994, pp. 154–7). On the debate between the rationalist Kasravi and the traditionalist Khomeini on this score, see Fischer, op. cit., pp. 132–3, and Wardi (1992), p. 232.

15. Schubel, op. cit., p. 2.
16. Victor Turner (1969) analyses the structure of rituals as a cycle of three phases, pp. 94–102. See also Victor Turner (1974), pp. 16–7, 23 and passim.
17. Schubel, p. 4
18. Ibid., pp. 4–5.
19. Fischer, op. cit., p. 100.
20. Ibid.
21. al-Wardi (1992), pp. 241–6.
22. Elizabeth Fernea, op. cit., p. 55.
23. Ibid., p. 96.
24. Ibid., pp. 69–70.
25. Ibid., p. 70 .
26. Ibid.
27. Ibid.
28. Ibid., p. 71.
29. Ibid.
30. Ibid.
31. Ibid., p. 72.
32. Ibid. p. 72–3
33. Karmali, op. cit., p. 235.
34. al-Wardi, op. cit., pp. 236–7, and 245–6
35. Nakash, 1994, p. 164.
36. Ibid., p. 173
37. Ibid., p. 179.
38. Interview with Salah Hithani and others who attacked the security service headquarters in Karbala during the 1991 uprising.

Chapter Eleven
1. Maull and Pick (eds) (1989), pp. 36–7, 60–6; O'Ballance (1988), p. 13 and passim.
2. A founding member of the Shi'ite Amal movement was quoted by Batatu as saying 'I saw Sayyid Muhammad Baqir al-Sadr at that time [1974]. He protested against the manner in which the judicial proceedings were conducted [by the Iraq government] but expressed his disapproval of the Da'wa. His opposition to this party derived from its links with the Shah of Iran.' Batatu, in Cole and Keddie (1986), p. 192.
3. Pachechi, interview.
4. O'Ballance, op. cit., p. 25; Slugletts (1990), pp. 140–4, 147; Marr (1985), pp. 221, 225; Axelgard (ed.) (1986), p. 87.
5. Tikriti (1983), pp. 49–50. The negotiations, in fact, took several weeks in January 1969. Marr, op. cit., p. 221; Khadduri (1978), p. 149.
6. Khadduri, op. cit., p. 150; Batatu (1978), p. 1085.
7. On the history of border agreements, see, Edmonds, AA, vol. 62, 1975, p. 147; El-Shazly (1995), p. 25. This dissertation on the Tanker War provides detailed maps of the Iraq-Iran border disputes, see pp. 26, 27, 28, 29, and 30.
8. Tikriti, op. cit., pp. 55–6.

9. Ibid., p. 58.

10. Ibid., p. 60; See also, Wiley, op. cit., p. 46; al-Sarraj, op. cit., pp. 248–9; *Liwa' al-Sadr* weekly, Tehran, no. 327, Year 6, 2 November 1987, Speech by Mahdi al-Hakim.

11. al-Sarraj, op. cit., p. 250; also interviews with al-'Askari, al-Khatib and Bahr al-'Ulum.

12. al-Sarraj, op. cit., p. 250 and passim; Tikriti, op. cit., p. 71; Akhavi, op. cit., p. 131; Slugletts (1990), p. 198; Mallat (1993), pp. 17–8; Wiley, op. cit., p. 46.

13. Ibn al-Najafi, Al-Khatib (1982), p. 96.

14. Amir Abdullah, and the architect Muhammad Makiya, interviews. Mallat, op. cit., p. 17. Abdullah recalls in his unpublished autobiography how al-Bakr was so adamant about confiscating the Kufa university funds that no argument could change his mind.

15. Tikriti, p. 55; Wiley, op. cit., p. 46.

16. The figures differ widely from one source to another. See, for example, Wiley, p. 48 and Khadduri, p. 150.

17. Bahr al-'Ulum, interview, and al-Sarraj, op. cit., p. 246.

18. For these and other measures, see al-Durra (1977), pp. 82–3 and 109; Slugletts, (1990), pp. 220–3.

19. al-Durra, ibid., p. 100.

20. Iraq Ba'th Party, 8th Congress, p. 110.

21. al-Durra, p. 109.

22. al-Sarraj, p. 253.

23. Jabar and al-'Askari, interviews.

24. al-Rubai'i, interview.

25. Reprinted in *Hay'at-e-Hakim* (The Life of Sayyed Muhsin al-Hakeem), Trs. by Murtaza Hussein, Karachi (1973), pp. 75–77, in Wiley p. 6–7.

26. al-Sarraj, op. cit., p. 239.

27. Mallat (1993), p. 18.

28. Interviews with al-Rubai'i, al-'Askari and Jabar.

29. Slugletts (1990), p. 197.

30. Nazari (1990), pp. 104–10; see also al-Ha'iri, op. cit., pp. 105–6.

31. DD PS, vol. 1, pp. 83–4.

32. Slugletts, op. cit., p. 168.

33. Uthman, interview.

34. Slugletts, p. 196.

35. This figure was cited by Saddam Hussein at the first meeting held by the higher committee of the National Patriotic and Progressive Front (NPPF) after the collapse of the Kurdish revolt in May 1975. Interview with ICP PB members Ajina and al-Ani.

36. Wiley, op. cit., p. 50.

37. Kedourie, AA, v. 62 (1975), pp. 140–2.

38. Interviews, al-Rubai'i, al-Khatib.

39. DD on 1974 executions; also DD, vol. 2, pp. 85–8; also, Da'wa Party, Qabdhat al-Huda, Tehran (1403).

40. Bengio, MES, v. 21, Jan. 1985, no. 1, pp. 1–14.

41. Jabar, interview.

42. Bengio, op. cit., pp. 1–14.

43. Bengio, ibid., also, Haim, in IOS, 10, 1980, pp. 165–72; Batatu, in MEJ, 35, 1981, pp. 578–94.

44. Haim, Ibid.

45. Batatu, in Stowasser, op. cit., p. 211.

46. Ibid.

47. The Ba'th party critically assessed the coercive student Ba'thization in the Report for the 9th Congress, 1983, p. 296 and passim.
48. Iraq News Agency, official announcement; see also, Haim, op. cit., p. 169.
49. DD, vol. 3, pp. 316–7; also: 'Abbas interview.
50. Ridha Zhahir, Siham Zhahir, 'Abbas and others, interviews.
51. Ibid.
52. Interview with the Najafi ritual leader al-Balaghi.
53. *al-Shahada*, 16 Sufar, 1404 (1982). Also, interview with al-Balaghi.
54. DD, vol. 3, p. 317.
55. 'Abbas, interview.
56. al-Din, interview.
57. Wiley, op. cit., p. 51.
58. DD, vol. 3, p. 317.
59. Bengio, in MES, op. cit., p. 3.
60. DD, vol. 3, p. 318.
61. Jassim al-Rikabi was the governor of the Najaf Province.
62. SAIRI communication on the anniversary of the Sufar Uprising, n.p, n.d.
63. Interview with Juburi, the acting foreign minister in 1979.
64. The figure was quoted by Saddam Hussein at a meeting of the higher committee of NPPF convened in Feb. 1977
65. Slugletts, op. cit., p. 198; Wiley, op. cit., p. 51.
66. *al-Jumhuriya* daily, 25 February 1977; Slugletts, p. 199; Stapelton, Barbara, p. 17; Bengio, p. 4. Conversation with various members of the al-Hakim family, including Sahib al-Hakim.
67. *al-Thawra* (daily), 25 February, 1977.
68. Haim, IOS, op. cit., p. 170.
69. Abdullah, interview.
70. Bengio, op. cit., p. 4.
71. Ibid., p. 4.
72. A family tree had already been manufactured for al-Bakr to claim a noble lineage.
73. Tilfah, K. (1968), v. 1, p. 175.
74. Faleh A. Jabar, in Yuval-Davis (ed.) (1991), pp. 211–18.
75. Hussein, Saddam, CW, 1978, v.3, pp. 157–71.
76. For details on the reshuffle, see Baram, IJMES, 21, 1989, pp. 447–93.
77. Details on ethnic, religious and regional composition of this body, consult, Slugletts (1990), pp. 210–11.
78. Marr, in MEJ, 24, 1970, pp. 283–301.
79. Marr (1985), p. 282.
80. Amnesty International Report, 'The Death Penalty: A Survey by Country', 26 September (1979).
81. DD, vol. 3, pp. 319–21.
82. Baram, IJMES, op. cit.
83. Barrak, op. cit., p. 143 and passim.
84. Haim, op. cit., p. 70.
85. Barrak, op. cit., pp. 148–58.
86. Jabar, al-Ruba'i, al-'Askari and al-Khatib, interviews.

Chapter Twelve
1. This chapter is mainly but not exclusively based on extensive interviews with Muhammad Hussaini Shirazi and his disciple Abu Saleh (Qum), Muhammad Taqi

al-Mudarisi and Muhsin al-Hussaini (Tehran), Ridha Jawad Taqi and Ahmad al-Khatib [*nom de guerre*] (London).
2. Hassan Shirazi (1964), p. 99.
3. Ibid., p. 125.
4. Ibid., p. 139.
5. Ibid., p. 139–40.
6. Ibid. p. 48, also pp. 72–3 and passim.
7. Hassan Shirazi's *al-wa'i al-Islami* [Islamic Consciousness] (1960). Also his *Kalimat al-Rasul al-Azam* [The Word of the Sublime Messenger of God] (1967).
8. My personal encounter with him for three successive days at his *husayniya* in Qum, April 1982.
9. Mallat (1993), p. 50.
10. This relies mainly on Taqi, PB member of the MAI.
11. Wardi (1991), vol. 1, pp. 21–3
12. Wardi, Ibid., pp. 22–3; see also, Heine, *al-Rafidayn*, Band III, 1995, pp. 7–17.
13. Shirazi, Muhammad (n.d.), Qawmiyat, pp. 5, 66–7; idem (1981), *Ila hukumat alf miliun muslim*, pp. 17–9.
14. Kho'i Foundation, interviews.
15. al-Katib, interview.
16. Picard (1993); See also, Norton, pp. 156–78, and Cobban, in Cole and Keddie (eds) (1986), pp. 137–55.
17. For Sayyid Qutb's ideas on Nasserism and nationalism, see Sivan (1985), pp. 21 and passim, 28–32; Kepel (1985), ch. 2, pp. 37–67.
18. As a prolific writer and lecturer, al-Mudarisi's works are numerous. Consult the bibliography.

Chapter Thirteen
1. Much emphasis has been placed on geopolitical and regional considerations of the Iraq-Iran war, yet the crucial factor is internal stability and regime's security. Consult Muhsin, Harding and Hazelton, in CARDRI, 2nd impression (1990), pp. 229–30; Marr (1985), pp. 292–3. Perhaps the best study on the differentiation between regime's security and nation-building factors in Iraq's two wars (1980, 1991) is Mohamedou (1998), pp. 104–5; El-Shazly (1995), pp. 60–7, and pp. 69–85. For a wider geopolitical, regional and international view, see, Maul and Pick (eds), ch. 5, pp. 45–59; O'Ballance, pp. 25–9; Cordsman and Wagner (1990), pp. 14–5, 29–33. The Iranian context is analysed by Halliday, in Cole and Keddie (eds) (1986), pp. 96, 102 and passim. For the relevant internal Iraqi landscape see, Jabar (1995), chapter 6, pp. 135–51; Tripp, in Hopwood, Ishow and Koszinowski (eds) (1993), pp. 91–115. For the official Iraqi perspective, see, Aziz (1981), pp. 9–10, 14–9.
2. Interviews with al-Juburi, al-Rubai'i, al-'Askari and others.
3. For a chronological line of revolutionary events between 1977–79, see Fischer, op. cit., pp. 184–213.
4. The same opinion was voiced by government and Ba'th party leaders in different meetings with the ICP in that period. The above- mentioned *al-Thawra* editorial was in response to a previous editorial run by the ICP organ *Tariq al-Sha'ab*, which hailed the mass movement and said success and prospects were hinging on the pivotal question as to who would provide leadership for the seemingly spontaneous movements: the 'Liberal Bazaar', the 'religious, petty-bourgeois radicals' (termed the 'Red Turbaned' by the Shah) or the left, the Tudeh and other groups. The name of Khomeini was not yet in circulation, and the phrase 'religious petty bourgeoisie'

denoted the current represented by Ayatollah Shari'atmadari, who made several public statements calling for the restoration of the 1906 Mashruta constitution.

5. This piece of information was conveyed by various ICP leaders Ani, Ajina and others.

6. Halliday, op. cit. p. 89. For analyses of the revolution, see, Halliday (1996), pp. 53–67.

7. Tripp, op. cit., p. 99.

8. Faleh A. Jabar, in Bersheeth and Yuval-Davis (eds) (1991), pp. 211–18; Tripp, Ibid.

9. CARDRI, op. cit., pp. 229–30.

10. Interview with al-Juburi, who confirmed Mahmud received a monthly salary of ID 70.

11. al-Mu'min (1993), p. 145.

12. Interview with al-Juburi, who described how far his superior, Saddam Hussein, was angered by this request which, if had been granted, would have changed history. Al-Juburi says Saddam Hussein retorted in anger: 'Are we his [the Shah's] employees? One day let Khomeini go. Another day let him not. He [Khomeini] is out of Baghdad, and out he will remain.'

13. DD, vol. 4, pp. 166–70, 172 and passim. Al-Mu'min, op. cit., refers to their lawyer, Sayyid Hassan Shubbar, as being in charge of liaising with al-Sadr. Another figure mentioned in this link is Abdul Hamid Abasia (possibly a *nom de guerre*), p. 160.

14. See for example, DD, vol. 2, pp. 463–4, or DD vol. 3, p. 158; vol. 3 pp. 163–6, vol. 3 p. 347, vol. 4 pp. 78–81.

15. Interview, al-Rubai'i.

16. al-Mu'min, op. cit., p. 147; Ja'far, op. cit., p. 519. The seminary who took the initiative is named Ahmad Kubba who admitted in an interview with Mullah Ali Asghar Ja'far that he acted contrary to the party instructions when he agitated for the march.

17. *A Group of Researchers* (1996), p. 97. Also: Interviews with al-'Askari, al-Rubai'i and other leading cadres from the Da'wa Party. The Da'wa still resents the position taken by Kho'i circles, not without Kho'i's knowledge, to distance themselves from the demonstrators.

18. Ibid., p. 97.

19. al-Mu'min, ibid., p. 147.

20. For the significance of the different wording, see: Mallat (1993), pp. 52–3.

21. *A Group of Researchers* (1996), p. 97.

22. These were reprinted by the Jihad Sazandegi establishment by al-Khayam printing house, Qum, Iran, 1399 AH. (the lunar year 1399 started on 2 December 1978 and ended on 20 November 1979). This means that the book was published sometime between March 1979, the date of writing, and November the same year. It is not clear whether or not the Iranian editions were published posthumously. For details see Ha'iri, Kazim (Qum, 1407 AH.) p. 68.

23. al-Ha'iri, K. op. cit., p. 115.

24. Interview with al-Rubai'i.

25. For example, al-Ha'iri (op. cit.) gives a detailed account of the cable sent by Khomeini asking al-Sadr not to leave Najaf, but never says a word that al-Sadr had such intentions at all (pp. 116–7). By contrast, al-Mu'min (op. cit., p. 165) quotes al-Sadr as saying he had no thoughts on leaving Iraq and he was depressed to learn that the Iranian leadership had been misinformed. See also *A Group of Researchers* (1996), p. 98.

26. al-Mu'min, op. cit., p. 165; al-Ha'iri, op. cit., p. 117; *A Group of Researchers*, op. cit., p. 98; Mallat, op. cit., p. 52. We have relied on Mallat's translation of the Arabic text

with few minor amendments.

27. Mallat, ibid., p. 53.

28. Interviews with al-'Askari and al-Rubai'i from the Da'wa leadership, and al-Khatib, a leading cadre of the MAI. The latter confirmed how the Arabic Radio Service in Tehran was under his party's control and never denied the encouragement by his organization to Khomeini to send the above cable.

29. Interview, al-Rubai'i.

30. Ibid.

31. Ha'iri, op. cit., pp. 116, 120–1.

32. Ibid., pp. 100–2.

33. Ibid., pp. 117–9.

34. Ibid., p. 119.

35. Shami (1992), p. 50.

36. Ha'iri, op. cit., pp. 120–1; al-Nu'mani (1997), p. 277; and *A Group of Researchers* (1996), pp. 497 and 508, 539.

37. With few amendments, the translation is taken from Mallat, op. cit., p. 52, but it was literally compared with the Arabic text: al-Ha'iri, K., op. cit., p. 123; also al-Mu'min, op. cit., p. 165.

38. Mu'min, ibid., pp. 169–71, Ha'iri, ibid., pp. 127–33; and *A Group of Researchers* (1996), pp. 100. 497 and passim; Shami, op. cit., pp. 51–3.; Mallat, TWQ, 10 (1988), pp. 728–9.

39. Al-'Askari, Sami, in *A Group of Researchers* (1996), p. 540.

40. Ha'iri, op. cit., pp. 53–5. Zaid Haider was accompanied by Abdul Razaq al-Habubi, governor of Najaf and a Ba'th leading cadre.

41. Baram, in Orient, 22. 1, March 1981, pp. 391–412; Indem, IJMES, 21, 1989, p. 447–93. And Bengio, MES, v. 21, January 1985, no. 1, pp. 1–14.

42. Bengio, Ibid.

43. The number and lists of the executed vary from one source to another. See, Wiley, op. cit., pp. 55–6, 160–1; Mu'min, op. cit., pp. 174–5; and Ferhad, op. cit., p. 274.

44. Mu'min, pp. 175, 185–6.

45. Ibid. p. 196. Sheikh 'Isa al-Khaqani, a Ba'th cleric, and Sayyid Ali Badr al-Din, a Lebanese Shi'i cleric, liaised with al-Sadr to convey the Ba'th government demands for denouncing the Da'wa and Iran and expressing support for Iraq.

46. Batatu, in MEJ, 35, 1981, p. 578.

47. al-Khatib explained how he, having to cross Syria several times to Lebanon, drew the attention of the Syrian security service. Upon his arrest, there were mediating efforts by Musa al-Sadr of Lebanon to have him released. During detention, he clarified his anti-Iraq positions and the interrogators offered him logistic backing, cooperation and co-ordination in organizing attacks against the Iraqi Ba'th.

48. Taqi, interview. There is also a different assessment to the bombing and assassination campaign. Al-Juburi, an ex-minister in the Ba'th cabinet, suggests the attack on Aziz was fake and stage managed by the Iraqi security.

49. *A Group of Researchers*, 1966, pp. 100, 499, 541.

50. There are different claims in this regard. One is that al-Sadr tape-recorded three statements calling for revolution (Ibid. p. 503). This claim is reiterated by Da'wa activists. al-Sadr's attendant, however, claims the statements were handwritten. Al-Nu'mani, 1997, pp. 274–6, 286–7, 304–7. For the text of the statements see *A Group of Researchers*, 1996, pp.761–5.

51. Mallat (1993), op. cit., p. 18; Batatu, in MEJ, p. 590.

Chapter Fourteen

1. For al-Mujahidin, see Batatu, in MEJ, 35 (1981), and Batatu, in Cole and Keddie (1986). The Mujahidin group was neither a party nor a well-disciplined group but rather a loose grouping of followers of the al-Hakim family financed and directed by Aziz al-Hakim who fled Iraq after the execution of al-Sadr in April 1980. With logistical support from Syria and Iran it planned and carried out several bombing attacks inside Iraq. The shadowy Mujahidin soon dissolved and had no mention whatsoever, the moment Baqir al-Hakim assumed leadership of SAIRI.

2. For details of these attempts at unifying the Iraqi groups see al-Mu'min, op. cit., pp. 256–9.

3. The first general secretary of the Jama'at was Murtadha al-'Askari, the second was Baqir al-Hakim. In 1985, Sheikh Muhammad Baqir al-Nasiri assumed leadership of the Jama'at al-'Ulama and was the first elected general secretary. Baqir Nasiri and Akram al-Hakim, interviews.

4. It was Muhammad Baqir al-Sadr who first envisaged the necessity to go beyond both sub- and supra-national limitations. In his three posthumously published declarations to the nation he addressed all Iraqis, Sunnis and Shi'is alike. For details, see, Sivan and Friedman (eds) (1990), pp. 95–125; Ha'iri, Kazim, op. cit., pp. 147–53; Mu'min op. cit., pp. 430–35.

5. Munazama, series no. 21, p. 17.

6. For a detailed discussion of these differences, see Mu'min, op. cit., pp. 256–7.

7. For details on the Qiyada Na'iba, see al-Ha'iri, Kazim, op. cit., pp. 159–60; also, al-Mu'min, ibid., p. 256.

8. Mallat, TWQ (1988), p. 270.

9. Mallat, Ibid. It seems that Baqir al-Hakim claimed he had been appointed by al-Sadr to carry out responsibility but this claim was challenged. Wiley, op. cit., p. 60.

10. Baqir al-Hakim, interview.

11. al-Mu'min, op. cit., p. 258.

12. These details on the set up of SAIRI is heavily dependent on information obtained from Akram al-Hakim, a leading member in the Majlis Shura of SAIRI. Other details were derived from conversation with Baqir al-Hakim, Muhammad Baqir Nasiri and Abu Ahmad al-Ja'fari (Ibrahim al-Ushaiqir).

13. The incomplete list of 65 with biographical details was provided in a letter handwritten by Akram al-Hakim, the head of SAIRI's office in London.

14. There are a number of preliminary studies on the contractual class which thrived under the Ba'th regime. They show how some tribal chiefs went up the social ladder by dint of state favours granted to them for their military or other services.

15. Akram al-Hakim, interview.

16. Baqir al-Hakim, *Ahadith*, pp. 11 and 13.

17. Akram al-Hakim, interview.

18. al-Mudarisi and Shirazi, interviews.

19. Abu Ahmad Ja'fari, interview.

20. al-Mudarisi and Muhammad Baqir al-Hakim, interviews.

21. al-Mudarisi, interview.

22. MAI, series 21, p. 17.

23. Ibid., p. 13 and passim.

24. Ibid.

25. Ibid.

26. Ibid., pp. 11–12.

27. Baqir al-Hakim, interview.

28. Baqir al-Hakim, *Ahadith*, p. 11.
29. Ibid., p. 13.
30. Muhammad Hussaini Shirazi, interview.
31. Akram al-Hakim, interview.
32. al-Mu'min, op. cit., pp. 326–7; and Wiley, op. cit., p. 63.
33. Conversations with some recruits in Badr who wish to retain anonymity. The size of Badr Army, according to them, was around 3,000. Another source put the figure at 7,000. In al-Mu'min's words, Badr Army 'was totally backed and commanded by the Iranian Revolutionary Guard, p. 327. The division, i.e. Badr, had a full brigade containing ex-Iraqi POWs. And it [the division] played a pivotal role on the south and north war fronts against Iraq (p. 327). The force sustained 500 injured and killed in action (p. 365).
34. *Tariq al-thawra*, No. 16, July, 1981, p. 20.
35. Mu'min refers to almost a dozen attempts, op. cit., pp. 334–349.
36. *al-Muwajaha* (The Confrontation), issued by *al-Markaz al-Islami lil abhath al-siyasiya* (The Islamic Centre for Political Research), no.6. (n.d) (n.p). The book contains available documents of Iraq military intelligence recording the activities of the Islamist groups within the army during the Iraq-Iran war in the service of the Iranian war effort. The centre is sponsored by the Da'wa.
37. Under these circumstances, the Iraqi Communist Party (ICP) and the pro-Syrian Iraqi Ba'th splinter group sustained political differences. A 'defensive' wing emerged in both organizations in favour of an alliance with the ruling Ba'th in Iraq, supporting the 'nationalist', 'defensive' fight of the Iraqi army against 'aggressive Iran'.
38. These proportions are generally held by so many dissident Iraqi high ranking officers. On Shi'is in the Iraqi armed forces, see, Zaidi, Ahmad, (1990), pp. 157–74.
39. Fischer, op. cit., pp. 88–95.
40. Interview with Muhammad Shirazi and his disciple Abu Salih (*nom de guerre*), the figure in charge of *Harakat al-Jamahir al-Muslima*. See also Faleh A. Jabar (1984), p. 54.
41. For details on Bahr al-'Ulum and the London based *Markaz alal-bait*, see Uwe-Rahe (1995), pp. 59–62.
42. On the Khalisi Family consult, Temimi (1996), pp. 188, 195; Wardi, 1976, v. 6, pp. 217–30.
43. Uwe-Rahe (1995), op. cit., p. 63 and passim.
44. Ibid., pp. 66–71.
45. For more details on the Intifada see, Jabar, in Hazelton (ed.) (1994), pp. 97–117. Kho'i's *fatwas* have been verified by the Kho'i Foundation in London.
46. On Jund al-Imam, see Uwe-Rahe, op. cit., pp. 88–9; also Muhammad A. Jabar, Ghanim Jawad, interviews.
47. Maududi's jahiliya concept (ignorance or barbarism) is applied to the Hindus who were, in his view, pagans because they worshipped animals, Qutb by contrast extended this concept to cover Muslims who embrace Western doctrines. For Maududi, see, Boulares (1990), pp. 76–9; Kepel (1985), pp. 62–3, 74–5; Sivan (1985) pp. 22–3.
48. For Qutb's doctrine see his *Ma'alim fil tariq* (Signposts on the Road) (1980). See also Diyab (1987); Sivan, op. cit., and Kepel, op. cit. (1985).
49. Jabar and \l-Nasiri, interviews.
50. Jabar, interview.
51. Baram, in Piscatori (1991), pp. 28–9.

52. Jabar, interview.
53. Interviews with cadres from the group.
54. al-Khatib and Taqi, interviews.

Chapter Fifteen

1. Iraqi Research and Documentation Project (IRDP), files 655: 163–65; 659: 986–87.
2. IRDP, on relations with Syria: see files 699: 410, 828: 865–66, 829: 368, 833: 700; on relations with Iran, see files: 699: 274, 539, 598 and passim.
3. O'Ballance, Edgar, op. cit. pp. xi–xvii.
4. On the play of nationalist and internationalist elements in Iranian foreign policy since 1979, see Fred Halliday's contribution in, Cole and Keddie (eds), *Shi'ism and Social Protest*, Chapter 3.
5. During that period opposition literature was optimistic that the fall of the Ba'th regime was pending.
6. Hobsbawm (1990) explains this interplay class and nationalism better than in any other account.
7. In his *Lamahat*, Volume 5, al-Wardi documents the common Shi'ite *mawakib husayniya*, (Hussain Processions), with Sunni Mawlid, the Prophet's Birthday Festivals, as a symbolic union of different communal groups under the newly constructed Iraqi national identity in the 1920s. Nationalism was still nascent, responsive to popular feeling. See also Ghassan Attiya and Y.Nakash (1994), who reassert the Bedouin Arab nature of Shi'ism in Iraq in contradistinction to Shi'ism in Iran.
8. On nationalism during this period, see Khalidi (1991); Phebe Marr (1985); Majid Khadduri, *Independent Iraq, 1932–58*, London, Oxford University Press, 1970.
9. For the Shi'ite role in the Ba'th party see, among others, Hani Fukaiki; Sluglett (1990) and Sluglett, in CARDRI (1986).
10. Religion is not so alien to nationalism in defining the nation as a community. On the role of religion as a national marker, see, Antony Smith (1971); Benedict Anderson and Sami Zubaida, in Littlejohn (1978).
11. Baram, 1991, *Culture and History*; Baram (1993); Faleh Jabar (ed.), *Nationalism*, London, Saqi Books, 1996.
12. Interviews with Iraqi Islamic leaders, London, March 1998.
13. Minutiae of Islamic-secular meetings in Damascus, 1988.
14. See my 'Why the Uprisings Failed' , in, Fran Hazelton (ed.), *Prospect for Democracy in Iraq*, London, ZED 1995.
15. Edward L. Morse, 'A New Political Economy for Oil', *Journal of International Affairs*, Fall 1999, No. 1, p. 161.
16. Fred Halliday, 'The False Answers of Saddam Hussain', *Le Monde Diplomatique*, Arabic Edition, November 1990. Halliday rightly argued that the questions raised by Baghdad were right but the answer was totally false.
17. See my 'Why the Uprisings Failed', op.cit.
18. See my 'The War Generation: A Case of Failed Etatist Nationalism', in Larry G. Potter and Gray G. Sick (eds), *Iran, Iraq and the Aftermath of War: Unfinished Business*, New York: Palgrave, 2003.
19. The official *al-Thawra* daily in Baghdad, ran in March 1991 a series of editorials that defamed the Shi'is and slandered on the Arab Marsh people. It circulated the term *ghawgha'iya* to describe the rebels as illiterate mob. The writer was believed to have been Deputy Prime Minister Tariq Aziz.
20. Different Iraqi groups contend that the uprising started in Basra; others claimed it

was initiated in Karbala. Majid Khadduri and Admund Ghareeb say it started in Nasiriya on 2 March 1999; see Khadduri and Ghareeb, *The Gulf War 1990–1, The Iraq-Kuwait Conflict and its Implications*, Oxford, Oxford University Press, 1997, p.190.

21. Ibid.
22. On the episode of Grand Ayatollah Abu al-Qassim al-Kho'i, see, among others, Yousif al-Kho'i, 'Grand Ayatollah Abu al-Qassim al-Kho'i: Political Thought and Positions', in Faleh A. Jabar (ed.), *Ayatollahs, Sufis and Ideologues*, London, Saqi Books, 2002; Charles Tripp, *A History of Iraq*, Cambridge University Press, 2nd ed., 2000; Khadduri and Ghareeb, *The Gulf War 1990–1*.
23. *Al-Thawra* daily, Baghdad, March 1991.
24. On Iraq under sanctions, the best accounts and analysis are to be found in Sarah Graham-Brown, *Sanctioning Saddam: The Politics of Intervention in Iraq*, London, I. B. Tauris, 1999.
25. See my *The Double-Edged Sword of Islam*.
26. *The Washington Post*, March 15, 2003, p. A14.
27. Ibid.
28. On the life of Sadr II, two books in Arabic appeared in London. See Fayiq Shaykh Ali, *Ightiyal Sha'b* (*A Nation Assassinated*), London, Al-Rafid Publishers, 2000; Mukhtar al-Asadi, *al-Sadr al-Thani, al-Shahid al-Shaheed* (*Sadr II: The Witness and the Martyr*), London, 1999.
29. Faleh A. Jabar, 'Clerics, Tribes, Ideologues and Urban Dwellers in the South of Iraq: The Potential for Rebellion', in Toby Dodge and Steven Simon, *Iraq at Crossroads*, Adelphi Paper 354, Oxford, Oxford University Press, 2003, p. 171.

Chapter Sixteen
1. See, for example, Sachedina (1981).
2. On *khilafa* and *imama*, see Imara (1983), p. 52 and passim; idem (1980), pp. 51–8; 'Ashmawi (1996), pp. 127–38; Raziq (1972), p. 113 and passim.
3. Zubaida, in ES, vol. 24, no. 2, May (1995), see section on the *'ulama* and the state, pp. 157–64.
4. Lewis (1988, 1991), pp. 113–4; Abrahamian (1982), p. 50 and passim. For a wider scope of Egyptian-Ottoman context, consult Lewis (1961) and Holt (1966).
5. Martin (1989), p. 178 and passim; Abrahamian, op. cit., pp. 83, 94–5; al-Ha'iri, Hadi (1977), pp. 114–20; Enayat (1982), pp. 164–75; Algar (1980), pp. 240–56.
6. Martin, ibid., p. 178.
7. Ibid., p. 184.
8. Ibid., p. 185.
9. Ibid., p. 182.
10. Ibid., p. 182.
11. Na'ini's text was translated to Arabic in Najaf in 1929 and was serialized by the Shi'ite review *al-Irfan* in Sydon, Lebanon, 1930–31. The Arabic translation was reprinted by *al-Mawsim* quarterly, year 2, no. 5, 1990, pp. 37–142.
12. Martin, op. cit., p. 184.
13. Ibid., p. 180.
14. 'Abdo, CW, v. 1., pp. 104–5.
15. al-Afghani, CW, v. 2, pp. 329–31; al-Afghani and 'Abdo (1957), pp. 13, 23; and Afghani, CW, v. 2., pp. 55, 66; Also 'Abdo, CW, v. 3, pp. 282, 300, 443, 492–6; 'Abdo, CW, v. 3. p. 355 and passim; also Imara (1985), pp. 285–9; Iraqi (1995), p. 53 and passim.
16. Hourani, (1962, 1991), pp. 126–9 and149–53.

17. Enayat, op. cit., pp. 125–34, and 139; Abrahamian, 1982, pp. 84–5.
18. Tauber, BJMES, v. 21, no. 2, 1994, see pp. 189–91; Kawakibi, CW, 1975, pp. 229–373.
19. Martin, op. cit., p. 120.
20. Hourani, op. cit., p. 67 and passim.
21. Abrahamian (1993), p. 17; Zubaida (1989), pp. 1–3.
22. DD, vol. 1, Usus, pp. 130–52; vol. 4, pp. 14–5.
23. al-Sadr's *Al-Islam yaqud al-hayat*, Qum, 1979, contained six tracts or parts. For their chronological order consult the bibliography.
24. Al-Sadr, *lamha fiqhiya*, p. 20.
25. Ibid., p. 20.
26. Ibid., p. 9.
27. Ibid., p. 4.
28. Ibid., p. 28.
29. Ibid., p. 5.
30. Ibid., p. 17.
31. Ibid.
32. Mallat (1993), p. 62.
33. al-Sadr, *Khilafat*, p. 132.
34. Ibid., p. 133.
35. Ibid., p. 134.
36. Ibid., p. 143.
37. The Qur'an, (1946).
38. The Qur'an (1991).
39. Mallat (1993), p. 63.
40. Ibid.
41. al-Sadr, *Khilafat*, p. 145.
42. Ibid.
43. Ibid., pp. 145–6.
44. Ibid., p. 146.
45. Ibid., p. 147.
46. Ibid., p. 161.
47. Ibid., p. 170.
48. Shirazi, *al-Hukum*, pp. 74–5,
49. Shirazi, *al-Hukum*, pp. 74–5.
50. Ibid., p. 82.
51. al-Mudarisi (1975), p. 413.
52. MAI, series no. 16, pp. 150, 152, 157–8, 165.
53. Fischer, op. cit., pp. 139–48.; Mottahedeh (1985, 1987) pp. 346–51.
54. Nakash (1994), pp. 6–7, 86–7.
55. Uwe-Rahe, in *al-Rafidayn* (1993), pp. 67–82 and Uwe-Rahe (1995), pp. 20–3; Heine, Peter, in *al-Rafidayn*, B.3 (1995), pp. 7–17.
56. See for example, Jabar, (1994); or his various articles in: *al-Mutamar* daily, London, No. 51, 6 May, 1994; *al-Hayat* daily, London, 21 March 1992; Iraqi Issues, Washington D.C., vol. 1, November, 1993.
57. See for example: Bahr al-'Ulum, Sayyid Dr Muhammad, a paper presented at SOAS 19–20 December 1994; Shams al-Din, Sheikh Muhammad (1954, 1991); *al-Nur* monthly, London, issue 42, November, 1994, pp. 8–9, and no. 69, February 1997; Bin Jadou, 1995, introduction; DF, issue 23, Summer 1995.
58. 'Ulum, Unpublished paper (1994), op. cit.
59. Ibid., p. 16.

60. Ibid., p. 5.
61. Jabar, M. in *al-Mu'tamar* weekly, London, no.51. May 6, 1994.
62. *al-Nur* monthly, London, no.42, November 1994.
63. Ibid.
64. Ibid.
65. Ibid.
66. Ibid.

Chapter Seventeen

1. See, Taleqani's *Islam and Ownership* (1983); Qutb's *Islam and Capitalism* (1951) or his *Social Justice in Islam (al-'Adala al-Ijtima'iya fil Islam)* (1958); On Islamic economics see Roy, Olivier (1994), pp. 132–46, Mitchell, op. cit., ch.9; Fishcer, op. cit., pp. 156–61; Mallat, 1993, his review of Sadr's Iqtisaduna and the usury-free banks; Katouzian, Homa, in Keddie (ed.) (1983). For a survey of Islamic literature from the mid-1950s, see, Siddiqi, Muhammad Nejatullah (1981) and Indem (1978). For a comparative approach, see, Rodinson's classical work *Islam and Capitalism* (1977); and Tahhan (1985).
2. Siba'i, Mustafa *Ishtirakiyat al-Islam (Socialism in Islam)* (1959, 1960).
3. Sa'ad, Ahmad Sadiq (1988), p. 9.
4. Ibid.
5. See, Siddiqi (1981), p. 2.; Mannan, 1970, p. 6; Choudhury and Malik (1992), pp. 1–2.
6. Khomeini (1987).
7. For a discussion of the *hisba* books of Abu Yusuf, Ibn Taimiya and others see, Sa'ad, Ahmad Sadiq, Mannan, Choudhury and Malik.
8. Siddiqi (1981), p. 54; Mannan, pp. 16, 87, Katouzian, op. cit., pp. 145–65; Fischer, op. cit., pp. 156–9; Mallat (1993), p. 111 and passim.
9. al-Sadr, *Iqtisaduna*, (1982).
10. al-Sadr, *al-Bank*, (1983).
11. al-Sadr, *al-Islam yaqud al-hayat*, op. cit., The economic tracts are: 1) *Sura 'an iqtisad al-mujtama' al-Islami* (An Image of the Economy of Islamic Society); 2) *Khutut tafsiliya 'an iqtisad al-mujtama' al-Islami* (Detailed Outlines on the Economy of the Islamic Society); 3) *Manabi' al-qudra fil dawla al-Islamiya* (The Sources of Power of the Islamic State); 4) A fourth tract may be added: *al-Tarkib al-'aqa'idi ail dawla al-Islamiya* (The Doctrinal Structure of the Islamic State).
12. On al-Sadr's economics consult Katouzian, op. cit; Tripp, paper, 1994, Fischer, op. cit; Siddiqi (1981); Rieck (1984).
13. Marx (1973), SW, vol. 3, pp. 13–30.
14. Marx *Das Kapital* (1976, 1982), vol. 1., pp. 283–4.
15. Ibid , p. 307 and passim.
16. On forms of land possession and ownership forms and legalities in early Islam see, Nasr Allah (1982), p. 49–58, 59–96; Tahhan, op. cit., pp. 61–7; Johansen, (1998), p. 11–12.
17. Marx, vol. 3, p. 965 and passim.
18. Marx, vol. 1, pp. 33–4, 265.
19. Ibid., vol. 3, pp. 350–1, 1039.
20. al-Mudarisi, (1975).
21. al-Mudarisi (1979).
22. In a lengthy Interview I videotaped in Tehran, April 1982, cited in some detail in Faleh A. Jabar (1984), pp. 71–3.
23. al-Mudarisi (1979), p. 10.

24. Ibid., p. 15.
25. Ibid., p. 81.
26. On cooperatives and their history consult, Bernice (1975).
27. al-Mudarisi delivered his views on cooperatives in lectures in Tehran in April 19802. See Note 48.
28. Shirazi, *Fiqh al-iqtisad*, 1400 AH.
29. Shirazi, *al-Iqtisad al-muqaran*, 1400 AH.
30. Shirazi, Hassan (1960). This book contains a chapter on economic statements and general principles which have no theoretical tone. It reiterates denunciation of both capitalism and communism and glorifies Islam as the only alternative to both Attacking the 'abolition of religion' in both systems is central to his argument. See, p. 13 and passim, p. 39, and p. 118 and passim.
31. *Fiqh al-iqtisad*, p. 13.
32. Ibid., p. 19.
33. Ibid., p. 121.
34. Ibid., pp. 82, 84.
35. Ibid., p. 117.
36. Ibid., p. 104.
37. Ibid., p. 111.
38. Ibid., p. 118.
39. Ibid., p. 97.
40. Ibid., pp. 155–6.
41. Ibid., p. 156.
42. Ibid., p. 144.
43. Ibid., p. 123.
44. Ibid.
45. Ibid.
46. Ibid., pp. 116–7.
47. Ibid., p. 175.
48. Criticism of bank interests is a regular theme in Islamic economics from moderates, radicals, Shi'is and Sunnis, populist or otherwise. See for example, *A Group of Researchers* (1983), pp. 224–33.
49. Siddiqi (1981), p. 54 and passim. Also, Mannan (1970), pp. 5–6, 63. In other words: 'Islamic Economics can be defined as the Area of Ethico-Economics', Choudhury and Malik (1992), p. 1, also pp. 12, 37 and passim.
50. *A Group of Researchers* (1983), p. 33.

Bibliography

Iraqi Government Publications and Archive Publications

Republic of Iraq, Planning Ministry, *Kitab al-Jayb al-Ihsa'i* (Statistical Handbook: 1960–70), Baghdad, 1972.

Republic of Iraq, Ministry of Planning, *Annual Abstact of Statistics,* 1988, Central Statistical Organization, Baghdad, 1988.

Republic of Iraq, Ministry of Planning, Central Statistical Organization, *Annual Abstact of Statistics* 1992, Baghdad 1993.

Ba'th Party, *Thawrat 17 Tammuz: al-Tajriba wal Afaq-al-Taqrir al-siyasi al-Sadir 'an al-Mu'tmar al-Qutri al-Thamin-al-Qutral-Iraqi* (The 17 July Revolution: The Experience and Prospects-The Political Report issued by the Eighth Regional Congress-Iraq Region-January 1974), Baghdad (n.d.).

Ba'th Party, *al-Taqrir al-Markazi lil Mu'tamar al-Qutri al-Tasi'* (The Central Report of the Ninth Regional Party Congress-June 1982), Baghdad, al-Dar al-Arabiya, January 1983.

Iraqi Gazette, different issues.

Ministry of Awqaf (Religious Endowments), A collection of laws and regulation on *awqaf*, Baghdad, April 1972.

Party Literature

Hizb al-Da'wa al-Islamiya (Islamic Call Party)

Bayan al-Tafahum (n.p.) 1980.

Barnamajuna, Al-Bayan wal Barnamaj al-Siyasi li Hizb al-Da'wa al-Islamiya, London, March 1992.

Thaqafat al-Da'wa al-Islamiya (Da'wa Doctrine), Manshurat Hizb al-Da'wa al-Islamiya, volume 1, 2nd edition, 1401 AH (1981)

Thaqafat al-Da'wa al-Islamiya, Manshurat Hizb al-Da'wa al-Islamiya, vol. 2, 1st. edition, 1401 AH (1981).

Thaqafat al-Da'wa al-Islamiya, Manshurat Hizb al-Da'wa al-Islamiya, vol. 3, 1st. edition, 1405 AH (1985).

Thaqafat al-Da'wa al-Islamiya, Manshurat Hizb al-Da'wa al-Islamiya, vol. 4, 1st. edition, 1409 AH (1989).

Thaqafat al-Da'wa, Political Section, Manshurat al-Da'wa al-Islamiya, vol. 1, Ringa Rang Press, Tehran, 1984.

Thaqafat al-Da'wa, Political Section, Manshurat al-Da'wa al-Islamiya, vol. 2, Ringa Rang

Press, Tehran, 1984.

Qabdhat al-Huda (The Martyrs of 1974), Tehran, 1403 AH (1983).

Al-Muwajaha (The Confrontation), Accounts of persecution against the Islamic movement as reflected in official documents. n.p.; n.d.

Harakat al-Kawader al-Islamiya, al-Maktab al-Siyasi (Islamic Cadre Movement-Political Bureau)

Al-Taqrir al-Siyasi (The Political Report), series no. 1, London, 24–25 January, 1996.

Al-Khutut al-'Aridha lil Mashru' al-Islami al-Musaqil (Outlines of the Independent Islamic Project), no. 3., London, July 1997.

Al-Hizb al-Islami al-Iraqi

Tarikh 'Iz (A Glorious History), edited by Basim Ibrahim al-'Azami, London. (n.p.; n.d.).

Munazamat al-Amal al-Islami (MAI)

Al-Qiyada al-Islamiya (Islamic Leadership), 2nd edition, series no. 16, 1980.

Al-'Iraq bayn al-Tanzimat wal Khiyarat (Iraq Between Different Organizations and Choices), series no. 21 n.p.; n.d.

Auqifu al-Irhab (Stop Terror) n.p.; n.d.

Jund al-Imam Haraka (The Movement of the Soldiers of the Imam)

Al-Mabadi al-Asasiya wal Tasawurat (Basic Principles and Conceptions) n.p.; n.d.

The Supreme Assembly for the Islamic Revolution in Iraq (SAIRI)

Al-Bayan al-Ta'sisi lil Majlis al-A'la lil Thawra al-Islamiya fil 'Iraq (The Declaration of the Foundation of SAIRI), Tehran, 17 November 1982.

Dima' al-'ulama fi Tariq al-Jihad (Blood of the *'Ulama* on the Road of Jihad), Tehran 1984.

Al-Tahjir Jarimat al-'Asr (Deportation [of Shi'is from Iraq]: The Crime of the Age), Tehran, 1984.

Al-Mashru' al-Siyasi al-'Askari (The Political and Military Programme), n. d., n. p.

Istratijiyatuna al-Mustaqbaliya (Our Future Strategy), a lecture delivered on 3 July 1991.

Ahadith Mukhtara (Selected Speeches) by Muhammad Baqir al-Hakim.

Interviews

1. 'Abbas, 'Adnan, ex-member of Central Committee (CC) of the ICP in charge of the mid-Euphrates organization in 1977–79. Interviewed in London, 22 March 1995.
2. Abdullah, Amir, ex-state minister under the Ba'th 1973–78), ex-member of Political Bureau (PB) and CC of the ICP. Interviewed in London, 10 March 1995.
3. Ajina, Rahim, ICP, P. B ex-member (d. 1996). Interviewed twice in London, 15 March 1995.

4. al-Ali, Salah Umar, ex-RCC member and Ba'th RC member until 1971. Interviewed twice in London, 3 and 10 April 1994.

5. al-Ani, Thabit Habib, ex-PB member of the ICP. (d. 1997). Interviewed in London, 12 March 1995.

6. al-Asifi, Muhammad Mahdi, spokesman of the Da'wa Party, interviewed in Tehran, 20 April 1982, telephone conversation and written questions and answers.

7. al-'Askari, Sami, Da'wa Party PB member (activist and author), interviewed in London, 25 March 1995.

8. al-Balaghi, Muhammad (Abu Yusra), activist in the Marad al-Ras 1977 episode, sentenced to death. Telephone interview, London, 8 July 1996.

9. al-Dalli, Abdul Ghani, ex-minister and governor of the industrial bank under the monarchy. Interviwed in London, 10 February 1995.

10. al-Hakim, Akram, Member of the Shura Council, SAIRI, in charge of SAIRI's London Office. Interviewed in London, 9 and 16 July 1996.

11. al-Hakim, Sayyid Hujjat al-Islam, Muhammad Baqir, SAIRI's Chairman. Interviewed in Tehran, 10 April 1982 (videotaped). The interview was done in collaboration with Zuhair Jazairi (writer) and Hikmat Dawud (filmmaker).

12. al-Hakim, Sayyid Sahib, human rights activist. Telephone interview, London, 10 July 1996.

13. al-Hithani, Salah, a poet from Karbala, participants in the 1991 Intifada. Interviewed in Den Haag, Holland, 6 April 1996.

14. al-Hussaini, Muhsin, Leading figure of the Munazama, interviewed in Tehran, 13 April 1982.

15. Ibrahim, Abu (*nom de guerre*), a leading cadre of the Shirazi-sponsored Harakat al-Jamahir al-Muslima, interviewed in Qum, 15 April 1982.

16. al-Iqabi, Hashim, academic and poet, interviewed in London, 22 January 1996.

17. Jabar, Muhammad Abdul, Da'wa leading cadre, co-founder of Kawadir al-Da'wa. Interviewed twice in London, 7 March and 19 December 1995 and 3 January 1996.

18. al-Ja'fari, Abu Ahmad (*nom de guerre*: Ibrahim al-Ushaiqir), PB, Da'wa member. Interviewed in London, 15 September, 1987.

19. Jamal al-Din, Sayyid Musatafa, poet and cleric, holder of a PhD. Interviewed in Damascus, 10 November 1989 and 20 May 1990.

20. al-Juburi, Hamid, ex-minister and ex-ambassador under Saddam Hussein, defected in 1994. Interviewed in London, 10 February 1995.

21. al-Katib, Ahmad (*nom de guerre*) activist, author and cleric (editor of the Shura monthly-London), leading activist of the Munazamat al-Amal al-Islami (MAI) Interviewed in London, 29 March 1995.

22. Kho'i Foundation in London. Various conversations with figures who wish to remain anonymous, March 1995–July 1997.

23. Makkiya, Muhammad, architect and chairman of the Kufa Gallery. Interviewed twice, London, 10 May 1991 and 5 March 1993.

24. al-Mudarisi, Sayyid Hujjat al-Islam, Muhammad Taqi, Leader of MAI. Interviewed in Tehran, 12 April 1982. (videotaped).

25. Muruwa, Karim, Lebanese Communist party, PB member and author. Interviewed in London, 10 September 1994, and Beirut 15 May 1997.

26. al-Nasiri, Ghanim, human rights activists, INC and Kho'i Foundation. Conversation and enquires in London, 5 March 1995.

27. al-Nasiri, Muhammad Baqir, general secretary of Tehran-based Jama'at al-'Ulama

al-Mujahidin fil Iraq. Interviewed in London 13 and 16 September1997.

28. al-Pachechi, 'Adnan, ex-foreign minister under 'Arif. Interviewed in London, 27 January 1995.
29. al-Rubai'i, Muwafaq (Dr), Da'wa Party PB ex-member. Interviewed in London 8 March 1995.
30. al-Safi, Abdul Razzaq, ICP, PB ex-member, lawyer from Karbala. Conversations in London, 6 February 1993 and 10 April 1994.
31. al-Shirazi, Ayatollah Sayyid Muhammad Husaini, based in Qum since 1980. The spiritual leader of the Munazama and Harakat al-Jamahir al-Muslima. Interviewed in Qum, 15 April 1982. (Recorded on tape.)
32. Taqi, Ridha Jawad, member of PB of the Munazama. Interviewed in London, 21 March 1995.
33. al-'Ulum, Sayyid Muhamad Bahr, leader of the Bahr al-'Ulum family, Chairman of Al al-Bayt Foundation in London, holds a PhD in Islamic jurisprudence, author and leading member of the opposition. Interviewed in London, 16 and 17 November 1995
34. Uthman, Hamid, KDP, PB ex-member, Kurdish activist. Conversations in London, 3 March, 1996.
35. al-Uzri, Abdul Karim, ex-foreign minister under the Hashimite union 1967–8. Conversations in London, 30 March 1991.
36. al-Zahir, Ridha, intellectual and writer from Twaireej. Interviewed in London 20 January 1996.
37. al-Zahir, Siham, teacher from Twaireej. Interviewed in London, 19 January 1996.
38. Zubair, Abdul Razzaq, General Director at the Agrarian Reform Ministry under Qassim. Interviewed in London, 11 November 1992.

Periodicals, Monthlies and Clandestine Organs

Periodicals and Monthly Reviews

Adhwa' Islamiya, monthly, Jama'at al-'Ulama Fil Najaf al-Ashraf, Najaf, 1960–63.
Dirasat Filistiniya (DF) quarterly, Beirut, Centre of Palestinian Studies.
Dirasat wa Buhuth, quarterly, Jama'at al-'Ulama al-Mujahidin fil 'Iraq, Tehran.
Al-Fikr al-Jadid (FJ) quarterly, Dar al-Islam, London, 1992–
Iraqi Issues, monthly, Washington D. C.
Al-Jihad, quarterly, Da'wa Party Information Committee, Tehran
Al-Mawsim, quarterly, Kufa Foundation, Holland
Al-Nahj, quarterly, Damascus. Centre of Socialist Research and Studies in the Arab World, 1983–
Al-Najaf, monthly, College of Theology, Najaf, 1966–
Al-Nur, monthly, London, Kho'i Foundation, 1990–
Qadhaya Fikriya (QF) ,Cairo, Annual Book, Edited by Mahmud Amin al-'Alim, 1985–
Al-Shura, monthly, issued by Ahmad al-Katib, May 1995; discontinued in 1996.

Arab and Iraqi Dailies

Al-Hayat, London-based.
Al-Iraq, government organ, Baghdad.

Al-Jumhuriya, government organ, Baghdad.
Al-Sharq al-Awsat, London based.
Al-Thawra, Ba'th party official organ, Baghdad.
Al-Hiyad, organ of the Islamic party, Baghdad, 1960.

Opposition Party Press

(Clandestine journals with no legal standing, issued by various organizations and groups. Unless indicated otherwise, all publications were started in 1980–81 in Tehran.)

Al-'Amal al-Islami (Munazamat al-'Amal al-Islami [MAI]), Tehran.
Al-Badil al-Islami, Kawadir al-Da'wa, Damascus (1987–ceased publication in 1990).
Al-Jihad (Da'wa Party) Tehran .
Liwa' al-Sadr (pro-al-Hakim, chairman of SAIRI), Tehran.
Al-Mu'tamar (INC), 1992–97.
Risalat al-Iraq, London, ICP.
Al-Shahada, The official organ of SAIRI, Tehran.
Sawt al-Da'wa, Iraq 1960–80,(issues nos 1–32, some of which are entirely missing).
Sawt al-'Iraq (Da'wa Party-Europe), 1981–
Tariq al-Thawra (Harakat al-Jamahir al-Muslima; [pro-Shirazi], Tehran.

Books in Arabic

'Abdo, Muhammad, *Al-'Amal al-Kamila* (Collected Works), ed. Muhammad Imara, Al-Mu'asasa al-Arabiya lil Dirasat wal Nashr, Beirut: vol. 1, *Al-Kitabat al-Siyasiya* (Political Writings), 2nd edition, 1979; vol. 2, *Al-Kitabat al-Ijtima'iya (Social Writings)*, 2nd edition, 1980; vol. 3, *Al-Islah al-Fikri wal-Tarbawi wal Ilahiyat* (Intellectual and Pedagogical Reform and Theology) 2nd edition, 1980.
Abda, Isa, *Wade' al-Riba fil Bina' al-Iqtisadi* (The Position of Usury in the Economic Structure), Dar al-Buhuth al-Ilmiya, Kuwait, 1392 AH, 1973.
Abdullah, Amir, *A Political Autobiography*, handwritten manuscript, London 1995.
al-Afghani, Jamal al-Din, and 'Abdah, Muhammad, *Al-'Urwa al-Wuthqa* (The Firm Bond), Dar al-Arab, Cairo, 23 July 1957.
al-Afghani, Jamal al-Din, *Al-'Amal al-Kamila, Al-Kitabat al-Siyasiya* (Collected Works: Political Writings), edited by Muhammad Imara, two vols, Beirut, al-Mu'asasa al-Arabiya lil Dirasat wal Nashir, 1981.
al-Alawi, Hadi, *Min Qamus al-Turath* (From the Dictionary of Tradition), Damascus, Ahali Press, 1988.
al-Alawi, Hassan, *Al-Ta'thirat al-Turkiya fil Mashru' al-Qawmi al-'Arabi fil Iraq* (Turkish Influences on the Arab Nationalist Project In Iraq), Dar al-Zawra, London 1988.
—— (1990), *Al-Shi'a wal Dawla al-Qawmiya fil Iraq* (The Iraqi Shi'is and the Nation-State, 1914–1990), 2nd edition, Dar al-Zawra, London.
Ali, Haidar Ibrahim, *Azmat al-Islam al-Siyasi, al-Sudan Numuthajan* (The Crisis of Political Islam in Sudan), Markaz al-Dirasat al-Sudaniya, Casablanca, Qurtuba Press, 2nd edition, 1991.
al-Ashmawi, Muhammad Sai'd, *Al-Khilafa al-Islamiya* (Islamic Caliphate), Cairo, Madbuli, 3rd. edition, 1416 AH, 1996.
al-Assadi, Mukhtar, *Al-Shahid al-Sadr Bayna Azmat al-Tarikh wa Thimmat al-Mu'arikhin*

(Martyr al-Sadr, Between The Crisis of History and the Honesty of Historians), published by the author (n.p.), Stara Press, 1418 AH, 1997.

al-Ayashi, Ihmayda, *Al-Islamiyun al-Jaza'iriyun bayn al-Sulta wal Rasas* (Algerian Islamists: Betwen Power and Bullets), Algiers, Dar Al-Hikma, 1993.

al-Azm, Sadiq Jalal (1982) *Naqd al-Fikr al-Dini* (Criticism of Religious Thought), Dar al-Tali'ah, Beirut, fifth edition.

al-Barrak, Fadhil (1984) *Al-Madaris al-Yahudiya wal Iraniya fil 'Iraq, Dirasa Muqarana* (Jewish and Iranian Schools in Iraq, a Comparative Study), Baghdad, Dar al-Rashid Press.

Basri, Mir, *'Alam al-Adab fil Iraq al-Hadith* (Literary Celebrities in Modern Iraq), volumes 1 and 2, London, Dar al-Hikma, 1994.

al-Bayati, Hamid (1997) *Shi'at al-Iraq bayn al-Ta'ifiya wal Shubuhat fil Watha'iq al-Sirriya al-Britaniya 1963–1966* (The Shi'is of Iraq Between Communalism and Suspicions in the British Confidential Documents), Al-Rafid, London.

Darniqa, Muhammad Ahmed (n.d.) *Al-Tariqa al-Naqshabandiya wa 'Alamuha* (Naqshabandi Order and its Figureheads), Jros Press, Lebanon.

Diyab, Muhammad Hafiz (1987) *Sayyid Qutb: Al-Khitab wal Idyulujya* (Sayyid Qutb: The Discourse and the Ideology), Cairo, Dar al-Thaqafa al-Jadida.

al-Duri, Abdul Aziz (1962), *Al-Juthur al-Tarikhiya lil Shu'ubiya* (The Historical Roots of the Shu'ubi Movement), Beirut, Dar al-Tali'a, February, 1962.

—— (1984) *Al-Takwin al-Tarikhi lil Umma al-'Arabiya-Dirasah fil Huwiya wal Wa'i* (The Historical Formation of the Arab Nation-A Study of Identity and Consciousness) Beirut, Markaz Dirasat al-Wahda al-Arabiya, 1st edition, September, 1984.

al-Durra, Sabah (1977), *Al-Qita' al-'Am: Dawruh, Tabi'atuh, Afaquh wa Mashakiluh* (Public Sector: Its Role, Nature, Prospects and Problems), Baghdad, Dar al-Ruwad.

Fadheel, Mahmud Abdul (1988) *Al-Tashkilat al-Ijtima'iya wal Takwinat al-Tabaqiya fil Watan al-'Arabi* (Social Formations and Class Structures in the Arab Homeland), Markaz Dirasat al-Wahda al-Arabiya, Beirut.

al-Fukaiki, Hani (1993) *Awkar al-Hazima, Tajribari fi Hizb al-Ba'th* (Dens of Defeat: My Experience in Ba'th Party), Dar Riyadh al-Rayis, London-Cyprus, March 1993.

al-Ghita, Muhammad Hussein Kashif, *Muhawarat al-Imam al-Muslih Kashif al-Ghita Muhammad Hussein ma'a al-Safirayn al-Britani wal al-Amriki fi Baghdad* (The Dialogue of the Reformer Imam Kashif al-Ghita with the British and American Ambassadors in Baghdad), Najaf, Haidariya press, 1954.

—— *Al-Muthul al-'Ulya Fil Islam La fi Bahamdun* (Sublime Ideals Are in Islam, Not in Bahamdun), Beirut, 5th edition, 1980. (First edition 1954).

—— *Asl al-Shi'a wa Usuluha* (The Origin and Fundamentals of Shi'ism), London-Rome, Bazaz Publications, 1994.

A Group of Researchers, *Sadr, Dirasat fi Hayatih wa Fikrih* (Sadr, Studies on His Life and Thought), Beirut, Dar al-Islam, Mu'asasat al-'Arif, 1996.

—— *Al-Tanmiya min Manzur Islami* ('An Islamic Perspective of Development'), seminar, Jordan, Amman, 9–12 July 191, volume 1, published in 1994.

—— *Nadwat al-Iqtisad al-Islami*, The Seminar on Islamic Economics, Institute of Research and Studies, Baghdad, 1403 AH, 1983.

Haddad, al-Tahir, *Al-Talim wa Harakat al-Islah fi Jami' al-Zaytuna* (Learning and Reformation in the Zaytuna Mosque Academy), Tunisia, al-Dar al-Tunisiya, 1981.

al-Ha'iri, Kazim, *Mabahith al-Usul* (Treatises on Methodology), Qum, Markaz al-Nashr, Islamic Information Centre, Rabi' Awal, 1407 AH, vol. 2, part 1.

al-Hamdani, Talib Aziz, *al-Imam al-Sadr: Fil Haraka al-Siyasiya wal Dawla al-Islamiya* (Imam al-Sadr: One Political Movement and the Islamic State), in A Group of Researchers, *Sadr, Dirasat fi Hayatih wa Fikrih* (Sadr, Studies on His Life and Thought), Beirut, Dar al-Islam, Mu'asasat al-'Arif, 1996. pp. 551–84.

Harbi, Muhammad (1987), *Ibn Taimiya, 'Alam al-Kutub*, Beirut.

al-Hashimi, Sayyid Mahmud, *Muhazarat fil Thawra al-Husainiya* (Lectures on Hussein's Revolution), published by the office of Sayyid Mahmud al-Hashimi, series no. 2 (n.p.), 1403 AH.

—— *Kitab al-Khums* (The Book on Payment of the Fifth Tax), published by the office of Sayyid Mahmud al-Hashimi (n.p.), Sha'ban 1409 AH.

al-Hassani, Sayyid Abdul Razzaq, *Al-Iraq Qadiman wa Hadithan* (Iraq Past and Present), Sydon, Lebanon, Irfan Press, 1948.

—— (1988) *Tarikh al-Wizarat al-Iraqiya* (History of Iraqi Cabinets), seventh edition, Dar 'Afaq 'Arabiya, Baghdad.

Hussein, Saddam, *Nazra fil Din wal Turath* (A Glimpse of Religion and Tradition), Baghdad, Hurriya Press, vol. 3, 1978.

—— *Al-Mu'allafat al-Kamilah* (Collected Works) Baghdad, Ministry of Culture and Information, 1989.

al-Hussaini, Muhammad, *Al-Imam al-Sadr: Sira Zatiya* (Imam al-Sadr: A Biography), in A Group of Researchers, *Sadr, Dirasat fi Hayatih wa Fikrih* (Sadr, Studies on His Life and Thought), Beirut, Dar al-Islam, Mu'asasat al-'Arif, 1996. p. 462–519.

Ibn al-Najaf, al-Katib (*nom de guerre*) *Tarikh al-Haraka al-Islamiya fil Iraq* (The History of Islamic Movements in Iraq), Beirut, Dar al-Maqdisi, 1982.

Ibn Taimiya, Ahmad, *Al-Jihad*, Beirut, Dar al-Jil, 1991.

Imara, Muhammad, *Muslimun Thuwar* (Revolutionary Muslims), Beirut, Al-Mu'asasa al-Arabiya lil Dirasat wal Nashir, 1971, 1979.

—— *Nazariyat al-Khilafa al-Islamiya* (The Theory of the Muslim Caliphate), Cairo, Dar al-Thaqafa al-Jadida, 1980.

—— *Al-Khilafa wa Nash'at al-Ahzab al-Islamiya* (The Caliphate and the Origins of Muslim Parties), Cairo, Kitab al-Hilala, 1983.

—— *Tayarat al-Fikr al-Islami* (Currents of Islamic Thought), Dar al-Wahada, Beirut, 1985.

al-Iraqi, Atif, *Al-Shaykh Muhammad 'Abdo, 1849–1905, Buhuth wa Dirasat 'an Hayatih wa Afkarih* (Shaykh Muhammad 'Abdo, 1849–1905, Studies and Research into His Life and Thought), Cairo, Al-Majlis al-Ala lil Thaqafa, 1995.

Jabar, Faleh A., *Al-Madiya wal Fikr al-Dini al-Mu'asir, Nazra Naqdiya, Numuthaj al-Iraq* (Materialism and Modern Religious Thought, A Critique: The Example of Iraq), Beirut, Dar al-Farabi, 1985.

—— *Al-Dawla, al-Mujtama' al-Madani wal Tatawur al-Dimuqrati fil 'Iraq* (State, Civil Society and Democratic Perspectives in Iraq 1968–1990), Cairo, Ibn Khaldun Centre for Developmental Studies, 1995.

Jabar, Muhammad Abdul, *Mustaqbal al-Dimuqratiya fil 'Iraq* (The Prospects of Democracy in Iraq), London, Dar Zayd, 1994.

Jaddo, Ghassan Bin, *Hiwarat ma'a Ayatollah Sayyid Muhammad Hussain Fadhlallah, Khitab al-Islamiyin wal Mustaqbal* (Dialogues with Ayatollah M. A. H. Fadhlallah: Islamists Discourse and the Future), Beirut, Dar al-Malak, 1995.

Ja'far, Mulla Asghar Ali Muhammad, *Al-Hayat al-Siyasiya lil Imam al-Sadr* (The Political Life of Imam al-Sadr), in A Group of Researchers, *Sadr, Dirasat fi Hayatih wa Fikrih*

(Sadr, Studies on His Life and Thought), Beirut, Dar al-Islam, Mu'asasat al-'Arif, 1996. p. 462–519.

Jamal al-Din, Sayyid Musatafa, *Al-Diwan* (The Poetry Book), Beirut, Dar al-Mu'arikh al-Arabi, 1995.

Jamil, Hussain, *Al-Iraq, Shahada Siyasiya* (Iraq: A Political Testimony), London, LAAM, 1987.

al-Jawahiri, Muhammad Mahdi(1988), *Thikriyati* (My Memoirs), volume 1, Dar al-Rafidayn, Damascus.

Al-Jumhuriya al-Islamiya (The Islamic Republic of Iran), *The Constitution of the Islamic Republic*, Tehran, translated by The Ministry of Guidance, 1st edition, 1403 AH.

al-Karmali, Anstas, *Lughat al-'Arab* (Arab Language), July 1912–June 1913, collected by Jamil al-Juburi, Ministry of Information, Baghdad, 1975.

al-Katib, Ahmad (*nom de guerre*) *Tajribat al-Thawra al-Islamiya fil 'Iraq* (The Experience of Islamic Revolution in Iraq, 1920–1980), Tehran, Dar al-Qabas al-Islami, 1402 AH, 1981.

al-Kawakibi, Abdul Rahman, *Collected Works (CW)*, edited by Muhammad 'Imara, al-Mu'assasa al-Arabiya lil Dirasat wal Nashr, Beirut, July 1975.

—— *Umm al-Qura* (The Mother of All Citites), Dar al-Ra'id, Beirut, 2nd ed., 1982.

—— *Taba'i al-Istibdad* (The Nature of Tyranny),

al-Kazimi, Nasir (*nom de guerre*), *Al-Hizb al-Shuyu'i wal al-Mas'ala al-Zira'iya fil Iraq* (The Communist Party and the Agrarian Question in Iraq), Damascus-Nicosia, The Centre of Socialist Research and Studies in the Arab World, 1986.

al-Khafaji, Sheikh Abdul Latif, *Al-Shahid al-Sadr: Thawrat Sha'b wa Masir Umma* (Martyr al-Sadr: People's Revolution and the Destiny of a Nation), Dar al-Ma'alim (n. p; n . d).

al-Khalili, Ja'far (author and editor) *Mu'asasa al-'Atabat al-Muqadassa* (The Encyclopaedia of Holy Shrines), Beirut, Lebanon, Mu'asasat al-Alami, 1407 AH (1987), 2nd edition, 10 vols, vols 6 and 7 (Najaf), vol. 8 (Karbala), and vol. 10 (Kazimain).

al-Khatib, Ahmad(1985), *Jam'iyat al-'Ulama al-Muslimin wa Atheruha al-Islahi fil Jaza'ir* (The Society of Muslim *'Ulama* and its Reforms in Algeria), Al-Mu'asasa al-Wataniya lil Kitab, Algiers.

Khomeini, Ruhollah, *Al-Hukuma al-Islamiya*, introduced by Sheikh Ja'far al-Muhajir, Beirut, Dar al-Quds (n.d.).

—— *Tahrir Al-Wasila (Tawdih al-Masa'il)* (Issues Explained), Damascus, The Iranian Cultural Centre, two volumes, 1407 AH, 1987.

al-Mallah, Abdul Ghani, *Tarikh al-Haraka al-Dimuqratiya fil Iraq* (The History of the Democratic Movement in Iraq), Beirut, Al-Mu'asasa al-Arabiya Lil Dirasat wal Nashr, 2nd edition, 1980.

al-Mawardi, *Al-Ahkam al-Sultaniya wal Wilaya al-Diniya*, Beirut, Dar al-Kutub al-'Ilmiya (n.d.).

al-Maududi (Maudoodi), Abul A'la, *Al-Hukuma al-Islamiya* (Islamic Government), trans Ahmad Idris, Cairo, Dar al-Mukhtar al-Islami, 2nd edition, 1980.

al-Mudarisi, Muhammad Taqi, *Al-Fikr al-Islami Muwajaha Hadhariya* (Islamic Thought: A Civilizational Confrontation), Beirut, Dar al-Jil, 2nd edition, 1975.

—— *Al-Islam Thawra Iqtisadiya* (Islam: An Economic Revolution), Beirut-Dubai-Bahrain, Dar al-Mashriq, 1979.

—— *Al-Mantiq al-Islami Usuluh wa Manahijuh* (Islamic Logic: Its Methodology and

Principles) (n.p.), 2nd, edition, 1401 AH, 1981.

—— *Al-Mujtama' al-Islami, Muntalaqatuh wa Ahdafuh* (The Muslim Society, its Basis and Ends) The Islamic Cultural Centre (n.p.) 1st edition, 1982, 1403 AH.

—— *Mustaqbal al-Thawra al-Islamiya* (The Future of Islamic Revolution) (n.p.), Islamic Cultural Centre, 1405 AH (1984)

—— *Afaq al-Haraka al-Islamiya* (The Prospects of Islamic Movement (n. p.) Islamic Cultural Centre, 8 Sha'ban, 1405 AH.

—— *Al-I'lam wal Thaqafa al-Risaliya* (Information and Messianic Culture) (n.p.), The Islamic Cultural Centre, 1405 AH.

—— *Al-Sahafa Tuhawir al-Mudarisi* (Mudarisi's Interviews in the Press), Iran, Dar al-Basa'ir, 1985.

—— *Al-'Amal al-Islami, Muntalaqatuh wa Ahdafih* (Islamic Activism: Its Basics and Targets), al-Markaz al-Thaqafi al-Islami, Tehran, 1981.

—— *Ru'a Islamiya fil 'Amal al-Thawri* (Islamic Visions in Revolutionary Action), lectures, al-Markaz al-Thaqafi al-Islami, lectures 20–40, Tehran (n.d.)

al-Mu'min, Ali *(nom de guerre), Sanawat al-Jamr: Masirat al-Haraka al-Islamiya fil 'Iraq* (Years of Hell: The March of the Islamic Movement in Iraq, 1957–86), London, Dar al-Masira, 1993.

Muruwa, Hussain, *Al-Naza'at al-Madiya fil Falsafa al-'Arabiya-al-Islamiya* (The Materialist Tendencies in the Arab-Muslim Philosophy), Beirut, Dar al-Farabi, 2nd edition, 1979.

al-Musawi, Ra'ad, *Intifadat Sufar al-Islamiya* (The Islamic Uprising in Sufar), n.p., 1402 AH.

al-Nafisi, Abdullah Fahad, *Dawr al-Shi'a fi Tatawur al-Iraq al-Siyasi al-Hadith* (The Role of the Shi'a in the Political Developemnt of Modern Iraq), Beirut, Dar al-Nahar, 1973.

—— (ed.), *Al-Haraka al-Islamiya:Ru'ya Mustaqbaliya* (The Islamic Movement: Looking at Perspectives), Cairo, Madbuli, 1410 AH (1989).

Na'ini, *Tanbih al-Umma wa Tanzih al-Milla* (The Admonition and Refinement of the People) Arabic translation, *Al-Mawsim*, year 2, no. 5, 1990, pp. 37–142. The book was authored in March-April 1909, translated and published in Arabic in 1930–31 in Sydon, Lebanon

Najaf, A *(nom de guerre), Dawr al-'Ulama fi Qiyadat al-Umma* (The Role of the *'Ulama* in Leading the Nation) (n.p.) (n.d.), published by Jama'at al-'Ulama al-Mujahidin in Iraq, no. 2.

—— *Al-Shahid al-Shahid* (The Witness and the Martyr), Information Centre, Jama'at al-'Ulama al-Mujahidin in Iraq (n.p.)[Tehran] 1981.

al-Naqib, Khaldun Hasan and Haido, Dawud (1988), *Al-Mujtama' al-Jamahiri wal Qita' al-'Am: Ru'ya Mustaqbaliya* (Mass Society and Public Sector, Future Perspective), Damascus, Dar Tallas.

Nasrallah, Muhammad Ali, *Tatawur Nizam Milkiyat al-Aradhi fil Islam, Numuthaj Aradhi al-Sawad* (The Development of Land Property in Islam, The Example of Sawad Land), Beirut, Dar al-Hadatha, 1982.

al-Nazari, Majid, *Abdul Sahib Dakhil wa Bidayat al-Haraka al-Islamiya al-Mu'asira* (Sahib Dakhil and the Beginnings of the Contemporary Islamic Movement), Beirut, Dar al-Furat, 1410 AH (1991).

Nazmi, Wamidh Jamal 'Omar (1984), *Al-Juthur al-Siyasiya wal Fikriya wal Ijtima'iya lil Haraka al-'Arabiya al-Qawmiya (al-Istiqlaliya) fil Iraq* (Political, Ideological and

Social Origins of Arab Nationalist Movement (for independence) in Iraq, Markaz Dirasat al-Wahda al-Arabiya, Beirut.

al-Nuʿmani, Sheikh Muhammad Ridha, *Al-Shahid al-Sadr, Sanawat al-Mihna wa Ayam al-Hisar* (Martyr al-Sadr, Years of Ordeal and Days of House Arrest), published by the author, Ismaʿilyan Press, 2nd edition (n.p.), 1417 AH. (1997).

Qassim, Abdul Hakim (1989), *Al-Mathahib al-Sufiya wa Madarisuha* (Sufi Doctrines and Schools), Cairo, Madbuli.

Qutb, Sayyid, *Al-ʿAdala al-Ijimaʿiya fil Islam* (Social Justice in Islam), 2nd edition, Cairo, Dar Misr, 1956.

—— *Maʿrakat al-Islam wal Raʾsmaliya* (The Battle Between Islam and Capitalism) Cairo-Beirut, Dar al-Shuruq (n.d.)

—— *Maʿalim fil Tariq* (Signposts on the Road), Cairo-Beirut, Dar al-Shuruq, 1980.

Raziq, Ali Abdul, *al-Islam wa Usul al-Hukm* (Islam and the Rules of Government), edited by Muhammad Imara, Beirut, Al-Muʾasasa al-Arabiya Lil Dirasat wal Nashir, 1972.

al-Ruhaimi, Abdul Halim, *Tarikh al-Haraka al-Islamiya fil Iraq: Al-Juthur al-Fikriya wal Waqi al-Tarikhi* (The History of Islamic Movement in Iraq: Ideological Roots and Historical Reality, 1900–24), Beirut, al-Dar al-Alamiya, 1985.

Saʿad, Ahmad Sadiq, *Kitab al-Kharaj li Abi Yusuf, Dirasah fil Mafahim al-Iqtisadiyya lada al-Mufakirin al-Islamiyyin* (The Book of Land Tax by Abi Yusuf: A Study of the Economic Concepts of the Muslim Thinkers), Beirut-Cairo, al-Farabi and al-Thaqafa al-Jadida, 1988.

al-Sadr, Ayatollah Sayyid Muhammad Baqir, *Falsafatuna* (Our Philosophy), Qum, Iran, Dar al-Kitab al-Islami, 10th edition, 1401 AH (1981).

—— *Iqtisaduna* (Our Economics), Beirut, Dar al-Taʿaruf, 1982.

—— *Al-Bank alla Rabawi fil Islam: Utruha lil Taʿwidh ʿan al-Riba* (The Non-Usurious Bank in Islam, A Treatise to Displace Usury), Beirut, Dar al-Taʾaruf, 8th edition, 1403 AH (1983).

—— *Al-Islam Yaqud al-Hayat* (Islam Guides Life), 2nd edition, Tehran. Islamic Ministry of Guidance, 1403 AH (1982).

—— *Al-Islam Yaqud al-Hayat*, Qum, Khayam Press, 1399ah. (1979) serialized in six tracts as follows:

1. *Lamha Fiqhiya ʾan Distur al-Jumhuriya al-Islamiya* (A Juristic View on The Constitution of the Islamic Republic; February 1979)
2. *Sura ʾan Iqtisad al-Mujtamaʿ al-Islami* (An Image of the Economy of Muslim Society); n.d.
3. *Khutut Tafsiliya ʾan Iqtisad al-Mujtamaʿ al-Islami* (Detailed Outlines on the esconomy of Muslim society; n.d.)
4. *Khilafat al-Insan wa Shahadat al-Anbiya* (Man as Caliph and Prophets as witnesses; 14 March 1979)
5. *Manabiʿ al-Qudra fil Dalwa al-Islamiya* (Sources of Power in the Islamic State; 19 March 1979)
6. *Al-Usus al-ʿAmma lil Bank fil Mujtamaʿ al-Islami* (The General Principles of Banks in Muslim Society). (n.d.)

—— *Bahth Hawl al-Wilaya* (A Treatise on Governance), Qum, Zahraʾ Press, 2nd edition, 1399 AH (1979).

—— *Risalatuna* (*Our Message*), Beirut, 2nd edition, 1981.

—— *Risalatuna* (*Our Message*), Tehran, Maktabat al-Najah, 3rd. edition, 1982.

Sa'id, Rif'at (1977, 1984), *Hasan al-Banna, mu'assis Jama'at al-Ikhwan: Meta, Kayf wa Limatha* (El-Banna, the Founder of the Muslim Brotherhood: When, How and Why?), Dar al-Thaqafa al-Jadida, Cairo.

Salim, Shakir Mustafa, *Al-Chebayish, Dirasah Anthrobolojiya Li Qarya fi Ahwar al-Iraq* (Al-Chibayish, An Anthropological Study of A Village in Iraq Marshes), Baghdad, al-'Ani Press, 2nd edition, 1970.

al-Sarraj, 'Adnan Ibrahim, *al-Imam Muhsin al-Hakim*, Beirut, Dar al-Zahra, 1993.

al-Shami, Hussain, *Azmat al-Iraq, Ru'ya min al-Dakhil* (The Crisis of Iraq: An Insight from Within), London, Dar al-Hikma, 1992.

Shams al-Din, Sheikh Muhammad Mahdi, *Nizam al-Hukm wal Idara fil Islam* (The System of Government and Administration in Islam), Beirut, al-Mu'asasa al-Dawliya lil dirasat wal nashr, 2nd edition, 1991 (1955).

Shararah, Wadhah (1996), *Dawlat Hizballah, Lubnan Mujtama' an Islamiyan* (The State of Hizballah: Lebanon as an Islamic Society), Beirut, Dar al-Nahar.

Sharif, Mahir (1980) *Al-Umamiya al-Shyu'iya wa Filistin* (Communist International and Palestine, 1919–1928), Beirut, Ibn Khaldun, 1980.

—— (1995) *Ba'dh Mazahir Azmat al-Markisiya* (Some Aspects of the Crisis of Marxism), Dar al-Yenabi, Damascus.

al-Shirazi, Sayyid Hassan, *Kalimat al-Islam* (The Word of Islam), Beirut (n. p.), 1964.

—— *Al-Wa'i al-Islami* (Islamic Consciousness), Najaf, al-Ghiri Press, 1960.

—— *Kalimat al-Rasul al-A'zam* (The Word of the Sublime Massanger of God), Beirut, Dar Sadir, 1967.

al-Shirazi, Ayatollah Sayyid Muhammad al-Hussaini, *Al-Hukm fil Islam* (Governance in Islam), Qum, Dar al-Qur'an al-Hakim, 1981.

—— *Fiqh al-Iqtisad* (Jurisprudence of Economics), Qum, Dar al-Qur'an al-Hakim, 1400 AH (1980).

—— *Al-Iqtisad al-Islami al-Muqaran* (Islamic Comparative Economics), Qum, Dar al-Qur'an al-Hakim, 1400 AH (1980).

—— *Fiqh al-Siyasa* (Jurisprudence of Politics), Qum, Sayyid al-Shuhada Press, 1401 AH (1981); reprinted as:

—— *Al-Siyasa*, Beirut, Dar al-'Ulum, 6th edition, 1987.

—— *Ila Hukumat Alf Miyun Muslim* (Towards the Government of One Million Muslims), Qum, Dar al-Qur'an al-Hakim, 1401 AH (1981).

—— *Al-Qawmiyat fi Khamsin Sana* (Nationalism in Fifty Years), Tehran, Dar Maythim (n.d.).

—— *Al-Sabil Ila Inhadh al-Muslimin* (The Way to Mobilize Muslims), Beirut, Mu'asasat al-Fikr al-Islami, 7th edition, 1414 AH (1994).

—— *A Collection of Communiques to the Muslim People of Iraq* (n.p.) 1401 AH (1981).

Shnawah, Ali Abid, *Al-Shibibi fi Shababih al-Siyasi* (Shibibi in His Political Youth), London, Dar Kufan, 1995.

al-Siba'i, Mustafa, *Ishtirakiyat al-Islam* (Socialism in Islam), Damascus, Mu'asasat al-Matbu'at al-Arabiya, 2nd edition, 1960.

Shubbar, Hassan, *Al-'Amal al-Hizbi fil Iraq* (Party Politics in Iraq, 1908–1958), Beirut Dar al-Turath al-Arabi, 1989.

—— *Tarikh al-Iraq al-Siyasi al-Mu'asir*, part 2, *Al-Taharuk al-Islami 1900–1957* (The Contemporary Political History of Iraq, part 2, The Islamic Movement 1900–1958), Beirut, Dar al-Muntada, 1990.

al-Tahhan, Zuhair, *Al-Nizam al-Iqtisadi al-Islami bayn al-Ra'smaliya wal Ishtirakiya* (The

Islamic Economic System between Capitalism and Socialism), Lazikiya, Syria, Dar al-Hiwar, 1985.

Ibn Taimiya, (1991), *Al-Jihad,* Dar al-Jil, Beirut.

al-Temimi, Khalid, *Muhammad Ja'far Abu al-Timman-Dirasa fil Za'ama al-Siyasiy*a (Muhammad Ja'far Abu al-Timman: A Study in Political Leadership), Damascus, Dar al-Warraq, 1996.

al-Tikriti, Hardan, *Muthakarat Wazir al-Difa' al-Asbaq* (Memoires of the ex-Defence Minister), Tripoli, Lybia, The General Directorate of Publication, Distribution and Advertisement, 1st. edition, 1983.

Tilfah, Khairullah, *Al-Iraq fi Sit Sanawat* (Iraq in Six Years, 1941–1963), part one, Baghdad, Al-Rashid Press, 1968.

—— Ayam min Hayati (Days in My Life), Abayechi press, Baghdad, 1997.

Tarabishi, George (1993) *Mathbahat al-Turath* (Destruction of Heritage), Dar al Saqi, Beirut.

al-'Ulum, Sayyid Muhammad Bahr, *Masadir al-Tashri' fil Islam* (Sources of Law-giving in Islam), Beirut, Dar al-Zahra, 1983.

——*Al-Ijtihad, Usuluh wa Ahkamuh* (Ijtihad: Its Methodology and Principles), Beirut, Dar al-Zahra, 3rd edition, 1991.

——*Al-Dirasa wa Tarikhuha fil Najaf*(History of Learning in Najaf) in Khalili, op. cit., vol. 7, ch. 8.

al-Uzri, Abdul Karim, *Mushkilat al-Hukm fil Iraq* (The Crisis of Government in Iraq), London (n. house), 1991.

Wahhab, Muhamad Bin Abdul, *Kitab al-Tawhid Allathi huwa Haq Allah 'ala al-'Abid* (The Book of Unity of God, Which The Demand of God Upon His Slaves), edited by Ahmad Muhammad Shakir, Beirut, Alam al-Kutub, 1st. edition, 1406 AH (1986).

al-Wardi, Ali (1991) *Lamahat Ijtima'iya min Tarikh al-Iraq al-Hadith* (Social Aspects of Iraq Modern History), six volumes, Kufan edition, London.

—— (1978), *Lamahat,* V. 5, Al-Adib Press, Baghdad.

—— (1976), *Lamahat,* V. 6. Al-Ma'arif Press, Baghdad.

—— (1992), *Dirasa fi Tabi'at al-Mujtama' al-Iraqi* (A Study in the Nature of Iraq Society), Amir Press, Qum.

English, French, German, Russian or Persian Books Translated into Arabic

al-Atiyya, Ghassan (1988) *al-Iraq: Nash'at al-Dawla* (Iraq: Emergence of a State), 1908–1921, translated by Ata Abdul Wahab, London, Dar LAAM, 1988. (Originally published in English as: *Iraq, A Political Study, 1908–1921*, Beirut, 1973.)

Bernice, Karl, *Dirasat Ishtirakiya fil Nazariya al-Ta'awuniya* (Socialist Studies in the Theory of Co-operativism), translated by Majid Mas'ud, Damascus, Dar al-Jamahir al-Arabiya, 1975.

Brook, Solomon (1986), *Ethnographic Processes, World Population on the Eve of the Twenty First Century*, Moscow, published by the editorial board of Social Sciences review. series no. 1.

Burgat, Francois, *al-Islam al-Siasi, Sawt al-Janub* (Political Islam: The Voice of the South), translated by Lorain Fawzi Zikra, Cairo, Third World Press, 1992 (The Original French: *L'Islamisme au Maghreb: La Voix du Sud*, Editions Karthala, 1988).

Cleveland, William L. (1983), *The Making of an Arab Nationalist, Ottomanism and Arabism in the Life and Thought of Sati' al-Husri*, [Princeton, Princeton University Press, 1971] translated by Victor Sahhab, Dar al-Wahda, Beirut.

Desmond, Stewart (1971, 1974 and 1981) *The Middle East, Temple of Janus*, Arabic translation, Dar al-Nahar, Beirut.

Dan, Uriel (1989) *al-'Iraq fi 'Ahd Qassim, Tarikh Siyasi*, two volumes, Sweden, Nabaz Publishing House. Translation, commentary and supplement by Fathalla, Jarjis al-Muhami (Original title *Iraq Under Qassem, A Political History, 1958–63*. (1969).

A Group of Researchers, *Tarikh al-Aqtar al-'Arabiya* (The History of Arab Countries), Moscow, Progress, 1975.

Ibrahim, Ferhad, *Al-Ta'ifiya fil 'Alam al-'Arabi, Numuthaj Shi'at al-Iraq* (Communalism in the Arab World, The Example of the Shi'a in Iraq), translated by Markaz Dirasat al-Tafa'ul al-Thaqafi Cairo, Madbuli, 1996. (German Original: *Konfessionalismus und Politik in der Arabischen Welt am Beispiel der irakischen Schiiten. Ein Beitrag zur Thematik Religion und Politik in den gegenwartigen Gesellschaften des Vorden Orients*, Berlin, 1994.)

Keido, Akram, *Mu'asasat Shaykh al-Islam fil Dawla al-'Uthmaniya* (The Institution of Sheikh of Islam Under the Ottoman Rule), translated by Hashim Ayubi, Tripoli, Lebanon, Jros Press, 1992.

Kepel, Gilles and Yan Richard (eds) (1990) *Al-Muthaqaf wal Munadhil fil Islam*, translated by Bassam Hajjar, London, Al Saqi, 1994. (In French: *Intellectuels et militants de l'Islam contemporain*, Editions du Seuil, Paris).

Kepel, Gilles (1992) *Yaum Allah, Al-Harakat al-Usuliya al-Mu'asira fil Diyanat al-Thalath*, translated by Nasir Mruwa, Cyprus, Limassol, Qurtuba Press (In French: *La revanche de Dieu: chrétiens, juifs et musulmans à la redonquête du monde*).

Kotlov, L. N. (1981), *Takawun Harakat al-Taharur al-Watani fil Mashriq al-Arabi* (The Formation of the National Liberation Movement in the Arab Mashriq-mid 19th century to 1908), translated by Sa'id Ahmad, Damascus, Ministry of Culture and Guidance.

—— (1975) *Thawrat al-Taharur al-Watani fil Iraq* (The National Liberation Revolution in Iraq), Beirut, Dar al-Farabi.

Mitchell, Richard P. (1969, 1977) *The Society of Muslim Brothers*, Oxford, Oxford University Press, translated by Abdul Salam Radhwan and Muna Anis (two volumes), Madboli, Cairo, May 1977.

al-Quchani, Sayyid al-Najafi, *Siyahat al-Sharq* (A Tour in the East), translated by Lujnat al-Huda (A Committee for Guidance), Beirut, Dar al-Balagha, 1992.

Techonova, T. P (1987), *Sati' al-Husri, Ra'id al-Manha al-'Ilmani fil Fikr al-Qawmi al-'Arabi* (Husri, The Pioneer of Secularization of Nationalistic Arab Thought) Progress Publishers, Moscow.

Vassiliev, A. (1986), *Tarikh al-'Arabiya al-Sa'udiya* (The History of Saudi Arabia), Progress Publishers, Moscow.

Essays and Articles in Arabic

'Abdullah, Amir, 'Haqa'iq 'an Masirat Khan al-Nus in Shubat 1977' (Facts Relevant to the Khan al-Nus Demonstrations in February 1977, *Risalat al-Iraq*, no. 21, September, 1997, p. 14.

al-'Alawi, Hadi, 'Masa'ir al-Islam al-Mu'asir' (The Prospects of Contemporary Islam), *al-Nahj*, no. 17, 1987, pp. 8–34.

al-'Askari, Sami, 'Al-Imam al-Sadr wa Dawruh fil Sira al-Siyasi fil Iraq' (Imam al-Sadr, His Role in Political Struggle in Iraq), in A Group of Researchers, *Sadr, Dirasat fi Hayatih wa fikrih* (Sadr, Studies on His Life and Thought), Beirut, Dar al-Islam, Mu'asasat al-'Arif, 1996, pp. 521–50.

al-Atiyya, Ghassan, 'Hizb al-Da'wa al-Islamiya' (The Islamic Da'wa Party), *Iraqi File*, London, no. 22, 1993.

Fadlallah, Muhammad Hussain, 'Hiwar Shamil' (Comprehensive Dialogue), *Dirasat Filistiniya* (Beirut) no. 23, Summer 1995, pp. 93–121.

—— 'Al-'Aza al-Husaini' (Hussain's Rituals of Mourning), *Al-Nur* (London), no. 75, August 1997, p. 46 and passim.

Jabar, Faleh A., 'Al-Naz'a al-Qawmiya al-'Arabiya wal Islam' (Arab Nationalism and Islam, 1890–1990), *Qadhaya Fikriya*, Cairo, Volume 13–14, October, 1993, pp. 329–45.

Jabar, Muhammad A., 'Ishkaliyat al-Da'wa Ila al-Islam Ba'idan 'an al-Idyulojya' ('The Problem of Islamic Call Beyond Ideology'), *al-Hayat*, London, Saturday, 21 March, 1992.

—— 'Afkar Hawl al-Dawla wal Dawla al-Islamiya' (Thoughts on the state and the Islamic state), *Iraqi Issues*, Iraqi Institution, Washington D. C., no. 11, November, 1993, pp. 12–15.

Al-Jami'ya al-Mu'asisa li Jami'at al-Kufa (1968) (The Society for Founding the Kufa University), *Jami'at al-Kufa, Fikratuha, Ahdafuha wa Manhajuha* (The Kufa University, Its Concept, Ends and Method), Baghdad, Al-Azhar Press.

al-Muwahhid, Nabil (*nom de guerre*), 'Zahirat al-Takhalluf al-Tanzimi fil Amal al-Islami al-Mu'asir', *Dirasat wa Buhuth* review, issued by Jama'at al-Uala al-Mujahidin in Iraq (based in Tehran), no. 2., year one, 1402 AH, January 1981, pp. 257–68.

al-Najjar, Ahmad, 'Azmat al-Bunuk al-Islamiya' (The Crisis of Islamic Banks), *Al-Sharq al-Awsat*, no. 5455, Thursday, 4 November, 1993.

al-Qaradhawi, Yousif, 'Al-Iqtisad al-Islami Nizam Akhlaqi' (Islamic Economics: An Ethical System, *al-Sharq al-Awsat*, no. 5476, Thursday 25 November 1993, p. 17.

al-Qazwini, Jawdat, 'Al-Haraka al-Akhbariya wa Haqiqat al-Sira al-Usuli-al-Akhbari', *al-Fikr al-Jadid*, vol. 1, no. 1, January 1992, pp. 206–66.

Sheikh from Baghdad (*nom de guerre*), 'Al-Shu'ubiya wal Shi'a: Hiwar bayn Sheikh min Baghdad wal Duktor M. A. Hatim min al-Qahira' (A Dialogue Between A Sheikh from Baghdad, and Dr. M. A. Hatim of Cairo), *Al-Mawsim*, Kufa Academy, Holland, no. 14, 1413h. (1993), pp. 105–58.

al-'Ulum, Sayyid Muhammad Bahr, 'Al-Islamiyun wa Khiyar al-Dimuqratiya' (Islamists and the Democratic Option), a paper presented at a seminar at SOAS, 19–20 January 1994.

Zubair, Abdul Razzaq, 'Dirasat fil islah al-Zira'i, Muraja'a' (Agrarian Reform Laws Revisited), manuscript of unpublished lectures of 144 pages, delivered at the Faculty of Law and Politics, Baghdad University in the academic year 1975–6.

Books in Other Languages

Abrahamian, Ervand (1982) *Iran Between Two Revolutions*, Princeton, N. J: Princeton University Press.

—— (1993), *Khomeinism, Essays on the Islamic Republic*, London: I. B. Tauris.

Akhavi, Shahrough (1980), *Religion and Politics in Contemporary Iran*, Albany, State

University of New York Press.

Algar, Hamid (1980), *Religion and State in Iran, The Role of 'ulama in Qajar Period 1785–1906*, Berkely, Los Angeles: University of California Press.

Anderson, Benedict (1983), *Imagined Communities: Reflections on the Origins and Spread of Nationalism*, London: Verso.

Amanat, Abbas (1988), Between the Madrasa and the Market Place: The Designation of Clerical Leadership in Modern Shi'ism, in Said Amir Arjomand (ed.), *Authority and Political Culture in Shi'ism*, Albany: State University of New York Press.

Amnesty International, International Report, *The Death Penalty, A Survey by Country*, 26 September, 1979.

Arjomand, Said Amir (ed.) (1984), *The Shadow of God and the Hidden Imam:Religion, Political Order and Societal Change in Shi'ite Iran, from the beginning to 1890*, Chicago: Chicago University Press.

—— (1988) *Authority and Political Culture in Shi'ism*, Albany: State University of New York Press.

—— (1989) *The Turban for the Crown, The Islamic Revolution in Iran*, Oxford: Oxford University Press.

Axelgard, Frederick W. (ed.) (1986), *Iraq in Transition: A Political, Economic and Strategic Perspective*, Boulder, Colorado: Westview Press.

Aziz, Tariq (1981), *Iraq-Iran Conflict, Questions and Discussions*, translated by Naji al-Hadithi, London, Third World Centre.

Azm, Sadik Jalal (1993), Islamic Fundamentalism Reconsidered: A Critical Outline of Problems, Ideas and Approaches, *South Asia Bulletin* (SAB), volume XIII, nos 1 and 2, 1993, pp. 1–55.

Bagley, F. R. C, The Azhar and Shi'ism, *The Muslim World*, vol. L, 1960, pp. 122–9.

Baldick, Julian (1989), *Mystical Islam*, London: I. B. Tauris.

Baram, Amatzia (1981) The June Elections to the National Assembly in Iraq, An Experiment in Controlled Democracy, *Orient*, 22, 1 March 1981, pp. 391–412.

—— (1983), Mesopotamian Identity in Ba'thi Iraq, *Middle Eastern Studies*, volume 19, no. 4, October, 1983, pp. 246–455.

—— (1989), The Ruling Elite in Ba'thi Iraq, 1968–1986: The Changing Features of a Collective Profile, *International Journal of Middle Eastern Studies*, 21, 1989, pp. 447–93.

—— (1990), Radical Shi'ite Opposition Movements in Iraq, in Emmanuel Sivan and Menachem Friedman (eds) (1990) *Religious Radicalism and Politics in the Middle East*, Albany:State University of New York Press.

—— (1991), *Culture History and Ideology in the Formation of Ba'thist Iraq, 1968–89*, Oxford: St. Antony's College, in association with Macmillan.

—— (1991), From Radicalism to Radical Pragmatism: The Shi'ite Fundamentalist Opposition Movements of Iraq, in James Piscatori (ed.) (1991) *Islamic Fundamentalism and the Gulf Crisis*, Chicago, The American Academy of Arts and Sciences.

Batatu, Hanna (1977), Class Analysis and Iraqi Society, in Saad Eddin Ibrahim and Nicholas Hopkins (eds) (1977) *Arab Society, Social Science Perspective*, Cairo American University Press.

(1981), Iraq's Underground Shi'a Movements: Characteristics, Causes and Prospects, *Middle East Journal*, 35, pp. 578–94.

(1986) Iraqs Shi'a: Their Political Role and the Process of their Integration into Society, in Barbara Frayer Stowasser (1986) *Islamic Impulse*, Washington, Georgetown

University Centre for Contemporary Arab Studies, 1987.

—— (1986) Shi'i Organizations in Iraq: Al-Da'wa h al-Islamiyah and al-Mujahidin, in Juan Cole and Nikki Keddie (eds) (1986) *Shi'ism and Social Protest*, New Haven, Yale University Press.

—— (1978, 1989) *Old Social Classes and the Revolutiuonary Movements of Iraq*, Princeton, N. J, Princeton University Press. Third paperback print.

Bayat, Mongal, Islam in Pahlavi and Post-Pahlavi Iran: A Cultural Revolution?, in John L. Espositio (ed.) (1980), *Islam and Development*, New York, Syracuse University Press.

Beblawi, Hazim and Lucciani, Giacomo (eds) (1987), *The Rentier State*, London, Croom Helm.

Bengio, Ofra, Shi'ism and Politics in Ba'thi Iraq, *Middle Eastern Studies*, vol. 21, no. 1, January 1985, pp. 1–14.

Berkey, Jonathan (1992), *The Transmission of Knowledge in Medieval Cairo*, Princeton, N. J., Princeton University Press.

Boulares, Habib (1990) Islam: *The Fear and the Hope*, London: Zed Press.

Bozzo, Anna, Islam and the State: Theory and Praxis for the Algerian 'ulama, *Journal of Algerian Studies* (JAS), vol. 1, 1996, pp. 51–64.

Calder, Norman, Zakat in Imami Shi'i Jurisprudence, *Bulletin of School of Oriental and African Studies*, Volume XLIV, 1981, pp. 468–80

—— Khums in Imami Shi'i Jurisprudence, *Bulletin of School of Oriental and African Studies*, vol. XLV, 1982, pp. 39–47.

CARDRI (Committee Against Repression and for Democratic Rights in Iraq) (1986) *Saddam's Iraq, Revolution or Reaction*, London, ZED.

Chartouni-Dubarry, May, The Development of Internal Politics in Iraq, in Hopwood et al. (eds) (1993)*Iraq:Power and Society*, Ithaca Press, Reading. pp. 19–36.

Chaudry, Kiren Aziz, On the Way to Market, *MERIP*, no. 172, v. 21, no. 3, May–June 1991, pp. 14–23.

—— The Myths of the Market and the Common History of Late Developers, *Politics and Society* (PS), V. 21, no. 3, September 1993, pp. 245–74.

—— Economic Liberalization and the Lineages of the Rentier State, *Comparative Politics* (CP) October, 1994, p. 1–25.

Choudhury, Masudul Alam and Malik, Uzir Abdul (1992) *The Foundations of Islamic Political Economy*, London, Macmillan, Hing Kong .

Cobban, Helena, The Growth of Shi'i Power in Lebanon, in Juan Cole and Nikki Keddie (eds) (1986) *Shi'ism and Social Protest*, New Haven, Yale University Press.

Cohen, Stweart A. (1976), *British Policy in Mesopotamia*, 1903–1914, Ithaca Press, London.

Cole, Juan R. I. (1983) Imami Jurisprudence and the Role of the *Umma*: Mortaza Ansari on Emulating the Supreme Examplar, in Niki R. Keddie (ed.) (1983) *Religion and Politics in Iran, Shi'ism from Quietism to Revolution*, New Haven, Yale University Press.

—— (1985) Shi'i Clerics in Iraq and Iran, 1722–1780: The Usuli Akhbari Conflict Reconsidered, *Iranian Studies*, Volume XVIII, No. 1, winter 1985. pp. 3–33.

—— (January 1985) Indian Money and the Shi'i Shrine Cities of Iraq, 1786–1850, *Middle Eastern Studies*, 22, January 1986, No. 4, pp. 461–480.

Cole, Juan and Keddie, Nikki (eds) (1986) *Shi'ism and Social Protest*, New Haven, Yale University Press.

Cole, Juan and Momen, Moojan, Mafia, Mob and Shi'ism in Iraq, *Past and Present*, 112, August 1986, pp. 112–43.

Cooper, John, The Muqaddas al-Ardabili on Taqlid, in Said Amir Arjomand (ed.) (1988), Ch. 12.

Cordsman, Anthony H. and Vagner, Abraham R. (1990), *The Lessons of Modern War, The Iran-Iraq War*, Volume II, London, Mansell Publishing House.

Cummings, John Thomas; 'Askari Hossein and Mustafa, Ahmad, *Islam and Modern Economic Change*, in John L. Espositio (ed.) (1980) *Islam and Development*, New York, Syracuse University Press.

Dickens, A. G. (1968, 1992) *The Counter Reformation*, Thames and Hudson. London

Dodge, Bayard, Al-Azhar, *A Millenium of Muslim Learning*, Washington D. C., The Middle East Institute, 1961.

Durkheim, Emile (1915, 1971) *The Elementary Forms of Religious Life*, London, Novello and Company, seventh impression. 1971

—— The Social Foundations of Religion, in Roland Robertson (ed.), *Sociology of Religion*, Penguin Education, 1976, pp. 42–54.

Edmonds, C. J., The Iraqi-Persian Frontier:1639–1938, *Asian Affairs*, vol. 62, 1975, pp. 147–54.

Eickelman, Dale F., *Moroccan Islam, Tradition and Society in a Pilgrimage Centre*, Austin, University of Texas Press1976.

Enayat, Hamid (1983) Khumaynis Concept of the Guardian of the Jurisconsult, in James Piscatori (ed.) (1983) *Islam in the Political Process*, Cambridge, Cambridge University Press.

—— 1982 (1988) *Modern Islamic Political Thought*, London, Macmillan.

Esposito, John L. (ed.) (1980), *Islam and Development: Religion and Sociopolitical Change*, New York, Syracuse University Press.

Fakhry, Majid, 1970 (1983) *A History of Islamic Philosophy*, London, Longman.

Farouk-Sluglett, Marion, From the Politics of Notables to the Politics of Parliamentary Government, Iraq 1921–31, 1993, unpublished paper.

—— The Meaning of Infitah in Iraq, 1992, unpublished paper.

Fernea, Robert A. (1970), *Shaykh and Effendi, Changing Patterns of Authority Among the El Shabana of Southern Iraq*, Cambridge, Massachusetts, Harvard University Press.

Fernea, Elizabeth W. (1965)1969 *Guests of the Sheikh: An Ethnography of an Iraqi Village*, Garden City, New York, Anchor Books.

Fischer, Michael J. (1980) *Iran From Religious Dispute to Revolution*, Cambridge, Massachusetts, Harvard University Press.

Fuccaro, Nelida (1997), Ethnicity, State Formation and Conscription in Postcolonial Iraq: The Case of Yazidi Kurds of Jabal Sinjar, *International Journal of Middle East Studies*, 29, 1997, pp. 559–80.

Gellner, Ernest (1981) 1989, *Muslim Society*, Cambridge, Cambridge University Press.

—— (1983) 1992, *Nations and Nationalism*, Oxford, Blackwell.

—— (1992), *Post-modernism, Reason and Religion*, London, Routledge.

Gilsenan, Michael, *Saint and Sufi in Modern Egypt: An Essay in Sociology of Religion*, Oxford, Oxford University Press, 1973.

Gotlieb, Yosef, Sectarianism and the Iraqi State, in Michael Curtis (ed.) (1981) *Religion and Politics in the Middle East*, Boulder, Colorado, Wetsview Press. ch. 12.

Graham, Robert (1987), *Iran: The Illusion of Power*, London, Croom Helm.

Haim, Sylvia G., ed. (1962) *Arab Nationalism, An Anthology*, University of California Press, Berkeley and Los Angeles.

—— 'Shi'ite Clerics and Politics: Some Recent Tendencies', *Israel Oriental Studies*, 10,

1980, pp. 165–72.

Ha'iri, Abdul Hadi (1977) *Shi'ism and Constitutionalism in Iran,* 'A Study of the Role Played by the Persian Residents of Iraq in Iranian Politics', Leiden, E. J. Brill.

Halliday, Fred, 'Iranian Foreign Policy Since 1979: Internationalism and Nationalism in the Islamic Revolution', in Cole and Keddie (eds), *Shi'ism and Social Protest* (1986).

—— (1995), *Islam and the Myth of Confrontation,* London, I. B. Tauris.

Harik, Iliya and Sullivan, Denis (eds) (1992) *Privatization and Liberalization in the Middle East,* Bloomington, Indiana University Press.

Hegel, W. F. (1967) *Philosophy of Right,* translated by T. M. Knox, Oxford, Oxford University Press.

Heikel, Mohamed (1982), *Iran: The Untold Story,* Pantheon, New York.

Heine, Peter, 'Zghurt und Schmurt, Zur gesellschaflichen Sturktur der Schiiten im Irak bis 1958', *Al-Rafidayn,* Jahrbuch zu Geschichte Und Kultur des Modernen Iraq, , Band 3, Hrsg. von Peter Heine, Wuerzburg, Ergon Verlag, 1995, pp. 7–17

—— 'Der Abriss des Minaretts, Ein Beitrag ueber den sunnitisch-schitishcen Konflikt im Iraq', *Al-Rafidayn,* Band 1, Wuerzburg, Ergon Verlag, 1991, pp. 63–8

—— 'Political Parties, Institutions and Administrative Structures', in Hopwood, Derek et al, eds (1993), *Iraq: Power and Society,* Ithaca Press, Reading.

Hill, Christopher (1972, 1991) *The World Turned Upside Down, Radical Ideas During the English Revolution,* Penguin Books, London.

Hobsbawm Eric (1990) *Nations and Nationalism Since 1870, Programme, Myth, Reality,* Cambridge, Cambridge University Press.

—— (1994, 1995) *The Age of Extremes,* Abacus, London.

Hoepp, Gerhard and Paetzold, Mathias, 'Arabs and the Great Revolution of the French. Impulses and Effects in the Nineteenth Century', *Asia, Africa Latin America* (AALA), Akademie-Verlag, Berlin, no. 25, 1989, pp. 57–70.

Holt, P. M. (1966) *Egypt and the Fertile Crescent, 1516–1922, A Political History,* London, Longmans.

Hourani, Albert (1962) 1991, *Arab Thought in the Liberal Age, 1798–1939,* Cambridge, Cambridge University Press.

—— (1991) *A History of the Arab People,* London, Faber and Faber.

Hudson, Michael C., 'The Islamic Factor in Syrian and Iraqi Politics', in James P. Piscatori, ed. (1983), op. cit. p.p 73–97.

Iraqi National Congress (INC) (1993), *Crimes Against Humanity,* London.

Jabar, F., 'Les origines et L'idéologie du Neo-Islamisme', *La Pensée,* 299, juillet-aout-septembre, 1994, pp. 51–8.

Changing Phases of Responsive Social Movements in Sunni Islam: A Contribution Towards Classification, in Association of Iranian Researchers (ACI), *Government and Religion,* A Seminar at the University of London held in February 1997, published in Paris, May 1997.

Jamali, Fadhil, 'The Theological Colleges of Najaf', *The Muslim World,* Hartford, volume 1, no. 59, January, 1960, pp. 15–22.

Jericho, A. and Simonsen, J. Baek, eds (1997) *Islam in a Changing World, Europe and the Middle East,* Curzon, London.

Johansen, Baber (1988), *The Islamic Law of Land Tax and Rents,* Croom Helm, London.

K. S. Jomo, ed. (1992) *Islamic Economic Alternatives, Critical Perspectives and New Directions,* London, Macmillan.

Katouzian, Homa, Shi'ism and Islamic Economics: Sadr and Bani Sadr, in Keddie, N.

Biblbiography

R., ed. (1983) *Religion and Politics in Iran.*

Kazemi, Farhad (1980) *Poverty and Revolution in Iran, The Migrant Poor, Urban Marginality and Politics*, New York, New York University Press.

Keddie Nikki R. (1980), *Iran, Religion, Politics and Society (Collected Essays)*, London, Frank Cass.

—— ed. (1983), *Religion and Politics in Iran: Shi'ism from Quietism to Revolution*, New Haven, Yale University Press.

—— (1983) *An Islamic Response to Imperialism, Political and Religious Writings of Sayyid Jamal ad-Din al-Afghani*, Berkeley, Los Angeles, University of California Press.

Kedourie, Elie, 'Continuity and Change in Modern Iraqi History', *Asian Affairs*, volume 62, 1975, pp. 140–6.

—— *The Iraqi Shi'is and their Fate*, in Martin Kramer (ed.) (1987) *Shi'ism, Resistence and Revolution*, Boulder, Colorado, Westview Press.

Kelidar, Abbas, ed. (1979), *The Integration of Modern Iraq*, London, Croom Helm.

Kepel, Gilles (1985) *The Prophet and the Pharaoh, Muslim Extremism in Egypt*, translated by Jon Rothschild, London, Al Saqi Books.

Khadduri, Majid (1969), *Republican Iraq, A Study in Iraqi Politics since the Revolution of 1958*, Oxford, Oxford University Press.

—— (1978), *Socialist Iraq, A Study in Iraqi Politics since 1968*, Washington D. C., The Middle East Institute.

Khalidi, Rashid et. al. (eds) (1991), *The Origins of Arab Nationalism*, New York, Columbia University Press.

Khalil, Samir (1989), *Republic of Fear*, Berkeley, University of California Press.

Kholberg, Etan (1988), *Imam and Community in the Pre-Ghayba Period*, in Said Amir Arjomand (ed.), *Authority and Political Culture in Shiism.*

Kienle, Eberhard (1990) *Ba'th vs. Ba'th: The Conflict between Syria and Iraq, 1968–1989*, London, I. B. Tauris.

Lewis, Bernard (1988) 1991, *The Political Language of Islam*, Chicago, University of Chicago Press.

—— (1961) *The Emergence of Modern Turkey*, London, Oxford Univeristy Press.

Longrigg, Stephen Hemsely (1953, 1956), *Iraq, 1900 to 1950, A Political, Social and Economic History*, Oxford, Oxford University Press.

Lukes, Stephen (1973) *Emile Durkheim*, Penguin.

Makiyya, Kanan (1993) *Cruelty and Silence*, London, Jonathan Cape.

Makdisi, George (1981), *The Rise of Colleges, Institutions of Learning in Islam and the West*, Edinburgh, Edinburgh Univesity Press.

Mallat, Chibli, 'Religious Militancy in Contemporary Iraq: Muhammad Baqer as-Sadr and the Sunni-Shia Paradigm', *Third World Quarterly*, 10, 1988, pp. 699–729.

—— (1993), *The Renewal of Islamic Law, Muhammad Baqer as-Sadr, Najaf and the Shi'i International*, Cambridge, Cambridge University Press.

Mannan, M. A. (1970) *Islamic Economics, Theory and Practice, A Comparative Study*, Lahore, Muhammad Ashraf.

—— (1982) *Islamic Perspective on Market Prices and Allocation*, Jeddah, International Centre for Research in Islamic Economics, King Abdul Aziz University.

Marr, Phebe Ann (1985) *The Modern History of Iraq*, Boulder, Colorado, Westview Press.

—— Iraq's Leadership Dilemma: A Study of Leadership Trends, 1948–68, *Middle East Journal*, 24, 1970, pp. 283–301.

—— The Political Elite in Iraq, in George Leczowski (ed.) (1975), *Political Elites in the*

372

Middle East, Washington D. C, American Enterprise Institute for Public Political Research.

Martin, Vanessa (1989) *Islam and Modernism: The Iranian Revolution of 1906*, London, I. B. Tauris.

Marx, Karl, 'Critique of the Goethe Programme, Marginal Notes to the Programme of the German Workers Party', in Marx, Karl and Engels, Friedrich (1970) 1973, *Selected Works*, volume III., Moscow, Progress Publishers, pp. 13–30.

—— (1976) 1982, *Capital, A Critique of Political Economy*, volume I, translated by Ben Fowkes, Penguin.

—— *Capital, A Critique of Political Economy*, volume III, translated by Davis Fernbach, Penguin, 1981.

Matthee, Rudi, The Egyptian Opposition on the Iranian Revolution, in Cole and Keddie (eds) (1986) *Shi'ism and Social Protest*, pp. 247–74.

Maududi, Abul A'la, *Capitalism, Socialism and Islam,* Kuwait, Safat, Islamic Book Publishers, 2nd edition, 1987.

Maul, Hans and Pick, Otto (eds) (1989) *The Gulf War*, London, Pinter.

Momen, Moojan (1985) *An Introduction to Shi'i Islam*, New Haven, Yale University Press.

Mohamedou, Mohammad-Mahmoud (1998) *Iraq and the Second Gulf War, State Building and Regime Security*, San Francisco, Austin and Winfield Publishers.

Mortimer, Edward (1982) *Faith and Power, The Politics of Islam*, London, Faber and Faber.

Mottahedeh, Roy (1985) 1987, *The Mantle of the Prophet, Learning and Power in Modern Iran*, Harmondsworth, Penguin.

Moussavi, Ahmad Kazemi, 'The Establishment of the Position of Marja'iyyat-i Taqlid in the Twelver Shi'i Community', *Iranian Studies*, volume XVIII, no. 1, winter 1985, pp. 35–51.

Muhsin, Jabr, Harding, George and Hazelton, Fran, *Iraq in the Gulf War*, in CARDRI, 1986, pp. 229–41.

Najmabadi, Afsaneh (1987), *Land Reform and Social Change in Iran*, Salt Lake City, University of Utah Press.

Nakash, Yitzhak, 'An Attempt to Trace the Origin of the Rituals of 'Ashura', *Die Welt des Islams*, 33 (1993), pp. 161–81.

—— (1994) *The Shi'is of Iraq*, Princeton, New Jersy, Princeton University Press.

Naqvi, S. N. H. (Syed Nawab Haider) (1985), *Ethics and Economics, An Islamic Synthesis*, Leicester, The Islamic Foundation.

al-Nasrawi, Abbas, *The Economy of Iraq, Oil, Wars, Destruction of Development and Prospects, 1950–2010*, Westport, Connecticut, Greenwood Press, 1994.

Newman, Andrew J., 'The Myth of the Clerical Migration to Safawid Iran', *Die Welt des Islams*, 33 (1993), pp. 60–112.

Niblock, Tim and Murphy, Emma (eds) (1993), *Economic and Political Liberalization in the Middle East*, London, British Academic Press.

Norton, Augustus Ritchard, *Shi'ism and Social Protest in Lebanon*, in Cole and Keddie (eds) *Shi'ism and Social Protest*, 1986.

O'Ballance, Edgar (1988) *The Gulf War*, London, Brasseys Defence Publishers.

Owen, Roger, Class and Class Politics in Iraq Before 1958: The Colonial and Post-Colonial State in Robert A. Fernea and Wm. Roger Louis, *The Iraqi Revolution of 1958: The Old Social Classes Revisited*, 1991, London, I. B. Tauris. ch. 9.

—— (1992), *State, Power and Politics in the Making of the Modern Middle East*, London,

Routledge.

Picard, Elizabeth, *The Lebanese Shi'a and Political Violence*, UNRISD, Discussion Papers, April 1993.

Piscatori, James P. (1983) *Islam in the Political Process*, Cambridge, Cambridge University Press.

Pool, David (1979) 'From Elite to Class: The Transformation of Iraqi political Leadership', in Kelidar Abbas (ed.) (1979), *The Integration of Modern Iraq*, London, Croom Helm.

The Holy Qur'an, translation and commentary by Abdullah Yusuf Ali (n.p.) Islamic Propagation Centre International, 1946.

The Holy Qur'an, translated by M. A. H. Shakir, Al-Kho'i Benevolent Foundation, 4th edition, 1991.

Reetz, Dietrich, 'Enlightenment and Islam: Sayyid Ahmad Khan's Plea to Indian Muslims for Reason', *Asia Africa, Latin America* (AALA), Akademie-Verlag, Berlin, no. 25, 1989, pp. 71–80.

Rieck, Andreas (ed. and trans) (1984), *Unsere Wirtshcaft*, Berlin, Kalus Schwarz.

Roberts, Hugh, 'The Zeroual Memorandum: The Algerian State and the Problem of Liberal Reform', *The Journal of Algerian Studies* (JAS), V. 1, 1996, pp. 1–19.

Robertson, Roland (ed.) (1969, 1976) *Sociology of Religion*, Penguin Education.

—— (1970), *The Sociological Interpretation of Religion*, Oxford, Basil Blackwell.

Rodinson, Maxime (1977) *Islam and Capitalism*, Penguin.

Roy, Olivier (1994), *The Failure of Political Islam*, translated by Carol Volk, London, I. B. Tauris.

Sachedina, Abdulaziz Abdulhussein (1981) *Islamic Messianism: The Idea of Mahdi in Twelver Shi'ism*, Albany, State University of New York Press.

al-Sadr, Ayatollah Muhammad Baqir, *Unsere Wirtschaft: eine gekurzte kommentierte des Buches Iqtisaduna von Muhammad Baqir as-Sadr*, trans. Andreas Rick, Berlin, Klaus Schwaz, 1984.

Said, Edward (1978), *Orientalism*, London, Routledge.

—— (1981), *Covering Islam, How the Media and the Experts Determine How We See The Rest of the World*, New York, Pantheon.

Salame, Ghassan (ed.) (1944, 1996), *Democracy Without Democrats? The Renewal of Politics in the Muslim World*, I. B. Tauris, London.

Schubel, Vernon James (1993) *Religious Performance in Contemporary Islam: Shi'i Devotional Rituals in South Asia*, Columbia, University of South Carolina Press.

Shiblak, Abbas F. (1986), *The Lure of Zion: The Case of The Iraqi Jews*, London, Al Saqi Books.

Sidahmed, Abdel Salam (1997), *Politics and Islam in Contemporary Sudan*, London, Curzon.

Siddiki, Muhammad Nejatullah (1978) *Contemporary Literature on Islamic Economics*, International Centre for Research on Islamic Economics, Jedda, King Abdul Aziz University, U. K, The Islamic Foundation.

—— (1981), *Muslim Economic Thinking, A Survey of Contemporary Literature*, London, The Islamic Foundation.

Sivan, Emanuel (1985), *Radical Islam*, New Haven, Yale University Press.

—— 'Sunni Radicalism in the Middle East and the Iranian Revolution', *International Journal of Middle East Studies*, vol. 21, no. 1, February 1989, pp. 1–30.

Sivan, Emanuel and Friedman, Menachem (eds) (1990), *Religious Radicalism and Politics in the Middle East*, Albany, State University of New York Press.

Slugletts (Farouk-Sluglett, Marion and Peter Sluglett), 'Some Reflections on Sunni/Shi'i Question in Iraq', *British Society for Middle Eastern Studies Bulletin*, vol. 5, no. 2, 1978, pp. 79–87.

—— 'Iraqi Bathism: Nationalism, Socialism and National Socialism', in CARDRI, 1986. op. cit., pp. 89–107.

—— (1990), *Iraq Since 1958, From Revolution to Dictatorship*, London, I. B. Tauris.

The Historiography of Modern Iraq, *The American Historical Review*, volume 96, no. 5, December 1991, pp. 1408–21.

The Social Classes and the Origins of the Revolution, in Robert A. Fernea and Roger Wm. Louis (eds) (1991), *The Iraqi Revolution of 1958*, London, I. B. Tauris, ch. 7.

Sunnis and Shi'is Revisited: Sectarianism and Ethnicity in Authoritarian Iraq, in Hopwood, Derek et al. (eds), *Iraq: Power and Society* (1993), Oxford, St. Antony's College, pp. 75–90.

Smith, A. (1971) *Theories of Nationalism*, London, Duckworth.

Solh, Camillia Fawzi El-, Egyptian Migrant Labour in Iraq: Economic Expediency and Sociopolitical Reality, in Hopwood, Derek et al. (1993), *Iraq: Power and Society*.

Springborg, Robert, Infitah, Agrarian Transformation, and Elite Consolidation in Contemporary Iraq, *Middle East Journal*, 40, 1986, pp. 33–52.

Stark, Freya (1938) 1992, *Baghdad Sketches*, Marlboro, Vermont, The Marlboro Press.

Stapleton, Barbara, *The Shi'a of Iraq, An Historical Perspective on the Present Human Rights Situation*, A Report to the Parliamentary Human Rights Group. Published by the Parliamentary Human Rights Group, London, March 1993.

Taji-Farouki, Suha (1996), *A Fundamentalist Quest: Hizb al-Tahrir and the Search for the Islamic Caliphate*, London, Grey Seal.

Taleghani, Ayatullah Sayyid Mahmud (1982), *Society and Economics in Islam*, translated from the Persian by R. Campbell, with an introduction by Hamed Algar, Berkeley, Mizan Press.

Taleqani, Seyyed Mahmood (1983) *Islam and Ownership*, translated from the Persian by Ahmad Jabbari and Farhang Rajaee, Mazda Publishers, Lexington.

Tauber, Elizer, Three Approaches, One Idea: Religion and State in the Thought of 'Abd Al-Rahman Al-Kawakibi, Najib Azuri and Rashid Rida, *British Journal of Middle Eastern Studies*, vol., 21, no. 2, 1994, pp. 188–98.

Tibawi, A. L. (1979), *Islamic Education, Its Traditions and Modernization into Arab National Systems*, London, Luzac and company.

Tripp, Charles (1993), The Iraq-Iran War and the Iraqi State, in Hopwood, Derek et. al. (eds), *Iraq: Power and Society*.

—— An Islamic Economics? Problems in the Imagined Reappropriation of Economic Life, Department of Political Studies, SOAS, University of London, *Conference on Identity, Modernity and Politics*, 14–15 September, 1994. Draft Paper.

Tritton, A. S. (1957), *Muslim Education in the Middle Ages*, London, Luzac.

Turner, Bryan S. (1983), *Religion and Social Theory, A Materialist Perspective*, London, Heinemann.

Turner, Victor (1974), *Dramas, Fields and Metaphors: Symbolic Action in Human Society*, Ithca, New York, Cornell University Press.

—— (1969), *The Ritual Process: Structure and Anti-Structure*, London, Routledge & Kegan Paul.

UN High Commissionar For Refugees, Geneva, November, 1994.

Uwe-Rahe, Jens, Die iraqischen Sunniten und Schiiten aus deutscher Perspektive (1927–41): Ein Konfessioneller Konflikt?, *Al-Rafidayn*, Band 2, 1993, Wuerzburg, Ergon, pp. 67–82.

Watt, W. Montgomery (1962) 1987, *Islamic Philosophy and Theology*, Edinburgh, University Press of Edinburgh.

—— (1988) 1989, *Islamic Fundamentalism and Modernity*, London, Routledge.

Weber, Max (1968) 1978, *Economy and Society, An Outline of Interpretive Sociology*, volume 1, edited by Guenther Roth and Clans Wittich, volume 1, Berkeley and Los Angeles, California, University of California Press.

Wiley, Joyce N. (1992), *The Islamic Movement of Iraqi Shi'as*, Boulder, Lynne Reiner Publishers.

Wilson, Rodney (1979), *The Economics of the Middle East*, Macmillan, London.

Zubaida, Sami, Is There A Muslim Society? Ernest Gellners Sociology of Islam, *Economy and Society*, volume 24, no. 4, May 1995, pp. 151–88.

—— *Community, Class and Minorities in Iraqi Politics*, in Robert A. Fernea and Wm. Roger Louis, *The Iraqi Revolution of 1958: The Old Social Classes Revisited*, 1991, London, I. B. Tauris. ch. 11.

—— (1989), *Islam The People and the State, Essays on Political Ideas and Movements in the Middle East*, London, Routledge.

—— (1978), *Theories of Nationalism*, in Littlejohn (ed.), *Power and the State*, London, Croom Helm.

Dissertations

Clark, Katharine Anne Mary, *The Development of Ethnic and Religious Sectarianism in Iraq Since 1968*, MA Dissertation, University of Exeter, September 1994.

Pool, David (1972) *Politics of Patronage: Elites and Social Structure in Iraq*, UMI, Dissertation Information Service.

al-Shazly, N. E., *The Tanker War Political Objectives and Military Strategy*, University of Exeter, June 1995.

Uwe-Rahe, *Jens Irakische Schiiten Im Londoner Exil, Eine Bestandsaufnahme iherer Organisationen und Untersuchung ihrer Selbstdarstellung (1991–1994)*, Philosophischen Fakultaet der Rheinischen Friedrich-Wilhelms-Universitaet zu Bonn, 1995.

Index